Identification and Child Rearing

Stanford Studies in Psychology, IV

Editors

Robert R. Sears
Leon Festinger
Douglas H. Lawrence

Identification and Child Rearing

Robert R. Sears
Lucy Rau
Richard Alpert

Stanford University Press, Stanford, California

Stanford University Press
Stanford, California
© *1965 by the Board of Trustees of the*
Leland Stanford Junior University
Printed in the United States of America
Original edition 1965
Reprinted 1967

Preface

This book reports a study of the interrelationships and child-rearing antecedents of several types of child behavior in four-year-olds, including dependency, aggression, adult role, gender role, guilt, and resistance to temptation. These behaviors were selected as dependent variables because we believed them to be the major aspects of personality influenced by, or influencing, the presumed processes of primary and defensive identification. When the study was begun, in 1956, these mechanisms had been but little examined outside the clinical setting, and a number of hypotheses stemming from both psychoanalytic observations and psychological theorizing were badly in need of testing. It is a tribute to the vitality of research in this field that only eight years later there are many more provisional findings that would influence our research design, and hypotheses that would be incorporated in it for testing, if the study were being planned today. There is also testimony to the complexity of the field of personality development in the fact that after eight years most of the original hypotheses remain untested and the questions we have asked of our data remain unanswered elsewhere.

The study was designed to provide methodologically independent measures of parents' methods and attitudes and children's behavior. Forty children and their fathers and mothers served as subjects. Both parents were interviewed, the mothers were observed in standardized interaction situations with their children, and the children were observed systematically both in the nursery school and in a large number of assessment situations. The separate measuring of parent and child behavior was designed to avoid the interpretive complexities that arise when, in the guise of an antecedent-consequent frame of reference, parents' judgments of their children are compared with other measures of the parents obtained from the parents themselves, or when children's reports of their perceptions of their parents are compared with other measures of child behavior obtained from the children themselves.

The research was performed at the Stanford Village Nursery School during the summer session of 1958. Eleven researchers, including the authors, designed the procedures and collected and processed the data. Because individual scientists' contributions to team research are too often lost in a unified final report, we wish to indicate here the responsibilities each of our co-workers undertook. We owe them much for their uniformly able and untiring assistance in a demanding program. Alphabetically cited, they are:

Clara Melville Baldwin, Research Assistant. Administration of permissive and deviation doll play; observer in resistance-to-temptation situations; observer in mother-child interactions; director of the nursery school during the last two weeks of the study.

Lyn Kuckenberg Carlsmith, Research Assistant. Behavior unit observer.

Anne Harsanyi, Research Assistant. Behavior unit observer; construction of observer rating scales.

John Hatfield, U.S.P.H.S. Postdoctoral Fellow. Design and performance of mother-child interaction (with Rau and Alpert) and red-light situation (with Rau).

Lucille Mlodnosky, Research Assistant, later Research Associate. Behavior unit observer; reliability studies of interviews; data analysis for Chapter 4.

Paul C. Vitz, Research Assistant. Behavior unit observer; analysis of behavior unit data.

Gerald Weinberger, Research Assistant. Design and performance of resistance-to-temptation situations; observer for mother-child interactions, and experimenter for hamster situation.

John C. Wright, Research Assistant. Design and administration of gender role measures and quoting-rules assessment; father interviews; preliminary data analyses.

We include ourselves to complete the record:

Robert R. Sears. General planning and supervision; father interviews; design of behavior unit observation procedure, quoting-rules assessment, and mother-attitude scales; data analysis for Chapters 2, 3, 5, and 7; preparation of the manuscript and index.

Lucy Rau (now at Michigan State University). Mother interviews; design of mother-child interaction (with Hatfield and Alpert); experimenter for red-light situation and quoting-rules assessment; data analysis for Chapter 6.

Richard Alpert (now at the Castalia Foundation, Millbrook, New York). Pilot studies, 1956–58; coordination and scheduling of project; father interviews; design and administration of hamster situation; design of mother-child interaction (with Hatfield and Rau); supervision of computer work.

Parent-child research in a nursery school setting places a great burden on both the parents and the nursery school directors and teachers. We are much indebted to the parents who collaborated with us, for our demands were great and required not only many hours of direct participation by the parents but also help in the scheduling of their children's activities.

To Dr. Edith M. Dowley, Director of the school, and Miss Patricia Rowe, Head Teacher, we express our deep appreciation for their skill and sensitivity in coordinating the needs of our research group with the needs of the children and the parents, and for demonstrating (Dowley, 1961, Rowe, 1961) how wise teachers can exploit a research operation to the positive benefit of the children on whose education the research experience impinges.

We express our appreciation also to some other colleagues: Gracie A. Barron, who supervised the assembly-line output of interview transcriptions and maintained the great file of working papers for the project; Janet Beavin, who coped with the intricacies of the 101, the 650, and the 704; Dorothea Ross, who designed the coding system for the taped records of the mother-child interaction situations, and did the coding; and Ruth Terrill and Marie Waterhouse, who coded the parent interviews.

Finally, we thank William W. Carver, of Stanford University Press, for his endless patience and skill in converting our complex report of this research to a readable and accurate book.

Interim reports have come from this research, as they inevitably do in a project taking this long to complete. There have been oral reports to Division 7 of the American Psychological Association and to the Society for Research in Child Development. There have been masters' theses and journal articles; these are included in the References, with asterisks to note them. There has been a half-hour television film (APA, 1963) that displays some of our methods and summarizes some of the findings.

There has been an article that presents some of the data on dependency; we are grateful to the University of Nebraska Press for allowing us to incorporate revised versions of some parts of that paper (Sears, 1963), in Chapter 2 of the present volume.

This study was inaugurated under a mental health research grant to the Laboratory of Human Development, Stanford University, from the Ford Foundation, and was completed with the aid of a grant (MH5398) from the National Institutes of Health.

R.R.S.
L.R.
R.A.

Stanford University, July 1, 1965

Contents

Tables

Identification and Child Rearing

1. *Problems and Methods*

During the last decade, interest in children's moral development, and in their learning of role-appropriate behavior, has focused a good deal of attention on the process of identification. This mechanism, first conceptualized by Freud (1917) to account for the pathology of melancholia, has seemed to have broad explanatory power for other types of behavior as well. Later, in connection with his formulation of the structural part of psychoanalytic theory, Freud (1921, 1923) extended and revised the concept in such a way as to make identification the process responsible for the development of the superego and ego-ideal, and for certain qualities of sex typing (1924). The gradual development of Freud's ideas on this subject, and the way in which he was led finally to postulate two separate mechanisms (*anaclitic* and *defensive* identification), have been ably described by Bronfenbrenner (1960) and need not be reviewed here.

As a hypothesized process, identification has been attractive to non-analytic psychologists because it has given promise of explaining several rather complex forms of behavioral development that have not yielded easily to theoretical analysis in terms of the more molecular or monadic learning theories. Increasingly, as research has revealed more and more of the subtleties that characterize the early stages of sex typing, adult role formation, self-control, self-recrimination, prosocial forms of aggression, guilt feelings, and other expressions of conscience, psychologists have sought higher-level conceptualizations. For the sake of parsimony, they have sought also to keep such concepts to the minimum, and have attempted to subsume as much to-be-explained behavior as possible under the effects of a single process.

The behaviors mentioned have three common aspects: they develop very early in life, they seem to occur spontaneously, and they become very strongly established. These similarities have lent impetus to inquiries into the nature of identification, i.e., into whether there may be a single unitary process of identification that accounts for the development of a seemingly quite heterogeneous set of complex responses.

Efforts at self-control, prosocial aggression, and the display of guilt feelings find expression very early in a child's life, and although they often give the appearance of having been modeled after the parents' behavior, their development also often appears to have been independent of direct tuition by the parents. Similarly, certain sex role behaviors, such as style of aggression or toy preference, not only occur very early but also give the impression of almost spontaneous development without parental intervention. A pervasive quality such as masculinity (or femininity) receives at least some intentional reinforcement by parents and peers, of course, but the training task required for creating this kind of role conformity seems too great to permit an explanation in terms of the direct reinforcement of each of the behavioral components that compose the roles. So far as strength of the role behavior is concerned, witness the difficulty of therapeutic modification of male character disorders that include severe passivity, or the intransigence of gender roles in pseudohermaphrodites whose ascribed roles are changed after the age of three. Thus, there is great temptation to assume the operation of some intermediary process which, very early in life, enables the child to *learn* without the parents' having to *teach,* and which creates a *self-reinforcing mechanism* that competes effectively in some instances with external sources of reinforcement.

If our presumptions are correct, and if there is a single mediating process governing the development of the various hypothesized behavioral products of identification, there should be some unity among them. One would expect them to develop at the same rate, and, at a given point in a child's life, to have developed to the same degree. In other words, within a group of young children there should be high positive correlations among the measures of the several so-called identification behaviors. The testing of this notion was one of the two main purposes of the present study.

The other purpose was to determine whether the child-rearing antecedents of such behaviors were those to be expected from identification theory; but to understand the implications of this part of the research, it is necessary to describe the theory.

Theories of Identification

Although Freud, from his clinical observations, provided the original induction of the identification process, his analyses of the presumed conditions under which it might be supposed to develop in infancy were incomplete, and were not couched in terms conducive to empirical investigation. There have been several attempts to reformulate the theory in more precise terms to facilitate behavioral research on sex typing and various aspects of moral development. In the main, these efforts have rested specifically on the basic principles of learning, making use of what is known concerning the effects of reward and punishment and the mechanism of secondary reinforcement. Perhaps for this reason they have dealt almost entirely with primary, or anaclitic, identification, since the concept of defensive identification (identification with the aggressor) was originally described in psychodynamic rather than developmental terms. In this section, we shall present briefly the two theories that have determined the form and substance of the present research.

Anaclitic Identification

Anaclitic identification is understood to be a mechanism, developed during the first three or four years of life, by which behaving like the parents—or perceiving the similarity between the self and the parents—becomes intrinsically rewarding. Various sources of reinforcement have been hypothesized to account for the establishment of this motivational system; basically, most of them reduce to gratification of dependency needs. The actions learned by the child, by imitation, are those which the parent performs in providing this gratification. The assumption has been made (Sears, 1957) that the child generalizes these actions into "being like" the rewarding parent. When he behaves in this fashion, his own performance possesses (acquired) reward value.

This development assumes that the earliest relationship between infant and mother is a caretaking one. The mother provides constant biological support for the child's needs; i.e., she nurtures him, and he in turn becomes both physically and emotionally dependent on her. She and all she does become environmental events that have reward value for the child. Once this dependency motive is established, he will seek her out and attempt to manipulate both her and other necessary parts of the environment in such a way as to keep her available to him by sight and sound and to instigate in her behavior all the qualities that have been associated with the primary rewards that have accompanied caretaking.

A second step inevitably follows. Gradually the mother must withdraw herself from the child. Early infant care is very demanding on time and energy; it takes the mother away from her husband, her work, her other children—and herself. If she has another baby, he will require the same effort as the preceding one, and she will have to transfer much of her time and energy to him. The upshot is that the by now emotionally dependent child is deprived of some of the maternal stimulation (secondary rewards) to which he has become accustomed.

The next step is the weakest link in the formulation. By some mechanism not yet satisfactorily described, the child begins to imitate the mother. Only the inception of this process is theoretically troublesome, and we would probably do well to follow the guidance of Bandura and Walters (1963) in simply accepting the fact that "observational learning," as they call learning by imitating a model, occurs early in life. The relevance of this imitation to identification theory is that the child, by performing acts which, in the mother's behavior repertoire, have become secondary rewards or reinforcers for the child, now has a mechanism by which he can reward himself. By imitating his mother, he can provide a substitute for her when she begins withdrawing affectionate interaction and nurturance from him.

This mechanism was first proposed by Mowrer (1950) in his study of talking birds. He suggested that the words of the nurturant trainer become acquired rewards; when the bird hears its own voice making the same sounds, it automatically rewards itself. Later, Mowrer (1960) suggested that *all* forms of proprioceptive feedback from imitative acts could serve the same function. Sears (1957) extended Mowrer's proposal to include among the acquired forms of self-reward the whole class of imitated maternal behaviors, such as gestures, postures, task performances, and expressions of feeling; and ultimately, as the child's cognitive capacities develop and he begins to perceive and absorb belief systems, values, and ideological positions, he imitates these aspects of his available models also.

To account for the apparently non-tuitional character of much of the learning from models, various theorists have postulated the establishment of a general habit of *role practice*. For example, Sears (1957) hypothesized the development of a secondary drive to behave like the parents (a construct that no longer seems useful), and Maccoby (1959) suggested that role playing develops as a generalized habit that permits the child to gain mastery of many responses he will be expected to perform as an adult. Bandura and Walters (1963), however, have questioned whether any such generalized habit need be hypothesized. In their view, there are so many models available to children that one need assume only the operation of "observational learning" to account for the efficiency with which children absorb the adult and sex-appropriate qualities of behavior. In either case—generalized habit or pervasiveness of opportunities for model imitation—the theory postulates that many of the absorbed qualities should develop simultaneously and at approximately the same rate, the rate depending on the extent to which the optimum conditions of nurturance, withdrawal of love, and modeling characterize parental behavior.

The kinds of behavior presumed to be adopted under these circumstances are those that characterize the behavior of the models. Since the most potent models for the very young child are those who are *nurturant* and who *control resources* (cf. Bandura and Walters, 1963, pp. 93–100), the qualities of the caretaker or caretakers largely determine those of the child. In every case in the present research, the caretakers have been the parents.

The two main classes of this imitative behavior are sex-appropriate and adult-like behavior. The latter includes a great variety of things, such as adult role play, prosocial aggression, resistance to temptation, achievement orientation (in American middle-class culture), rule quoting, labeling of actions as "right" or "wrong," and various inhibitions of changeworthy behavior, including infantile sexual and dependency actions. Furthermore, since the child incorporates the parental strictures on misbehavior, he not only tends to behave, but also feels it to be wrong when he does yield to temptation, and at such times expresses reprehension of himself just as the parents would. In short, he experiences what is commonly called guilt, and tends to respond to his feeling by conventional methods of confession and restitution.

Inherent in this theory is a set of developmental principles that dictate a wide range of individual variation in the rate at which the identification process develops, and the ultimate strength it reaches. By hypothesis, rapid and strong development should be related positively to the following five variables:

1. *High early dependency in the child.* The dependency system plays two roles. It exists as a set of supplicative habits that are instigated both internally and externally. It is also the dyadic system in which the nur-

turant, affectional, and attention-giving acts of others serve as secondary reinforcers. Thus, the dependency habits and their reactional reinforcements constitute a feedback system, in that the child is encouraged (and retains the now reinforced supplications in his habit set) or discouraged (and modifies or replaces them). The stronger the system becomes, as measured by the frequency of dependency-expressive acts, the more of these environmental events (reinforcers) are necessary to avoid frustration. Hence, if the mother is reducing her responsiveness to the supplications, in her press toward developing the child's independence, there will be more occasions for the child to be forced to discover new imitable acts, and to secure self-reward by performing these acts. On the other hand, although a massive, sustained, reward program by the parents forestalls frustration, it is also destructive to the child's strivings for acceptably imitative behavior. Ultimately, of course, the social necessity for the mother to reduce her responsiveness does produce the frustration required for establishing the imitation.

2. *High parental nurturance.* The child's urge to imitate the behavior of the parents derives from the rewarding quality of that behavior. The degree of reward afforded should be a function of the frequency, intensity, and obviousness with which the parents respond to supplications. In the present context of parental behavior measurement, these attributes are interpreted as being represented by interview ratings of the parents' warmth, caretaking, affectional demonstrativeness, and reward of dependency.

3. *High parental standards of conduct.* The more demanding the parents' standards are, the more the child must do to attain them; hence the less frequently will he receive reinforcement, and the stronger will be his learning of whatever acts are reinforced—in this case, the imitated parental behavior. This reasoning rests on the principle that *intermittent* reinforcement provides greater habit strength than *continuous* reinforcement. High standards of conduct, as indicated by requirements for obedience, neatness and orderliness, table manners, bedtime schedules, reward or pressure for independence, and pressure for achievement, are interpreted as measures of the extent to which the parents require frequent practice of mature forms of behavior in order to secure rewarding parental responses.

4. *High use of love-oriented techniques of discipline.* The use of parental love and affection, rather than material rewards, in shaping a

child's behavior should increase the child's dependency, and should serve to label the parents themselves as the rewards to be sought. Likewise, the use of isolation (punishment by non-nurturance) should be more efficient in strengthening dependency supplications and in requiring the imitation of the absent parents' acts than physical punishment, which undoubtedly has some nurturance-depriving quality but which emphasizes physical pain rather than withdrawal of love.

5. *Clear presentation of models and of labels of appropriate behavior.* Labeling increases the discriminability of the behaviors that are to be imitated, and reference to the parents as models for defining "good" (i.e., rewardable) behavior should increase both the rate of learning and the extent to which the totality of parental behavior becomes the model to be imitated.

For the present research, we have assumed that the mother provides the main model during a child's first two or three years of life, and that the father becomes increasingly significant as a model in the later preschool years. We have assumed further that defensive identification is a secondary mechanism arising in these later preschool years as a product of primary (anaclitic) identification.

Defensive Identification

The secondary form of identification (Freud, 1923) is conceived to be a defensive process in which the already established anaclitic identification produces an internalization of the punitive and restrictive qualities of a threatening parent; Freud limited his exploration of the process to its development in the boy, and hence emphasized the boy's threatening father. This kind of identification is a defense in the sense that it reduces the anxiety engendered in the boy by his own Oedipal hostilities. The immediate motivation is fear of castration by the father in retaliation for the boy's libidinal feelings toward the mother and hostile, competitive feelings toward the father. As a solution to the Oedipal dilemma, this identification with the aggressive father arises only if the boy has a strong, albeit ambivalent, attachment to the father, i.e., if his hostility toward the father is intermingled with affection and love. The boy admires his father and wishes to be like him, but also wants him out of the way. The latter wish is repressed in response to the fear of castration, but remains as an unconscious source of guilt. Associated with this repression and guilt is the product of the conflicting love impulse toward the father, namely, an identification with the mother's role *in relation* to the father, an identification that adds a feminine component to his personality. These two solutions are not alternatives to each other, of course, but occur in combination, and are responsible for the continuing residue of femininity that accompanies masculinity in the male.

Three hypotheses can be derived from this theory, with respect to the development of strong defensive identification in the boy. First, there should be a negative relationship between the masculinity of a boy and the amount of aggression he displays toward his father. This follows from the reasoning that the mechanism of defensive identification will produce both inhibition of such aggression and a masculinization of his gender role. Second, there should be a positive relationship between self-aggression and resistance to temptation or other measures of impulse control (including aggression toward the father), since the incorporated attitude of derogation toward the self comes from the father, who disapproves aggression directed toward himself. Third, the amount of aggressive behavior expressed at the fantasy level should vary positively with the strictness and aggressiveness of the father. Normally the punitive quality of the father should inhibit overt expression of aggression toward him, but under the disinhibiting conditions of permissive doll play, the aggression should appear. These hypotheses will be examined and tested in Chapters 4 and 6.

The Problems

The two main problems with which the present research is concerned have already been mentioned. The first was to discover to what extent several types of behavior that are all presumed to be products of identification are correlated with one another in four-year-old children. Our reasoning has been that parents may be expected to differ in the degree to which they provide the optimum child-rearing experiences for the development of strong and rapid identification. Thus, their children should vary in the rapidity with which they develop identification-induced behaviors. The fifth year of life is a time when both types of identification should be particularly influential, and hence we should expect high positive correlations among the various behavioral products of the process. The child behaviors we have chosen for the test are adult role performance (including nurturance), appropriate sex role performance, prosocial aggression, resistance to temptation, and guilt reactions to experimentally induced transgressions.

The second problem was to discover the child-rearing attitudes and practices of the parents that were associated with such behavioral developments in the children. This second inquiry did not depend on the outcome of the first, for if we were forced to conclude that there was no evidence for positing a unitary process of identification, we could still test various additional hypotheses concerning the relation between child rearing and the separate forms of behavior we measured in the children.

The Methods

The plan of our investigation was to secure several measures of each kind of behavior from each of 40 children attending a nursery school, and to obtain child-rearing information from both mother and father. The child measures were drawn from (1) behavior unit observations made during the regular nursery school sessions, (2) several standardized assessment situations, (3) ratings by observers, (4) permissive doll play, (5) story-completion doll play, (6) observations of the child during two half-hour standardized mother-child interaction sessions, and (7) by interview, parental reports of the child's behavior at home. These procedures provided measures of both "real" (social-interactive) and fantasy behavior under varying degrees and types of social stimulation.

The parent measures were drawn from (1) interviews with both mother and father, (2) observations of the mother during the mother-child interaction sessions, and (3) mother-attitude scales (questionnaires). The interviews were designed to provide measures of a large number of child-rearing practices and attitudes, and several behavioral characteristics of the children as perceived by their parents. The mother-child interactions covered part of the same ground, as did the mother-attitude scales.

In the sections below, we shall describe the setting and overall procedure of the research, and the techniques of measurement. Some of the standardized assessment situations (those that were designed to be specific to certain action systems, such as adult role), will not be described here; to keep the measurement information as close as possible to the reports of findings, these situations will be described in the chapters devoted to the topics for which the situations were relevant. The descriptions of measurement methods given in the text (special assessment or otherwise) are sufficient for the reader's understanding of the findings, and more technical details are given in the various appendixes, as noted in the text.

Setting and Procedure

This research was performed in the Stanford Village Nursery School during the eight-week summer session of 1958. Since the research required extensive collaboration from the parents and teachers, considerable time and attention were given to explaining to all those concerned (except, of course, the children) just what was being done, the purposes of the research, and the amount and kinds of assistance that would be required. Parents were informed of the plans before they registered their children for the summer session. The night before school began, a meeting of all the parents and teachers was held for final discussion of the procedure. Cooperation was excellent, and virtually every measure was obtained from every parent and child. The details of this planning, and the effects of such an intensive and large-scale research project on the nursery school program and on the teachers have been published elsewhere (Dowley, 1960; Sears, 1960; Rowe, 1961; Vitz, 1961).

The Nursery School

All the research was done in the nursery school, except for the father interviews, most of which were held in Owen House, a comfortable old residence on the Stanford campus used as laboratory office space.

The nursery school building was a converted Quonset structure, with one very large room and one small room for school activities, two small rooms for research purposes, and the customary utility spaces. The building was set in one corner of a fenced play-yard (130 × 130 feet) to which, during the summer, there was continuous free access from the main room through permanently open double doors. The weather was regularly warm and sunny during the eight weeks, and the inside-outside flow of children was determined entirely by their interests or by (subtle) curricular influences.

One of the two research rooms (A) opened directly off the main room. It was 15 × 16 feet, with one corner cut off diagonally to form an observation chamber with a one-way mirror. There was a single entrance to the room itself, and a separate outside entrance to the chamber. The other room (B) was down a long hall, separated by some 50 feet from the main nursery school room. It was 10 × 20 feet. The entrance door from the main nursery school area was at one end of this narrow room, and mirrors for an observation chamber extended the width of the opposite end. There was an additional door leading outside in the left-hand side wall near the mirror. Entrance to the observation chamber was from the outside.

The social and psychological atmosphere of the school was a function of both its community setting and the educational philosophy of its staff. The school was established immediately after World War II, under the supervision of E. R. Hilgard (1949), in a large married-student housing area that had previously been an army general hospital. For some years, most of the pupils were the children of graduate students and younger faculty. By 1958, supplementary housing for students and an increase in the school's capacity permitted about half the children to be drawn from families outside the student housing area and unconnected with the university. The school nevertheless remained a focus of interest among the student parents, and the Director and Head Teacher were widely and well known. Community attitudes toward the staff, and hence toward the research, were warm and positive.

The educational philosophy of the school is best described in the Director's own words (Dowley, 1960):

The curriculum is planned in careful detail to meet not only the group needs of nursery age children, but also the particular needs of each individual in the nursery school. To do this the teacher makes available a wide variety of carefully selected materials and experiences, and encourages the children to choose their own activities rather than to follow a predetermined program. Children move freely indoors and out, from one center of interest to another, pausing to observe briefly in one area, perhaps, or to do a thorough job of exploration in another. There is enough dependability in the sequence of daily events, and enough orderliness in the arrangement of materials and equipment, to build feelings of confidence in the children and adults, while at the same time children are protected from over-demanding time schedules and from arbitrary conformity to group desires and activities.

The teacher sets the stage, in an atmosphere of relaxed informality, in such a way that the environment directs, guides, and determines the limits for child behavior. The environment tells the child what is appropriate for him to do when living and learning in a group of children. The utilization of the environment in the control of behavior in the nursery school reduces the need for and the amount of directing and controlling of children by teachers, students, and participating parents, and permits of adult-child relationships which are based on mutual trust, personal warmth, and affectionate friendliness.

The school atmosphere was relaxed, informal, and relatively permissive, but with sufficient structure to prevent boredom, desultory play, and lack of stimulation to exploration. The teaching staff was composed of the Head Teacher and two assistant teachers. Voluntary participation of the children's mothers was expected, and at each session there were from two to four of them assisting the teachers.

School was in session five mornings a week, from 9:00 to 11:45. The same staff taught all five mornings, although the total enrollment of sixty children was divided into two groups of thirty, one of which attended two sessions a week (Tuesday, Thursday) and the other, three sessions (Monday, Wednesday, Friday). Both groups were equally divided by sex, and their age ranges were similar, from two years and eight months to five years and six months.

Subjects

Only the twenty oldest children in each group participated in the research, the youngest of these, in each case, being four years and one month. In the M,W,F research group there were nine girls and eleven boys; in the T,Th group there were ten of each sex. Except for one brother-sister pair in the T,Th group, no two children were from the same family.

Thus, so far as adult staff and age and sex of peers were concerned, the children of the two groups had similar environments, but the actual peer bodies involved were different for the groups. One group of children had only two days' school experience per week while the other had three; in addition, four of the children in the M,W,F group had not previously attended this nursery school, whereas twelve of those in the T,Th group had not. These differences are of significance primarily in connection with the behavior unit observations, which were made in the social context of the school activity itself. A careful examination of these data has shown no significant differences between the two groups, in either means or distributions, in any of the categories we recorded; hence, no differentiation between children of the two groups will be made hereafter.

The mean age of the twenty-one boys was four years and nine months, and of the nineteen girls, four years and ten months. Five were the only children in their families, twenty-two were the oldest, nine were in the middle, and four were the youngest; these were about equally divided by sex. The mean age of the forty fathers was 32.7 years, with a range from 22 to 45; for the mothers, the mean was 31.2, with a range from 22 to 41.

Occupational, educational, and financial characteristics of these families were fairly typical of university nursery school populations. Twenty-eight of the fathers had had some graduate or professional training, and only one had stopped with a high school education. Half the mothers were college graduates, and all but four of the remainder had had some college. Occupationally, twenty-one of the fathers were classed as professional, twelve as students, and the other seven as managerial. Fewer than one-fourth of the mothers had never worked. The median family income was in the $6,600–8,500 bracket; only the students had incomes in the (low) $2,600–4,500 bracket. Religious backgrounds were predominantly non-devout, about two-thirds of them Protestant, less than one-fourth Catholic, and one-tenth Jewish.

Not all these demographic characteristics of the subjects are important for an understanding of the findings to be reported, but two of them are. *Sex* and *age* must be examined in connection with the study of both the organization and the antecedents of any motivational system in young children. These two variables are of such obvious relevance to the nature and extent of reinforcements occurring in the family, the expectancies both of parents and of other children, and cultural expectancies, that no examination either of behavioral organization or of child-rearing antecedents can ignore them. In a group of children of relatively homogeneous age, such as the twenty-month range of the present group, the influence of age can sometimes be ignored, but the influence of sex can never be. *All data analyses in this report will be presented separately by sex of child.*

Data Collection Program

Except for the information supplied in the father interviews and the mother questionnaires, all data were collected in the daytime at the nursery school. During the first week, the ten observers and experimenters became acquainted with the children, trying especially to assist in a rapid and healthy acculturation of the new ones. The main data collection was carried out during the subsequent seven weeks. In the mornings, while school was in session, four observers made continuous ten-minute samplings of the behavior unit categories. The selection of which child was to be observed by which observer, at what time of the morning, and in what sequence, was carefully randomized. With due attention to avoiding interference with this observation program, six experimenters kept busy taking one child after another to one of the research rooms for the various assessment situations. Except for a few scheduling emergencies that resulted from absences due to chicken pox, no child was taken to a research session more than once in a morning. The order in which the various assessment situations were performed varied unsystematically from child to child, except that the resistance-to-temptation and guilt-induction situations were kept at least a week apart.

The school was vacant in the afternoons, and hence was used for further assessment situations, mother-child interaction sessions, and mother interviews. There were two of these mother-child afternoon sessions for each pair, a week apart. The sessions each began with a half-hour mother-child interaction. Thereafter, the child was taken in charge for "playing games" with experimenters while the mother devoted an hour and a half to the interview.

The mother-attitude scales and other questionnaires were distributed to the mothers at the end of the summer. They were filled out at home and returned shortly thereafter.

Parent Measures

The data drawn from the interviews, interactions, and questionnaires produced a great many measures, or variables, for subsequent analysis. Appendix C lists these variables, and cites all text references to them.

Parent Interviews

To secure measures of the parents' attitudes and practices in connection with child rearing, to get estimates of certain of their personality qualities, and to obtain measures of their perceptions of some of their child's in-the-home behavior, each father and mother was interviewed with a standard set of open-ended questions. These interviews were recorded on tape and then transcribed to typescript. Two coders, working independently, rated each mother's interview on 161 scales and each father's on 119. These ratings, averaged for the two coders, constituted the final measures from the interviews.

The *content* of the interviews was directed toward those aspects of parental behavior that we conceived to be relevant to the development of a child's identification. These included the parents' caretaking activities during the child's infancy and childhood; their methods of handling early feeding, toilet training, disobedience, sexual activity, dependency, and aggression; their expressed attitudes concerning the child's independence, achievement, and moral behavior; their methods of discipline; their feelings about self-control, responsibility, and adult-typed and sex-typed role behavior; and a number of other qualities more related to family atmosphere and attitudes toward themselves and each other than toward their child. The full scope of the subject matter can best be assimilated by reading through the question sequence of the interviews, as given in Appendix A.

The forms for the mother and for the father were similar, but not identical. The mother's was somewhat longer than the father's. As nearly as was feasible, the same questions and probes were used for covering identical material, but the fathers were not asked for information on early feeding and toilet training, the mothers were less intensively asked about the child's interactions with the fathers, and there were many minor differences dictated by pre-test experience in approaching men and women on such matters as sex and aggression.

In general, the method of organization followed that of the mother interview used in *Patterns of Child Rearing* (Sears, Maccoby, and Levin, 1957), although the content was extended beyond that of the earlier study. There were 58 main questions in the mother's interview, and 40 in the father's. Each question was followed by a number of probes that the interviewer could introduce if the response to the main question did not include all the information required for rating the scales depending on that question.

All the mother interviews were performed by a woman (Lucy Rau); the fathers' were conducted by three men (Richard Alpert, Robert Sears, and John Wright). The mothers were interviewed at the nursery school, in the afternoon, immediately following the two half-hour sessions of mother-child interaction. The interview was carried on in an office, with the recording equipment in full view. The first session lasted about an hour and one-half, the second—a week later—about an hour or a little more. The fathers were commonly interviewed in the evenings or late afternoons, in a single two-hour session. Some were conducted in the father's home, but most were conducted at Owen House, in a small interviewing room.

In all instances, so far as we could tell, the parents took very seriously their responsibility for giving information and assisting the research. It was easy to sense the earnestness—and the freedom—with which they approached the task. What little self-consciousness there was disappeared very quickly; the recording process seemed to have no inhibiting effect after the first few moments. Half-hour tapes were used, and interruptions to change tapes created reactions of entirely predictable kinds, depending on the content at the instant. Some interruptions caused no comment or apparent discomfort, but others were frustrating and distressing because they struck at moments that were tense with feeling.

From time to time, unconscious defensiveness displayed its signs, and occasionally there were passages conveying a sense of boredom. But in almost every instance, the interview was followed by an expression of amazement at how much ground had been covered, and in many instances by gratitude for "the opportunity to think this all through." In the two years following, many parents—perhaps thirty or more—found occasion to express their pleasure at having been interviewed in this way.

Although there can be no question that defenses do enter such a standard interview procedure, many of the qualities that induce freedom of expression in therapeutic interviews are also present here. The picture of the parent gained in a couple of hours is undoubtedly different from that which would be gained by 100–400 hours of psychoanalysis, and one must face the question of validity. Where there is no single criterion against which validity can be checked, as is the case with parent behavior qualities, the validity of any one method of data-gathering can be evaluated mainly by its capacity for providing predictive or retrodictive tests of propositions.

This is not to say that the problem of validity with retrospective interviews can be ignored. Obviously we have chosen this method for practical reasons; it is relatively inexpensive compared with either psychoanalysis or prolonged direct observations of the parents and their child in the home. We suspect (without evidence) that interviews are less valid than direct observation for some types of variables (e.g., kinds of discipline used), but that they may be more valid with respect to some other parental qualities, especially ones that have more direct representation in the parents' language systems and verge on the area of values (e.g., sex and aggression permissiveness). We do know, from recent evidence (Robbins, 1963), that retrospective interviews have very poor validity with respect to factual historical matters such as age of weaning or use of scheduled feeding, but we did not have this evidence when we started the research. As will be seen later, these early-infant-experience variables have proved to be quite unsatisfactory, and have not even provided proper replications of previous research findings. Certainly with respect to such qualities of the parents as ambivalence and self-image, we would expect psychoanalysis to provide more valid information than structured interviews; therefore, with rare exceptions, we have not attempted to include variables of these types.

In sum, we have interpreted our ratings from the interviews as fallible measurements of actual parental behavior, recognizing that their validity is imperfect and unknown—and probably unequal from one variable to another, as well as from one father or mother to another—but assuming that there is sufficient correspondence between the rated variables and the parents' actual behavior and feelings to warrant the investigation we have undertaken.

About half the rating scales used for analyzing and quantifying the interviews were identical with scales constructed for the study reported in *Patterns of Child Rearing*. The remainder were specific to new content areas included in the present research.

The scales, as rated by the two independent coders, ranged from three to seven points each, the great majority being five-point scales. In nearly all instances, each point on a scale was defined by a brief description; this set of labels served to define the dimension being measured by the scale. Regardless of the number of points on a given scale, the final distribution of ratings, obtained by combining the judgments of the two coders, was converted to a nine-point scale in order to increase the fineness of the distribution. The mechanics of this process, together with details concerning the reliability of the coding, are given in Appendix B, and reliability coefficients are given in Appendix C. In general, the inter-coder reliability was quite satisfactory. The per cent of agreement within one scale point on the 159 scales retained for use in the study ranged from 78 to 100 per cent, with a median of 98 per cent.

The problems of trait consistency and validity both arise in connection with the interview data. There is no method of estimating trait consistency of the parents from the interviews. The only satisfactory method for this would be a re-interviewing procedure some months later. The likelihood of some inconsistency was, of course, assumed in many of the behavioral dimensions measured. The scales themselves simply represented efforts to place the parent on each dimension somewhere between all or none. For example, permissiveness for aggression toward mother is a quality that can prevail all the time (rated 5) or none of the time (rated 1) or somewhere in between.

Mother-Child Interaction (MCI)

Our mother-child interaction procedure was modeled after the techniques described by Merrill (1946), Bishop (1951), and Smith (1958). It consisted of bringing a mother and her child into a room and leaving them together for a half hour to perform two pre-planned activities about which the mother had been instructed in advance. When the two of them had completed the first activity, the mother was to begin the second immediately. There were two such sessions, with different activities in each, thus providing four quarter-hour samples of interaction under somewhat standardized conditions. Tape recordings and direct observations from behind the one-way mirror provided protocols from which 24 mother scales and 24 child scales were rated.

When the mother and child arrived at the nursery school, an assistant greeted the child and took him to another playroom for the few minutes required by the observer to give the mother her instructions. The mother was told that we had had ample opportunity to observe the child with other adults and with children, but that we wanted a sample of his behavior with his mother. The mothers were all familiar with the observation room and its one-way mirror, and a reminder was given that we would be observing and recording.

The child was then brought to Room A, and the mother assumed charge. Both sessions of the interaction were carefully structured for the mother, and she was responsible for carrying them through once the observer had left the room. In the first half of Session I, the mother was asked to sit down at a table and fill out a questionnaire asking for factual information about the family. At the other end of the table were two sheets of white paper and five colored crayons. Her task required about fifteen minutes. Its purpose was to provide a sample of a "mother busy" condition during which the child had nothing stimulating to do. This situation was designed to elicit interrupting and dependency behavior from him, and to give us an opportunity to observe the mother's reactions to such behavior.

The second part of Session I was a telephone game. Two adjoining booths were set up on a low table in such a way that the child, sitting in one, could face the mother through a plate-glass window as she sat in the other. Each booth contained a standard Western Electric hand-set telephone that had been reconstructed with a squeeze button in the handle. When both mother and child gripped the phones, holding down the buttons, they could talk together; the phones were battery-powered.

The mother had been instructed to have the child make five telephone calls to her. He was to be, first, himself, calling his mother; second, his mother, calling whomever he wished; third, his father, with the same freedom; fourth, a child of his own sex, phoning his mother to tell her he had done something wrong; and fifth, a child of the opposite sex, phoning mother to tell her what he had been doing at nursery school. (The fourth and fifth situations, that is, were to bear no reference to the *real* mother or child.) These role-playing situations provided behavior from the child that could be evaluated with respect to adult role, sex typing, and guilt over deviation. The specific scales relevant to each of these will be described in connection with the results.

In Session II, the first part was a "mother attentive" situation; the mother was instructed to sit with the child while he solved some jigsaw puzzles. The two sat at a low table under a window. There were current magazines on the table if the mother chose to look at them. She was told she could help the child if she wished, since we were interested in *how* he worked under these circumstances, not in a performance score. This situation was designed to provide a contrasting stimulus setting to the "mother busy" setting created in the first part of Session I, and to provide conditions suitable for arousing achievement motivation in the mother.

The second part of Session II was a fishing game. A large galvanized-metal tub, resting on a six-inch-high standard, was filled to the brim with water. In the bottom were seven hollow metal fish about five inches long, each with a loop in the nose and a number of openings into the hollow body. Mother and child were each provided with a fishing rod having a hook on the end of the line with which the loop on the fish could be snagged. Raincoats, hats, and fishing boots were also provided. After the mother was shown how to "catch the fish" with the line and hook, she was instructed to teach the child how, and to keep him fishing for the full quarter-hour. A pile of newspapers was stacked nearby, and a large and a small mop were leaning against the wall. The fish were designed to drip long and sloppily every time they were lifted from the water. It was quite a messy business. This situation was designed to provide a stimulus to restrictive, cleanly, directive behavior by the mother, and coordinately, a chance to see how the child would respond to such control.

On each of these two occasions, as soon as the mother and child went into the experimental room and closed the door, the assistant joined an observer in the observation chamber to watch through the mirror. Carefully adjusted hanging microphones in the experimental room were connected to earphones worn by both the observer and the assistant, and to a tape recorder. During the session, the observer dictated into a second tape recorder a running commentary designed to supplement and clarify the main tape-recording. At the end of the session, the observer and the assistant independently rated the mother on eight scales and the child on five.

A typescript of the observer's running description of the session was used in parallel with the mother-child tape to score the two sessions on the mother and child behavior-rating scales. The two recordings had been carefully matched by time signals, and hence it was possible to break a full session into small time units for development of the various ratings. For all the scales that were intended to provide measures covering either the full hour of interaction or any one of the four parts (e.g., "mother busy"), a rating was made for each three-minute period. A subject's final score on one of these scales was the mean of all the three-minute-period ratings on that scale. The exceptions to this method of scoring were the judgments made on six of the child behavior-rating scales respecting telephone behavior; each of these involved a single rating (e.g., resistance to adult role behavior).

The reliability of these ratings was calculated in terms of per cent agreement between two independent raters, in a fashion similar to that used with the parent interviews, on the protocols of five mothers and five children. The obtained values for the 24 mother scales ranged from 55.5 to 100 per cent, with a median of 84.2 per cent; comparable values for the 24 child scales were 50 to 90 per cent, and 72.8 per cent. Since these reliability indicators were of satisfactory size, the remaining 35 protocols were rated by a single rater.

Mother Questionnaires

Three types of questionnaires or attitude scales were given to the mothers at the end of the summer. The first was a scale designed by Winterbottom (1953) for measuring the strength and urgency of a mother's pressure on her child to develop independence. The scale consists of forty items that describe tasks a child must learn while he is growing up. Examples are "To stand up for his own rights with other children," "To be willing to try new things on his own without depending on his mother for help," and "To make decisions like choosing his clothes, or deciding how to spend money, by himself." A mother is asked to make two decisions about each task: (1) at what age she wants her child to have achieved it, and (2) whether the child should have achieved it by age ten. Scores based on the two judgments provide alternative measures of the same thing—how early and how rapidly independence is to be developed.

The second questionnaire was a behavior-maturity scale adapted from a preliminary form of the Cain-Levine Social Competency Scales (1963). The scale was designed to secure an overall measure, through the mother's perceptions, of her child's behavioral maturity. For each of twenty tasks (e.g., putting toys away, eating, care of clothing) there were listed four or five stages of maturity. For example, under "Putting toys away" were listed: "(1) Puts toys away only when directed to do so, (2) Usually puts toys away if reminded and occasionally puts them away without being told, (3) Usually remembers to put toys away without being told, (4) Always puts toys away without being told." For each of the twenty tasks, the mother was asked to indicate which of the four or five items represented the *most characteristic* behavior of the child at that time. Although the scaling in this early form of the scale may not be very precise, the cumulative total of the levels of performance attributed to all the tasks provides a rough measure of the child's maturity as his mother sees it.

The third questionnaire was a set of five mother-attitude scales (Sears, 1965) designed to measure five of the same variables on which information had earlier been sought in the mother interview. Four were permissiveness scales (indoor nudity, masturbation, social sex play, and aggression to parents) and the fifth was a punitiveness scale (aggression to parents). These additional measures were obtained to supplement the interview measures, because we knew from previous experience that these crucially important variables are among the most difficult to measure by interview.

The five mother-attitude scales were composed of 79 attitudinal statements about sex and aggression (in children) culled from the mother interviews that formed the basis for the report published as *Patterns of Child Rearing* (Sears, Maccoby, and Levin, 1957). Each quotation was preceded by a five-point scale ranging from "strongly agree" to "strongly disagree." A score for each of the five scales was calculated simply by summing the ratings made by a mother on the statements belonging to a particular scale. Spearman-Brown corrections of the odd-even reliability coefficients (r's) of these five scales were, in the order listed above, .92, .92, .94, .86, and .86.

Child Measures

The procedures for developing three sources of child measures (the mother-child interactions, the parent interviews, and the behavior maturity scale) have already been described. We have also stated that discussion of the standardized assessment situations will be taken up where each becomes appropriate, in later chapters. Three child-measure areas remain to be described: the behavior unit observations, the observer ratings, and the doll play. The section concludes with a brief discussion of some methodological problems arising in the development of child measures. Again, all the measures, or variables, selected for the study are listed in Appendix C, with an index to text citations.

Behavior Unit Observations (BUO)

Some of the behavior qualities having theoretical importance for the present study occur so often in a nursery school setting that measures of them can be obtained just by watching a child and recording how often he acts in a particular way. This was the case with three main categories of action in which we were interested—dependency, aggression, and adult role behavior.

To make such observations accurately, there must be a set of precise definitions of the behavior categories to be observed. For the present purpose, we defined five of dependency, twelve of aggression, and ten of adult role. These categories were mutually exclusive, and were intended to be exhaustive within their classes, i.e., to include all possible acts a child could perform that belonged to the more general class in which they belonged (e.g., dependency). The formal definitions, and behavioral examples of each, are given in Appendix D, along with a detailed description of the procedure, observer reliability, trait consistency, and method of constructing scores.

The behavior unit observations were made by four observers who worked continuously at this one task during the seven weeks of data collection. They were trained in advance to an acceptable level of agreement on recognizing the various categories. Each observer was equipped with a clipboard on which a small battery-powered timer provided a brief flash of light from a small bulb at thirty-second intervals. The observations were made according to a time-sampling procedure that required the observer to record the main category of behavior a child performed during each of twenty consecutive half-minute intervals. Every child was observed for at least three such ten-minute periods each week. His final score on each category was calculated by dividing the number of half-minute intervals in which that particular act occurred by the total number of half-minute intervals he was observed during the seven weeks. These *relative-frequency* measures are the scores described as *BUO scores* in the later chapters.

Observer Ratings

During the summer, the four observers spent almost 90 hours observing the children in connection with the BUO. Thus they probably knew the children's behavioral qualities better than anyone else. In order to quantify observer judgments, six five-point rating scales were constructed for use at the end of the summer. These scales, which related only in part to the BUO variables, measured masculinity-femininity, aggression, physical-contact seeking, attention getting, physical activity, and amount of social interaction. An average of all four observers' independent ratings on each scale was used as a final score for that scale. The reliability coefficients were quite satisfactory, as can be seen from the more extended description in Appendix E.

Doll Play

Two kinds of doll play were used to secure manipulative fantasy behavior from the children. The first, comprising two twenty-minute sessions, was the kind of permissive play that has been used frequently in studies from our laboratories (P. Sears, 1951; Sears, Whiting, Nowlis, and Sears, 1953). An experimenter presented the child with an open-topped doll house containing five rooms (kitchen, living room, bathroom, parents' bedroom, and children's bedroom), a garage, and an area defined as "daddy's shop." There were five dolls (father, mother, boy, girl, baby). The child was told he could show just what the family did in the house. His actions were recorded in terms of successive behavior units, but without time intervals as used in the BUO. The final score on each of the many variables measured was a per cent score indicating the relative frequency with which a given variable was noted. The frequency of occurrence of a given category was divided by the total frequency of behavior units recorded. Scores for all variables were calculated separately for the two sessions.

The categories of doll-play behavior for which scores were obtained are listed in the appropriate section of Appendix C, and the details of procedure, observer reliability, and trait consistency are presented in Appendix F. The variables that are of particular relevance to adult role, aggression, conscience, and sex typing will be discussed further in the later chapters.

The second kind of doll play was a more structured kind. At a single session, the experimenter used the doll house to present six incomplete stories in which a doll—the child doll of the same sex as the subject—committed a deviant act, something disapproved of in our culture. The child was asked to complete each of the stories, telling "what happens next" (cf. Wurtz, 1959).

Our interest lay in what dispositions the child might show to express behavior and feelings related to guilt. Such categories as confession, physical punishment, and fixing seemed relevant. The scoring categories are listed in Appendix C, and the procedural details in Appendix F. The main reference to deviation-doll-play variables will be found in Chapter 6.

A Methodological Problem

It is clear that our various behavior measures—obtained from the BUO, the MCI, the doll play procedures, and the assessment situations—are all directed toward securing estimates of relatively stable trait qualities in the children. If a quantitative comparison is to be made between children with respect to a consistent behavior quality (conceived as a potentiality for action), the stimulus conditions under which the behavior is sampled must be constant from one child to another. The obvious reason for this requirement is that the frequency of a given kind of behavior varies systematically with the immediate instigation to it, as well as with differences in the child's potentiality. For example, as will be seen in the discussion of dependency in the next chapter, the number of bids for attention when mother was busy was, on the average, about twice as great as when she was attentive. This finding exemplifies the principle that frustration induced by non-responsiveness of the mother is one of the determinants of attention-seeking. From a methodological standpoint, however, the finding points to the fact that external stimulating conditions can make very great differences in a child's behavior, and thus can introduce distorting influences on presumed measures of trait qualities if the stimulating conditions are not held constant for all children, or at least are not varied in a truly random fashion.

Standardized assessment situations have the virtue of providing relatively constant stimulation for all the children exposed to them. Of course, since they are relatively expensive of investigative time, the sampling of behavior under naturalistic conditions, as with our BUO procedure, has a substantial advantage to offer. Moreover, if a sufficiently large sample of behavior is obtained in the BUO procedure, the fortuitous differences in the immediate stimulus setting tend to cancel out one another. In the present study, the stability over the summer of individual children's displays of dependency, adult role behavior, and aggression (as indicated in Appendix D) suggests that the sample of behavior obtained was sufficiently large to provide the canceling out.

One systematic source of bias enters any such measurement, however, and whereas it may produce no difficulties or distortions in some types of data analysis, it may in others. Regardless of how large a sample of behavior is obtained, there is one kind of stimulus that varies systematically from child to child—namely, who the other children are in his immediate play area. Boys characteristically choose certain areas for play more often than girls do, and vice versa. This means that boys are relatively more often the companions of boys, and girls of girls. Since there are certain highly significant differences in the behavior of the sexes—e.g., with respect to frequency of antisocial aggression—it is clear that there is always some systematic difference in the stimulus environs of the two sexes. As will be seen in Chapter 5, this source of error has not seemed to influence the stability or size of any of our BUO measures, but it is a potential source of difficulty that should be kept in mind.

Plan of the Book

The succeeding chapters in this book present the data obtained concerning the six major types of child behavior measured. Dependency is not one of the identification products, of course, but it plays such a central role in anaclitic identification theory that it required as extensive study as the other forms. The discussions of resistance to temptation and of guilt reactions are combined in the chapter on conscience. Within each topical chapter, a brief description is given of the measures used for that kind of behavior (as obtained from BUO, MCI, doll play, and special assessments), and then consideration is given, in order, to sex and age differences, the correlations among the various measures obtained, the correlations of that general type of behavior with the types treated in preceding chapters, and the relations of child behavior to parental behavior. In the final chapter, the findings are assessed with respect to the light they cast on identification theory, and on the contribution of child rearing to children's personalities.

2. Dependency

Dependency, in identification theory, is the principal source of reinforcement of the imitative behavior that leads to adult role adoption. When the maturing but still dependent child suffers gradual withdrawal of parental nurturance and love, he is stimulated to role practice by his need to regain control of the parental resources, especially the expression of love. In the absence of dependency motivation, identification would not develop; with unusually high dependency, other things being equal, identification should develop very rapidly. Thus, it follows from anaclitic identification theory that there should be high positive correlations between measures of a child's dependency and measures of the behaviors that we have considered to be products of identification. The need to test this hypothesis was the first reason for including dependency among the child behaviors to be measured.

A second reason stemmed from our realization that little more was known about the structure and genetics of dependency than about identification. If, as presumed, the latter is derived from the former, then much the same questions needed answering about both. Hence, the present chapter reports our findings concerning the organization of dependent behavior, tests of some hypotheses concerning its child-rearing correlates, and some new antecedent-consequent hypotheses that have been induced from the data.

Dependency Theory

Dependency is considered to be an action system in which another person's nurturant, helping, and caretaking activities are the rewarding environmental events. Dependency *actions* are actions that elicit such events. To the extent that these actions are organized into a cluster—perhaps serving as alternative methods of securing the dyadic responses—dependency can be considered a *trait*. Whether one can usefully postulate a dependency *drive,* as a source of internal instigation to supplicative actions, depends, at present, largely on theoretical predilection.

This last question has been debated for several years, and has led to vigorous argument over whether *drive* is a necessary construct at all, and, if so, how it can be defined. Some investigators have conceptualized dependency as a secondary drive, an intervening variable modeled quite directly after such primary drives as hunger and sex. Presumably, this view has been taken because of the spontaneous character, and persistence, of young children's seeking for attention, affection, and reassurance from their parents, the seeming increase in strength of such supplication when nurturance or affection is withheld, and the reduction of such striving when a substantial amount of nurturance has been given. If we acknowledge, as we must, that there is no critical evidence to support the drive conception, then we must ask what alternative explanations can be used to account for these phenomena.

Gewirtz (1961) has presented a persuasive argument for the view that dependent behavior is, rather, an operant activity in response only to cues previously associated with the reinforcements that followed dependent supplication (and presumably also, he suggests, to cues that function for stimulus generalization). He finds no need for a drive construct, but rests with a statement of stimuli and learned responses. The differential implications of these two interpretations have yet to be derived in the kind of detail that will permit an empirical determination of where the truth lies. Either is satisfactory for purposes of identification theory.

One fact must be kept in mind. Whichever theory ultimately proves more efficient, the data from which inferences are made come always from *observations of overt dependent behavior.* For the moment, we shall keep the drive hypothesis as one of the two reasonable possibilities, recognizing clearly that the overt behavior from which this hypothesis is inferred is learned according to the same principles that govern the strengthening and weakening of operant actions in response to cue stimuli.

In its current usage, the notion of dependency as a motive stems mainly from two sources, Murray's *n* Succorance (1938) and Whiting's analysis of help seeking as a reaction to frustration (1944). Murray described succorance as being behaviorally exemplified by crying or pleading for nourishment, love, aid, and protection; the need was not limited to food, but included the associated caretaking and affectional nurturance that go with both infant feeding and other forms of infant care.

Whiting, also, emphasized the oral quality of dependency, suggesting that the association of hunger gratification with supportive and help-giving maternal behavior leads to the development of an acquired drive for which such behaviors are the appropriate rewards. Perhaps more important, Whiting pointed to the inevitability of dependency supplication as a reaction to frustration; since the satisfaction of early food needs was associated with affectionate care, later frustrations served as cues to elicit the same kind of supplication for help that had been learned initially. Thus, whereas Murray made a point of the drive (or need) quality of dependency, Whiting added another step by specifying a state of affairs (frustration) that could activate dependency behavior.

The conditions under which dependent behavior is presumed to be established in a child were described in detail in *Patterns of Child Rearing* (Sears, Maccoby, and Levin, 1957). They involve mainly the child's interaction with his original caretaker. The mother's caretaking behavior provides both the manipulanda required for the child's responses and the reinforcing stimulation that shapes those responses into a stable pattern of dependent behavior. On the child's side, there are operant responses from the beginning; the first of these are limited largely to sucking or mouthing movements, clutching and grasping reflexes, seemingly random vocalizations, and postural adjustments to being moved and held.

On the mother's side, the operant behavior is very complex, of course, since it is designed to achieve many caretaking ends—feeding, bathing, cleansing, warming, and so on—and also many mother-gratifying experiences, such as cuddling, fondling, being clutched at and sucked at, hearing, smelling, and even tasting the baby.

On neither side do we have a truly definitive list of these actions, even for one mother-baby pair, nor have we much notion of the similarities and differences across individuals or cultures. At the moment, we can do no better than use examples, such as those above, to evoke for each reader his own casual observations of the interaction topography. This is a terrain of almost infinite variety so far as the mother is concerned, but since her behavior is constantly guided by the conscious and unconscious purposes of her actions, this operant multiplicity channels into controlling systems that have definité shaping value for the baby's behavior. His operant repertoire increases as his capacities for more complex and more directed behavior multiply.

One apparent result of this mutually satisfying relationship is the creation of *secondary rewards* or *reinforcers* for both members of the pair. That is, the mother's talking, patting, smiling, and gestures of affection or concern are constantly being presented to the baby in context with primary reinforcing stimulations, such as those involved in eating and caressing.

It is not known whether the initially neutral maternal stimuli have any primary reinforcement quality at all; perhaps they are considered neutral because they seem to elicit so little response from the baby at first. It is pure inference, of course, that they gain all their later reward value from association with primary reinforcing stimuli. On the other hand, children of different mothers seek to produce such thoroughly idiosyncratic behaviors that one finds it difficult not to interpret their responses as the product of learning rather than of the maturation of some stimulus sensitivities.

A second consequence of mother-baby interaction is the development of *expectancies* on the part of both members. Each learns to respond to the other's characteristic actions and aspects not only with reactions suitable to the manipulandum and stimulus properties of the behavior, but also with an expectation of subsequent events. For example, a six-month-old baby who has been bottle-fed fairly regularly at the time of evening when his mother starts her work in the kitchen will respond to the preliminary sounds of pans on the sink, or the opening and closing of the refrigerator door, with gruntings and wigglings characteristic of the instant before the bottle is presented. As the food approaches, he will begin sucking movements, and these are often so strong in the early stages of learning that they interfere seriously with getting the nipple into his mouth. In keeping with the shaping conception of the influence of these experiences, however, the anticipatory responses soon disappear if they do in fact interfere with securing final gratification, i.e., with performing the act that produces the reinforcing stimulation being sought.

The child's expectancy is an inferred internal response to signals from the mother, and is essential to organizing his responses into purposeful activity. If the mother fails to perform the expected act from her own repertoire, the baby will suffer frustration and express resentment by crying or thrashing about or whatever he has so far learned to do in frustrating circumstances. Thus, if the mother performs all the initial acts that normally culminate in placing the nipple in his mouth, but then hesitates at the critical instant—interrupting the flow of her own behavior and hence not performing the environmental event that is reciprocal to the child's flow of behavior—an angry bellow is likely to ensue. The development of mutual expectancies molds the mother and baby into a dyad, a unit which can operate effectively only as long as both members perform their accustomed roles in expected fashion.

For the child, the upshot of this infantile experience is that a certain number of operant responses become firmly established to the various instigators that have been commonly associated with primary gratifications or reinforcing stimuli. The child learns to "ask" for the mother's reciprocal behavior. *These asking movements are the dependency acts whose frequency and intensity we use as a measure of the dependency trait (or dependency action system).* More precisely, we assume that the effectiveness of this learning process varies under different conditions and schedules of reinforcement, and that therefore children differ in the amount and kinds of such behavior.

If this view is correct, there are two sets of antecedents that should be related to the frequency of dependency behaviors at age four. One is the amount of reinforcement in infancy; the other is the amount more or less continuously provided after the habits are firmly established. In the earliest stages of learning, everything else being equal, the strength of the dependency response should vary positively with the amount of reinforcement. Thus one might expect that maternal indulgence and responsiveness toward the child's infantile supplications would be associated with more immediate development of a strong dependency action system, and with stronger dependency at a later age. Nothing in nature is ever equal, however, and the failure of the latter part of this oversimple prediction will occasion no surprise for the learning theorist. In fact, the *frequency and timing* (i.e., *scheduling*) of reinforcements in infancy appear to be much more potent determinants of ultimate response strength than sheer *amount*; intermittent schedules produce stronger responses than concentrated schedules. Whatever the relative *rates of development* of dependency responses in early infancy (such rates were not studied in the present research), the asymptotic strength finally achieved is more likely to be related to early intermittence than to early amount of reinforcement. Since, as will be seen, the measures from the retrospective interviews that we can use to infer *amount* of reinforcement in infancy are essentially the opposite ends of rating scales from which we would infer the degree of *intermittence* of reinforcement, only one of these two variables can be positively related to response strength.

Once the dependency response strength has become asymptotic, two antecedent variables are relevant—one to strength as defined by frequency of occurrence of dependency responses, and the other to strength as defined by both frequency and resistance to extinction. The former variable is *permissiveness* and the latter *scheduling.* The greater the number of exciting or exacerbating instigators the environment presents, the more frequently may the response be expected to occur. Conversely, the fewer the inhibiting or diverting instigators are, the less frequently alternative responses will replace the given response. Thus, for dependency, sex, or other positive-affective dyadic action systems, we would expect frequency of dependency responses to be related positively to such measures as permissiveness and reward, and negatively to non-permissiveness and punishment.

Again, however, the problem of intermittence of reinforcement arises. Coldness, remoteness, and non-responsiveness can serve not only as inhibitions to the child's dependency supplications, but also as conditions for a high degree of intermittence of reward. The more intermittent the scheduling, the stronger the responses.

Since we do not yet know how these several variables—amount of reinforcement, permissiveness, and intermittence—are represented in the measures obtained from the parent interviews, predictions of antecedent-consequent relationships cannot be made with great precision. The findings from the present data have helped to refine the indices of the variables, however, and we shall accordingly consider these theoretical problems further after a report of the data.

Measurement of Dependency

Four types of measurement were used. Two were introduced for methodological purposes and have not been retained for the present analysis; these were measures of the child's dependency drawn from the parents' interview ratings and from the observers' ratings. The two types of measure that have been retained are the behavior unit observations (BUO) of five categories of dependency occurring in the nursery school, and three measures of dependency exhibited toward the mother in the mother-child interaction (MCI) sessions. There were no special assessment situations designed for measuring dependency. (The numbers associated with the variables on the following pages, and throughout the remainder of the book, are keyed to the master list of parent and child variables presented in Appendix C.)

Behavior Unit Observations

The general procedure for the BUO was described in the first chapter, and further details are given in Appendix D. The five BUO categories of dependency were ones that had been used previously by Sears *et al.* (1953); the sum of the five was computed also. The categories are as follows:

Negative attention seeking (187): Getting attention by disruption, aggressive activity with minimal provocation, defiance, or oppositional behavior (e.g., opposing and resisting direction, rules, routines, and demands by ignoring, refusing, or doing the opposite).

Reassurance seeking (188): Apologizing, asking unnecessary permission, or seeking protection, comfort, consolation, help, or guidance.

Positive attention seeking (219): Seeking praise, seeking to join an in-group by inviting cooperative activity, or actually interrupting a group activity in progress.

Touching and holding (220): Non-aggressive touching, holding, clasping onto others.

Being near (221): Following or standing near a particular child or a group of children or a teacher.

Total observed dependency (224): The sum of all five categories, each weighted in accordance with its raw frequency.

The observers also recorded, for each dependent act, who the object of the supplication was—a boy, a girl, the teacher, another adult, a group, or whatever. About 95 per cent of the supplications were directed to an individual, i.e., to one of the first four of these objects.

Mother-Child Interaction

Three measures of child dependency were obtained from the MCI. The first (variable 335) was an overall rating of the amount of dependent supplication *of all kinds* displayed during the two half-hour sessions. This measure was obtained by rating each consecutive three-minute section of the interaction, the rater using both the typescript of the observer's dictated commentary and the tape recording of the interaction itself. The final score for each child was the median rating of the approximately twenty three-minute ratings thus secured.

The other two MCI dependency measures were rated while MCI sessions were in progress. Both ratings were with reference to frequency of *bids for attention.* One of these (336) was obtained during the first part of the first session, while the mother was filling out the questionnaire, and was designed to measure bids for attention *when the mother was busy.* The other measure (337) was taken during the first part of the second session, while the mother was watching the child work on the jigsaw puzzles, and was designed as a measure of bids *when the mother was attentive.*

Organization of Dependency

Sex Differences

In Table 1 are shown the mean frequency scores, by sex, on all our dependency measures, together with the standard deviations of the distributions, and the p value for the mean sex differences as derived from t-tests. The values for the BUO categories are per cent frequency of occurrence; those for the MCI measures are ratings. Of the nine measures, only one shows a clearly significant sex difference; boys displayed more negative attention seeking in the open nursery school situation than girls did. There were slight but insignificant differences favoring the girls on reassurance seeking and being near, and an equally noticeable one favoring boys on bids for attention (mother busy) in the mother-child interaction.

These findings are similar to those reported in an earlier study (Sears *et al.*, 1953), except that in that study the difference favoring boys in negative attention seeking was negligible—perhaps because the girls in that research group, judging from doll-play aggression scores, were somewhat more aggressive than the usual Iowa nursery school population. Since negative attention seeking and antisocial aggression are positively correlated (in the earlier study, p. 158, girls .31, boys .49; in the present study, girls .33, boys .35), it seems likely that the sex difference in negative attention seeking revealed in the present study was obscured

TABLE 1

Dependency Measures: Means, Standard Deviations, Significance of
Sex Differences, and Correlations with Age

*(Values for BUO measures are actual per cents; others are ratings.
An asterisk on the p-value indicates girls greater than boys.)*

Dependency Measures	Var. No.	Boys Mean	S.D.	Girls Mean	S.D.	p (2-tail)	r with Age Boys	Girls
Behavior Unit Observation								
Negative attention seeking .	187	.40	.44	.14	.25	<.05	−08	16
Reassurance seeking	188	.98	.83	1.42	.93	n.s.°	−27	−17
Positive attention seeking . .	219	2.27	1.39	2.38	1.78	n.s.°	−17	15
Touching and holding . . .	220	1.36	2.17	.95	.98	n.s.	24	−26
Being near	221	1.43	1.54	2.47	3.19	n.s.°	−11	−46
Total observed dependency .	224	6.50	3.41	7.47	4.59	n.s.°	−09	−39
Mother-Child Interaction								
Child's dependency	335	5.67	2.36	5.21	2.17	n.s.	06	−34
Bids for attention: mother busy	336	5.14	1.67	4.21	1.88	n.s.	−26	−50
Bids for attention: mother attentive	337	2.67	1.32	2.63	1.53	n.s.	06	−11

in the former by some variation in sampling. However, with this one exception, none of the differences in the present study is sufficient to suggest any stable sex difference in sheer frequency of dependent behavior in the nursery school.

The case is quite different with respect to *objects* of dependent supplication, however. Positive attention seeking is the only category (other than total observed dependency) for which object comparisons can be made; on the other categories there were too many children with zero scores to permit meaningful comparison. The left half of Table 2 presents mean percentages of positive attention seeking and total observed dependency acts directed toward each of four kinds of person: boys, girls, teacher, and other adults.† In supplication of teachers and of other adults, there is relatively little sex difference: the proportion of such acts

† "Other adults" consists of casual visitors, experimenters, observers, and other children's mothers who assisted temporarily in the school. A child's own mother was excluded from the category "other adults" as presenting too high a stimulus to dependency; we tried not to schedule the BUO when a child's own mother was present, but were not always successful. Siblings (who occasionally visited the school, especially when the mother was participating) were excluded from the boy object and girl object categories for the same reason. These exclusions, plus occasional instances in which an observer forgot to record the object, prevent the percentage figures given in Table 2 from adding to exactly 100.

TABLE 2

Objects of Dependency: Mean Per Cent of Responses Toward Four
Object Classes, with Confidence Level of Sex Difference

*(Confidence levels are 2-tailed, by t-test. In the boy-girl comparison, the difference score of boy
objects minus girl objects is used. Re-analyses of the Iowa data are given for comparison.)*

Object of Dependency Behavior	Positive Attention Seeking			Total Observed Dependency		
	By Boys	By Girls	Differ- ence p	Of Boys	Of Girls	Differ- ence p
	Stanford Data					
Boy	18.9	7.5		15.8	5.4	
			.02			.07
Girl	11.6	20.4		12.6	13.5	
Teacher	34.8	32.7	n.s.	39.2	41.6	n.s.
Other adult	31.7	32.5	n.s.	24.2	25.8	n.s.
	Iowa Data					
Boy	39.3	19.2		35.6	13.4	
			< .001			< .001
Girl	15.4	32.0		13.8	24.8	
Teacher and other adult . . .	40.2	43.7	n.s.	45.0	57.9	< .05

to the whole is about the same for boys as for girls. In supplication of
other children, however, there are large and significant sex differences:
for both categories, the sex difference can be generalized by the proposition that objects of dependency are more often children of the same sex
than children of the opposite sex.[*]

These results replicate those reported in the Iowa study (Sears *et al.*,
1953, p. 196). A re-analysis of those data, given here in the bottom half of
Table 2, shows that for both positive attention seeking and total observed dependency the above proposition holds true, and that, as at
Stanford, the boys directed their dependency acts toward children and
adults in about the same proportions as the girls. The two groups do
differ in one respect; the Iowa children directed relatively much more
of their positive attention seeking toward other children than toward
adults. This is scarcely surprising, for the teacher and one observer were
the only adults present when the Iowa observations were made, whereas
not only teachers but from six to ten other adults were present in the

---

[*] This same principle holds for negative attention seeking, touching and holding, and
reassurance seeking, if we consider only those children who made one or more such
responses. For being near, it applies to girls but not to boys.

Stanford Nursery School, and several of these were researchers who made it a point to be in frequent and friendly contact with the children. In the Stanford data, 33.8 per cent of the adult objects of positive attention seeking were teachers, and 32.0 per cent were other adults.

These large variations are reminders that BUO measures taken in the open nursery school are essentially estimates of operant level. The many influences representative of action principles are inevitably present in differing amounts from child to child, day to day, nursery school to nursery school, and culture to culture. It would be hazardous indeed to make any generalizations outside our own rather narrow subculture about the relative attractiveness of teachers (adults) vs. children as objects for positive attention seeking, or even of like-sexed vs. unlike-sexed children. We have mentioned earlier the tendency for children to select play areas according to sex; hence the available objects at any moment are more likely to be children of the same sex.

However, the fact that these two studies, performed ten years apart in different parts of the country (but both in university research nursery schools), agree on (1) the lack of any large sex differences in total frequencies of dependent behavior, and (2) the relative preference for like-sexed children as objects, may suggest that in these subcultures there are fairly stable qualities producing the observed similarities.

Age Differences

The age range was twenty months for the boys, and eighteen for the girls. This difference is sufficient, in the preschool years, to permit rather substantial variations in experience and level of maturation. One might expect concomitant variations in dependency behavior, since presumably parents direct the socialization process toward eliminating certain early (changeworthy) forms of behavior and developing more mature affiliations, independence, and responsibility.

Some such changes were noted by Heathers (1955) in his comparison of the dependency behavior of two- and five-year-olds. The older children showed less touching and holding and being near with adult objects, although there was no change in the frequency of these responses to other children. The older children also exhibited more positive attention seeking by verbal methods. This included asking questions, calling attention to performance, and asking for praise, behaviors that Gewirtz (1954) discovered formed a single factor in a factor analysis of several measures taken during an experiment on dependency in four- and five-year-old children. In *Patterns of Child Rearing* also, there was evidence, rather indirect, that such infantile forms of behavior as clinging, wanting to be near the mother, and objecting emotionally to the mother's leaving the house had been substantially stronger and more frequent earlier in the children's lives than at the time the mothers were interviewed (when the children were five). These various findings suggest that a child's operant activities for securing nurturance and attention not only change as he grows older, but also develop to some degree independently of one another.

The distribution of ages in the present sample is too curtailed to permit a successful test of this hypothesis. In general, the correlations between age and the various dependency categories and measures range from zero to negative, the size of the relationships being greater for the girls than for the boys (Table 1). None of the measures for the boys correlates to anywhere near a .05 level of confidence. Several of the girls' measures have a clearly negative coefficient, but only two are at the .05 level (being near and bids for attention when mother is busy).

An examination of the scatter plots suggests that these correlations may not be telling quite the whole story, however. With respect to both touching and holding and being near, the highest-scoring girls are younger than the highest-scoring boys. On each of these categories, the top six boys form a cluster, and the top six girls a second cluster; in both cases, the boys' cluster is higher on the age ordinate than the girls', though the mean difference in age of the clusters is not significant by *t*-test. (Among the boys, there is only one common member of these extreme groups on the two dependency measures, whereas the corresponding six-girl groups have four members in common.) This rather crude comparison suggests that the girls may have been developing a little more rapidly than the boys, and therefore that—following Heathers' interpretation—we can regard touching and holding and being near as representing less mature forms of dependency supplication.

Our conclusion is that there is probably some general tendency for the more contactual and more intimate forms of dependency behavior to decline gradually during the preschool years, but that certain child-rearing variables are more important than age in determining their frequencies; within the age range we are dealing with here, age may be pretty largely disregarded so far as dependency is concerned.

Activity Level

Not all categories of behavior require bodily activity for their occurrence, but a good many do. Among the BUO dependency categories, being near tends to receive more frequent mention if a child does not move much. By contrast, positive attention seeking is inherently an active process; a child cannot seek without seeking! Since children vary considerably, and self-consistently, in their basal rate of moving around in their environment, some children have more, or less, opportunity than others to exhibit certain behaviors. Thus, the prevailing activity level has some influence on any behavioral measure based on sheer frequency of occurrence of a given type of act, as is true with our BUO categories.

In the report of the Iowa study, this influence was interpreted as a contaminating factor, and teacher ratings of the children's activity levels were obtained in order to permit its removal by use of partial correlations. For example, in that study the raw frequencies of observed dependency and aggression (essentially the same as our present BUO measures) were positively correlated .32 and .49 for boys and girls, respectively, but eliminating the influence of activity level by partial correlation dropped these figures to $-.09$ and .28. A similar procedure was followed in the present study, the ratings of activity level being obtained from the observers. Again we find reductions in the correlations between positive attention seeking and antisocial aggression; the zero-order coefficients in the Stanford data are, for boys and girls, respectively, .11 and .62 (for raw frequencies) and .06 and .36 (for the partials). Again the girls have the higher correlation, both before and after activity level is partialed out.

We have become somewhat skeptical of the significance of these findings, in spite of the seeming logic of the initial argument. The observers in the present study, all graduate students in child psychology, were familiar with the earlier findings and accepted the reasoning. In making their ratings of activity, they already "knew" that the more active children must have shown more aggression, more active dependency, and more adult role behavior. And the relationship is obviously reversible—the more these kinds of behavior occurred during the BUO, the more active a child must be. This could introduce a spurious element into the ratings: namely, activity *ratings* could be influenced as easily by the observers' knowledge of the frequency of the substantive forms of behavior (aggression, etc.) as the children's *behavior* could be influenced by the prevailing activity level.

This possible source of error occurred to us only after an elaborate data analysis of both the organization and the child-rearing antecedents of dependency, an analysis that essentially duplicated—with partial correlations to hold activity constant—the analysis presented in the remainder of this chapter. The partialing led to no significant relational differences from the analysis to be presented here, in terms of zero-order coefficients of correlation. To test our hidden-bias hypothesis, we examined, separately by sex, the correlations between activity ratings and two other kinds of measure: the ratings of sex typing, aggressive behavior, and two kinds of dependency behavior, and the BUO categories of these same four variables. In all but one of the eight comparisons, activity correlated higher with rating than with BUO category. This is not conclusive evidence for our suspicion that the activity ratings were contaminated by the observers' knowledge of substantive behavior frequencies, but it is certainly congruent with such an interpretation. In any case, we shall present our findings without introducing a special control for activity level.

Relations among Dependency Measures

As in so many other respects, boys and girls differ in the degree of correlation they show between the various measures of dependency. Table 3 provides a matrix of coefficients for these measures. In general, correlations among the five BUO dependency categories center around zero for the boys, but are mainly small and positive for the girls. The slightly higher interrelationships for the girls are represented also by higher correlations of the separate categories with their sum (total observed dependency); the median for these correlations is .45 for the boys, .61 for the girls.

The positive relations between the two categories touching and holding and being near, in both boys and girls, and the slight negative relations of these with positive attention seeking in boys, add some support to the suggestion made earlier that these represent, respectively, immature and mature forms of dependency. When age of child is partialed out of these interrelations, however, there is no significant change in any coefficient. Thus, although it may be convenient to characterize these behaviors as "mature" and "immature," these labels ought properly to be reserved for contrasts over broader age ranges than are represented

TABLE 3

Intercorrelations among Dependency Measures

(Girls above the diagonal, boys below)

Dependency Measures	Var. No.	Variable Number								
		187	188	219	220	221	224	335	336	337
Negative attention seeking	187	°	06	10	15	37	29	−13	−15	37
Reassurance seeking	188	−24	°	25	19	26	57	−10	−09	44
Positive attention seeking	219	23	−11	°	11	−03	62	10	23	62
Touching and holding	220	04	14	−16	°	71	61	−14	19	44
Being near	221	−03	12	−15	13	°	67	−04	23	42
Total observed dependency . .	224	20	39	46	45	56	°	06	31	71
MCI: child's dependency . .	335	02	−28	−07	27	−07	−02	°	74	10
MCI: mother busy	336	09	06	28	−04	−21	12	33	°	12
MCI: mother attentive	337	05	15	−32	−04	22	04	18	00	°

here. Perhaps "active-passive" or "verbal-physical" would be better than "mature-immature" for indicating the contrast.

In general, we must conclude that the five BUO dependency categories represent almost entirely independent action systems for boys, and are organized only very slightly into an overall trait of dependency in girls.

The remaining three measures are those obtained during the mother-child interaction. One of these is an overall dependency rating. For neither sex does this relate significantly to any other measure of dependency. The other two measures are ratings that combine frequency and intensity into single measures of bids for attention; one rating was made while the mother was busy with the questionnaire, the other while the child was solving the jigsaw puzzles. For the boys, neither of these relates significantly to any other dependency measure. Among the girls, however, the mother-attentive puzzle period correlates significantly with three of the five BUO categories. Again, the girls show some slight consistency among dependency expressions, and the boys do not.

Summary of Organization

The following statements summarize our findings with respect to the organization of dependency:

1. In sheer frequency of dependency supplications in the nursery school setting, the only significant sex difference was the boys' higher incidence of negative attention seeking.

2. There was no difference between boys and girls in the relative frequency with which they directed dependency acts toward children, nor was there where such acts were directed toward adults.

3. When dependency was directed toward another child, the object was significantly more often a child of the same sex.

4. There was a very slight positive interrelationship among the dependency measures (particularly the BUO categories) for girls, but none for the boys.

5. Touching and holding and being near related more highly to each other than to positive attention seeking in girls; this differentiation of immature and mature types of dependency was only very slightly suggested in the boys' data.

6. There was some very slight evidence that the girls had matured earlier than the boys, as measured by the shift from immature to mature forms.

7. The evidence for a basic trait of dependency behavior is unsatisfactory for girls and clearly lacking for boys; for both sexes, each of the five BUO dependency categories should be considered separately with respect to its origins.

Reinforcement in Infancy

In our search for child-rearing correlates of the children's dependency behavior, we began with the hypotheses mentioned above. They had been suggested by the Iowa study, which examined the relation of several child-rearing variables to measures of dependency obtained by both observation and teacher ratings in the nursery school. The present study permits a test of these hypotheses.

The first proposed that the more frequently an infant is rewarded for making dependent responses toward his parents, the more of these responses he will make at age four. This hypothesis is deceptively simple, however. In fact, dependent supplications of the kinds made during the first year of life cease almost entirely by the fifth year, so that only in the most general sense can "dependency" be compared at the two ages. Hence, the measured responses must be considered to be either products of response generalization or representations of a dependency drive, the strength of which should vary positively with reinforcement (and, as we have just seen, the evidence for a basic trait of dependency is unsatisfactory or clearly lacking). Furthermore, we would be hard pressed to determine which, if any, of our interview measures of child rearing reflect amount of reinforcement.

There are two ways in which reinforcement may vary in infancy; one is in amount of reward given, the other in amount of operant behavior required for a given amount of reward, i.e., in amount of intermittent reinforcement. As an example of the first point, a child separated frequently or continuously from a parent during infancy should have less opportunity to establish dependent responses toward that parent. As an example of the second, scheduled feeding (as opposed to demand feeding) should require more operant activity for the ultimate reward, and hence should create more dependency.

Consider amount of reinforcement first. Table 4 presents correlations between the various measures of dependency and several relevant child-rearing variables. It can be seen that severity of early separation from either parent (variables 5 and 6) is not significantly related to any of the dependency measures; none of the coefficients reaches the .10 level of significance, and their patterning seems quite random. The correlations with each parent's scale are, in fact, so low that partial correlations holding each parent scale constant (so that the effects of the other parent may be determined) produce no significant change in the size of any of these relationships. Perhaps a relationship here would be too much to hope for, inasmuch as the range of experiences was quite narrow in this respect (as was the case in the Iowa study, which also gave no indication of a relation between separation and dependency).

A second measure of amount of reinforcement is duration of breast feeding (variable 13). It might be supposed that the longer a child is fed at the breast, the more reinforcement he will receive for his dyadic controlling behavior. The supportive evidence in Table 4 is limited to boys' negative attention seeking, which will be discussed later. For the other measures, the relationships are mainly zero or even negative.

Turning now to the other way of evaluating reinforcement—the proportion of times that a given operant behavior receives reward—we would presume that intermittent reinforcement leads to a stronger response, because the child must perform a greater number of acts to secure reward. In this respect there are two other aspects of infant feeding, besides duration of breast feeding, that may be relevant—rigidity of scheduled feeding (14) and severity of weaning (16).

TABLE 4

Infancy Experiences: Correlations with Dependency Measures

Dependency Measures	Duration of Breast Feeding (13)	Rigidity of Scheduled Feeding (14)	Severity of Weaning (16)	Severity of Early Separation		Proportion of Caretaking in Infancy		Caretaking (Partial)[*]	
				Mother (5)	Father (6)	Mother (11)	Father (12)	Mother	Father
GIRLS									
Negative attention seeking	−07	−07	02	15	−23	−49	47	−43	41
Reassurance seeking	−03	−10	04	−06	08	−02	16	02	16
Positive attention seeking	−07	−27	02	−04	−17	−62	17	−61	03
Touching and holding	28	11	−46	07	01	26	22	34	30
Being near	21	−07	−50	−02	−03	13	08	16	12
Total observed dependency	03	−19	−24	−01	07	−23	16	−20	10
MCI: child's dependency	−35	22	12	−04	31	21	−46	12	−43
MCI: mother busy	−28	12	−33	−29	27	12	−31	05	−29
MCI: mother attentive	14	−15	00	02	−21	−29	12	−27	05
BOYS									
Negative attention seeking	43	−19	45	18	−26	11	02	17	14
Reassurance seeking	−31	16	29	−05	08	−37	14	−38	−18
Positive attention seeking	23	08	26	−16	26	18	−49	−26	−51
Touching and holding	−32	−16	−07	28	−23	−41	21	−37	−12
Being near	−21	−22	15	02	03	20	−19	10	−07
Total observed dependency	−13	−12	38	08	06	−03	−28	−34	−42
MCI: child's dependency	08	08	−27	22	29	−06	32	24	39
MCI: mother busy	30	41	−15	−08	18	−34	42	−08	27
MCI: mother attentive	21	00	10	−06	−01	17	23	48	50

[*] Partial correlations in which the proportion of caretaking by the other parent is held constant.

Both were measured and their relation to dependency examined in the Iowa study. There, the extent to which the mother used self-demand (rather than a rigid schedule) was interpreted as a positive measure of the pure *amount* of reward the child had received for making supplications. However, results just the opposite from those expected were found —the observed dependency in nursery school was somewhat *inversely* related to self-demand feeding, the relation in girls being stronger than in boys. In the present study, this would correspond to a *positive* correlation between rigidity of scheduled feeding and total dependency. However, Table 4 shows virtually no relation at all between scheduling and any of our observational measures of dependency; the columns of coefficients for both sexes strike us as entirely random in size and direction. The essential point of these results, we believe, is that the findings from the previous investigation are not replicated in the present one.

With regard to severity of weaning, it can be reasoned that a gentle, well-prepared-for weaning to the cup takes into account the child's wishes and provides a more regular reinforcement of supplication, with less effort on the child's part, than a severe weaning that involves a determined refusal by the mother to respond to the child's requests, a method that should maximize intermittent reinforcement and strengthen dependency actions. Thus, severe weaning should produce more dependency. In the Iowa study, observed dependency showed no relation at all to severity of weaning, but dependency as rated by the teacher was quite clearly *positive* in its relation to weaning severity, as we would expect from the hypothesis. The findings from the present study (Table 4) are equivocal; for girls, there is a fairly consistent negative relationship, whereas for boys, as the hypothesis proposes, the relations are predominantly positive. So far as the Iowa teacher's ratings of dependency are concerned, then, the Stanford boys replicated the findings, but the girls did not and indeed were more strongly related in the opposite direction.

Several investigators have expressed doubt whether infant oral or feeding experiences have any influence at all on behavior in the later nursery school years. The present findings do nothing to allay such doubts, so far as nursery school behavior is concerned. Not only are the expected relationships notably missing, but the relatively small relationships found in the earlier study receive no replication in the present one.

The case is quite different for another (but non-oral) indicator of infant reinforcement. The proportional amount of caretaking in infancy by the mother (11) and by the father (12) do provide some rather substantial correlations. The two scales are the same as those used for this purpose in *Patterns of Child Rearing*, and consider the proportion of total caretaking performed by sitters and relatives, as well as by the other parent. In the Stanford data, the correlation between the two parents' proportions is −.70 for boys and −.24 for girls; the difference is significant at the .05 level. The smaller negative correlation for girls' parents suggests that they made more use of babysitters or relatives than the boys' parents did. At such times as the mothers were not doing the caretaking for their sons, the fathers evidently were, whereas when the mothers were not caring for their daughters, the fathers might or might not have been. Both fathers and mothers tended to do less caretaking of girls than of boys, but neither sex difference is significant.

These correlations correspond to *r*'s of −.64 and −.46, respectively, in the earlier study, which do not differ significantly. The rather large difference between the two present correlations may be a sampling variation, although we cannot be confident of this because all the information for both parents was obtained from the mothers in the former study, whereas the parents reported separately in the present one. Another difference between the two studies was the time in world affairs when they were performed; the *Patterns* children were infants just at the end of World War II, when sitters were hard to find, families were perhaps displaced from the locus of relatives, and incomes were often precarious as fathers made the transition from military to civilian occupations. Since non-parental caretaking was easier to obtain and more frequently used by the present group of parents, and since it was drawn upon more for girls than for boys, we would tend to expect the lower negative correlation for girls in the present study. These substantial and differing correlations between the two parent caretaking scales make partial correlations worth examining; the last two columns of Table 4 show partial *r*'s between the dependency measures and each parent's proportional amount of caretaking, with the other parent's proportional amount held constant.

The most notable relation for both sexes is between the BUO category of positive attention seeking and the amount of caretaking by the same-sexed parent; these correlations are significantly negative, indicating that the greater the proportional amount of infant caretaking by the same-sexed parent, the less the positive attention seeking in nursery school. Several of the other correlations are rather substantially negative also, although those for boys' dependency in the mother-child interaction are positive with father caretaking. The overall indications appear to be in opposition to the hypothesis that amount of caretaking positively reinforces dependency behavior. On the contrary, this parental variable seems to represent a measure of interference or frustration—the less the frustration (the higher the caretaking), the less the dependency—and the more important influence apparently stems from the same-sexed parent. This finding will be considered further in the discussion of positive attention seeking.

Our conclusion is that amount of reinforcement in infancy may or may not be influential for later dependency; present measurements of both child-rearing and child-behavior variables are unable to demonstrate or refute any such influence. The one antecedent that does show a significant and consistent relationship for both sexes (proportional amount of caretaking by same-sexed parent) is related *oppositely* to the expected direction, and appears to measure intermittence rather than amount of reinforcement. It seems unlikely that early reinforcement is entirely irrelevant to the development of the cathectic dyadic relation between mother (or father) and child, but our measures of dependency are not suitable for estimating cathexis. They are quantitative estimates of operant activity. Such behavior is learned in the context of securing rewarding responses from others, or avoiding punishing ones; its strength (frequency, duration, intensity, resistance to extinction or interference) is therefore a function of both the total amount of reinforcement received through the child's entire life history and the amount of internal and external instigation impinging on him at a given time. Furthermore, we may expect that the particular dependent acts learned will be those permitted and encouraged by the parents, not simply acts emanating at random, and that the concurrent level of excitation or inhibition of these specific acts will influence their operant strength.

Current Reinforcement and Frustration

We turn now to the two hypotheses concerning the maintenance of dependency response strength. One says that greater current excitation by parents leads to greater frequency of dependent acts; and the other that greater intermittence of reinforcement leads to greater frequency of dependent acts.

Excitation and non-inhibition, as measured by parent scales indicating permissiveness, should increase the frequency of dependency acts as responses to parents or to any other stimulus objects (e.g., teachers or children) who fall with the parents on some dimension that allows stimulus generalization.

Frustration of dependency interactions, as indicated by parental punishment, coldness, or distance, should compel the child to work harder —to supplicate more—in order to obtain dyadic rewards. Aperiodic intermittent reinforcement thus operates to increase habit strength. Although the frequency of dependency acts toward the non-responsive parent should diminish eventually, we would expect the frequency of such acts in the non-punitive and accepting nursery school environment to reflect the increased habit strength.

The procedure chosen for analyzing the present data has two purposes. One is to test these two hypotheses; the other is to discover, if possible, additional antecedents that have not hitherto been used in formulating concrete hypotheses. In what follows, we shall present lists of all the correlation coefficients of .05 significance level between each of the five BUO dependency categories and the 197 parent measures secured from the interviews and mother-child interactions. We shall then examine these lists to see whether some of the relationships seem to support the hypotheses, and what theoretical sense can be made of those that do not.

This method has some dangers, for it risks capitalizing on purely chance correlations; there would be about ten significant correlations with each dependency measure if correlations among the 197 antecedent measures were purely random. Since these relations are *not* random, there is no way to estimate what a purely chance yield of .05-level correlations would be. Fortunately, however, since we are seeking definite evidence of permissiveness and frustration—rather than simply random antecedents—the question of chance yield seems unimportant. In general, the risks of such a procedure can be minimized if one's interpretations of the antecedent variables are not allowed to stray too far from some preformulated theory. Although this technique of data analysis may be expected to lead to a quasi-test of the hypotheses, it also serves the second purpose, which is to increase the precision of the theory by providing new hypotheses as well as testing old ones. In this respect, the procedure is essentially inductive rather than deductive in character and intent.

Negative Attention Seeking

Negative attention seeking has an aggressive quality and is not always easily distinguished from plain aggression. In the BUO scoring, a disruptive, disobedient, irritating act was categorized as negative attention seeking rather than aggression if the observer judged that it was performed mainly to get attention. In the Iowa study, there were significant positive correlations for both sexes between negative attention seeking and both total observed aggression and the total of other forms of dependency; the relation to aggression in boys was reduced from .49 to .21 when activity level was partialed out, whereas the same process for the girls reduced the figure only slightly, from .31 to .27.

In the present study, the relation of negative attention seeking to other forms of dependency is minimal for both sexes (Table 3); this fails to replicate the Iowa findings. However, with respect to total observed antisocial aggression (no distinction was made between prosocial and antisocial aggression in the Iowa study), the present results are very similar to the earlier ones. For boys, the correlation here is .35, which is reduced to an insignificant .18 by partialing out activity level, whereas for girls, the partialing reduces the correlation only from .33 to .32. It seems evident that negative attention seeking is a more integral part of the aggression system in girls than in boys, a conclusion reached on quite different grounds in the earlier study (Sears *et al.*, 1953, pp. 158–59). The low correlations with other forms of dependency, on the other hand, do not support the earlier suggestion that negative attention seeking is more closely allied to dependency in boys than in girls. Prosocial aggression shows no relation at all to negative attention seeking.

We turn now to the antecedents. In the Iowa study, only one major contributor to negative attention seeking was discovered—a mother-interview scale measuring the amount of nurturance the mother gave when she was busy. The relationship was negative; if she was non-responsive to the child's supplications, he tended to develop the disruptive types of attention seeking defined as negative. This scale was not used in the present study, so the replicability of that finding cannot be tested. However, two segments of the mother-child interaction provide a comparison of "mother busy" and "mother attentive" as the stimulating conditions, and permit measurement of the child's "bids for attention." The relevant data are given in Table 1. The last two lines in the table give the mean ratings of the frequency and intensity of the child's efforts to secure attention under the two conditions. "Mother busy" results in a significantly higher rating than "mother attentive." These ratings were made independently by two observers at every session, and were based on objective definitions of "bidding" that unfortunately did not distinguish between negative and positive methods. No matter; there was almost no negative attention seeking during the mother-attentive condition, when the mother was helping the child solve puzzles, and much of the bidding for attention during the questionnaire period was definitely negative in type, especially toward the end of the period. Thus, although these data are not a reproduction of the Iowa data, they do show, at the *action* level if not at the *learning* level, that withdrawal or withholding of attention increases the amount of negative attention seeking.

A second major determinant of negative attention seeking for both sexes appears to be a general permissiveness and lack of standards or demands for mature behavior. The evidence for this may be seen in the lists of scales given in Table 5, which include all the measures from the parent interviews and mother-child interaction situations that correlate with the BUO category of negative attention seeking at a significance level of .05 or better; this level is indicated by a correlation of .43 for boys, .46 for girls.

There are two indications for this suggested relationship, one being the correlations with a factor-analytic constructed score of mother's non-permissiveness, the other the correlations with the relevant individual scales used for scoring both the mother and the father interviews. The factor score (variable 173) was derived from the summing of standard scores on nine of the scales shown by Milton (1958) to have loadings greater than .30 on the primary factor of permissiveness-strictness. A number of individual scales that are components of the factor score, or are at least congruent with that dimension, are in the lists also.

In contrast to the general permissiveness that seems evident in the reported treatment of *both* sexes, there are also qualities of child-rearing experience that seem to affect the sexes differentially. For girls, several of the related antecedent scales characterize the father's behavior or attitudes. He seems to be an important person in the girl's life. For example, negative attention seeking is associated with high father and low mother caretaking in infancy, with severity of current separation from the father, and with his rewarding of dependency. *His* permissiveness, as well as the mother's, is influential. Several other father variables not quite at the .05 significance level are not included in the table: low use of ridicule, low use of modeling of good behavior, high satisfaction with the child's socialization, and high empathy for the child's feelings.

The negative-attention-seeking little girl was apparently "daddy's girl" from the beginning; she formed a strong attachment to her father, and separation from him produced an aggressive type of dependent supplication. Why aggressive? Because she had been masculinized by her close association with her father. The picture is strikingly similar to that of twelve-year-old girls who have high aggression anxiety, as is apparent from a comparison with findings from a follow-up study of the *Patterns* children (Sears, 1961). An examination of the early socialization experiences of those girls revealed a strong emphasis on father caretaking in infancy and early childhood, and high expression of aggression toward the parents at kindergarten age. They had apparently been treated more

TABLE 5

Negative Attention Seeking (187):
Correlations with Parent Interview and Mother-Child
Interaction Measures at Level $p < .05$

GIRLS

7. Severity of child's current separation from father (pooled)	51
8. Stability of current home situation (pooled)	−59
11. Mother's proportion of caretaking in infancy	−49
12. Father's proportion of caretaking in infancy	47
18. Level of demands for table manners	−55
30. Mother's permissiveness for masturbation	60
32. Mother's permissiveness for sex play among children	52
37. Openness about sex shown by mother's parents	−52
43. Father's pressure for neatness and orderliness	−48
56. Father's demand for aggression toward peers	−50
112. Mother's expectancy of sex differences in behavior	−46
127. Father's use of reward for dependency	60
164. Spaciousness of living space	47
173. Mother's non-permissiveness: factor score	−54

BOYS

13. Duration of breast feeding	43
15. Severity of child's reaction to weaning	54
16. Severity of weaning	45
21. Frequency of current bedwetting	43
26. Amount of child's social nudity (mother)	55
38. Mother's sex anxiety	−52
43. Father's pressure for neatness and orderliness	46
105. Father's use of punishment for independence	−49
115. Father's use of reward for sex-appropriate behavior	−55
117. Child's expression of affection toward father	−53
173. Mother's non-permissiveness: factor score	−46

like boys than most little girls are, and their own aggressive reactions created aggression anxiety. In the present group of girls, negative attention seeking is positively related (.33) to observed antisocial aggression in the nursery school, and, more critically, is negatively related (−.47) to the total measure of feminine sex typing (cf. Chapter 5).

Although the father's role in this process is clear, the mother also is involved, for negative attention seeking is significantly related to her low expectation of sex differences in behavior at this age (112). When we discover that there is a correlation of −.43 with father's evaluation of mother, the picture becomes a little clearer, perhaps. The father took over much of the child rearing because of his lack of confidence in the mother—or perhaps he expressed such low esteem as justification for the fact that he *had* taken over!

We suggest the hypothesis that the parents of the high-negative-attention-seeking girl are somewhat slack in their pressures on her, and that the father, lacking confidence in the mother's rearing activities, takes on much of the responsibility himself. This attitude of the father, and the mother's indifference to feminizing the girl, tend to masculinize her, and she behaves aggressively. At the same time, the infantilizing effect of low socialization demands leaves her relatively dependent in her reactions to others, and she combines the aggression and dependency into negative attention seeking. (Not surprisingly, the correlation with number of children in the family is −.43; there is little opportunity for the high-negative-attention-seeking girl to be corrected by siblings!)

The negative-attention-seeking picture for boys is less sharply defined. The effect of permissiveness is quite clearly indicated, but there are two other parental elements that differ from those relevant to girls who exhibit this behavior. First, there are significant correlations with two infant socialization measures that are unrelated to each other in either sex: the high-negative-attention seekers were fed longer at the breast and were more severely weaned. There is a suggestion here of early socialization pressures.

The second element concerns the father's influence. The high-negative-attention-seeking boy shows little affection for his father, who is characterized not only as permissive but also as neither expecting sex differences in behavior at this age (−.42) nor rewarding masculine behavior when it occurs (−.55); since the two father scales are positively related (.69), they evidently represent facets of the same quality. It would seem that the fathers of these high-negative-attention-seeking boys were neglectful of their sons, rather than lovingly permissive, like the girls' fathers. There is no evidence that this treatment was destructive to the process of sex typing, however, for negative attention seeking and masculinity are only slightly negatively correlated in boys ($-.14$).

To summarize these findings in the form of a hypothesis, we suggest that negative attention seeking in the boy is the product not only of general permissiveness by the mother, but also of severe infant socialization by the mother and a neglectfully permissive attitude toward the boy by the father, an attitude resulting in a low affectional attachment to him by his son.

Reassurance Seeking

Since the frequencies of reassurance seeking and negative attention seeking are entirely unrelated to one another in girls, and are even slightly negatively correlated in boys, it comes as no surprise to find that the child-rearing correlates of the two categories are quite different. With reassurance seeking, moreover, the apparent antecedents for boys are strikingly unlike those for girls (see Table 6).

Consider the girls first. Once more the father seems the salient figure. The mother's permissiveness is almost entirely unrelated to the measure; only one restrictiveness scale (house and furniture) has a moderate correlation ($-.44$) with reassurance seeking, and the non-permissiveness factor score has almost none ($-.15$). But the father's sex behavior is represented strongly by his low modesty in the home ($-.57$), and moderately by high giving of sex information to the child ($.41$) and high permissiveness for indoor nudity ($.41$). The father, in his open way, seems to present a rather strong sexual stimulus to the little girl. Why should this lead her to seek reassurance?

The answer seems reasonably straightforward if we assume that sexual arousal by the opposite-sexed parent is likely to promote insecurity in a child's relationship with the same-sexed parent. This is essentially the rivalrous condition described by Freud as the Oedipus situation. Certainly in American culture there is ample opportunity for a girl to learn that sexual responsiveness to either parent is forbidden. If the father displays himself freely and also gives sexual information to the child, he is providing cue stimuli that may arouse sexual impulses in her. Certain consequences are to be expected: reassurance seeking is only one, and perhaps a minor one at that. We should expect a lack of affection—a remaining at arm's length—with respect to the mother. The evidence for this is strong; reassurance seeking correlates negatively ($-.60$) with expression of affection toward the mother. We should also expect the child to be generally sensitive to the deviation behavior implicit in her feelings toward her father, to be emotionally upset or to express guilt; and this does occur, correlating at .56 with the summary guilt measure obtained from the two assessment situations described in Chapter 6. A more detailed discussion of this Oedipal relationship is given in that chapter.

But lest the Oedipus explanation be given too ready credit for the full force of these relationships, consider the mother's behavior. She is no lay figure standing idly by to be imbued with whatever projected hostilities her daughter may develop. She has qualities of her own that affect the child's emotions; in this instance it is clear that her behavior increases her daughter's insecurity and encourages the "unaffectionateness" we

TABLE 6

Reassurance Seeking (188):
Correlations with Parent Interview and Mother-Child
Interaction Measures at Level $p < .05$

GIRLS

29. Father's modesty . . . . −57
64. Mother's use of reasoning 52
84. Father's stress on importance of teaching right and wrong   49
116. Child's expression of affection toward mother . . . . . . −60
133. Mother's achievement standards for child 53
134. Father's achievement standards for child 45
322. Mother's pressure for child's independence 58
332. Mother's involvement in telephone game 63

BOYS

18. Level of demands for table manners 53
23. Mother's permissiveness for indoor nudity . . . . −58
25. Mother's pressure for modesty indoors 58
28. Mother's modesty 57
32. Mother's permissiveness for sex play among children . . . −50
35. Extent mother gives sexual information to child . . . . . −55
38. Mother's sex anxiety 61
51. Extent mother keeps track of child 49
167. Mother Attitude Scale: permissiveness for sex play among children . . . . −44
173. Mother's non-permissiveness: factor score 67
322. Mother's pressure for child's independence . . . . −66
326. Mother's directiveness toward child 49
330. Mother's warmth toward child . . . . −49

have already seen. In the correlation list are the mother's reported high standards of achievement, and (from the mother-child interaction) her pressure for the child to show independence and her involvement in the telephone game, which was an achievement-oriented teaching task. To these can be added several unlisted items: in her efforts to secure productive, cooperative behavior from her daughter, she rewards both achievement (.44) and adult role behavior (.44), uses reasoning (.52), is consistent in her caretaking policies (.42), and (in the mother-child interaction) was judged to reward dependency (.39). She is persuasive rather than demanding, but her high standards would appear to be the proper setting for a certain contingency in her giving her love.

Three final correlations indicate that the father is not simply a sex object to the little girl: he is seen by her as the source of power in the family (−.40, father low on this measure); he feels it important to teach her the meaning of right and wrong (.49); and he, too, has high achievement standards (.45).

We suggest the hypothesis, then, that the little girl's seeking for reassurance is a reaction to an insecurity aroused in her—especially in her relation with her mother—by her father's sexual attractiveness, by her mother's strong efforts to train her, and by pressures from both parents for maturity, morality, and achievement.

The apparent antecedents for the boy are similar in one respect, but strikingly different in another. The opposite-sexed parent is again the primary influence; without exception, all the correlations that reach the .05 level of significance are to scales referring to the mother. But the mother-son relationship is quite the opposite of the father-daughter relationship in terms of the directions of correlation. The mother whose son seeks reassurance is cold, non-permissive, and anxious about both sex and aggression (.40), and has high conflict over the mother role (.40). She keeps track of the child but seldom makes constructive efforts to train him; in the mother-child interaction, she did not press for independence or reward it (−.41), nor did she even reward dependence (−.40). She was concerned with the water play (.40).

This provides a picture of a relatively ineffectual mother, a conception supported perhaps by the father's low evaluation of her (−.40) and his tendency to interact with the child (.40).

We see no indication here of an Oedipal influence. On the contrary, reassurance seeking in boys seems to be a product of persistent coldness and restrictiveness, perhaps even neglect, in the sense that neither dependence nor independence is rewarded.

Being Near

Being near, one of the two immature (or passive or physical) forms of positive dependency behavior, is characterized by the child's efforts to get close to another child or to a teacher, and to remain there without necessarily engaging in verbal contact. Table 7 gives the correlates.

Among the girls, there was a close correlation with the other immature form, touching and holding, and a moderately close one with negative attention seeking. Moreover, there is a noticeable similarity between the latter and being near in terms of antecedents reaching the .05 level of significance, especially those that imply a permissive treatment with low

TABLE 7

Being Near (221):
Correlations with Parent Interview and Mother-Child
Interaction Measures at Level $p < .05$

GIRLS

1.	Age of child	−46
16.	Severity of weaning	−50
32.	Mother's permissiveness for sex play among children	50
35.	Extent mother gives sexual information to child	48
38.	Mother's sex anxiety	−46
43.	Father's pressure for neatness and orderliness	−47
53.	Extent of overt aggression in home by mother	−54
103.	Father's use of reward for independence	−47
137.	Extent of mother's influence on child	55
145.	Mother's caretaking consistency (with this child)	54
342.	Mother's use of punishment for child's aggression	46

BOYS

24.	Father's permissiveness for indoor nudity	−45
48.	Mother's expectancy of responsibility	−59
51.	Extent mother keeps track of child	50
80.	Extent of sex stereotyping in parents' roles (father)	43
86.	Father's use of people as models of good behavior	−48
135.	Extent child resembles mother (pooled)	−44
153.	Mother's evaluation of father	−45
155.	Strictness of mother's parents	−46
170.	Child Behavior Scale: maturity (mother)	−44
171.	Winterbottom Scale: mean age of expected independence (high = low pressure for independence) (mother)	68
330.	Mother's warmth toward child	−54

demands and expectations for mature behavior. But although the father's low demands are in evidence, there is an important difference between this list and the list for negative attention seeking: there is no indication here of an especially close relationship to the father. Furthermore, negative attention seeking is unrelated to the child's age, whereas being near is significantly related to age, the younger girls showing the behavior more frequently. On the other hand, none of the antecedent scales relevant to being near remotely approaches a significant relationship with age; it appears then that younger girls who receive permissive treatment tend to be more infantilized by the experience than older girls, if we consider being near a sign of infantilization. Although femininity tends to be negatively associated with being near (−.25), there is no indication that any especially strong participation of the father in the child-rearing process is responsible.

For boys, the correlates of being near do not reflect the maternal permissiveness seen in the girls, but there is some indication of a similar tendency toward infantilization. Although there is no relation to age (−.11), there is a significant negative correlation with maturity as evaluated by the mother on the semi-objective checklist of skills the child has attained. This measure is itself related only moderately to chronological age (.34), but correlates −.41 with keeping track of the child; i.e., mothers who keep track most vigilantly rate their sons as less mature. Since keeping track and low pressure for neatness and orderliness are both significantly associated with being near, we suggest that low demand and high supervision by the mother may tend to infantilize the boy. His infantilization is exhibited not only by his mother's judgment of his maturity level, but also by his frequent use of being near as a form of dependency toward other children and teachers.

The father appears prominently among the measures related to being near. His role is interesting; he is non-permissive with respect to indoor nudity, and reports a clearly stereotyped masculine role for himself by drawing a firm distinction between the sex roles of the parents. Wives whose husbands make this strong distinction do not evaluate their husbands highly (−.64); hence it is to be expected that boys who score high on being near have fathers who receive low evaluation from their wives (153). Finally, there is an almost significant correlation (.42) with a measure of discrepancy between the two parents' child-rearing attitudes.

These relationships suggest that the father may be rather ineffectual in his child rearing—ineffectual because he lacks the respect of the mother and operates in opposition to her. Her slackness in pressing for maturity, then, becomes a significant determinant of the boy's low level of maturity, as exhibited in frequent use of being near. One might speculate further that early disagreement between the parents may have retarded the child's maturity by making him unsure about what kind of behavior would be rewarded, and that the mother's infantilizing treatment may have been a result, rather than a cause, of the slow development. There is no way to test this notion within the present body of data.

Touching and Holding

Touching and holding is the other form of immature but positive dependency behavior. Since in girls it correlates strongly (.71) with being near, it is not surprising to find considerable similarity in the lists of associated antecedent scales, although several of the scales that reach the .05 significance level in correlation with being near fail to reach that level in correlation with touching and holding (e.g., touching and holding correlates −.26 with age, .26 with mother's permissiveness for sex play, .42 with giving sex information to child, −.43 with mother's sex anxiety, −.27 with father's rewarding of independence, .44 with mother's feeling of influence on the child, and .40 with mother's caretaking consistency). On the other hand, two of the scales that relate significantly with touching and holding correlate in the same direction with being near but do not reach the .05 significance level for being near: father's reward of sex-appropriate behavior (−.45) and the Winterbottom Scale, number of items checked (.36). Thus, there is nothing to add, for girls, concerning the antecedents of touching and holding that has not been said about being near (see Table 8).

For boys, the correlation between being near and touching and holding is much lower (.13), and the two categories are clearly differentiated with respect to antecedents. The scales correlating significantly with touching and holding, as well as several others just failing to reach significance, suggest that the father is an active and affectionate influence on the boy, but that the mother is non-interactive if not actually neglectful. The conditions for an active form of immature dependency are presented by the father's lack of anxiety and by his possibly child-oriented attitudes, and by high current separation from the mother (.51) and low current separation from the father (−.38). The effect here of the

TABLE 8

Touching and Holding (220):
Correlations with Parent Interview and Mother-Child
Interaction Measures at Level $p < .05$

GIRLS

16. Severity of weaning . . . . −46
53. Extent of overt aggression in home by mother . . . . . −58
115. Father's use of reward for sex-appropriate behavior . . . −50
172. Winterbottom Scale: number of items checked (high =
high pressure for independence) (mother) 50

BOYS

2. Child's behavior: correspondence between MCI and home
(mother) . . . . −43
41. Father's restrictions on house and property . . . . −44
63. Father's aggression anxiety . . . . −48
90. Mother's expectancy of conscience . . . . −45
97. Father's use of tangible reward . . . . −58
99. Father's use of psychological (vs. tangible) reward . . . 58
112. Mother's expectancy of sex differences in behavior . . . . −46
123. Child's dependency on father 58
142. Severity of child's current separation from mother (pooled) 51
156. Strictness of father's parents . . . . −57
163. Number of children in family 47
359. Mother's pressure for and reward of adult role behavior . −50
368. Mother's use of models with child . . . . −54

father's low anxiety is in marked contrast to the apparently inhibiting effect of his sex anxiety on the passive quality of being near. In both cases, the mother's undemanding standards tend to produce infantilization, but the father's role seems crucial in determining whether the infantilization is expressed actively or passively. Mother separation and the greater competition present among children in a larger family are also undoubtedly conducive to the active quality of touching and holding.

Positive Attention Seeking

Positive attention seeking is the most mature (or verbal or active) form of dependency behavior, although it correlates with neither chronological age nor the mother's objective estimates of maturity. It is primarily a verbal form of dependency, and involves efforts to secure approval of others.

In girls, the measure shows a zero relation to negative attention seeking and the two immature positive forms of dependency, but is positively related to reassurance seeking. As will be seen later, it is also positively related to real adult role behavior (.67).

Among child-rearing antecedents (Table 9), we find again an emphasis on sex permissiveness by the mother, low proportional caretaking by the mother during infancy, and high current separation from her. The mother rewards the girl for dependency and sees in her a resemblance to herself. She expresses affection for the child (.42), as does the father (.45). This permissiveness concerning sex and dependency does not extend to aggression, however; both parents are strict on that score. The net impression is of a mother who is affectionate, tolerant of sex and dependent behavior, restrictive with respect to aggression, and inclined to see the little girl as an extension of herself—but who has tended to spend less time with her daughter than most mothers. The mother who combines these behaviors provides both high interference and high reinforcement, a combination we could expect to draw forth the most concerted efforts toward dependency behavior.

The reasons for expecting such a maximal effect from this combination

TABLE 9

Positive Attention Seeking (219):
Correlations with Parent Interview and Mother-Child
Interaction Measures at Level $p < .05$

GIRLS

11.	Mother's proportion of caretaking in infancy	−62
28.	Mother's modesty	−48
33.	Sexuality in child (mother)	54
37.	Openness about sex shown by mother's parents	−51
58.	Mother's permissiveness for aggression toward parents	−49
61.	Father's use of punishment for aggression toward parents	48
126.	Mother's use of reward for dependency	50
128.	Mother's use of punishment for dependency	−63
135.	Extent child resembles mother (pooled)	63
138.	Mother's directiveness toward child	−46
142.	Severity of child's current separation from mother (pooled)	53

BOYS

4.	Mother's tension concerning MCI	−49
12.	Father's proportion of caretaking in infancy	−49
27.	Amount of child's social nudity (father)	−45
39.	Father's sex anxiety	50
60.	Mother's use of punishment for aggression toward parents	54
111.	Extent child imitates parents (pooled)	52
152.	Extent of child's acquaintance with father's work (pooled)	−52

of influences are drawn from two separate theories—action theory and learning theory. Action theory is a set of principles that account for the facilitation and inhibition of action *at the time it occurs.* These principles make use of such variables as strength of instigators, number of competing responses aroused and degree of conflict between these responses, amount of reward expectancy aroused, and frequency of response by the dyadic partner. High interference in the present context means low responsiveness from the mother—hence a greater number of dependency responses by the child before he secures a nurturant response from her. Learning theory, on the other hand, is a set of principles that account for changes in the *potentiality* for action. These principles make use of such variables as reinforcement and extinction, and the various possible combinations of the two that are implied by the term "scheduling of reinforcement." High reinforcement of dependency responses means a strengthening of the dependency habit, a strengthening that can be seen by an observer only in an increased vigor, frequency, duration, or resistance to extinction of the overt dependency response in question. Since overt behavior (exemplified here by our BUO measurements) is the only index of the effect of variables belonging to both action theory and learning theory, there is sometimes great difficulty in determining whether a child is behaving in a certain way (e.g., with increased positive attention seeking) as a result of the particular constellation of stimuli impinging on him at the moment (an action theory interpretation) or as an outcome of a sequence of reinforcements (a learning theory interpretation). Since both kinds of theory would predict the correlations obtained between positive attention seeking and its antecedents, we do not know how much influence should be ascribed to learning theory principles and how much to action theory principles. (For a discussion of the two kinds of theory, see Sears, 1951.)

Positive attention seeking in boys has a small positive correlation with negative attention seeking, and a slight negative relation to the immature forms of dependency. In boys, as in girls, there is a substantial positive relationship to real adult role behavior (.42).

Antecedent information is sparse. Again we see the low proportion of infant caretaking by the same-sexed parent, but in association with high sex anxiety (low rather than high permissiveness) on the father's part. As with girls, the mother does not permit aggression. The boy is also felt to be little acquainted with his father's work. The combination of low permissiveness for both sex and aggression might seem to suggest a feminizing process, but the correlation of positive attention seeking with masculinity is only −.14. Clearly, then, we cannot conclude that positive attention seeking represents feminine behavior brought on entirely by the same experiences that produce non-masculine sex typing (cf. Chapter 5).

It is interesting to note that the high-positive-attention-seeking boy is said by his parents to imitate them quite often, although there is no evidence from their statements that he especially resembles either of them. This imitation is also positively related to adult role behavior, both real and fantasy, which reinforces our interpretation of positive attention seeking as a maturity-seeking kind of behavior. In view of the strict parental control of both sex and aggression, the status of being a child probably has little to recommend it to the boy, and positive attention seeking serves to bring him into a more favorable relationship with his parents. To parents who dislike open sexual and aggressive behavior, the mature quality of positive attention seeking is no doubt reassuring, perhaps because of its emphasis on verbal interchange.

In this connection, a special comment should be made about the two parent-interview ratings of proportional amount of caretaking in infancy. As can be seen from Table 10, these scales are negatively correlated with sex anxiety in *both* parents of boys; i.e., the fathers and mothers who were judged to have sex anxiety tended to avoid caretaking of the infant boy. There is little relation between these variables in either parent of girl babies. The boy seems to represent more of a sex symbol to parents that have high sex anxiety; if we consider that holding, feeding, and diaper changing are the major *required* functions in taking care of an

TABLE 10

Correlations Between Parents' Sex Anxiety and Proportions
of Infant Caretaking

Interview Scale	Boys' Parents		Girls' Parents	
	Mother's Sex Anxiety (38)	Father's Sex Anxiety (39)	Mother's Sex Anxiety (38)	Father's Sex Anxiety (39)
Mother's proportion of caretaking (11)	−46	−07	00	00
Father's proportion of caretaking (12)	18	−45	−30	−09

infant, it is understandable that these parents should avoid the caretaker role.

These relationships make clearer what is implied by the low relative caretaking by the same-sexed parent. The girls received less caretaking from the mother not because she had high sex anxiety, but *independently* of her feelings about sex. Low maternal caretaking of the infant girl thus gains clear status as a relevant antecedent variable in its own right, and not as a correlate of the sex-permissiveness syndrome. By contrast, low paternal caretaking of the infant boy appears to be simply part and parcel of the general non-permissiveness and anxiety about sex that are the associates of high positive attention seeking.

We assume that the absolute amount of caretaking was sufficient for all these children, of both sexes, to have established both an affection for and a dependency interaction system with both parents. We then propose the following interpretation and hypotheses.

For the girl, low maternal caretaking represents a withholding of full satisfaction of the dependency interaction; when overlaid by two later influences—strictness toward expression of aggression, and high current separation—its effect is to force the girl to unusual efforts to please and attract the mother in a mature and feminine way. If we may take the mother's estimate of how much the little girl resembles her as in part, at least, a measure of the mother's goal, then evidently positive attention seeking (correlated .63 with the resemblance variable) is associated with the mother's goal. Thus the girl's positive attention seeking represents a reaction to a long-term frustration (in the form of contingent love response).

Our reasoning about the boys is somewhat different. We interpret low caretaking by the father as part of a more general picture of rejection, which is reflected also in the judgment that the boy at preschool age had little acquaintance with his father's work outside the home. These two father scales have no relation to one another (.10), and hence represent different measures of the rejection. The father's rejection and the mother's strictness toward aggression combine to produce continuous frustration —unallayed in this case by the guidance toward social progression provided for the girl by her mother's permissiveness with respect to sex and dependency. Thus the boy's positive attention seeking is also interpreted as a response to a long-term frustration, but the lack of an associated "invitation to dependency" leaves him free—or forces him—to develop other responses as well (autonomy, avoidance, independence) to signals of impending nurturance.

Data obtained in the mother-child interaction tend to confirm these hypotheses. For both sexes there was a small positive correlation (.23 for the girls, .28 for the boys) between positive attention seeking and the number of bids for attention elicited by the mother-busy situation; the "withholding" stimulation was effective. But when the mother-attentive situation was presented, the correlation was .62 for the girls, and −.32 for the boys; when attention was proffered, the girls grabbed for it, and the boys rejected it. A similar contrast arises with respect to total independence shown during the four sections of the interaction; the correlation between this category and positive attention seeking is very low (.18) for the girls, whereas the correlation for the boys (.44) is significant at the .05 level. This independent behavior is perhaps one of the alternatives learned by the boy in the relative absence of the dependency conditions provided by permissiveness, reward, and low punishment.

Total Observed Dependency

Total observed dependency is simply the additive combination of the other five BUO dependency categories, with whatever weighting occurred in nature. The relative contribution of each of the five categories is suggested by its correlation with the total score (Table 3). For both sexes, negative attention seeking contributes relatively little to the total, whereas the other four categories contribute more substantially and in about equal portions, again for both sexes.

As is to be expected, the total score maximizes the common elements among the antecedents of the five component categories, and cancels out the variables related only to individual categories. Thus for the girls there is clear evidence (Table 11) of the general correlates of sex and dependency permissiveness or non-permissiveness: there are six sex-permissiveness scales, two scales implying high reward or low punishment for dependency, two representing low pressure for independence or obedience, and one (lack of hostility) suggesting a happy relationship between mother and daughter.

This leaves uncounted two very revealing scales—mother's satisfaction with the girl's socialization, and mother's judgment that the child resembles her. The two suggest the flavor of the mother-daughter relation perhaps better than the other correlates that are so broadly represented.

TABLE 11

Total Observed Dependency (224):
Correlations with Parent Interview and Mother-Child
Interaction Measures at Level $p < .05$

GIRLS

28. Mother's modesty . . . . −47
29. Father's modesty . . . . −46
30. Mother's permissiveness for masturbation 46
38. Mother's sex anxiety . . . . −46
81. Source of power in home: mother high (pooled) . . . . −52
106. Mother's satisfaction with child's socialization 66
128. Mother's use of punishment for dependency . . . . . . −47
135. Extent child resembles mother (pooled) 53
140. Mother's hostility to child . . . . −52
328. Mother's use of reward for child's dependency 53
329. Mother's use of punishment for child's dependency . . . . −49
341. Mother's pressure for child's obedience . . . . −46

BOYS

19. Severity of toilet training 48
24. Father's permissiveness for indoor nudity . . . . −63
25. Mother's pressure for modesty indoors 59
27. Amount of child's social nudity (father) . . . . −45
32. Mother's permissiveness for sex play among children . . . −49
39. Father's sex anxiety 44
44. Mother's strictness about bedtime behavior 55
47. Mother's use of democracy . . . . −46
61. Father's use of punishment for aggression toward parents . −44
86. Father's use of people as models of good behavior . . . . −51
91. Father's expectancy of conscience . . . . −48
97. Father's use of tangible reward . . . . −48
99. Father's use of psychological (vs. tangible) reward . . . 54
112. Mother's expectancy of sex differences in behavior . . . . −46
114. Mother's use of reward for sex-appropriate behavior . . . −50
155. Strictness of mother's parents . . . . −50
171. Winterbottom Scale: mean age of expected independence
(high = low pressure for independence) (mother) . . . 48
322. Mother's pressure for child's independence . . . . −49
330. Mother's warmth toward child . . . . −56
332. Mother's involvement in telephone game . . . .−43

The mother of the very dependent girl is pleased, by and large, with her daughter's development, sees her daughter as becoming like herself, and feels she has some influence on her daughter (.44). Another substantial contributor to the basically dependent quality of the child's behavior is separation (.40) from this non-hostile, rewarding, tolerant, and well-satisfied mother. The little girl's dependency is reinforced by a successful dyadic relationship, and dependency is becoming a normal way of life. It is amusing to note in this connection that in the telephone episode of the mother-child interaction, the more dependent girls showed less willingness to play the "bad child" role ($-.47$) and more enthusiasm for playing their own true role ($.46$). They liked themselves and did not want to be different—especially, to be bad!

From both a learning and an action standpoint, then, the data on girls' dependency seem to be in accord with theoretical principles derived from experimental studies. Permissiveness provides opportunity for practice, and reward following operant activity provides reinforcement. Moreover, permissiveness for sex behavior represents the conditions needed for encouraging the child to make her dependent responses involve approaches to another person, whether physical or verbal; this holds for all varieties of dependency behavior except negative attention seeking, and occasionally even that. The seeking of closeness, of intimacy, can be either dependent or sexual, and is probably usually both in the little girl. If the mother is not free of sex anxiety, these approaches could be threatening to her own defenses and discomforting to her sense of the proprieties of interpersonal relationships. Thus, sex permissiveness may be considered a measure of the broad range of opportunities for practice. Finally, the severity of current separation from the mother represents a measure of interference with the dyadic interaction, and offers the appropriate circumstances for facilitation of the operant activity, as described earlier in this chapter in the discussion of intermittent reinforcement.

A comparable analysis of boys' total dependency is by no means so easy, and for good reason. The virtual lack of intercorrelation among the five component categories has raised the serious question of whether one can justify ascribing any such *general* rubric to them. It may well be that our search for antecedents should stop with the separate examination of the categories. Certainly a review of the six lists presented does not reveal any common element comparable to sex permissiveness in the socialization of girls. If boys' total dependency possesses any one reasonably widespread relationship, it is with sex non-permissiveness on the part of one or both parents.[*] There is a vague hint of an inhibited and ineffectual mother, and to some extent the same sort of father, who pro-

---

[*] This judgment must exclude negative attention seeking, which is associated with high permissiveness, as it is in girls.

vides little freedom for the boy, and little incentive for rapid maturing.

This admittedly inadequate induction is somewhat strengthened by the list of correlates given in Table 11. Both parents are inhibited and restrictive with respect to sex. There is an atmosphere of over-control (sex and bedtime) and domination (low democracy). Both parents are low in certain expectancies (conscience, sex differences in behavior) that one would suppose might be helpful to the boy in learning mature ways. There is an aura of neglect or ignoring by both parents; there is little in the way of positive rewarding (praise, tangible rewards) or presenting models of good behavior, i.e., little guidance. The mother appeared cold in the mother-child interaction with her son, and on the Winterbottom Scale she expressed willingness to wait quite late for the achievement of the various elements of independence.

The difference between the boy and girl antecedents is very striking, even though our description of the pattern for boys suffers a certain inexactness. The girls appear to be learning to be dependent as a normal progressive aspect of their socialization; the child-rearing conditions are what we would expect in the circumstances. If our interpretations are correct, the boys receive little support for such learning; it is as if dependency for them were a *regressive* rather than *progressive* form of response, a reaction to chronic frustration.

Summary of Dependency Antecedents

The major child-rearing correlates of the various measures of girls' nursery school dependency are those referring to the mother's permissiveness for sex and dependency. These are present in some degree for all but one of the BUO categories, and are emphasized in the list of parent variables significantly correlated with total observed dependency. The more special antecedents related to each of the component categories are as follows:

1. For negative attention seeking, low demands and restrictions plus high participation of the father in the girl's rearing.

2. For reassurance seeking, high demands for achievement from both parents, plus possibly sex anxiety produced by the father's sex permissiveness.

3. For being near and touching and holding, low demands and restrictions without the masculinizing entrance of the father into the girl's rearing.

4. For positive attention seeking, low infant and current caretaking by the mother and a non-permissive attitude toward aggression.

The parent variables correlated with boys' dependency are all but unspecifiable because of the lack of coherence in the action system. There is a suggestion of a cluster implying coldness, slackness of standards, and neglect by the mother, without any real permissiveness, and a generally non-permissive attitude—especially about sex—by the father. The one definite exception to this statement is provided by negative attention seeking, which in boys, as in girls, is associated with maternal sex permissiveness; there is also a special cluster of variables for boys that implies early severity of socialization. The only detectable special variables relevant to the other categories are as follows:

1. For touching and holding, some unspecified influence of the father.

2. For positive attention seeking, low father participation and high aggression control by the mother.

Discussion of Dependency

We began this investigation with four hypotheses concerning the structure and development of dependent behavior. The first was that children of nursery school age possess a cluster of associated habits, or *dependency* responses, having a common quality—a quality that arises from their all having been reinforced by parental nurturant behavior. The hypothesis is testable by determining whether there is positive intercorrelation among the five dependency categories measured in the BUO. The test gives a questionably affirmative answer for girls, but a clearly negative one for boys. The median intercorrelation for girls is .17, which does not even approach statistical significance, and the median for boys is exactly zero. These values are not significantly modified (.24 and .02, respectively) by holding a measure of activity level constant, using partial correlation.

Apparently, then, these kinds of behavior do not represent aspects of a trait or any other unified behavior quality that can be defined solely by intercorrelation among responses. This conclusion gains additional support from the "trait consistency" measure presented in Appendix D. The median intercorrelation between the three parts of the summer was only .36, and although the Spearman-Brown correction for the reliability of the full seven weeks' measure raises this value to .63, the former figure is probably a more meaningful representation of the temporal consistency of total observed dependency. (The comparable consistency measures for the five categories were not calculated because of the great frequency of zero scores.)

There are other possible conceptions of a trait, of course—conceptions based on operations other than intercorrelation—that are not susceptible to test with our data. One such conception postulates the dynamic substitutability of one response for another. Operationally, this might suggest, for example, that if available time for making a response and amount of stimulation were held constant, there would be inverse relations between the frequencies of occurrence of the various behavior types; i.e., given a constant level of stimulation to dependent responses during, for example, a ten-minute interval, any stimulus increasing the frequency of one category (such as negative attention seeking) would decrease the frequency of the others. The testing of such a hypothesis would require experimental rather than naturalistic procedures.

Another possible interpretation is that the quite small positive correlations among the several dependency categories are a function of a common antecedent learning situation. If certain of the child's actions secure nurturance or attention from others, then any consistency in either the conditions of learning or the level of current stimulation could account for whatever consistency exists in the child's behavior. The list of dependency categories, in this case, would represent only what has become discriminable to psychologists as the most usual ways in which nurturance or attention is sought. There could be many other ways, many of them perhaps unique to an individual child, and the actual structure of dependency for each child would be a function of the behavior that has been rewarded by his parents and peers. Following this reasoning, one would also have to consider an opposing implication, namely, that not all behavior satisfying dependency needs has only this end in view. We have commented earlier, for example, on the apparent fusion of aggression with dependency that results in negative attention seeking. It may well be that each of our categories is so multiply instigated that the commonality resulting from the so-called dependency antecedents is too small to result in measurable intercorrelations among the consequent categories.

If this interpretation is correct, we should eventually discover other behaviors that properly belong in the list of dependency categories. In the next chapter we shall present a strong candidate for such a transfer, namely, *real adult role behavior*. That category correlates more highly with positive attention seeking than some of the other dependency categories do, and there are some similarities in its child-rearing antecedents as well. What other behaviors may be suitable for inclusion seems, at present, a matter for empirical inquiry based on the notion that *it is parental consistency in offering nurturance and attention as rewards for specific kinds of child behavior that determines the structure of a given child's dependency trait, or habit hierarchy*. This leads to a consideration of the second of our four hypotheses.

From a general theory of learning, one would expect the behaviors of the child that elicited the strongest (intermittent) reinforcement by parental responses to be the most strongly established. Clinical observation and psychoanalytic theory have long emphasized the importance of early oral activity, or the oral stage, in the development of dependent qualities. Feeding and caretaking—the *giving* of rewards—are predominant parental activities during the first twelve to eighteen months of the child's life. During this period he is essentially passive—simply a recipient, so far as food and loving handling are concerned. He presumably learns to expect care, and his operant behaviors that immediately precede gratification become strengthened. If a dependency *drive* is formed by these experiences, it should instigate behavior leading to a maintenance of his passivity and to the securing of rewards from the parents. If a drive in fact existed as a continuous instigator, one would anticipate that new actions would gradually develop as the child's motoric and perceptual capacities matured and as his increasing age and status stimulated new expectancies of him by his parents. Such behaviors as being near and touching and holding, and eventually the verbal forms of dependency behavior (reassurance seeking and positive attention seeking), should replace the smiling, arching, mouthing, and passive offerings of his body for caresses and holding that compose his first repertoire of dependency supplications.

In an effort to test the hypothesis that oral or other caretaking experiences establish dependency response strength, we compared the frequency of occurrence of our five BUO dependency categories with three measures of oral experience that seemed to be possible antecedents. We reasoned that high reinforcement would create the equivalent of fixation, and that later dependency behavior would be more frequent as a result. There is no evidence whatever to support the hypothesis, nor do the rather small antecedent-consequent relationships we obtained replicate those found in the Iowa study. The crudity and inexactnesss of our antecedent measures make us hestitate to consider this failure crucial to the hypothesis, but we have felt it worth reporting in order to discourage other investigators from wasting time on this method of examining what is in fact a very complex theory and at present a very poorly defined one.

However, from this effort to find evidence of the effect of early reinforcement on later behavior, we did discover a significant *non-oral* relationship—between positive attention seeking and proportionately low infant caretaking of the child by the same-sexed parent. In spite of a negative correlation between the latter measure and a companion estimate of caretaking by the opposite-sexed parent, only the same-sexed parent's caretaking is significantly correlated with the child's behavior. Since the correlation is large for both boys and girls, we are inclined to give the obtained relationship serious credence.

But why the same-sexed parent? The caretaking scales are based on caretaking during the first few months of the child's life, and were rated from the responses of the first ten minutes of each parent's interview. It is hard to believe that the father's low responsiveness to his son at that age could have served more effectively than the mother's as a source of aperiodic intermittent reinforcement to increase the strength of operant responses directed toward securing nurturant attention. The answer may be elsewhere, we think—specifically, in the father's sex anxiety. The part of the interview from which the quality was rated was separated from the discussion of the child's infancy by twenty minutes or so and by the statement "Now let's come up to the present." The child's sex behavior and the parents' attitudes were explored at some length— sufficiently to permit the later rating of a dozen different scales—and sex anxiety was rated on the basis of the total sex discussion. As we have demonstrated, sex anxiety is related negatively to infant caretaking of boys in both the father ($-.45$) and the mother ($-.46$). Sex anxiety of the father forms part of the frustration and withholding-of-love syndrome associated with positive attention seeking in the boy; this latter more pervasive and continuing quality of the father's personality may be responsible for the dependency behavior, and the low caretaking in infancy may be simply a by-product. However, when sex anxiety is held constant by partial correlation, the relation of caretaking to positive attention seeking drops only from $-.49$ to $-.35$; although this direction of change fits our suggested interpretation, the drop is not wholly convincing.

Even if valid, this interpretation leaves unexplained the effect on the *girl* of the mother's low caretaking in infancy. We would ascribe the effect to the influence of intermittent reinforcement, if there were some immediate reason we could see why the same effect should not apply to boys. Possibly it does, as the data in Table 4, for *boys*, might suggest. Although a tiny opposite effect occurs with the zero-order correlation (mother caretaking vs. positive attention seeking), we see in the adjacent column (partial-correlation coefficients for each parent's caretaking, with that of the other parent held constant) a change from the zero-order .18 to a first-order partial r of $-.26$, not significant but in the right direction to encourage the inference that boys, too, are influenced somewhat by the opposite-sexed parent's intermittent reinforcement.

These various findings provide some support, ambiguous though it is because of the intercorrelations among the child-rearing variables, for the hypothesis that aperiodic intermittent non-oral reinforcement in infancy (i.e., low caretaking) increases the operant level of positive attention seeking at age four. More detailed consideration of this matter will be given in Chapter 3, where the close relation of caretaking and adult role behavior require a similar analysis.

This brings us to the third and fourth hypotheses, which must be considered together. These are that (1) continuing permissiveness for sexual and dependent behavior, and (2) frustration through the withholding of love and affection, serve as instigators and/or reinforcers of dependency behavior. The permissiveness hypothesis is direct; the more opportunity the child is given for practice, and the more frequently he is rewarded, the stronger his responses will become. The frustration hypothesis is more complex. Coldness and non-permissiveness are conditions that might be expected to operate in the opposite way, but these withholdings of reward are, of course, in no conceivable sense complete, but only relative, and hence may be presumed to provide the quality of aperiodic intermittent reinforcement. Thus, the child with a non-permissive and non-rewarding father has fewer opportunities to practice and to be rewarded for his dependency responses, but the scheduling of the rewards he does receive operates to increase the strength of the operant responses.

One difficulty with this use of frustration as an antecedent for strengthened dependency is its immediate facilitating influence on frequency and intensity of response. In terms of action theory, frustration operates in the same direction as it does by this learning principle. An analysis of the kind of data available from an interview cannot possibly disentangle these two effects; both principles predict an increase in dependency operants with greater frustration (non-permissiveness, non-reward or punishment, coldness).

So far as girls are concerned, all of our dependency measures reflect clear support of the permissiveness hypothesis, whereas support for the frustration hypothesis is reflected only in positive attention seeking. For boys, there is support for the frustration principle, but not for the permissiveness principle. Support for the frustration principle rests on our interpretation of three elements—the mother's coldness and her slack standards and the father's sex non-permissiveness—as frustrations.

At first blush, these affirmations of the two hypotheses appear contradictory. How can a positive correlation with a given scale support one hypothesis and a negative correlation with that scale support another—when the consequent measure is the same for both correlations? Obviously, this situation could not arise in a single group of subjects, but here we are dealing with two groups, boys and girls, and with antecedent measures derived from fathers in one group and mothers in the other. Again, as with infant caretaking, we are dealing with the influence of the same-sexed parent. So the finding of significant correlations with opposite signs is mathematically possible; the logic still needs explanation.

The difficulty stems from an ordinarily unspecified assumption that opposite signs on correlation coefficients, or on any other measures that indicate relational *direction*, are the indicators of affirmation or negation of a proposition. The problem is an old one for those who have sought to verify psychoanalytic theoretical propositions. Experimenters have often complained, for example, that there is no way to disconfirm the principle of the Oedipus conflict because it can predict "either" outcome of the boy's emotional reaction to his father: he loves him or he hates him. If we disregard the superficiality of such a gross description of the dependent variables ("love" vs. "hate"), we must insist that both these outcomes do support or confirm the theory. The error lies in applying the word "either" to love and hate. They are not alternatives for this theory. They are *an* alternative to something else—no emotion at all. For the Oedipus theory, the disconfirming outcome would be a boy's total indifference toward his father.

Similarly, with our two hypotheses concerning the relation of child dependency to parental permissiveness, the *disconfirming* result would be a *lack* of correlation between the variables. Many of our 197 parent measures never appear in the lists of variables significantly correlated with the forms of dependency. With few exceptions, for example, the measures of disciplinary techniques are not to be found. Neither is the cluster of ratings that refer to parental self-esteem (esteem or disesteem for the spouse, yes, but not self-esteem), nor the control of adult role behavior, nor the regulation of moral conduct. In other words, there are non-correlations between dependency measures and theoretically irrelevant child-rearing variables that stand in contrast to both positive and negative correlations with the theoretically relevant variables.

On these grounds, then, the third and fourth hypotheses gain support from the data. The sex differences in the variables that have proved relevant, however, and the lack of clear intercorrelational evidence for a single trait of dependency, suggest that the relationships between child rearing and the several types of dependent behavior are more complicated than these hypotheses have implied.

The positive relation of maternal sex and dependency permissiveness to four of the girls' dependency measures, and the negative relation of paternal sex permissiveness to three of the boys', suggest a possible difference in the reinforcement conditions for the two sexes. Dependency, sociability, verbal responsiveness to the mother—all represented by positive attention seeking—appear to be associated with the mother's satisfaction with her daughter; these are appropriate for the sex typing of the girl. Thus, dependency in girls seems to be acceptable or even desired, and mothers who encourage intimacy achieve their aims. For boys, however, dependency seems to be associated with coldness in the mother, slackness of standards, and a rejection of intimacy by the father. It is as if the dependency supplications were efforts to overcome indifference and neglect, as if they represented reactions to some kind of insecurity stemming from withdrawal or withholding of parental affection. Thus, the same overt behavior may be interpreted as *progressive* in girls and *regressive* in boys.

One final point worth noting is the similarity between the sexes in the list of child-rearing correlates of negative attention seeking. In this respect, the boys are like the girls: a high amount of such behavior is associated with a sexually permissive mother and an infantilization by both parents. The boys have a history of weaning and toilet-training difficulties and a current disaffection for the father, whereas the girls are masculinized by their close relation to the father. This suggests two quite different mechanisms for the creation of such an infusion of aggression into dependency: in the girl, an adoption of the aggressive component of her father-induced masculinity; and in the boy, a resentment toward the father for interfering in the boy's affectional relationship with the sex-permissive mother. The implications of this hypothesis for our concept of the theory of the Oedipus complex will be considered further in Chapter 6.

3. *Adult Role*

In a sense, all the qualities of behavior that a child adopts from his supposed identificand are representative of the adult role. Our so-called identification behaviors—expressing responsibility, resistance to temptation, self-condemnation for deviation, prosocial aggression, appropriate sex typing—are all characteristically portrayed by the parents, and hence are adult in form. The present chapter is devoted to none of these, but to an additional area of adult role—a group of behaviors not commonly considered part of the legacy from adults, but which we have thought might represent another cluster of intercorrelated adult-like action tendencies.

Constructs of this sort are essentially hypotheses. They are defined and given labels because the various measures of each (e.g., of gender role) are expected to intercorrelate more highly with one another than with those of other behavior constructs. At any given stage in the development of behavior theory, such constructs are chosen on the basis of whatever information is then available. Thus, to take another example in the present research, the notion of resistance to temptation has seemed potentially useful to us because previous studies utilizing several measures of it (e.g., Hartshorne and May, 1928) have shown small but seemingly stable intercorrelations. Since our present data provide similar intercorrelations (as will be seen in Chapter 6), we will continue to use this construct until new data force its reorganization. The previous chapter, on the other hand, has given us an example of a construct—dependency—that has now had some doubt cast on its value. The concept of *adult role*, as used in this chapter, represents an effort to combine a number of behavior qualities into a single construct that would be distinct from the others we have used, but that would describe behavior belonging in the general category of the hypothesized products of identification. That this effort is promising but seriously oversimplified will become evident when the intercorrelations among our different measures are examined.

A previous study (Maccoby, 1961) used the concept in a similar theoretical context. In a follow-up study of the children whose child-rearing experiences before age five had been reported in *Patterns of Child Rearing*, Maccoby constructed two questionnaire scales, suited to children aged twelve, that defined behaviors called "rule enforcement" and "adult-child role choice." The former was designed to measure a child's attitudes toward enforcing adult-type rules on other children. A high score was interpreted as an indication that a child had adopted an adult attitude. The other scale was composed of some items that permitted the youngster to choose between two roles in the same setting (one an adult role and the other a child role), and some that allowed him to express feelings of sympathy with either an adult or a child in a conflict situation. The two scales were included in a large battery of tests presented to 525 sixth-grade children. They were correlated .34 among the boys, and .25 among the girls.

The behaviors called adult role in the present study are several that characterize maturity of manner or social interaction—adultness—in contrast with immaturity or childlikeness. They include actions on a realistic level, such as assisting the teacher, performing chores in a helpful manner, giving information to others, being nurturant and supportive, and suggesting proper standards of conduct. On a less realistic level, they include fantasy-like play involving the assumption of adult roles and the performing of adult occupations or recreations that are not in fact available to children. Mimicry of adult speech or mannerisms—with or without any evident intention to be funny—is still another type. The full meaning of the adult role construct will become clear with a description of our measures of it, particularly the BUO categories.

Theory of Adult Role

In our consideration of dependency, we emphasized the description of dependent acts as operants that presumably had received reinforcement from dyadic interactions with the child's main caretakers in infancy and very early childhood. The retrospective reports provided by the parent interviews lent no evidence for this reinforcement process, however, and we were left with the demonstration only that the strength of dependency acts characteristic of four-year-olds is more closely related to current parental attitudes and practices than to earlier ones. This conclusion was congruent with the findings from the Iowa study (Sears et al., 1953).

So far as identification theory is concerned, however, this failure to confirm the genetic theory of dependency is unimportant. Identification theory requires only that children do become dependent very early in life, and that they begin imitating parental role behavior as an instrumental technique for maintaining the dependent-nurturant dyadic relationship with the parents. According to the theory, the more dependent children should display a stronger tendency to adopt the adult role.

However, this proposition assumes a prior proposition—namely, that the various types of adult role behavior correlate reasonably well with one another. Indeed, this is crucial, for the essence of the theory of primary identification is that the child imitate the caretaking parent in all ways that are not impeded by other sources of learning; i.e., that he adopt the totality of the role of being adult. Those of our *a priori* choices of behavior categories that are most reflective of actual adult behavior should be those accorded the highest frequency or intensity in the children's performances.

There is an alternative theory of the development of adult role behaviors that should be kept in mind, a theory that relies not on role practice as the source of such behavior, but simply on imitation of the specific acts (including attitudes, values, expressions of feelings, etc.) that are reinforced by the parents' nurturant behavior. The reinforcement need be neither direct nor immediate, of course, for stimulus and response generalization of both excitation and inhibition can operate to spread the effects of reinforcement, non-reinforcement, and punishment to many instigators and response systems beyond those directly associated. The question is similar to that raised in connection with the creation of dependency. (We noted there, for example, that children of different parents learn thoroughly idiosyncratic behaviors with the same apparent ease as they do more generalized adult behaviors.) There is the possibility, in other words, that adult role behavior can be accounted for by direct tuition of imitated acts favored by the parents, rather than by the intervening variable of role practice.

The difference between dependency and adult role behavior lies in three things, according to this view. First, there is a different *content* to the child's behavior. The various types of dependent behavior render the child more or less subordinate to the parent, whereas adult role activity involves the playing of a role superordinate to that of other persons or the performance of adult-like actions that provide independent manipulation of the environment. Some types of dependency (e.g., positive attention seeking) are not necessarily childlike, but are supplicative. Adult role behavior may or may not be supplicative in intent, but its manifest form is not.

Second, the two groups of behavior differ with respect to their dyadically interlocked *reciprocal parental needs.* Whereas dependency instigates nurturance in the caretaker, and serves as the required environmental event to fulfill or complete the caretaker's nurturant action system, adult role behavior provides reinforcement for the parent's motive to socialize the child. Almost all parents wish to "bring up" their children, to see them become increasingly independent and able to handle their environment without material help; training in mature ways (caring for themselves, playing or working with others, taking responsibility) is a pervasive part of the socialization process. To *rear* children is to *push* them upward. Toward what? Obviously toward the values, tastes, and methods and standards of conduct that characterize the older members of their species. Parents *want* their children to grow into adulthood, and reinforce appropriate behaviors so that they *will.* They offer models; they instruct and reward. They have value systems of their own and perceive their children's behavior as being congruent or incongruent with those systems. Adult role behavior, for our discussion, provides the environmental events for the parents' motive to socialize.

Third, dependency and adult role behavior differ in *the nature of the reinforcing event.* For dependency, we have hypothesized (though we have not been able to demonstrate) that original reinforcement stems mainly from such primary sources of gratification as touching, holding, fondling, feeding, and other aspects of the caretaking process. Our data suggest, however, that dependency is further reinforced and maintained by secondary reinforcements belonging to the dyadic dependency-nurturance system. Adult role behavior develops later than dependency, and the nurturance, affection, and contingent giving of love—depending for their influence as reinforcers on the prior development of the dyad— are likely the main adult role reinforcers. Whatever may be preponderant in the establishment of the dependency system, there seems little doubt that, in the establishment of adult role at age four, parental rewarding of desired behavior by the giving of attention and affection is more common and more influential than the giving of food or physical caretaking.

Thus, nurturance and affection expressed toward the child for his

performance of mature, adult-like actions is the condition for their establishment. He has observed these actions in the parents. The stronger the
child's dyadic expectancy of nurturance—as measured by the frequency
and intensity of his dependency supplications—the stronger his adult role
behavior system.

If this hypothesis is correct—and if the hypothesis of total role practice is therefore invalid—the question can be raised whether adult role is
not, in fact, one form of dependency. In both cases, the constituent acts
are instrumental to gaining nurturance. Since the chief difference between adult role and dependency lies in their *content*, as discussed
above, the separate labels must be considered provisional until the empirical evidence of similarity is examined.

Measurement of Adult Role

Measures of adult role behavior were made in several settings, including the open play of the nursery school. Obviously, our list of BUO categories does not exhaust all possible actions that fit the definition of adultness, but it does include a major portion of those commonly exhibited in
a nursery school setting. The single assessment situation used was designed with the objective of evoking but one kind of such behavior. The
measures to be considered in this chapter, then, constitute a set of adult-
like actions we originally suspected might be rather highly correlated
with one another, actions which, if the identification theory were correct,
would correlate positively—if less strongly—with dependency, with the
other presumed products of identification, and with the same child-rearing antecedents.

The five sources of measures were the Behavior Unit Observations, an
assesssment situation designed to elicit the quoting of adult-imposed
rules to a younger child, two sessions of permissive doll play, the parent
interviews, and two games in the mother-child interaction situation.
These sources permitted measures ranging from socially oriented behavior in the naturalistic setting to fantasy activity under quite precisely
controlled conditions, and drew upon behavior occurring in the home as
well as in the play group.

Unlike dependency, adult role has little history in the study of personality development (cf. Maccoby, 1961). The abundance of measures
we have used is an indication of our uncertainty concerning what we
might reasonably expect to find correlated with what. The listing is

simply a first approximation to an operational definition of adult role, and represents an exploration of the construct's properties as much as it does a set of consequent measures to be used in testing the hypotheses about child-rearing sources of the behavior.

Behavior Unit Observations

There were ten BUO categories of adult role behavior (see Appendix D). Seven of these are what we have called "real AR," i.e., adult role behavior apparently intended to have physical or social consequences appropriate to the needs and abilities of the child qua child. For example, real adult work is action of a responsible kind that helps to maintain nursery school activities in progress, such as bringing out the juice, straightening and arranging paints on the easels, or mopping up some water. Three other categories are "fantasy AR," i.e., adult-like actions performed as play or "pretend," with apparent recognition that the action does *not* produce work or stimulation to others, but that it would were an adult to perform the "real" counterpart. For example, fantasy adult work is work or activity appropriate to an adult but in a play context, such as pretending to be a man driving a car, or a cowboy rounding up cattle, or a mother getting dinner or cleaning house.

Only four of the real AR categories occurred with sufficient frequency that usable distributions were obtained. These are:

Giving facts or demonstrating knowledge (175): Teaching or guiding another with the intent of helping to train.

Real adult mannerisms (176): Employing characteristically adult postures, gestures, tone of voice, language, vocabulary, etc.; exhibiting interpretive or indirect imitation, or pseudosophistication.

Real adult work (179): Spontaneously assuming the responsibility of work appropriate to an adult, including tasks necessary to maintain activity in progress in the nursery school.

Nurturance (182): Voluntarily guiding or assisting another with the intent of being helpful or performing a service.

The rare instances of the remaining three real AR categories were added to these four, however, to provide:

Total real AR (184): Summary score of seven real AR measures.

The fantasy AR categories fared little better; only two of the three could be retained for more detailed analysis. These are:

Fantasy adult mannerisms (177): Acting like an adult in a "pretend" context (a context composed largely of dressing up in adult clothes).

Fantasy adult work (180): Performing work appropriate to an adult, in a play context.

Again we combined the instances of the used and unused categories, to obtain:

Total fantasy AR (185): Summary score of three fantasy AR categories.

(The master list of variables is presented in Appendix C.)

Several summary scores combining real and fantasy scores on a given category (e.g., adult mannerisms) were constructed, but do not appear in the master list of measures in Appendix C. Their use was abandoned early in our data analysis because there appeared to be systematic differences in both child-behavior and child-rearing correlates of real and fantasy forms of behavior. The same reasoning accounts for our separate use of first- and second-session doll-play scores, and the absence of any combined scores from the two sessions.

Quoting Rules (QuRu)

The QuRu test situation, which yielded a single AR measure (variable 212), was designed to measure the extent to which a child would adopt adult-like behavior in order to control the behavior of a younger child who was breaking a rule. (The test is described in detail in Appendix G.) The subject child was taken into a room by the experimenter and shown some exceptionally fine toys that were "not to be played with because they belonged to another nursery school group and they might get broken. But I have a very nice surprise for you, and I will go get it from the car if you will just wait here in the room for a few minutes." Two minutes after the experimenter left, a younger child was sent into the room —after having been told by another researcher that there were "some marvelous toys in there that you can play with."

The two children were left together in the room for five minutes, and of course the younger child tried to play with the toys. The older child, believing this to be forbidden, was faced with the task of controlling his companion. The extent to which he tried to enforce the rule, and the degree of adult-like quality in his methods, constituted the adult role behavior measured. Observers behind the one-way mirror used a fairly complex but reliable rating scale to record the measure.

The behavior exhibited by the research children in this situation

ranged from highly responsible control of the younger child for the full
five minutes, with the use of ingenious methods of distraction and reasoning, to an almost immediate giving in and collaboration in the forbidden play. Detailed examples of the two extremes are given in Appendix G.

Permissive Doll Play

Two twenty-minute sessions of permissive doll play were used to
measure a number of variables, including fantasy AR (as represented by
the relative frequency of use of the adult dolls as agents) and certain
adult-thematic behavior categories. The procedure was essentially the
same as that used in a number of previous studies (e.g., P. Sears, 1951).
Full details are given in Appendix F.

The doll house contained the conventional five rooms (living room,
kitchen, bath, and two bedrooms) and two additional room-like spaces—
a garage and a shop. A standard doll family (father, mother, boy, girl,
baby) was used. A medium level of experimenter-child interaction was
maintained.

Behavior unit recording was performed by the woman experimenter.
The events scored for each unit in each of the two sessions were (1)
agent, (2) object, (3) category of behavior, and (4) location. The behavior categories included three items relevant to adult role—*nurturance*
(286, 287), equivalent to BUO nurturance variable (182), above; *total
adultlike routine activity* (284, 285); and *frequency of use of adult
agents for routine acts in doll play* (250, 251). (The variable numbers
given are for the first and second sessions.)

The two latter categories were recorded with sex differentiation (father vs. mother, and male-typed vs. female-typed work), but only the
totals will be considered in the present chapter. The sex-differentiated
quality of both work and agents will be reserved for discussion in Chapter 5, where the implications for gender role can be considered also.

Parent Interviews

Two rating scales were based on information pooled from both parent interviews. The two scales—*resemblance to mother* (135) and *resemblance to father* (136)—referred to the number and importance of behavior characteristics in which the child seemed to be like each parent.

Mother-Child Interaction

Two scales, based on the children's taped behavior, are directly relevant to adult role. Both make use of behavior occurring only during the telephone and fishing games, i.e., from half of each of the two MCI sessions. The first scale is *interest in AR behavior* (360), i.e., interest in anything either the child or the mother referred to as being done by adults, such as making telephones calls "like daddy," mopping up, cooperating in wearing proper fishing costume, describing himself as behaving like an adult, or derogating childlike behavior ("I'm not a little fisherman—I'm a *big* fisherman!"). The correlations between AR interest ratings for the two kinds of session are .18 for boys and .02 for girls. Obviously the responses were situationally determined.

The behavior measured by the second scale, *resistance toward AR behavior* (361), was evidenced by the child's resisting the assumption of parental roles in the telephone game, being passive and letting the mother take the lead, willfully playing the roles childishly, or referring to himself as *not* an adult. The correlations between ratings for the two settings are .17 for boys and −.24 for girls.

In addition to these various measures, we used the *behavior maturity scale* (170), a measure of the child's behavioral maturity as reported by the mother.

Organization of Adult Role

Sex Differences

The mean scores for all the AR measures are given in Table 12. All but one of the real AR BUO categories were found insignificantly more frequently in girls; giving facts was more frequent in boys, but the difference is not significant. There are no sex differences worth noting among the fantasy AR BUO measures, nor are there on either of the mother-child interaction scales.

An interesting though not very significant sex difference was found with respect to the quoting rules (QuRu) assessment situation, however. In this case, also, the girls behaved more maturely than the boys. They quoted the restrictive rules more frequently and more emphatically, and persisted in their distraction techniques more effectively. It is our impression they were more verbal, too, although no separate notation was made of this.

The sex difference in the QuRu scores is more impressive than its

TABLE 12

Adult Role Measures: Means, Standard Deviations, Significance of Sex Differences, and Correlations with Age

(Values for BUO and doll-play measures are actual per cents; all others are ratings. An asterisk on the p-value indicates girls greater than boys.)

Adult Role Measures	Var. No.	Boys Mean	S.D.	Girls Mean	S.D.	p (2-tail)	r with Age Boys	Girls
Parent Interviews								
Imitates parents	111	4.19	1.87	5.37	2.06	< .10°	−41	04
Resembles mother	135	4.62	1.70	5.47	1.14	< .10°	08	−04
Resembles father	136	4.95	1.29	3.37	1.69	< .01	−19	02
BUO Real AR								
Giving facts	175	.82	.69	.50	.42	< .10	60	06
Adult mannerisms	176	.66	.77	.68	.65	n.s.°	22	05
Adult work	179	.69	.69	.72	.52	n.s.°	00	−01
Nurturance	182	1.20	1.12	1.53	1.24	n.s.°	17	14
Total real AR	184	3.73	1.93	4.03	2.39	n.s.°	48	13
BUO Fantasy AR								
Adult mannerisms	177	.53	.52	.40	.41	n.s.	−02	12
Adult work	180	7.09	4.33	9.07	8.59	n.s.°	−01	27
Total fantasy AR	185	12.41	6.75	12.56	9.93	n.s.°	−11	24
Quoting Rules (QuRu) . . .	212	5.24	2.78	7.11	3.43	< .10°	23	23
Permissive Doll Play								
Adult as routine agent, I . .	250	18.52	10.79	28.63	8.99	< .01°	−14	−04
Adult as routine agent, II . .	251	13.05	9.73	26.05	11.66	< .001°	03	16
Total routine AR, I	284	8.29	6.60	13.21	5.12	< .02°	−16	00
Total routine AR, II . . .	285	7.52	6.42	12.00	8.52	< .10°	04	32
Use of nurturance, I . . .	286	1.43	2.04	3.95	3.50	.01°	57	16
Use of nurturance, II . . .	287	1.67	1.91	4.05	4.78	.05°	09	08
Mother-Child Interaction								
Interest in AR	360	5.33	2.32	5.16	2.18	n.s.°	−22	−05
Resistance to AR	361	3.71	2.99	4.53	2.98	n.s.°	11	−08
Behavior Maturity Scale . . .	170	5.00	2.71	5.79	2.07	n.s.°	34	41

size indicates, for one slightly contaminating factor in the measures worked against the difference and favored the boys. This was the maturity level of the stooge child; on a five-point rating scale, this level was .63 higher on the average for the girls. The relevance of this is that, for both sexes, the more mature stooges tended to require less control and therefore to decrease the subject children's scores on the QuRu measure. Neither the mean sex difference in stooge maturity nor the two intra-sex correlations (girl QuRu with stooge maturity, boy QuRu with stooge maturity) are significant, but whatever influence this factor had was in the direction of minimizing the sex difference on the mean QuRu score itself. Thus we have little hesitation in judging the difference genuine, though it may be a function of some kind of social maturity level that is more influential at this age than during the period of middle childhood; Maccoby (1961) did not find a significant sex difference in attitudes toward rule enforcement at age twelve.

The most notable sex differences are those among the doll-play measures. The girls used the adult dolls as agents of routine action much more often than the boys did. They also tended to perform more adult-like routine actions, and to display more nurturance. Within these classes of adult acts, there were differences, as well, in the relative frequency of using father and mother dolls, and in the relative frequency of performing male- and female-typed adult work, but these data will be presented in connection with sex typing in Chapter 5. It is more relevant, here, to emphasize that the girls were generally more adult-like than the boys in their choice of agents and action categories.

In one other area—the parent interview measures—there are also interesting sex differences in means. Girls were judged to show significantly more resemblance to their mothers than to their fathers ($p <$ .001). This is hardly surprising, but the findings on the boys are. On the average, the boys resembled the father more than the mother but the difference is slight and not significant. If we compare boys and girls on each of these two scales, we note that boys resembled the father very significantly more than girls did, but although girls resembled the mother somewhat more than boys did, the difference was of minimal significance.

The parents would seem to perceive their daughters to be significantly more sex-typed than their sons, as judged by resemblance to the parents. Although one dislikes to consider parental perceptions strictly objective, because of their obvious susceptibility to cultural stereotypes, these findings do support the general prediction following from identification theory that girls should mature more rapidly than boys toward the sex-typed differentiation of behavior that characterizes adulthood, and that an early childhood representation of such differentiation would be noted in the girls' stronger similarity to their mothers than the boys' to their fathers.

Age Differences

Table 12 indicates no significant unilinear relationships between age of girl and the amount of AR behavior shown. The scatter plots of these relationships suggest, however, that the correlation coefficients are masking a tendency toward curvilinearity; the youngest and oldest girls show the least adult role behavior on nearly all the measures, the trend being stronger on the fantasy BUO measures than on the real BUO measures or the various other categories.

A similar trend occurs with the boys, although in the real AR categories the correlations correctly reflect a linear positive relationship. However, two or three extreme cases are responsible for the two larger coefficients (giving facts and total real AR), and it seems doubtful that within the age range of our sample there is evidence for any very significant variation with age. What indications there are for such evidence may be interpreted as we interpreted the minor age variations in dependency—namely, that the girls perhaps go through an adult role stage a little earlier than the boys—and in our sample the fantasy forms among older children of both sexes had begun to drop out already.

Objects of Adult Role

The issue of the objects involved in adult role behavior—i.e., the objects toward which or to whom the behavior is expressed—arises mainly in connection with nurturance. There is nothing particularly revealing about our findings. As noted in Table 12, the girls were slightly more nurturant than the boys, and, as with dependency, there was a preference for children of the same sex as objects; the boys more often chose boys, and the girls chose girls. Only the latter difference is significant, however. Girls were also slightly more often nurturant to animals, but a somewhat higher proportion of boys' nurturant acts were so directed; neither difference is significant.

Relations among Adult Role Measures

Examination of the correlations among our various AR measures implies a search for a trait. Since situational determinants of the AR behavior may be expected to have played some part in determining the size of the correlations, it seems appropriate to start with intercorrelations within each of the separate types of measurement.

TABLE 13

Intercorrelations among Adult Role Measures

(Girls above the diagonal, boys below)

Adult Role Measures	Var. No.	Variable Number											
		111	135	136	175	176	179	182	184	177	180	185	212
Parent Interviews													
Imitates parents	111	*	46	20	20	23	35	39	36	05	19	14	22
Resembles mother	135	−08	*	07	42	57	34	52	65	39	32	44	40
Resembles father	136	36	23	*	20	01	29	02	−01	26	−23	−20	18
BUO Real AR													
Giving facts	175	17	−10	03	*	49	18	61	68	52	−29	−09	−16
Adult mannerisms	176	15	−06	−08	24	*	46	61	76	61	42	53	−10
Adult work	179	15	15	−11	−08	−03	*	32	51	54	39	35	−04
Nurturance	182	06	09	01	13	17	−03	*	87	32	11	16	−18
Total real AR	184	23	−03	−02	64	57	24	63	*	59	27	34	−15
BUO Fantasy AR													
Adult mannerisms	177	28	−20	33	17	−20	−29	09	−07	*	34	47	−07
Adult work	180	28	−30	−49	22	14	49	12	35	−07	*	95	25
Total fantasy AR	185	39	−31	−03	17	−11	−05	27	12	78	51	*	31
Quoting Rules (QuRu)	212	17	29	04	04	66	15	43	55	−13	−06	−16	*
Permissive Doll Play													
Use of adult as routine agent, I	250	25	−02	−29	−15	−01	51	06	14	−13	32	12	17
Use of adult as routine agent, II	251	−37	−01	−48	−22	−07	45	02	−01	−55	34	−19	−18
Total routine AR, I	284	35	21	05	02	06	27	−13	09	−01	26	19	07
Total routine AR, II	285	20	30	−22	16	−04	69	−16	16	−34	40	−09	−08
Use of nurturance, I	286	−12	32	23	65	02	17	08	43	−22	−02	−31	12
Use of nurturance, II	287	21	−15	00	38	−13	31	−06	27	07	27	21	−28
Mother-Child Interaction													
Interest in AR	360	02	−21	−19	−02	17	−05	12	06	−42	08	−30	−02
Resistance to AR	361	−51	13	−18	−10	−38	07	−30	−40	19	05	18	−46
Behavior Maturity Scale	170	−02	37	27	23	00	−17	22	16	19	−35	−06	03

TABLE 13 (continued)
Intercorrelations among Adult Role Measures
(Girls above the diagonal, boys below)

Adult Role Measures	Var. No.	250	251	284	285	286	287	360	361	170
Parent Interviews										
Imitates parents	111	-01	-11	-01	-33	-08	-08	-12	05	24
Resembles mother	135	-10	-08	-19	-31	10	-10	-16	42	-07
Resembles father	136	40	14	26	13	-34	29	-10	-11	-13
BUO Real AR										
Giving facts	175	-19	-38	02	-16	09	00	-40	07	15
Adult mannerisms	176	-22	-06	-31	-13	05	-04	-16	06	38
Adult work	179	-35	19	-24	23	-29	-07	00	-17	42
Nurturance	182	-21	-18	-02	-13	19	-14	-26	-07	48
Total real AR	184	-12	-09	-17	-07	10	-21	-19	07	53
BUO Fantasy AR										
Adult mannerisms	177	15	06	02	34	08	20	-01	01	23
Adult work	180	-09	20	-25	07	10	-01	12	-11	42
Total fantasy AR	185	-12	-09	-28	01	12	04	05	-06	34
Quoting Rules (QuRu)	212	03	-17	-06	-23	-21	-03	08	09	-22
Permissive Doll Play										
Use of adult as routine agent, I	250	✱	44	28	25	05	25	06	28	06
Use of adult as routine agent, II	251	47	✱	33	60	01	09	-02	15	04
Total routine AR, I	284	71	17	✱	33	04	01	-39	06	-14
Total routine AR, II	285	60	60	52	✱	-05	14	-32	-24	11
Use of nurturance, I	286	-26	-07	-14	14	✱	63	-02	28	13
Use of nurturance, II	287	28	22	22	36	34	✱	14	07	-01
Mother-Child Interaction										
Interest in AR	360	08	11	-06	07	-15	-39	✱	-17	-10
Resistance to AR	361	-06	31	-05	12	00	13	-41	✱	-32
Behavior Maturity Scale	170	-34	31	-36	-09	22	-16	01	01	✱

The intercorrelations among real and fantasy AR BUO measures are shown in Table 13; as with dependency, the sex difference in the apparent degree of organization is very great. The median r for girls on real AR measures is .47, whereas for boys it is virtually zero. The two fantasy AR measures are positively related in girls (.34) but unrelated in boys (−.07), and the crosscorrelations between the real and fantasy categories show similar differences. Thus it would seem reasonable, for girls, to use the combined scores of total real AR and total fantasy AR as measures of adult role behavior in the nursery school, whereas the propriety of using such combinations for boys might seem questionable.

When we examine the specific BUO measures for boys more closely, however, we find what may be a fundamental difficulty in the definition of adult role, as well as a partial explanation of the apparent lack of organization of the trait in boys. The problem arises from the sex-typed character of certain forms of adult role behavior. Among the intercorrelations of real AR BUO categories in boys, all three of those involving real adult work are zero. Furthermore, fantasy adult work is positively correlated with its real counterpart (.49), and is unrelated to the other fantasy measure. In other words, the qualities measured by adult work do not seem to be those measured by the other social-situational measures of adult role. Furthermore, adult work is the only social-situational measure of adult role that relates positively to the doll-play measures. Thus, in boys, there appears to be a cluster of three types of adult role measures that may represent a tendency toward display of *feminine* adult behavior; these are real and fantasy adult work and the various (highly intercorrelated) measures of adult work in doll play.

The resemblance-to-father measure, moreover, has no relation to the BUO measures, except that it is *negatively* related to both adult work categories, significantly so for the fantasy measure. This finding strengthens the suggestion that adult work in the nursery school may be a feminine type of activity, and in fact both real and fantasy adult work are *negatively* related to the overall measure of masculine sex typing (real −.61, fantasy −.29). Adult work thus appears not to be measuring *masculine* adult qualities in boys, and the question therefore arises whether it can be used, without special qualification, as a measure of adult role behavior. This matter will be considered further in Chapter 5.

The same problem does not arise with girls, of course, because their adult role behavior coincides with feminine-typed behavior. Although the intercorrelations between the two adult work categories and the other BUO AR measures are lower than those among the others themselves, they are nevertheless predominantly positive.

The interview measures of resemblance to the two parents are of interest in this connection. In boys, neither is related to masculinity (mother .09, father .16), nor to any of the other AR measures—BUO, QuRu, doll play, or mother-child interaction—except negatively to adult work, as mentioned above.

For girls, the situation is quite different. Both parental resemblance scales are slightly related to femininity (mother .33, father .35), and resemblance to mother is positively and substantially correlated with all the BUO measures and with the QuRu score. Interestingly enough, both the mother resemblance scale and the BUO measures are negatively related to the occurrence of female-typed adult work in doll play (cf. Chapter 5). This suggests that doll play may serve as an alternative way for little girls to express their impulses to act in an adult way. For boys, however, as we saw above, doll play appears to reflect the feminine-typed behavior tendency seen so clearly in the BUO adult work categories.

QuRu is still another measure that seems to have a strong flavor of *maternal*—if not altogether feminine—quality. In both sexes, it is positively related to resemblance to mother and not at all to resemblance to father. In neither sex is it related to any of the measures of sex typing. It seems to measure mother-like behavior, as it was intended to do.

The positive correlations between QuRu and the BUO real AR measures in boys reinforce our suspicion that what we are measuring in many of these instances is maternal (i.e., feminine adult role) behavior. However, for the girls there is no such relation between QuRu and the BUO AR measures, even though there is a substantial correlation of QuRu with resemblance to mother, and this rating in turn correlates highly with all the BUO AR measures.

Summary of Adult Role Organization

All these rather complex relationships lead to the following conclusions concerning the structure of adult role behavior in children of this age. First, for girls, there is a constellation of action tendencies, observable in both the home and the nursery school, that can be labeled adult role. There is evidence, however, that such tendencies are sex-typed, for the nursery school adult role behavior is correlated with resemblance to mother but not with resemblance to father, and real AR is significantly related to femininity. Thus, the measures of adult role appear to be confounded with measures of sex typing. The maturing girl is becoming both more adult and more feminine, and at least some of the measures seem to be measuring both qualities at once. Thus, the final estimate of adult role—especially as reflected in the BUO real AR categories—is the product of a mixture of the two correlated developmental trends, and there is no clear way of discovering to what extent the adult role constellation exists independently of gender role.

Second, for boys, there is clear evidence of a similar confounding, in that certain of the AR measures appear to be predominantly measures of feminine adult role behavior, as shown by their negative correlations with both masculinity and resemblance to father. For boys, however, both adult role behavior and masculinity represent measures of maturity in behavioral development, and hence—to the extent that the adult role is an indication of femininity—the two behavior tendences influence the so-called AR measures in opposite directions. That is, developing maturity should be toward both masculinity and adultness, but our measures of the latter appear to be contaminated with femininity. The net result is a chaotic mélange of obtained correlations that average zero or close to it.

Third, the significance of fantasy adult role behavior differs for the two sexes, too. What we have called "fantasy" in the BUO categories bears little relation to the fantasy represented by permissive doll play. In girls, the former is simply part and parcel of adult role behavior in the social situation, while in boys it is as unrelated to other forms of adult role behavior as are all the other femininity-contaminated measures.

On the other hand, the doll-play measures of adult role are somewhat negatively related to real AR measures in girls, and may represent an alternative form of expression. In boys, the feminine real adult work categories are positively related to doll-play female-typed adult work, giving further support to the conclusion that adult role in boys is too confounded with sex-typing to be examined fruitfully alone.

Relation of Adult Role to Dependency

In the previous chapter, evidence was presented to show that positive attention seeking is differentiated from the other forms of dependency not only with respect to intercorrelations among the BUO measures, but also with respect to child-rearing antecedents. It was interpreted as a more mature form of behavior, and touching and holding and being near as less mature forms. The relationships between adult role and dependency add further support to this differentiation, and also aid in clarifying the distinction between the two immature forms of dependency (see Appendix K, Table K4).

In both sexes, positive attention seeking is more closely associated with real AR measures than with the other forms of dependency. In girls, the median correlation with the four BUO AR measures is .53, and that with total real AR is .67. Partial correlations in which rated social activity level is held constant reduce these figures somewhat but not significantly. In boys, the same generalization may be made, though the obtained correlations are smaller (total real AR, .42). Total fantasy AR and QuRu are not significantly related to any measure of dependency in either sex.

Nurturance and Dependency

There is an important difference between the sexes with respect to nurturance, however. In girls, the r with positive attention seeking is .75, the highest correlation involving an AR measure. In boys, the corresponding value is just zero. This sex difference becomes of some theoretical importance when we note that nurturance by boys is strongly associated with touching and holding (.60) but has a slightly negative correlation with being near ($-.22$), although these two supposedly immature dependency behaviors are mutually unrelated (.13). Nurturance by girls shows no relationship to either of these two forms of dependency.

The significance of nurturant behavior for girls appears to differ markedly from that for boys. For girls, it is simply one element of the behavior constellation otherwise defined by high intercorrelations among positive attention seeking, real AR, feminine sex typing, and resemblance to mother.

For the boys, however, nurturance has a more complicated role, and to understand it we must go back to the distinction between touching and holding and being near. The former, it will be recalled, is positively related to rated activity level, whereas the latter is strongly negatively related. Although there are reasons for considering both behaviors immature, it is clear that they are mutually distinguishable along an activity-passivity dimension. The hypothesis was presented earlier that touching and holding is an active form of early dependency and being near is a corresponding passive form. The different child-rearing measures associated with the two seemed to offer additional support for this view; touching and holding is associated with dyadic frustration (separation from mother, and number of siblings), a state of affairs which could be expected to exacerbate seeking for contact, whereas being near is associated with maternal infantilizing and a negative attitude on the part of the father, both of which might be expected to inhibit a child's active seeking of contact. The positive relation between nurturance and touching and holding seems to bear out this interpretation, since both are correlated significantly with rated activity levels.

Some aspects of aggression are also pertinent to the relation of nurturance to dependency in boys. In Chapter 4, categories of aggressive behavior are combined into larger summary scores in two ways: the first combines aggression measures of antisocial quality into one summary score, and those of prosocial quality into another; the second way combines one prosocial and two antisocial aggression measures into a direct interpersonal aggression summary measure (but makes no such summary use of the indirect aggression measures). The first way of differentiating component aggression measures into summary scores is consonant with the theoretical position from which our research began—namely, that high identification with his parents would lead a child to express his aggression in the mature and socially acceptable forms that characterize adult discipline. Prosocial aggression is a combination of tattling and verbal disapproval. A more detailed definition of these aggression variables is given in Chapter 4.

All three summary scores show substantial positive relation to real AR in both sexes; the uncombined indirect aggression categories have much lower relations to real AR.

The significance of these findings for the activity-passivity problem is that, in boys, both nurturance and touching and holding show the same positive relations to direct interpersonal aggression, whereas being near shows negative relations, thus adding further support to the interpretation of the latter as a passive form of immature dependency behavior.

In sum, then, nurturance in girls is simply one of several forms of mature feminine behavior, apparently part of an extensive system of actions having the common end of maintaining a satisfying relationship with the mother. In boys, however, nurturance is associated with the active form of the so-called immature dependency behaviors, although greater emphasis must be placed on the active aspect than on the immature, for as we have seen in Chapter 2, touching and holding is not so clearly an indication of immaturity in boys as it is in girls.

Summary of Relation to Dependency

So far as girls are concerned, adult role behavior as defined by our BUO categories appears to be a form of mature dependency behavior quite similar to what we have described as positive attention seeking. The overt actions defined by the AR categories are of course discriminably different from those of positive attention seeking, but some girls do a good deal of both and others do little of either. Both kinds of behavior are, in turn, closely associated with all forms of direct interpersonal aggression (especially the prosocial), with social interaction level, and with feminine sex typing. There is one difference worth noting in anticipation of the discussion of child-rearing antecedents, however; high AR is related to high behavioral maturity as judged by the mother (.53), while positive attention seeking is not so related. In the main, though, girls have a well-integrated set of behaviors that seem designed to bring a girl to the favorable notice of her mother; this trait, if we may call such a cluster a trait, displays qualities of maturity, femininity, and active social interaction.

For boys, on the other hand, the concept of adult role is ambiguous. The maturing boy is in conflict over his choice of roles. His mother is an important adult model, but maturity also implies the adoption of masculine actions. The boy who is maturing most rapidly may also be becoming more feminine—or at least more like his mother. Yet the pressure toward masculinity must be great if he is indeed maturing rapidly, for masculinity is his ultimate goal.

The measures of adultness we used are, in varying degrees, measures of feminine role behavior. Adult work in a nursery school is essentially women's work—preparing food, cleaning and ordering the household and its equipment, helping small children, admonishing and gently disciplining, caring for hurts and disasters, and planning for the morrow. The boy who eagerly adopts this adult work gets a high score on adult role, but not so high a score on masculinity—an equally relevant aspect of the maturing process. The ultimate upshot for our limited measures is a confusion between two somewhat incompatible behavior tendencies —and many very low intercorrelations among the measures.

Nevertheless, there is a good reason for continuing the analysis of these behaviors in boys, for they provide a reliable indication of the complex outcome of the conflictual learning the boy is doing. Our results show clearly a fairly high degree of individual consistency in the total real AR score over the seven weeks of observation (see Appendix B). Whatever confusion is present lies in the boy, not in the measuring instruments, for the latter show the resolution of his conflicts to have some stability over this relatively brief time. Furthermore, Vitz (1961) has shown that the BUO scores for adult role increased during the period of nursery school attendance, which is what we would expect in an environment we have concluded to be conflict-producing for boys with respect to the feminine aspect of adult role behavior.

Correspondence to Identification Theory

Our original expectations, based on identification theory, were that adult role behavior would be positively associated with (1) the child's own dependency, (2) the warmth of the parents, (3) the high demands by one or both parents, (4) the use of reasoning, isolation, praise, and withdrawal of love as disciplinary techniques, and (5) the use of the parents as models of good behavior. The first three of these hypotheses were tested by Maccoby (1961) in her follow-up study. She found that attitudes favoring rule enforcement were stronger in twelve-year-old boys whose mothers had placed high restrictions (demands) on them in the preschool years. This effect was significantly greater among boys whose mothers were warm and who judged their sons to be high in dependency. Similar results were obtained with the girls, though the restrictiveness variable was replaced by punitiveness, and warmth was not found to be influential.

Maccoby's measure of adult role (rule enforcement) was taken at age twelve, and her items were specifically applicable to the sex of the child being tested. In the present study, the contamination of the boys' AR measures by gender role makes difficult a simple and direct test of the five propositions in boys, but the propositions can be rather easily tested in girls by examining separately the correlations between three of the measures (total real AR, total fantasy AR, QuRu) and the child-rearing measures obtained from the interviews and mother-child interactions.

Total Real Adult Role

The dependency hypothesis is clearly supported; high real AR is associated with high positive attention seeking in both sexes, and high nurturance in boys is associated with high touching and holding.

The second proposition, that for parental warmth, is disconfirmed, however. Table 14 shows all the parent variables from the interviews and the mother-child interaction that correlate significantly ($p = .05$ or better) with either total real AR or total fantasy AR; only one of the six available measures of warmth—estimated mother's warmth in the mother-girl interaction—appears in the list for either sex, and the coefficient in this single case is significantly *negative* with total fantasy AR.

The third proposition, concerning high demands, is more difficult to evaluate. There are many areas of conduct in which parents can set up high levels of performance for their children to strive toward. These include control of sex, dependency, and aggression; development of appropriate table manners, neatness, orderliness, responsibility, and conscience; and so on. The demands may be expressed by parents in either or both of two ways: by attempts to inhibit changeworthy behavior (as in non-permissiveness or punishment for aggression or dependency), or by demands for mature behavior (as in table manners). Among the scales drawn from our interviews there are 27 that measure demands of an inhibiting type—18 measures of mothers' demands and nine of fathers' demands. There are also ten mother scales and six father scales relating to positive achievements or to attitudes of pressure toward maturity. In Table 14, for girls' real AR, only two of the significantly correlated scales (58 and 91) belong to these classes. The case is better for the boys; two of the expected scales (31 and 83) appear in the list, both related in the expected direction, and one other scale (89) might be interpreted similarly. A scanning of the more than forty remaining correlations—those below the .05 level of significance—adds little to these findings, however, and our conclusion is that there is some but not strong support for the high-demand hypothesis in its present general form.

The fourth proposition, concerning love-oriented disciplinary techniques, is clearly disconfirmed. The only expected disciplinary technique in the correlation list (Table 14) is mother's praise for girls, and this correlation is in the negative direction.

The fifth hypothesis, respecting the use of parents as models, can be tested with three scales: a pooled rating of the extent to which the child

TABLE 14

Total Adult Role, Real (184) and Fantasy (185) (BUO): Correlations with Parent Interview and Mother-Child Interaction Measures at Level $p < .05$

(Where a sign alone is shown, the r is larger than .25 but less than .46 for girls or .43 for boys.)

	Real (184)	Fantasy (185)
GIRLS		
4. Mother's tension concerning MCI		48
11. Mother's proportion of caretaking in infancy	−50	−
13. Duration of breast feeding		−46
24. Father's permissiveness for indoor nudity		−48
27. Amount of child's social nudity: father		−75
32. Mother's permissiveness for sex play among children	−	−48
38. Mother's sex anxiety	+	47
46. Father's pressure for conformity to standards	−	−70
58. Mother's permissiveness for aggression toward parents	−57	
75. Relative strictness of parents: mother high (pooled)		51
85. Mother's use of people as models of good behavior	−	−56
91. Father's expectancy of conscience	47	
94. Mother's use of praise	−51	
96. Mother's use of tangible reward	−56	
115. Father's use of reward for sex-appropriate behavior	49	61
123. Child's expression of dependency toward father	49	+
135. Extent child resembles mother (pooled)	65	+
153. Mother's evaluation of father	−	−50
160. Extent of mother's current dissatisfaction with her life		50
170. Child Behavior Scale: maturity (mother)	53	+
330. Mother's warmth toward child		−54
333. Mother's involvement with puzzles	−51	
BOYS		
1. Age of child	48	
12. Father's proportion of caretaking in infancy	−61	
29. Father's modesty	51	
31. Father's permissiveness for masturbation	−46	
32. Mother's permissiveness for sex play among children		58
39. Father's sex anxiety	61	
59. Father's permissiveness for aggression toward parents		−52
69. Mother's use of deprivation of privileges		46
83. Mother's stress on importance of teaching right and wrong	46	
89. Signs of conscience as reaction to wrongdoing (pooled)	58	
105. Father's use of punishment for independence		43
124. Mother's permissiveness for dependency		−67
126. Mother's use of reward for dependency	+	−54
128. Mother's use of punishment for dependency	−	61
139. Father's directiveness toward child		43
159. Extent father disowns grandparents' child-rearing policies	44	−
326. Mother's directiveness toward child		−57

imitates the parents, and two measures of the extent to which the parents refer to themselves or others as models of good behavior. For both sexes, all three correlations are nonsignificant.

In general, then, we must conclude that of the five hypotheses deriving from identification theory, only one—that relating real AR behavior to the child's dependency—receives unequivocal support from the total real AR measure.

Total Fantasy Adult Role

The findings for fantasy AR are somewhat less discouraging for identification theory. Suppressive control of dependency and aggression in boys and of sex in girls supports the hypothesis concerning high demands (of an inhibiting kind), but the low pressure by the father for conformity in girls is in the opposite direction. The dependency hypothesis, confirmed by the real AR measure, is here disconfirmed, as was noted earlier in the discussion of the relation of adult role to dependency.

Quoting Rules (QuRu)

There is little if any relation between girls' adult role behavior as measured in the QuRu assessment situation and as measured in the BUO observations of real AR. Not surprisingly, therefore, there is no similarity in the list of significantly correlated child-rearing variables (Table 15). But so far as the four theoretical predictions are concerned, this dissimilarity makes little difference. Only one—warmth—gains clear support; father's, not mother's, warmth correlates .73 with QuRu. There is also a little evidence for modeling, but although QuRu correlates .47 with mother's use of models in the mother-child interaction, there is no indication of such a relation with any of the three interview measures.

With boys, QuRu correlates .55 with real AR, and the significantly correlated interview variables are confined to the demands hypothesis, as they are with respect to real AR. Father's control of sex and mother's achievement standards bear out the expectation, but the lenient treatment of dependency by both parents is in contradiction to the prediction.

Summary of Correspondence to Identification Theory

The hypothesis that dependency is associated with adult role behavior is clearly supported by the real AR measure, but not by either fantasy AR or QuRu; congruent with this statement is the correlation of nurturance with touching and holding, in boys. The other four hypotheses

TABLE 15

Quoting Rules (QuRu) (212):
Correlations with Parent Interview and Mother-Child
Interaction Measures at Level $p < .05$

GIRLS

94. Mother's use of praise	49
96. Mother's use of tangible reward	50
119. Father's warmth toward child	73
132. Father's empathy for child	48
141. Father's hostility to child	−56
149. Father's self-esteem	57
325. Mother's use of punishment for child's independence	46
326. Mother's directiveness toward child	46
368. Mother's use of models with child	47

BOYS

8. Stability of current home situation (pooled)	−51
31. Father's permissiveness for masturbation	−45
39. Father's sex anxiety	53
56. Father's demand for aggression toward peers	48
83. Mother's stress on importance of teaching right and wrong	45
124. Mother's permissiveness for dependency	44
126. Mother's use of reward for dependency	50
128. Mother's use of punishment for dependency	−53
129. Father's use of punishment for dependency	−49
133. Mother's achievement standards for child	44
144. Continuity of mother's goals with the mother role	−43

stemming from identification theory obtain no consistent support, although the findings for parents' demands are somewhat suggestive and not unlike those obtained by Maccoby (1961).

A Direct Reinforcement Theory

An alternative theoretical possibility deserves consideration—namely, that adult role behavior receives direct reinforcement by the parents. Information obtained in the interviews permitted us to rate each parent on permissiveness for, reward of, and punishment of both adult role behavior and independence in the home. None of these six scales for either parent is significantly related to real or fantasy AR or to QuRu, nor are any of five possible mother scales that relate to similar variables in the mother-child interaction.

An Inductive Analysis

In the absence of previous explorations and analyses of the adult role concept and its manifestations in preschool-age children, the present attempt to link such a hypothetical trait to the equally hypothetical process of identification was obviously a risky leap, both theoretically and empirically. So far as identification theory is concerned, we are now no farther ahead than when we began, for we cannot know whether the failure to confirm our antecedent-consequent hypotheses stems from a lack of coherence in the adult role concept or from inaccuracy in the hypothesized relationships. The obtained data have a particular value, however, since the extensive surrounding information about both the children and their parents provides a good source for an inductive analysis of the parent-child relationships that eventuate in so-called adult role behavior. Our purpose here is to shift from hypothesis testing to hypothesis forming.

Total Real Adult Role

Although we are more accustomed to finding differences than similarities between the sexes, both in child-behavior correlates and in parental antecedents of any given behavior, there is one striking parallel displayed in the two lists of Table 14. For both boys and girls, high real AR is significantly associated with low infant caretaking by the parent of the same sex. This close association between parent and child variables was also seen—with the same child-rearing antecedent—for positive attention seeking.

High infant caretaking is an index of two of the child-rearing dimensions isolated in *Patterns of Child Rearing*—permissiveness and warmth. High degrees of both these dimensions are associated with high caretaking of the opposite-sexed child, but not necessarily of the same-sexed child. An infant, tiny though it may be, apparently already has a sex-role stimulus value for the parents.

Since caretaking by the two parents is to some extent an either/or matter, one might expect that the negative relation between real AR and caretaking by the same-sexed parent would be paralleled by a positive relation to caretaking by the opposite-sexed parent. This is not the case for fathers and girls ($-.22$), however, and is but slightly so for mothers and boys ($.23$). Indeed, if the influence of caretaking by the same-sexed parents is held constant by partial correlation, these two values become $-.39$ and $-.29$, respectively. We may conclude, then, that real AR is associated with non-caretaking by both parents, but especially by the same-sexed parent.

For the mothers of girls, Table 14 presents a picture of non-permissiveness for aggression and low use of praise and rewards. Some of the nonsignificant (hence not listed) coefficients add an impression of nonpermissiveness about sex, a low evaluation of the mother role, and high achievement standards. These various restrictions and demands are evidently directed toward producing more behavioral maturity in the child, for the mother judges this to be high, and sees her daughter as resembling herself.

For boys, high real AR has an implication of feminization, and the low caretaking by fathers is associated with father's sex anxiety. As has already been mentioned (Chapter 2), this sex anxiety tends toward a feminizing of both sons and daughters, so that, for real AR, one might be inclined to interpret the relation with infant caretaking as essentially an index of the influence of sex anxiety. However, partialing out the influence of either caretaking or sex anxiety, one on the other, leaves a residual r of .48; hence, both variables apparently have some independent relationship to real AR.

In the list for boys (Table 14), one other variable appears that is related to father's sex anxiety—namely, mother's belief in the importance of teaching right and wrong. Interestingly enough, this scale correlates significantly for each parent with the *spouse's* sex anxiety but not with the parent's own! One cannot help wondering whether the sex anxiety of one spouse creates a moralistic attitude in the other. In any case, the mother's belief, in the present context, may be considered a part of the father's sex-anxiety constellation.

For boys, there is one additional complex of variables associated with real AR. This complex includes age of child, mother's pressure for neatness and orderliness, child's conscience (an interview measure), disowning paternal grandparents' child-rearing policies, and the amount of living space in the child's home. The last measure is negatively related to the others and to real AR. This cluster of variables is consistently intercorrelated in the $p = .10 > .01$ range, and there seems to be no way to disengage its member variables to determine which, if any, is most genuinely connected with real AR.

Because of the unwieldy structure of our findings for total real AR, we will do well to summarize. In girls, the development of high real AR is somewhat parallel to that of positive attention seeking, and seems to be the product of maternal restrictiveness and expectation of maturity, a kind of shaping and pressuring toward the goal of drawing the girl out of her infancy.

In boys, real AR is a somewhat feminized (or perhaps maternalized!) form of behavior, as is positive attention seeking, and tends to be induced by the father's sex anxiety; the boy is showing his feminine development by behaving in a "womanly" fashion.

Whether the low amount of caretaking in infancy by the father is an index of a continuing detachment from the boy—as the mother's appears to be from the girl—is not determined, but if the caretaking variable has significance beyond its implication of sex anxiety, this must be the case; it is difficult to imagine that the infant experience could of itself have such a profound effect. It is possible, too, that the reciprocal effect on the mother is more important than the figures reveal. For example, mother warmth is correlated −.53 with amount of father caretaking; some such variable as this might represent a supplement to the feminizing influence of father's sex anxiety, though in this case warmth itself has little relation (−.12) to masculinity in boys. But a search of our maternal child-rearing variables reveals no likely candidates for this possible reciprocating effect.

Total Fantasy Adult Role

Fantasy AR behaviors, which constitute about three-fourths of all adult role behavior observed, were not differentiated with respect to sex appropriateness. They included playing house, washing dishes, caring for the baby, giving a party, dressing up in adult costumes, playing cowboy, bandits, cops and robbers, gas station attendant, or truck or racing driver, and so on. Generally, though by no means exclusively, girls played feminine adult roles, and boys played masculine adult roles.

The frequency of fantasy play occurrence is unrelated to the overall measure of sex typing in either sex, however, and there is even a slight tendency for children who rank high in this play to spend their time in sex-inappropriate areas (−.31 for boys, −.19 for girls). In spite of this, the observers rated boys more masculine (.56) and girls more feminine (.32) if they had high scores on fantasy AR. One might say the observers were seduced into their ratings by the manifest sex-appropriateness of this play. In any case, the appearance obscured the underlying irrelevance of such role play. Or perhaps it was not irrelevant; perhaps in some instances it was a reflection of a child's desire to be more adult and more sex-typed than he or she was permitted to be by the parents.

This hypothesis would suggest a search for parental attitudes that suppressed the children's effort to secure autonomy, independence, and

adultness. The list of correlated variables in Table 14 might be interpreted as partial support of this notion. For girls, there is evidence of
strong suppression of sex expression by both parents, and for boys, evidence of suppression of both aggression and independence by the father
and dependency by the mother. The single important coefficient contra-
dicting this generalization in boys is probably fortuitous; mother's permissiveness for sex play is the only sex scale that correlates greater than
.23 with fantasy AR, and the remainder average just zero. Furthermore,
the mother attitude scale measuring the same variable relates not at all
($-.07$) to this behavior.

There would seem to be some merit in pursuing further the hypothesis
that fantasy forms of adult role behavior represent efforts to overcome
suppressive attitudes of the parents.

Quoting Rules (QuRu)

In examining the relations of QuRu behavior to other forms of adult
role and to aggression, dependency, and sex typing, we were led to the
conclusion that rule quoting is essentially a form of maternal, rather than
simply feminine, behavior. In neither sex is it at all related to any of the
direct measures of sex typing.

The list of significantly correlated parental measures (Table 15) reveals a clear picture for both sexes. For girls, the father's warmth and
empathy are salient correlates; there is also an unlisted but almost significant positive correlation with father's caretaking in infancy ($.43$). The
mother is interactive with her daughter, praising and rewarding her, but
in the mother-child interaction she was guiding and controlling. The picture is that of a loving, affectionate father, a mother taking positive actions toward her daughter's development, and a little girl who resembles
her mother ($.40$), has a conscience ($.41$), is overtly aggressive toward her
mother in the home ($.44$) but indirectly so in the mother-child interaction ($-.47$), and is not necessarily aggressive toward her father ($.20$).
Possibly she is adopting her mother's behavior as a device for maintaining the love of her father.

In boys, QuRu correlates highly with two of the four real AR categories and with willingness to play the adult role in the telephone game
in the mother-child interaction. The child-rearing correlates are similar,
as might be expected: high sex anxiety in the father, relatively low infant caretaking by the father ($-.38$), and high importance placed on

teaching right and wrong by the mother. In addition, the QuRu antecedent list includes significant correlations with permissiveness and non-
punitiveness of dependency by both parents, and high achievement
standards of the mother. These variables are insignificantly correlated
with real AR, but the directions are the same.

These dependency relationships are of particular interest, because (as
seen in Table 14) they are oppositely directed from those for fantasy AR.
The adoption of maternal behavior in real situations would seem to be
perhaps a function of the boy's being allowed to be dependent toward
the mother, whereas if this form of closeness and intimacy is suppressed,
the boy goes off by himself or with other children and plays the fantasy
roles.

Adults as Routine Agents in Doll Play

Because of the moderate correlations between first and second sessions of doll play, in frequency of use of adults as routine agents, there
is considerable similarity in both the child-behavior correlates and the
child-rearing correlates. The correlations between sessions were .47 for
boys, .44 for girls. There is also a surprising similarity between boys and
girls in respect to the correlates. Table 16 shows the variables from the
interviews and the mother-child interaction that correlate at the .05
level of significance, or better.

For both sexes, the use of adult agents in doll play is negatively related
to activity level and interpersonal aggression, and positively and strongly related to resistance to temptation. The difference between the sexes
lies in the associated maturity level and the degree of sex typing; for
boys, the use of adult doll agents correlates with orality, with the passive
immature forms of dependency, with non-masculinity, and with the feminine forms of social adult role behavior (adult work), whereas for girls
the associated behaviors definitely exclude both the narcissistic orality
of the boys and the distortion in sex typing. The correlations of adult
agents with femininity are just zero.

The child-rearing correlates include for both sexes a pervasive restrictiveness about both sex and dependency, a pressure for conformity,
and demands for aggression toward peers. In addition, the girls are
severely restricted on aggression and are subjected to physical punishment by the father. Indeed, the father's influence is greater in the girls'
list in Table 16 than in the correlate list of any other form of behavior we

TABLE 16

Use of Adult as Routine Agent in Permissive Doll Play (250, 251):
Correlations with Parent Interview and Mother-Child
Interaction Measures at Level $p < .05$

(Where a sign alone is shown, the r is larger than .25 but less than .46 for girls or .43 for boys.)

	Session I (250)	Session II (251)
GIRLS		
6. Severity of child's early separation from father	47	
11. Mother's proportion of caretaking in infancy	48	+
22. Amount of thumb-sucking child has shown (pooled) . .	−	−50
26. Amount of child's social nudity (mother)		−46
28. Mother's modesty	56	64
30. Mother's permissiveness for masturbation	−	−52
31. Father's permissiveness for masturbation	−	−50
43. Father's pressure for neatness and orderliness	58	
46. Father's pressure for conformity to standards	53	
54. Extent of overt aggression in home by father	46	
56. Father's demand for aggression toward peers	+	46
59. Father's permissiveness for aggression toward parents . .	−55	
61. Father's use of punishment for aggression toward parents	53	
68. Father's use of physical punishment	61	
73. Relative frequency as agents of discipline: mother high (mother)		−55
75. Relative strictness of parents: mother high (pooled) . .	−64	
76. Strictness of mother	+	61
77. Strictness of father	54	
86. Father's use of people as models of good behavior . . .	50	
88. Extent child confesses wrongdoing (father)		−50
106. Mother's satisfaction with child's socialization		−56
107. Father's satisfaction with child's socialization	−46	−51
109. Father's use of reward for adult role behavior		52
113. Father's expectancy of sex differences in behavior		−51
117. Child's expression of affection toward father		−48
124. Mother's permissiveness for dependency		−55
125. Father's permissiveness for dependency	−54	−55
126. Mother's use of reward for dependency		−55
128. Mother's use of punishment for dependency		57
129. Father's use of punishment for dependency	49	63
140. Mother's hostility to child		57
150. Mother's sociability	53	47
156. Strictness of father's parents	−	−64
169. Mother Attitude Scale: permissiveness for aggression toward parents	−54	
173. Mother's non-permissiveness: factor score	48	+
322. Mother's pressure for child's independence	60	+
330. Mother's warmth toward child	50	
331. Mother's responsiveness to child	50	
332. Mother's involvement in telephone game	50	

TABLE 16 (continued)
Use of Adult as Routine Agent in Permissive Doll Play (250, 251)

	Session I (250)	Session II (251)
BOYS		
3. MCI seen by mother as achievement situation for child .	−49	
6. Severity of child's early separation from father		−45
9. Mother's resentment of this pregnancy	−46	−
13. Duration of breast feeding	−56	−47
22. Amount of thumb-sucking child has shown (pooled) . .	+	49
23. Mother's permissiveness for indoor nudity	−	−54
25. Mother's pressure for modesty indoors	+	54
36. Extent father gives sexual information to child	−50	
55. Mother's demand for aggression toward peers	45	
98. Mother's use of psychological (vs. tangible) reward . . .		−52
101. Father's permissiveness for independence		−44
109. Father's use of reward for adult role behavior		−48
117. Child's expression of affection toward father	72	47
121. Father's affectional demonstrativeness toward child . . .	+	47
129. Father's use of punishment for dependency		43
136. Extent child resembles father (pooled)	−	−48
142. Severity of child's current separation from mother . . .	45	+
146. Mother's child-rearing anxiety		−45
161. Age of father		51
163. Number of children in family	+	65
167. Mother Attitude Scale: permissiveness for sex play among children	−	−43
324. Mother's use of reward for child's independence	−52	−
328. Mother's use of reward for child's dependency	−43	
329. Mother's use of punishment for child's dependency . . .	+	52
330. Mother's warmth toward child	−59	−43
331. Mother's responsiveness to child	−45	−

have measured. Nevertheless, these little girls who used adult dolls as agents were not forced into masculinity, nor is there any evidence of the sex anxiety that seemed apparent with the dependency category of reassurance seeking. Neither is there evidence of negative attention seeking (−.56 and −.24), nor of injury to objects (−.15 and .08), which will be shown in Chapter 4 to be a masculine form of aggression associated with the father's intrusion into the girl's rearing.

The reasons for the lack of either anxiety or masculinity as associates of the use of adult agents probably lie in the nature of the father's relationship to the girl. Table 16 indicates that the mother was the chief caretaker in infancy (father: −.45 and −.16, for the two sessions), that she showed warmth and involvement in the mother-child interaction, and that the daughter was reported not to show affection to the father. The latter fact is scarcely surprising when one notes the overwhelming list of restrictions, punishments, and demands imposed by the fathers. On the basis of these findings, we suggest the hypothesis that heavy use of adult agents in doll play is a sign of passivity, immaturity, and fear produced by a restrictive and punitive parent-child relationship.

Discussion

Our conception of adult role derived initially from our theory of identification. We reasoned that children learn to imitate their parents in order to secure or maintain the affectionate, nurturant responses that have been the reinforcing stimuli for infantile dependency behavior. We presumed that this imitation generalizes beyond the specific parent-pleasing forms of mature behavior to all forms of parental behavior; the child practices the adult role as he sees it exhibited in the behavior of his chief adult models—his parents. The behavioral concept of adult role was essentially an abstraction of the common elements of adult behavior we had seen performed by children. These included mannerisms, chores or work, imparting facts or knowledge, nurturance, and the controlling of other children's impulses toward deviant behavior. The generalized concept of adult role, then, was simply the sum of these various acts, a common denominator of adult behaviors that we presumed could be seen in most young children. Essentially, we hypothesized the existence of a trait that would have the same content for all children, for we excluded from our categories anything that would be idiosyncratic to a particular parent and child.

This *a priori* conceptualization has received some support from our observations, though not all the categories we defined are correlated with one another in the ways anticipated, and the familiar difference between sexes arises again in the structure of the trait. For example, in girls the four categories of real AR correlate with one another to a fairly substantial degree, and seem to be part of a constellation that includes positive attention seeking, feminine sex typing, prosocial and interpersonal aggression, and a resemblance to the mother. The controlling of other children's impulses to deviant behavior, as measured in the QuRu assessment situation, does not belong in this constellation, however.

In boys, on the other hand, there is little or no evidence of a trait structure composed of the four categories of real AR behavior, if we may judge from their intercorrelations. We have adduced some evidence from the correlations of these variables with measures of sex typing that suggests the particular categories we have used are partly indicators of the adoption of maternal adult role; hence, the adult qualities of behavior are confounded with feminine qualities. The QuRu measure of mature controlling of other children is part of this same rather confused boys' constellation, in a rather surprising way: it correlates much more strongly with two of the observational categories than any two of the four categories correlate with each other.

The sex difference in trait structure is emphasized by some other relationships as well. Nurturance in girls is part of the main feminine real AR constellation, whereas in boys it is part of a pattern that includes the active immature form of dependency (touching and holding), and is unrelated to sex typing. Also, almost every measure of girls' adult role behavior is correlated with the mother's interview rating of resemblance to mother; but none of the boys' behavior is related positively to resemblance to father, and one observational category (adult work) is significantly related in the negative direction.

These examples illustrate not only the sex differences in the structure of the adult role trait, but also the difficulty facing any simple test of our five initial hypotheses concerning the child-rearing origins of adult role. Only the first proposition—dependency—responds easily. We do find, for both sexes, that observed real AR actions occur more frequently in children who also rank high in positive attention seeking. Only in girls (and there but to a minor degree) is this relationship influenced by the rated social interactiveness of the children; the relationship appears to be an inherent aspect of the behavior categories themselves and not a by-product of activity level. This finding is in accord with our first identification hypothesis. Another finding that fits this hypothesis, but one that is limited to the boys, is the strong relationship between nurturance (an AR category) and touching and holding (a dependency category); this relationship, too, is independent of the influence of activity level.

The child-rearing variables that correlate significantly with the dependency measures tend, on the whole, to correlate in the same directions with the real AR measures, including nurturance. The similarities are worth repeating. For both real AR and positive attention seeking in girls, there are correlations with non-caretaking in infancy by the mother, non-permissiveness for aggression toward parents, permissiveness for dependency, and perceived resemblance to the mother. For boys, the real AR variables correlate with non-caretaking in infancy by the father (again the same-sexed parent) and with the father's sex anxiety.

There are some differences in the lists, however, that seem to make sense in terms of the differences in actual observed forms of dependency and adult role behaviors. (The existence of these differences is particularly important because of the otherwise close similarity of positive attention seeking.) In girls, the behavior maturity rating made by the mother shows a positive relation to real AR behavior, and so does the rating of the mother's achievement standards (.42). Neither of these is related to positive attention seeking. The father enters into the AR picture too, in a way that he does not with positive attention seeking; he expects conscience development, rewards sex-appropriate behavior, and is an object of dependency for his daughter. These correlations suggest that he is pressuring her toward maturity; the mother, who uses little praise or tangible reward, evidently is also. Between them, the parents seem to be getting results.

The major variable associated with positive attention seeking that does not appear in the girls' real AR list—severity of mother's current separation from the child—may be responsible for the child's repeated efforts to make social contact in the form of positive attention seeking.

For boys, the difference between the two lists is the little cluster of variables comprising age, conscience, and disowning paternal grandparents' child-rearing policies that appears in the AR list but not in the positive-attention-seeking list. Age and conscience are understandable bedfellows here if the latter is interpreted as a development depending on the former (.39). Moreover, the grandparents' policies scale is correlated significantly with age. However, age is related strongly to only one of the four real AR categories—giving facts or knowledge (.60)—and the (cognitive) capacity for this behavior does undoubtedly increase with age. The correlation between age and total real AR is a product solely of the weighting given to this one category in the total. Why age should not influence the girls in the same way as the boys is not clear.

The reasonably direct tests we made of the high-demand and love-oriented-discipline hypotheses were essentially non-confirmatory. The tests consisted in counting the number of potentially relevant interview scales that are significantly correlated with the child-behavior variables. It is evident that these tests, at least so far as the demands area is concerned, are too simple. The constant recurrence, in the dependency and adult role lists of child-rearing correlates, of low infant caretaking by the same-sexed parents, sex anxiety of boys' fathers, permissiveness for dependency by girls' mothers, and inhibition of aggression by one or both parents, suggests that both the substantive character of the child's behavior to which the parents respond and which parent does the responding, may be important determinants of these forms of child behavior. Sex, dependency, and aggression are powerful action systems, and they are repeatedly aroused by the conditions of family living. In infancy and early childhood they all have primitive and changeworthy forms of expression. Their control inevitably represents an extensive and pervasive aspect of the interaction between the child and his parents. These three systems are important not only in the development of adult role behavior, but also (as will be seen in Chapter 6) in the so-called internalizing of impulse control. Perhaps it is only to be expected that such significant developing systems as adult role, resistance to temptation, emotional reaction to deviation, and that subtle shaping of great areas of behavior called sex typing should rest on the methods by which parents cope with and direct the most powerful and pervasive systems of primitive action, rather than on the methods the parents use to control the less strongly motivated activities, such as table manners and care of house and property.

4. Aggression

The relation of aggression to identification theory is more complex than the relation we have posited for adult role. Whereas adult role was derived hypothetically from the primary identification process alone, aggression is presumed to be influenced by both the primary (anaclitic) and secondary (defensive) processes.

With respect to primary identification, aggression is similar to such other presumed behavioral products as adult role, resistance to temptation, and sex typing in that it has adult forms that must be adopted by the child, and for which the parents provide the main models. Aggression appears first in infantile forms viewed as distinctly changeworthy by most parents. The early angry outbursts, cryings, obstinacies, and disobediences must become shaped and modified into socially acceptable forms of aggression that serve useful purposes in the control of others, or at least into forms that hurt in ways not too severe for the cultural milieu to tolerate. In simplest terms, the child must develop the forms of aggressive behavior used by his parents.

Adult aggression has an almost infinite variety of forms, and its strength and style are determined by several major variables. One general dimension along which it clearly differs from childhood aggression is the prosocial-antisocial. In very young children, the immediate situational instigator often appears to be some form of frustration. The angry reaction is usually a hitting out, either in retaliation or in an attempt to remove the frustrating object, or it may be sheer expression, such as crying or yelling. As the youngster gets older, his aggressive acts become more attenuated and more directed toward hurting the person who is interfering with him or failing to support him. Such behavior may or may not appear to an observer to have an aim of social control. In any case it is usually destructive, or at least unacceptable, to adults; it is considered antisocial. By contrast, adults express a great deal of aggression for purposes the culture defines as desirable. These prosocial aggressions include, very prominently, disciplinary action and verbally expressed disapproval for actions or attitudes that are anti-social, i.e., alien to the common values of the culture. Since prosocial disciplinary action is a form of behavior peculiarly adult, and is more commonly displayed to young children by their parents than any other form of adult aggression, we have judged it a likely candidate for the list of behaviors attributable to primary identification. Hence, if such a process is operative, we would expect to find the frequency of pro-social aggressive acts in the nursery school positively associated with frequency of adult role behavior, appropriate sex typing, and so on. Likewise, the child-rearing correlates should be of the same classes we proposed for adult role in Chapter 3—namely, parental warmth, high demands, love-oriented discipline, and the use of parents as models of good behavior. In addition, the amount and severity of the parents' dis-cipline (i.e., their prosocial aggression) should be related, since that is the behavior for which the parents serve as models.

The expected influence of defensive identification on aggressive be-havior is less clear. Freud (1924) conceived identification as a mecha-nism used by boys to resolve the Oedipal conflict. The boy, loving his father but fearing castration as punishment for his forbidden desires toward the mother and his hostility toward the father, identifies with the father and thus secures the paternal role and power. The boy mas-ters his own aggressive impulses by "becoming" the father, a role in which he need no longer be subject to his own rivalrous hostilities. This defensive identification appears to make use of the already established anaclitic (primary) identification, and occurs in the Oedipal context as a procedure for retaining the nurturant and affectionate support of the father. With respect to process, then, identification with the aggressor appears to be simply a special instance of identification, but its impor-tance lies in the fact that the father-object is male and thus provides the boy with an appropriately sex-typed identificand in place of the mother, with whom the primary identification process was first learned. The significance of this theory is more relevant to the development of conscience and of sex typing than to the nature of aggression, and we will return to the matter in the next chapter.

One implication must be considered here, however; to the extent that defensive identification inhibits aggression toward the father, there should be a generalization of inhibition to other stimulus situations.

Hence, we would expect a low level of antisocial aggression to be associated with indications of an affectionate and happy relation with the father.

The general course of the child's development—with or without a theory of defensive identification—involves the gradual increase of prosocial aggressive acts and the reduction of antisocial acts. One might expect, therefore, that a parallel set of relationships (but with negative rather than positive correlations) would be found between antisocial acts in the nursery school and the same parent variables presumed to be relevant to the development of prosocial aggression. Such a hypothesis brings immediately to mind, however, the appalling complexity of the set of interacting variables responsible for the frequencies of the various types of aggressive acts. The presumption of prosocial aggression as a product of primary identification implies a construct of habit or trait, a developed potential for a particular form of response. The behavioral measures we have obtained are conceived as indices of the strength or prepotency of such a structure.

In fact, of course, the overt behavior is a function of many different instigators, some of which are internal, some external. Their effects depend on the existence of appropriate trait or habit structures, but in the case of aggression we can specify *several* sources of variation in the nature and strength of these structures, rather than simply that arising from the strength of a hypothesized primary identification process. First, there is frequency of evocation and reinforcement of aggression; such experiences as frustration, permissiveness, and punishment during the child's life history are known to establish excitatory and inhibitory variations in his potentiality for response. Second, differential sex typing by the parents, whether conscious or not, creates different overall strengths and styles of aggression in the two sexes, and in the case of boys produces confusion by combining social maturing with the feminizing influence of the mother, as we saw with adult role behavior. Third, the various kinds of models to whom the child is exposed—siblings and peers as well as parents—present various kinds of influences. Fourth, by hypothesis, defensive identification (identification with the aggressor) establishes a special pattern of aggressive response potential.

These four major sources of variation are based on the social learning process; there are also certain sources that must be dealt with in terms of action principles, i.e., sources that create individual differences among children in the strength of instigation at the time of occurrence of the measured behavior. A major influence of this kind is probably the strength of the conflict-produced drive arising from current frustrations and punishments, current inconsistency in discipline and standards imposed by the parents (either intra-parentally or by disagreement between father and mother), and differential standards between home and nursery school. Beyond the positive instigation to aggression provided by these frustrations, there are differences in the level of inhibitory stimulation provided by different environments; the customary warning signals that inhibit aggression can vary in strength with the social atmosphere and the persons present in the child's field of stimulation. The facilitating effect of conflicts has been shown to influence the frequency of aggressive acts differentially among children (Sears, Whiting, Nowlis, and Sears, 1953), as have variations in inhibitory stimulation (Hollenberg and Sperry, 1951); hence, some of the variance in observed behavior derives from these sources as well as from the trait structure.

With respect to the BUO measures, there is another possible source of variability—namely, the systematic differences in immediate social stimulation resulting from the children's selecting their own moment-by-moment environment in the nursery school. Since boys tend to play more with boys (who are more aggressive and hence more frustrating), the obtained sex differences in certain types of aggression are perhaps not fully accounted for by differences in the "natures" (trait structures) of "boys" and "girls." Not all boys select masculine play areas to the same extent, of course, so that even among the children of a single sex, there are uncontrolled sources of variability in the amount of moment-by-moment excitation and inhibition of aggression. In our present data we find a low correlation (.23) between nursery school aggression and masculinity of play areas, however, so we seem to be spared this contaminating factor—at least as a source of constant error, if not of random error.

It is to be expected, of course, that the several kinds of antecedents described above will have differential effects on the various types of aggressive acts we have measured. It has been shown, for example (Sears, 1961), that severity of punishment for aggression toward parents in the preschool years is associated at age twelve with a prosocial increase and an antisocial decrease in aggressive feelings. The present data offer an opportunity to examine some of these other influences on aggression, as well as those more directly related to identification, and also to test the replicability of some of the findings reported in previous research on aggression in young children.

Measures of Aggression

A variety of aggression measures was obtained by six methods. By no means all the aggression variables measured are relevant to identification theory; the main such variable is prosocial aggression. However, the cost of a reasonably complete survey of aggression was so small that we intentionally went well beyond our interest in identification theory to obtain data relevant to several other processes and propositions relating to aggression and its antecedents.

Behavior Unit Observations

There were eight BUO categories of antisocial aggression and three of prosocial. Although the observers recorded and were prepared to score both real and fantasy forms of each of these eleven categories, almost none of the behavior was of a fantasy character. Of the 40 children, 22 showed none at any time, and the maximum frequency of fantasy aggression for any child was 2.8 per cent. This figure contrasts with 18.2 per cent for real antisocial aggression and 6.0 per cent for real prosocial aggression. The fantasy form has therefore been ignored in our analysis.

Of the antisocial categories, only four (direct physical aggression, direct verbal aggression, injury to objects, and mischief) occurred with sufficient frequency and normality of distribution to permit meaningful analysis. Only two of the three prosocial categories (verbal disapproval and tattling) were similarly usable.

To avoid complete loss of the data obtained for the rare categories, however, two summary scores have been used, one combining all eight antisocial categories, the other all three prosocial categories. Each is simply the sum of all observations of its component categories; we have labeled them total antisocial aggression and total prosocial aggression.

In addition to these *a priori* combined scores, one other combination scale was constructed. Preliminary analysis of the intercorrelations among the six usable categories showed that three of them (direct physical, direct verbal, and verbal disapproval) were highly correlated with one another in both boys and girls. These three, which include one prosocial and two antisocial categories, were combined in a summary score labeled direct interpersonal aggression.

There are, then, nine BUO measures of aggression. Six of them are the four antisocial and two prosocial component categories. Two of the summary scores reflect the totals of these two main *a priori* types of aggression, and the third is an empirically derived score cutting across the prosocial-antisocial dimension to establish the different dimension of direct interpersonal aggression. The nine variables are as follows:

Direct physical aggression (189): Hitting, throwing, withholding objects, pulling, taking things away from a child, i.e., the use of force toward another person.

Direct verbal aggression (191): Name calling, jeering, threatening, uttering angry talk, derogating status, commanding vigorously.

Injury to objects (192): Displaced or non-person-directed aggression, such as smashing constructions or spilling paints.

Mischief (193): Mischievous disobedience, such as throwing cups in the wrong place or spilling sand.

Total antisocial aggression (194): Summary score (including unused categories).

Verbal disapproval of behavior (196): "That's bad!"

Tattling (197): Calling attention to another child's misbehavior.

Total prosocial aggression (198): Summary score (including the unused category).

Direct interpersonal aggression (Z): Summary score for variables 189, 191, and 196.

Mother-Child Interaction

There were eight MCI measures of aggression, all based on the full tape recordings of both sessions. They are listed as variables 344 to 351 in Appendix C. Seven of them are measures of amount of aggression of different types directed at various objects, and the eighth is a measure of the relative directness of the child's aggression toward the mother. Four of the scales (disobedience, direct aggression toward mother, indirect aggression toward mother, and outer-directed physical aggression) correlate so highly with one another (range = .33 to .88) that they have been combined into a single summary scale called *real outer-directed aggression (MCI)* (variable Y). A fifth scale (outer-directed verbal aggression) is equally highly correlated with the other four in girls, but is not in boys (consistently low positive) and was therefore left out of the summary scale score.

Four MCI measures (real outer-directed aggression in the MCI, relative directness of aggression toward mother, direct self-aggression, and fantasy aggression) have been retained for the present analysis.

Permissive Doll Play

There are 22 aggression scores available from the two doll-play sessions. Ten of them are percentage scores measuring, separately for the two sessions, the relative frequency of aggressive acts committed by each of the five doll agents. The remaining twelve measures are combinations of these: by sex of agent, by adult or child agent, total use of antisocial aggression, and total use of thematic aggression. Too few prosocial acts occurred to justify prosocial-antisocial differentiation in the analysis; 27 children displayed no prosocial aggression in either session.

Deviation Doll Play

There are three "punishment" categories drawn from completion of the doll-play stories that may properly be considered aggression (verbal and physical punishment, and isolation), but they will be examined in Chapter 6, in connection with guilt reactions to forced deviation.

Parent Interviews

The fathers' and mothers' interviews were scored separately on the scale measuring amount of aggression in the home expressed toward parents (cf. *Patterns of Child Rearing*, p. 507, Scale No. III, 29), and both ratings have been retained for the analysis. A rating that pooled the reports of both parents was also constructed, but since the correlations between the two parents' scores were $-.07$ and $-.05$, for parents of girls and boys, respectively, there seemed no obvious reason for pursuing its analysis.

Observer Rating

Two five-point scales were used by the four observers for their ratings of aggressive behavior. The first was an estimate of the frequency and extent of acts directed against other children and adults; some of the examples given were pinching, hitting, pushing, throwing and grabbing things, ruining others' work, teasing, and threatening. The second scale was designed to reflect the frequency and extent of non-personal acts or acts directed at objects, such as deliberately spilling water or paint or beads, tipping over blocks, sweeping things off a table, or knocking down planks. The scores on the two scales were averaged to secure a single measure of aggressiveness for which the inter-rater reliability, corrected by the Spearman-Brown formula, was .87. For each child, then, this single measure reflects eight separate ratings—the estimates of two forms of aggression by each of four observers.

Limitations on Analysis

Even without the 22 permissive doll-play measures and the three punishment scores from deviation doll play, there are seventeen useful measures of aggression remaining after various eliminations and combinations in the BUO list, the mother-child interactions, and the observer ratings. Not all are relevant to the theoretical formulations to be tested, and the examination of child-rearing correlates for all of them would be unwieldy, laborious, and unrewarding. The measures to be used in this chapter, therefore, are only those that appear to us to have some theoretical importance, either for identification or for aggression itself.

Organization of Aggressive Behavior

Sex Differences

The sex differences in seventeen measures of aggression are shown in Table 17. There is clear replication of the common finding that boys display significantly more antisocial aggression than girls, both in the nursery school (Dawe, 1934; Green, 1933; A. Siegel, 1956) and in permissive doll play (Bach, 1945; P. Sears, 1951; Durett, 1959). In the mother-child interaction, however, the obtained differences are much smaller, the combined scale of real outer-directed aggression reflecting a difference with a p of $<.10$. Fantasy aggression in the MCI was significantly higher for boys, but self-aggression was not. The slim overall sex difference in the mother-child interaction is similar to that found by Bishop (1951) in a comparable situation, and the lack of difference in self-aggression is similar to the result obtained by Sears (1961) in twelve-year-olds, with a questionnaire method. Neither of the parent interview measures shows a significant sex difference, and the same

TABLE 17

Aggression Measures: Means, Standard Deviations, Significance of Sex Differences, and Correlations with Age

*(Values for BUO and doll-play measures are actual per cents; others are ratings.
An asterisk on the p-value indicates girls greater than boys.)*

Aggression Measures	Var. No.	Boys Mean	S.D.	Girls Mean	S.D.	p (2-tail)	r with Age Boys	Girls
Parent Interviews								
Aggression to mother . . .	W	5.24	1.51	4.53	1.14	n.s.	16	−01
Aggression to father	X	5.38	1.25	4.95	1.54	n.s.	05	16
Behavior Unit Observation								
Direct physical	189	2.92	2.01	.88	.96	<.001	15	46
Direct verbal	191	2.01	1.05	.94	.99	<.001	−20	51
Injury to objects	192	1.92	1.12	.61	1.03	<.001	−05	−07
Total antisocial	194	9.58	5.04	3.28	2.41	<.001	−08	44
Verbal disapproval	196	.60	.43	.91	1.05	n.s.°	−04	15
Tattling	197	.20	.23	.15	.20	n.s.	47	03
Total prosocial	198	.91	.58	1.23	1.38	n.s.°	12	00
Direct interpersonal	Z	5.17	2.90	2.73	2.47	<.01	−01	44
Observer Rating	214	5.95	2.55	3.53	2.11	<.01	07	51
Mother-Child Interaction								
Directness	347	5.48	2.59	6.16	2.18	n.s.°	34	02
Self-aggression	350	2.62	1.43	2.00	.92	n.s.	−36	−04
Fantasy aggression	351	4.24	3.35	2.05	1.82	<.02	14	09
Real outer-directed	Y	20.62	7.63	15.58	10.22	<.10	−15	−14
Permissive Doll Play								
Total thematic, I	290	31.52	18.16	12.58	12.37	<.001	17	37
Total thematic, II	291	39.48	17.86	22.47	17.02	<.01	−19	16

mother interview measure gave the same results in the *Patterns* study (Sears, Maccoby, and Levin, 1957).

Of greater interest is the slight reversal of this relationship in the measures of prosocial aggression in the nursery school. In these categories, the girls displayed slightly but non-significantly more aggression than the boys. In the doll play, equal proportions of the girls' and boys' groups showed one or more instances of prosocial aggression. Previous studies have not measured prosocial aggression (as so labeled) in the nursery school, but sex differences have been found favoring the girls with respect to verbal aggression in the nursery school (Jersild and Markey, 1935) and in doll play (Bach, 1945; P. Sears, 1951; Durett, 1959). Moreover, Johnson (1951) found a significantly higher frequency of prosocial aggression in girls' doll play than in boys', in two slightly older groups (five to six and eight to nine years). This finding was replicated at ages four and six by Moore and Ucko (1961).

We conclude that, in the nursery school setting, interpersonal aggression and injury to objects are more typically masculine, whereas verbal and prosocial aggression are more typically feminine (or else do not differentiate the sexes). In the mother-child interaction, however, these sex differences are much less noticeable, and are reflected hardly at all in the parent interview reporting of home behavior, if indeed, they do exist under the stimulus conditions of the home.

Age Differences

Table 17 shows that there are some age differences in aggression within the sixteen-month range of our sample. In girls, interpersonal aggression in the nursery school increased with age, a relationship reflected in the observer ratings as well as in the time sample measures. In boys, tattling increased.

Relations among Aggression Measures

In the description of the aggression measures, it was mentioned that certain of the BUO categories and certain of the MCI scales formed clusters that suggested the usefulness of category summing to provide "combined" scores. The bases for this decision are shown in Appendix K, Tables K1 and K2, which give the intercorrelations among these two sets of measures.

For girls, the range of intercorrelations among the four antisocial aggression categories is −.31 to .66, with a median of .19. The comparable figures for boys are considerably higher, with a range of .23 to .63 and a median of .41. The two prosocial categories, however, correlate higher for the girls (.47) than for the boys (.15). Among the eight correlations between the four antisocial and two prosocial categories, four are significant for the girls but only two are significant for the boys, although the relation between the total scores for these two classes is about the same for both sexes.

What is especially worth noting is that, among girls, injury to objects correlates with none of the other BUO measures; indeed, it correlates with no other measure of aggression we obtained. Its occurrence is very infrequent among girls, much more frequent among boys. Moreover, it correlates —.35 and .23 with the summary sex-typing scores of femininity and masculinity, respectively; thus there would seem to be ample reason for characterizing injury to objects as a peculiarly masculine form of aggression.

A somewhat parallel phenomenon is to be found among the boys' intercorrelations, where tattling correlates with no other measure of aggression, either in the nursery school or elsewhere. It is significantly related to age, however, and somewhat to masculinity (.26), which is also significantly related to age (.44); but if age is held constant by partial correlation, the relation of tattling to masculinity drops to .06. Tattling is related to femininity in girls (.48) but not to age, and is significantly correlated with three of the other five BUO categories. Thus, we suspect that tattling is a reflection of maturing verbal behavior—a normal part of the girls' repertoire of (more verbal) aggressive acts, but an independent aspect of aggression in boys, depending more on verbal development than on overall aggressiveness.

Both injury to objects and tattling seem therefore to deserve separate consideration in our analysis. On the other hand, the three categories that correlate highly with one another in both sexes (direct physical, direct verbal, verbal disapproval) have been combined into a single summary scale Z for later analyses.

Similar contrasts occur among the measures taken in the mother-child interaction (see Appendix K, Table K2). Four of the measures have been combined into the summary score Y, real outer-directed aggression, because all of the girls' intercorrelations, and all but two of the boys', are significant in size. Three of the remaining scales are worth separate consideration because of their importance for the problem of displacement. These include directness of aggression toward mother, self-aggression, and fantasy aggression. With a single exception, none of the three correlates significantly with any of the other MCI aggression measures, nor (except for self-aggression in girls) with anything else among the aggression measures obtained.

The only other setting in which multiple scores on aggression were obtained was the permissive doll play. A detailed report of the relations among the various agent-usage measures would require too long an analysis for our present purposes, and we have reserved that problem for a later report. As overall measures of the extent to which the children expressed aggression in these standardized fantasy situations, we have retained a pair of total thematic aggression variables, one for each session.

The Main Variables and Two Syndromes

The final—and now manageable—group of aggression variables selected for analysis is the list of fourteen shown with their intercorrelations in Table 18. These measures provide estimates of the children's aggressiveness in four settings: the home, the nursery school, the structured mother-child interaction, and the doll play. They also offer variation with respect to the objects of aggression, the modes of expression (verbal or physical), the directness of aggression toward the mother and toward self, and the degree of attenuation of the aggression (i.e., whether outer-directed or fantasy).

Whereas girls appeared to have more coherent and more stable traits of dependency and adult role, Table 18 suggests that boys have a more highly integrated trait of aggression. Among the dozen measures that are independent of one another (i.e., disregarding the antisocial and prosocial summary scores), there are ten intercorrelations for the boys but only six for the girls that reach the .05 significance level. The intercorrelations among the BUO measures (Table K1) and among the MCI measures (Table K2) both showed a slight tendency for higher correlation among the girls' measures. Thus the intercorrelations of Table 18 not only reverse the BUO and MCI tendency, but also exhibit a sharper sex differentiation. One possible inference from these variations is that, for aggression, girls are more subject to the influence of specific situational stimulus conditions, and boys to the influence of trait structure.

But whatever the origins of the boys' intercorrelations, there is clear evidence of a five-variable syndrome of aggressive behaviors. Four of the variables intercorrelate positively and one negatively. The four positive measures are direct interpersonal aggression in the nursery school (Z), real outer-directed aggression in the MCI (Y), injury to objects (192), and the observer rating of nursery school aggression (214). The negative contribution is made by the father's perception of the boy's aggression toward the parents in the home (X). The six intercorrelations for the four positive measures range from .44 to .83 (all significant), with a median of .50. The negative correlations between the

TABLE 18

Intercorrelations among Fourteen Aggression Measures

(Girls above the diagonal, boys below)

Aggression Measures	Var. No.	Variable Number													
		W	X	192	194	197	198	Z	214	347	350	351	Y	290	291
Parent Interviews															
Aggression to mother	W	◦	−07	11	36	02	−04	17	−20	03	05	11	28	17	05
Aggression to father	X	−05	◦	01	27	39	11	24	19	−47	37	23	−14	−18	−33
Behavior Unit Observation															
Injury to objects	192	07	−58	◦	15	−18	−03	−15	−23	−22	13	−10	−12	−23	−37
Total antisocial	194	01	−59	75	◦	44	52	86	64	−03	−22	13	09	25	16
Tattling	197	13	−04	−06	12	◦	62	62	24	14	−18	−20	−01	−20	07
Total prosocial	198	01	−31	31	55	49	◦	76	43	26	−24	−08	−09	17	02
Direct interpersonal	Z	−04	−48	48	85	22	72	◦	72	13	−24	16	06	35	21
Observer Rating	214	11	−35	51	78	32	61	83	◦	−10	−19	10	03	46	36
Mother-Child Interaction															
Directness	347	14	44	−23	−35	12	−26	−23	−03	◦	−18	−17	−09	25	28
Self-aggression	350	09	−21	26	22	−17	−19	−05	−04	−26	◦	35	06	−36	−65
Fantasy aggression	351	−09	14	02	08	−01	−10	20	15	15	02	◦	16	05	06
Real outer-directed	Y	−03	−42	47	58	06	17	44	52	−20	−04	35	◦	15	23
Permissive Doll Play															
Total thematic, I	290	17	−38	47	27	06	02	11	03	17	35	−21	06	◦	53
Total thematic, II	291	31	−12	24	19	−07	12	04	−06	−03	24	14	35	42	◦

father's report and the other four variables range from −.35 to −.58 (three of the four significant), with a median of −.45. The implications of this negative relation for the theory of defensive identification will be discussed later, in connection with the more detailed examination of the other behavioral correlates of this syndrome and its child-rearing antecedents.

The other seven measures of aggression in boys are unrelated to the measures composing the syndrome, and with one exception are independent of each other. The one exception is the positive correlation between the father's report and the directness of the boy's aggression toward the mother in the interaction situation; the more aggressive the boy is at home (at least to the extent perceived by the father), the more directly aggressive he is toward the mother in the MCI. As we shall see later, this directness is positively related to permissiveness and warmth in the parents, but we should not overlook (in Table 18) the non-significant negative relations with the other syndrome measures. It may be hypothesized that the father's perception of aggression in the home is reasonably accurate, and that such aggression, deriving from permissiveness, does not spread to the nursery school situation or even to the mother-child interaction, but *is* accompanied by a tendency to be expressed—when it does occur—in a direct and uninhibited fashion.

In the girls, there is much slighter evidence for a clustering of aggression categories. The nursery school aggression is of an interpersonal character, with tattling replacing the boys' injury to objects as the additional correlated category. For reasons that will be discussed later, we conceive this feminine aggression syndrome to be based on affiliative needs.

One other possible important difference between boys and girls, in the structuring of their aggression, is suggested by the *negative* correlation between father's perception of the girl's aggression toward the parents in the home and the directness of her aggression toward the mother in the MCI. This is just the reverse of the boys' relationship. When we note, further, that the father's report is positively related to the girl's tattling and to her self-aggression in the MCI, we cannot help wondering whether the girl's home aggression may be primarily indirect, and somewhat attenuated in comparison with the boy's home aggression. Unfortunately, we failed to query the parents in this matter.

There is little to be noted about doll-play aggression in this context.

In boys, it is slightly correlated with self-aggression and injury to objects, and negatively to aggression toward father, suggesting that it may represent a form of displaced aggression, but the relationships are too small to be conclusive. In girls, the correlations with other variables are a little higher, and the directions of correlation suggest that doll-play aggression is not a displaced form but, rather, part of the general outward display of aggression.

One final point needs comment. The observers evidently based their aggression rating primarily on the amount of interpersonal aggression the children expressed. Although the rating correlates .51 with injury to objects in boys, the two variables are slightly negatively related in girls, and in neither sex is there more than a small positive relation to tattling.

In summary, then, there is a clear syndrome of aggression in boys; it includes direct interpersonal aggression in the nursery school and toward the mother in the interaction situation, and also aggression toward impersonal objects, but an apparent inhibition of aggression toward the father in the home. There is a similar but less clear syndrome in the girls that includes tattling in place of injury to objects.

Relation to Dependency and Adult Role

We can now widen the scope of our examination of these syndromes and the other forms of aggression by noting some of their correlates among the two classes of behavior described in the previous chapters. The data for the following discussion are presented in Appendix K, Table K5.

In general, for both sexes, the several measures of aggression in the nursery school are closely related to activity level as rated by the observers. The one exception is injury to objects by girls, which, as we have already seen, is not related to other BUO aggression categories. In the boys, outer-directed aggression in the MCI is also related to activity level, as might be expected from its presence in the syndrome.

One other generalization, following from expectations based on primary identification theory, can be made for both sexes. Both real adult role and prosocial aggression were hypothesized as deriving from primary identification, and hence should be positively correlated with one another; they are, to the extent of .47 in boys and .60 in girls. The other forms of nursery school aggression are closely related, in girls, to real adult role, but in boys much less so, in spite of the fact that prosocial and antisocial aggression are equally related within the two sex groups.

The reason for this difference probably lies in the different roles aggression plays in boys and girls. For boys, antisocial aggression is a representation of masculinity but prosocial aggression is not, and neither is related to positive attention seeking. In girls, interpersonal aggression of an antisocial type is part and parcel of the need-affiliation syndrome. It shows no relation to femininity, but is closely related to positive attention seeking and negatively related to the immature forms of dependency. It is found more frequently in older girls than in younger ones. In other words, although the overtly aggressive children of both sexes avoid the immature and passive display of dependency, all forms of the girls' aggression are associated with mature dependency. On the other hand, boys' prosocial aggression is associated with nurturance and adult role, neither of which is related to masculinity. For boys, then, prosocial aggression appears to belong to the maternally defined area of adult role behavior, and antisocial aggression to the competing pressure toward masculinity.

In our discussion of the components of adult role, in the last chapter, we were led to conclude that the boy at this age, forced to mature in a mother-dominated environment, finds himself in conflict in selecting between two forms of "mature" behavior: the *maternal* adult role and the *masculine* role. It was shown, for example, that real adult work (mainly maternal in form) was negatively correlated (−.61) with masculinity. Now in the first column of Table K5, it will be noted, *all* the aggression measures (even the prosocial) show non-significant negative correlations with real adult work.

The positive relationships in girls between dependency, aggression, and activity level replicate those reported by Sears, Whiting, Nowlis, and Sears (1953). For boys, however, there is no such replication; there is, in fact, a complete lack of such relationships, whereas, in the earlier study, the boys showed substantially less intercorrelation among these measures than the girls, but did show some—if non-significantly.

One further matter—mother's estimate of amount of aggression toward the parents in the home—deserves comment. In Table 18 we saw that this measure correlates with no other measure of the children's aggression, not even with the father's report. Our suspicion has been that there are certain forms of aggressive behavior that irritate mothers especially, and that the child who displays them sensitizes his mother, leading her to describe his aggressiveness more extravagantly than she might otherwise be inclined to do. The suspicion may get a little support from these data. The significant positive correlation between the QuRu score and mother's report of aggression—for both sexes—suggests that bossy little rule-enforcers may be the special irritants!

In summary, then, the following propositions appear reasonable:

1. In boys, prosocial aggression belongs with a cluster of behaviors (nurturance, real adult role) arising from the influence of the maternal model, whereas antisocial aggression represents masculine maturing.

2. In girls, aggression that is specifically *typical* of girls is part of a need-affiliation syndrome that includes positive attention seeking, nurturance, and real adult role, but has no relationship to sex typing. This is the cluster of qualities described in Chapter 2 that seem to mature under the aegis of dependency on the mother.

Theoretical Antecedents

There are a number of hypotheses concerning antecedents of aggression that can be tested with the available data. In addition to primary identification, such variables as infant and current home frustrations, parental punishment or permissiveness for aggression, methods of punishment for aggression and various other acts, and defensive identification may influence the style and frequency of aggressive behavior in different places and under different stimulus conditions. We shall test some of the hypotheses involving frustration, punishment, and permissiveness as antecedents; the possible influences of defensive identification will be considered later, in connection with conscience development (Chapter 6).

Infant Frustrations

From a theoretical standpoint, there are four sources of frustration to be considered. First, there is that of early infancy, which ensues either from rigid caretaking or from neglect. Scheduled feeding, tentative or prolonged weaning, coldness and non-responsiveness to crying or dependency supplications, severe and demanding toilet training, and frequent parental absence are among the conditions that seem relevant. The influence of such experiences may be presumed to be imposed through a learning process by which repeated stimulation (of the forms described) elicits and permits reinforcement of aggressive actions, the degree of reinforcement depending of course on the effectiveness of the aggression in eliminating the frustration. There has been little evidence to support this hypothesis, although the immediate effects of coercive toilet training have been shown to include aggressive expression (Huschka, 1942; Sears, Maccoby, and Levin, 1957), and one previous study (Sears *et al.,* 1953) presented minor indications of a positive relation between severe toilet training and later nursery school aggression. In a follow-up study of the *Patterns of Child Rearing* children, when the children were age twelve, there was a slight indication of greater self-aggression in boys who had been severely toilet-trained (Sears, 1961). Early feeding frustrations have shown no relation to later aggressiveness (Sears *et al.,* 1953).

In the present interviews, information about infant experience was sufficient to permit ratings on seven scales that could easily be identified as measures of infant frustration. A table of correlations between these seven scales and the fourteen aggression measures was searched for patterns of relationships. The following tabulation shows the significant correlations:

Severity of early separation from mother (5). Boys: prosocial aggression (.49).

Severity of early separation from father (6). Boys: tattling (.47), fantasy aggression in MCI (.45).

Mother's resentment of this pregnancy (9). Boys: self-aggression in MCI (−.46).

Father's resentment of this pregnancy (10). Girls: direct interpersonal aggression in nursery school (.65), prosocial aggression (.59), injury to objects (−.46), tattling (.47).

Rigidity of scheduled feeding (14). Boys: self-aggression in MCI (−.60), fantasy aggression in MCI (−.47), directness of aggression toward mother in MCI (.47); Girls: direct interpersonal aggression in nursery school (−.51), antisocial aggression (−.48), prosocial aggression (−.51), observer rating (−.47).

Severity of weaning (16). None.

Severity of toilet training (19). Boys: Tattling (−.47).

The actual number of significant correlations here (eight of 98 for each sex) is hardly beyond what can be accounted for by chance and by the non-independence of the aggression scores.

Two of the findings, however, do tempt interpretation. In boys, the effect of scheduled feeding appears to have been to produce a high degree of directness and a low degree of displacement or attenuation of aggression in the mother-child interaction. In girls, the daughter whose father resented this pregnancy was distinctly non-aggressive. Neither of these infantile experience variables has here any unique theoretical implications, so far as we can see, and we are led to examine suspiciously the possibility that the measures may be indices—whether by substance or by chance—of something else in the parents' behavior that could more reasonably be interpreted as causative. Our suspicions are, in fact, borne out; rigidity of scheduled feeding is associated (for the boys' parents) with a father who is warm (.46), permissive of dependency (.53), and empathic toward his son (.51), and with a mother who performed relatively little infant caretaking (−.53), is cold (−.35 with interview measure of warmth), punishes aggression severely (.46), uses ridicule as discipline (.46), and is non-permissive toward aggression (−.47, Mother Attitude Scale). Later analyses will show these variables to be more cogent than scheduled feeding. Likewise, the resentment of this pregnancy by the girl's father probably achieves its correlation by being an index of two other paternal qualities that are related to it: severe punishment for aggression (.62) and low use of praise (−.65). These variables, rather than the correlated resentment, are no doubt those actually relevant to an understanding of girls' interpersonal aggression.

It would be wrong to assume that none of the infant frustrations was important in influencing the later aggression, but the evidence is certainly heavily against any interpretation that infant frustration *per se* is an important antecedent.

Current Separation from Parents

A second cause of frustration is separation from the parents. Children in most homes develop a clear dependency on their parents, especially the mother; presumably, frequent or prolonged absences of the parents should frustrate the dependency supplications and instigate aggression (among other responses). In the absence of correlated suppressive control by the parents, the aggressive behavior should increase both at home and in the nursery school.

Severity of current separation from each parent was rated from the parent interview responses. (Both parents' estimates of the father's separation were pooled for one measure, both parents' estimates of the mother's separation for the other.) The scale for mothers yielded a good distribution, ranging from a high rating of 5 ("Has almost full-time job; definitely a part-time mother with mother-centered attitudes," (five cases) to a low rating of 1 ("No evidence of mother absence; cautious about leaving without child's consent; no trips," (six cases). The father separation scale, however, was poorly distributed; eighteen of the forty fathers were rated at the low end, which is not surprising in a sample with heavy weighting on young academic people.

There is no evidence of any influence on aggression from current separation. Only one of the fourteen aggression measures relates significantly to either scale for girls, and only one for boys. The observer rating of girls' aggression correlates .49 with severity of mother's separation. Since there is a correlation of .30 between mother separation and the age of the girl, and since nursery school aggression in girls correlates significantly with age, this obtained relation between separation and aggression can perhaps be accounted for by age mediation. Among the boys, directness of aggression in the MCI is negatively related ($-.50$) to mother separation. However, there is no evidence that this correlation between parent separation and child aggression was due to a suppressive effect from some correlated punitiveness or non-permissiveness. Neither of the separation scales was correlated with any of the four punishment and permissiveness (for aggression) scales or with the mother's non-permissiveness factor score.

We are inclined to think that the nature of our sample should be looked to in this context—that children become reasonably easily accustomed to the kind of planned and regular occasions of parental absence from home that characterize a stable middle-class household, and that, in fact, the children are not frustrated by these absences. Somewhat indirect evidence from a study of effects of maternal employment on children's behavior by McCord, McCord, and Thurber (1963) suggests that maternal separation in stable homes actually reduces sibling rivalry and produces no indication of peer aggressiveness. In unstable homes, on the other hand, such absence is more frequently perceived as rejection, and at later ages the boys tend to show a higher delinquency rate. Thus, we are disinclined to relinquish the original hypothesis, though we must conclude that the child's *perception* of the mother's absence (as perhaps capricious or rejecting), rather than the mere fact of the absence, is probably the significant determinant of aggressive behavior.

Pressure and Restrictiveness

A third form of frustration can arise from high levels of demand for conformity to parental values and from restrictions placed on the child's behavior in connection with household routines. Ordinarily, a child is pressed toward more mature ways of behaving at a rate consonant with his maturing abilities. Unusual pressure for more rapid development— a quality so characteristic of the upward-mobile middle-class intellectual—can go beyond the child's tolerance for rate of change or growth, and can produce a degree of frustration that serves to instigate rebellious aggressive responses.

This proposition has been tested twice before. In the Iowa study, pressures for cleanliness and orderliness, avoidance of dangerous situations, and good table manners were presumed to be likely indices of current frustration; both teacher ratings and time-sample observations were used as measures of aggression in the nursery school. There was no evidence in the correlations among these measures to support the hypothesis (Sears, Whiting, Nowlis, and Sears, 1953, pp. 211–12). The second test was with the data reported in *Patterns of Child Rearing*, in which a congeries of household restrictions was combined to form a frustration score, and the mother's report of her child's aggression in the home was used as the consequent measure. When the suppressive effect of a correlated quality of non-permissiveness for aggression was eliminated by partial correlation, there remained no effect of the household frustrations (Sears, Maccoby, and Levin, 1957, pp. 263–64).

Much the same results must be reported from the present data, so far as sheer frequency of significant correlations is concerned. There were eight father scales and thirteen mother scales (to be listed below) that were designed to reflect the pressures, restrictions, and demands placed on the children. An examination of the 294 correlations between these 21 interview-derived parent measures and the fourteen of aggression in the children shows that only twelve of the 294 for girls and thirteen for boys are of significant size ($p = .05$ or better). The list of scales examined, with the significant aggression correlations for each, follows:

MCI seen by mother as achievement situation for child (3). Boys:

outer-directed aggression in MCI (.44). Girls: self-aggression in MCI (.55).

Level of parents' demands for table manners, as reported by mother (18). Boys: doll play I (−.44).

Mother's pressure for modesty indoors (25). Girls: fantasy aggression in MCI (.60).

Mother's restrictions on house and property (40). None.

Father's restrictions on house and property (41). None.

Mother's pressure for neatness and orderliness (42). Girls: injury to objects (−.47), antisocial aggression (n.s., −.43).

Father's pressure for neatness and orderliness (43). Boys: tattling (−.48). Girls: injury to objects (−.51).

Mother's strictness about bedtime behavior (44). Girls: self-aggression in MCI (.48).

Mother's pressure for conformity to standards (45). Girls: antisocial aggression (n.s., −.43).

Father's pressure for conformity to standards (46). Boys: outer-directed aggression in MCI (−.50). Girls: observer rating (−.46).

Mother's expectancy of child's taking responsibility (48). Boys: direct interpersonal aggression (.67), injury to objects (.49), antisocial aggression (.62), observer rating (.69), outer-directed aggression in MCI (.49). Girls: injury to objects (−.46).

Father's expectancy of child's taking responsibility (49). Girls: tattling (.46).

Extent mother's standards of obedience are realistic (50). None.

Strictness of mother (76). Girls: outer-directed aggression in MCI (.47), doll play II (−.55).

Strictness of father (77). Boys: doll play I (−.50), doll play II (−.67).

Mother's stress on importance of teaching right and wrong (83). Boys: direct interpersonal aggression (.43).

Father's stress on importance of teaching right and wrong (84). Girls: outer-directed aggression in MCI (.49).

Mother's achievement standards for child (133). None.

Father's achievement standards for child (134). Boys: mother's perception of child's aggression toward parents in the home (.55).

Mother's directiveness toward child (138). None.

Father's directiveness toward child (139). Girls: tattling (.50).

The number of significant correlations is slightly less than the fifteen that would be expected by chance, even if there were complete independence of measures within both the frustration and the aggression subsets. Furthermore—and as one would expect by chance—approximately half of the correlations for each sex are positive and half negative. Certainly there is no evidence for the simple proposition that current restrictions, pressures, and demands increase aggressiveness in any general way.

However, there is a noticeable pattern in the *direction* of the effects— a pattern that contrasts the aggression of the two sexes. If the aggression measures are divided into two groups, one of attenuated or indirect forms (tattling, self-aggression, fantasy aggression, and the aggression of both doll play sessions), and the other of the more direct forms, the sex difference becomes apparent. For the boys, all eight of the positive *r*'s occur among the direct-aggression measures, and four of the five negative *r*'s are among the indirect or attenuated forms. It is as if a higher level of frustration were tending to focus aggression toward outward direct expression and away from inward or indirect expression. Just the opposite is found with the girls; six of the seven negative *r*'s are found among the direct forms, and five of the seven positive *r*'s are among the indirect forms. It is as if the restrictions and pressures were serving as inhibitors of direct aggression and facilitators of indirect expression.

If one recognizes that the restrictions and pressures described by these parental scales not only serve as frustrations but also carry implied threats of punishment for non-compliance, then the interpretation that girls are inhibited, and boys excited, in their outward aggressive expression is seen to be congruent with the finding by Sears, Whiting, Nowlis, and Sears (1953) that punishment is positively correlated with nursery school aggression in boys, but in its more severe degrees tends to inhibit the girls' aggression.

Tension and Instability in the Home

A final cause of frustration that might conceivably have consequences for aggression is the tension sometimes created in the home by disagreement between parents or by a sense of impermanence about the living situation. These sources seemed best described by the following four scales:

Stability of current home situation (pooled response) (8). Girls: injury to objects (−.64).

Extent of parents' disagreement about child rearing (78). Boys: doll play II (−.46).

Mother's caretaking consistency (with this child) (145). Girls: prosocial aggression (−.47).

Parental discrepancy score (147). Girls: fantasy aggression (.48).

This last score, 147, is an average difference between the parents' responses on eleven scales on which both were rated; the scales were important ones concerning sex, aggression, dependency, and various disciplinary techniques.

There is nothing in the pattern of correlations between these four scales and the fourteen aggression measures that provides a clue to a possible relationship.

Summary of Frustration

This extended analysis of the relations between children's aggressions and the various measures of presumed frustration drawn from the interviews has not been supportive of any simple proposition based on either learning theory or action theory. Infancy frustrations, current separations from parents, and current sources of tension in the home show seemingly minor and random relationships to the child behavior measures. Only the scales relating to current pressures, demands, and restrictions provide a meaningful pattern of relations. The pattern does not represent a simple frustration-aggression correlation, but appears to incorporate two possible functions, one for each sex of child. For boys, these variables appear to be evocative of more outer-directed aggression and less inner-directed or attenuated aggression. For the girls, however, the influence seems to be the opposite. This difference has been interpreted as indicating that such restrictions and pressures imply a contingent threat, and that girls, being more responsive to punitive signals, respond with less outer-directed aggression but with more of the alternative forms. This interpretation must be accepted with caution, however, even though the data appear to replicate a previous finding, for the cluster of correlations on which the statement is based represents no more than the number to be expected by chance.

Severity of Punishment

There are three major aspects of punishment—severity, method, and agent—that must be considered here. All three have been studied in previous investigations, and we shall compare our present findings with the previous findings where the present data can serve in some degree as a test of replicability. The agent aspect will be considered in connection with both severity and method.

The very nature of punishment is such as to make it a form of frustration for a child. The action itself is painful, by definition, and in many instances interferes with strongly motivated child activity. The child who is sent to his room, or brought in the house, or deprived of a toy or a trip, or ridiculed is being frustrated directly and obviously. Even physical punishment, which in theory seems to be simply the infliction of pain, often has far more severe frustration quality in the ego derogation or loss of autonomy implied. From a learning standpoint, the *threat* of interference that develops as a product of repeated punishment may be assumed to cause the child to hesitate when he is instigated to perform the punished act. From an action standpoint, therefore, both the past history of punishment and its current frustrating effect should be conducive to a stronger instigation to aggression.

Punishment is a deterrent to angry behavior in some instances, however. To the extent that it elicits avoidance responses that compete successfully with the punished act, it should reduce the frequency of performing the punished act. The earliest forms of aggression tend to be destructive, painful, and irritating to the parents. When the parents retaliate with punishment, the child has various options. His immediate frustration-induced instigation to further aggression increases, but the nature of the punishment may be such that he cannot tolerate the greater frustration it induces. He can learn to apologize, fix up the situation, appeal for sympathy, or flee—or he can shape his aggression into more acceptable forms. It has been shown, for example, that the more severe the punishment for aggression in early childhood, the less antisocial (and more prosocial) the aggressive feelings expressed at age twelve (Sears, 1961).

This phenomenon of a shift away from the punished acts is presumed to rest on two principles—stimulus generalization and response generalization. Stimulus generalization should lead to the performance of similar acts in situations sufficiently different from that in which punishment occurs that the inhibition instigated by the stimuli associated with punishment would not be aroused. This statement assumes the validity of the well-known formulation by Miller (1948) that the gradient of inhibitory generalization is steeper than that of the excitatory.

Response generalization should lead to acts—even in the original punishment setting—that are sufficiently dissimilar in apparent form or content to have escaped the inhibitory influence brought to bear on the original acts.

The additional frustration created by the punishment itself adds one further determinant of behavior, a conflict-produced drive (Whiting and Child, 1953). This source of increased instigation should serve to facilitate whatever aggressive responses do occur as products of stimulus and response generalization, producing the overdetermination in strength so characteristic of the displacement process. It would seem a profitable hypothesis that projection operates in accordance with the same principle, the difference from displacement being that the act involved is perceptual rather than motoric.

In two previous studies, support has been found for the proposition that punishment for aggression increases aggressive behavior. Our present data, generated by quite similar methods in some respects, provide an opportunity to test for replication.

Facilitation in the home. In *Patterns of Child Rearing*, it was reported that a mother-interview rating of children's aggressiveness toward their parents (*Patterns*, III, 29) was correlated .16 with a rating of mother's severity of punishment for aggression. When this value was calculated separately by sex of child for a reduced follow-up sample (Sears, 1961), the r's were .11 for boys and .18 for girls (both significant; there were 76 boys, 84 girls).

Although the inter-rater reliability for the aggression measure used was only .52 (corrected, .67), the scale was added to the code list for the present study simply to provide an opportunity to test the replicability of the significant positive correlation found in the former study. The reliability was but little higher in the present instance (.63; corrected, .77).

For the present study, we used four measures of punishment for aggression, three for the mother and one for the father. The interview scale, which is the same as that used in *Patterns* (III, 31), was applied to the father and mother interviews separately. There were also a Mother Attitude Scale for the same dimension and a rating of the mother's behavior in the mother-child interaction situation.

Table 19 shows the correlations of these four scales with the fourteen aggression measures, including the ratings of the mothers' and fathers'

TABLE 19
Punishment for Aggression Toward Parents:
Correlations with Fourteen Child Aggression Measures

Aggression Measures	Var. No.	Mother Interview (60)	Father Interview (61)	Mother Attitude Scale (168)	MCI (342)
		GIRLS			
Parent Interviews					
Aggression toward mother	W	17	30	07	28
Aggression toward father	X	11	39	−12	−27
Behavior Unit Observation					
Injury to objects	192	−16	−26	−18	−02
Total antisocial	194	02	40	−08	−37
Tattling	197	39	72	−10	−23
Total prosocial	198	32	44	13	−29
Direct interpersonal	Z	23	44	04	−44
Observer Rating	214	−12	07	−12	−52
Mother-Child Interaction					
Directness	347	22	03	06	−32
Self-aggression	350	03	−15	−20	−10
Fantasy aggression	351	32	−12	50	14
Real outer-directed	Y	−15	−18	−38	09
Permissive Doll Play					
Total thematic, I	290	−13	−25	00	−31
Total thematic, II	291	−05	−06	10	03
		BOYS			
Parent Interviews					
Aggression toward mother	W	23	−10	−52	−45
Aggression toward father	X	25	32	01	−15
Behavior Unit Observation					
Injury to objects	192	07	−06	−18	−02
Total antisocial	194	15	−13	−07	−06
Tattling	197	01	16	−24	−27
Total prosocial	198	35	00	21	−25
Direct interpersonal	Z	22	−10	16	02
Observer Rating	214	33	20	−05	−04
Mother-Child Interaction					
Directness	347	−01	33	−09	−10
Self-aggression	350	01	−40	−07	−23
Fantasy aggression	351	−13	−27	−10	34
Real outer-directed	Y	04	−12	−23	28
Permissive Doll Play					
Total thematic, I	290	−14	−17	−22	−26
Total thematic, II	291	23	−44	−16	−17

reports of amount of aggression shown toward the parents (W and X). The coefficients corresponding to the .11 and .18 previously obtained are .23 and .17, and thus provide reasonable replications in size and direction, though not in relative significance, of course. The findings with respect to father's report and father's punishment are similar, although there is one negligible negative correlation, that between father's punishment and mother's report of aggression, for boys. In all, seven of the eight relevant *r*'s for the two sexes and the two parents indicate small positive relationships of the sort expected, but the correlations are too small to be considered important beyond the fact of replication.

Facilitation and inhibition at school. In another study, Sears, Whiting, Nowlis, and Sears (1953) measured aggression in 40 preschool children by a behavior unit observation method in the nursery school and by the same permissive doll-play procedure used in the present study. The children's mothers were interviewed, and a rating of their punitiveness was obtained. For 21 boys, there was a significant (.60) correlation between maternal punitiveness and nursery school aggression. For 19 girls, the correlation was −.41.

No comparable scale of overall punitiveness is available in the present study, but substituting for it the mother-interview rating of punishment for aggression, and using the interpersonal aggression score (Z) as a measure of nursery school aggression, we obtain corresponding coefficients of .22 and .23. These fail to replicate the earlier findings. An examination of the relevant scatter plots suggests the possibility that the two most severely punished girls may have suffered some generalized inhibition, but the findings are too tenuous to warrant further consideration.

Displaced, attenuated, and projected aggression. In the Iowa study, measures were obtained of the frequency of aggression in doll play (projected aggression), and a rating of "displaced aggression" was secured from the nursery school teachers. The latter measure was not used in the present study, but the same doll-play procedure was used as before, and an identical measure of total frequency of doll-play aggressive acts was recorded.

The Iowa girls who showed little aggression in the nursery school nevertheless showed a great deal in doll play. This finding was interpreted as support for the principle of conflict drive. More generally stated, the amount of displaced, projected, and attenuated—or indirect—

aggression should vary positively with the severity of punishment for aggression. We tested the proposition for both boys and girls with the present data.

There are eight variables in the aggression list (192, 197, 198, 347, 350, 351, 290, and 291) that might be expected to be influenced by such a principle. So far as boys are concerned, there is no evidence in Table 19 to support the proposition, however. Indeed, all but one of the eight doll-play correlations are negative, one of them significantly so. The girls' correlations are equally unsupportive, although there is a surprisingly high correlation between tattling (and the tattling-inclusive prosocial aggression summary score) and father's punishment. Whether this represents support for the attenuation concept, or whether it is a product of the high general integration of the nursery school aggression in girls, is impossible to say. (There is also a fairly high correlation with interpersonal aggression in the nursery school, Z.) A careful examination of the scatter plots has revealed nothing that could be interpreted as heightened fantasy aggression on the part of the more severely punished children of either sex. With respect to prosocial aggression, which may reasonably be interpreted as an attenuated form, there is some slight positive evidence for our hypothesis in the five out of six positive correlations with the two parent interview scales and the Mother Attitude Scale. This positive relationship was also found by Sears (1961) in the *Patterns* follow-up study.

We must conclude, however, that the present data on the relation of doll-play aggression to parental punishment do not replicate the Iowa findings.

Method of Punishment

A number of earlier studies have shown a relation between various forms of aggression and the use of physical punishment in children of different ages. Glueck and Glueck (1950), McCord and McCord (1956), and Bandura and Walters (1959) have all reported the greater use of such punishment among delinquent boys, and recently Lefkowitz, Walder, and Eron (1963) have demonstrated a clear positive correlation for eight-year-old children in a large population of normal families. By ingenious comparisons, these investigators showed that non-physical punishment, though correlated with the use of physical methods, was not responsible for the higher aggression of the physically punished children. The findings applied to boys and girls equally well, and showed no apparent differentiation between father and mother as agents of discipline.

In *Patterns of Child Rearing*, physical punishment was found positively associated (.22) with mother's perception of aggression toward the parents in the home. In the follow-up sample, the obtained figures were .22 for boys and .23 for girls. The same physical-punishment scale (*Patterns*, III, 46) was used separately with the father and mother interviews in the present study. The results of our attempted replication of the earlier results are shown in Table 20, which presents the correlations between three methods of punishment and the fourteen aggression measures. Intercorrelations among the punishment measures are given in Appendix K, Table K3.

The relevant comparisons with the *Patterns* data on physical punishment are the correlations (with mother's report) of .06 and .18 for boys and girls, respectively, which are too small to represent replication. There are other relationships between physical punishment and aggression that are of substantial size, however, and well worth noting.

The parent interviews yielded measures of four methods of punishment: isolation, ridicule, physical punishment, and deprivation of privileges. Isolation was used too infrequently by fathers to justify its retention; we have, however, retained mother's use of isolation. Neither parent used deprivation of privileges appreciably, and we have accordingly abandoned both deprivation measures in the analysis.

For the five scales retained, the corrected reliabilities of scoring by the two raters range from .75 to .91, with a median of .79. A glance at the intercorrelations among the three mother scales (Table K3) evokes the impression that whereas the *boys'* mothers used physical punishment in conjunction with both isolation and ridicule, the *girls'* mothers combined physical punishment with ridicule only, somewhat avoiding its use with isolation. We have mentioned that mothers and fathers of girls punish aggression to more similar degrees than mothers and fathers of boys do. It is interesting to note that the same difference is reflected, at the .05 level of significance, in a higher mean parent discrepancy score for boys than for girls. Whether this greater disparity in parental behavior with boys can be generalized to other samples, or whether it is just a sampling variation in our group, we do not know. One might hypothesize that a father is more inclined to follow the other parent's

TABLE 20
Isolation, Ridicule, and Physical Punishment:
Correlations with Fourteen Child Aggression Measures

Aggression Measures	Var. No.	Mother Isolation (66)	Mother Physical Punish-ment (67)	Father Physical Punish-ment (68)	Mother Ridicule (71)	Father Ridicule (72)
GIRLS						
Parent Interviews						
Aggression toward mother	W	09	18	10	06	−37
Aggression toward father	X	12	−16	−30	−06	36
Behavior Unit Observation						
Injury to objects	192	−05	−11	05	08	−06
Total antisocial	194	05	14	03	−04	−10
Tattling	197	03	44	35	09	42
Total prosocial	198	−19	49	34	25	−05
Direct interpersonal	Z	−13	36	12	11	00
Observer Rating	214	−15	05	−21	−09	−07
Mother-Child Interaction						
Directness	347	−01	20	12	38	−07
Self-aggression	350	02	−13	−34	−04	18
Fantasy aggression	351	−31	01	−11	07	16
Real outer-directed	Y	09	−23	−21	−63	−14
Permissive Doll Play						
Total thematic, I	290	−27	−15	−41	04	−43
Total thematic, II	291	−35	00	−03	−05	−13
BOYS						
Parent Interviews						
Aggression toward mother	W	−16	06	04	−17	26
Aggression toward father	X	−39	14	49	40	−01
Behavior Unit Observation						
Injury to objects	192	10	−17	−28	−38	−15
Total antisocial	194	47	−09	−37	−49	04
Tattling	197	−09	−11	−20	−05	57
Total prosocial	198	45	09	−17	−18	31
Direct interpersonal	Z	62	10	−16	−41	20
Observer Rating	214	51	22	08	−34	33
Mother-Child Interaction						
Directness	347	−42	−08	25	24	−04
Self-aggression	350	02	−18	−09	−30	−11
Fantasy aggression	351	−15	00	08	−38	28
Real outer-directed	Y	32	27	−40	−35	25
Permissive Doll Play						
Total thematic, I	290	−06	−23	−42	−14	−40
Total thematic, II	291	−10	−01	−61	−06	−14

lead with girls than a mother is with boys. In any case, the greater mean discrepancy score for the boys' parents evidently reflects no special strain; the disagreement between parents over child-rearing policies is no greater with boys than with girls.

The effects of the three forms of punishment may be traced through consistencies in the correlations in Table 20. For boys, the mother's use of isolation, which is somewhat associated with physical punishment, tends to reduce the expression of aggression in the home. What is especially notable, however, is that isolation in the home increases aggression in the nursery school and in the mother-child interaction. In the latter case, the aggression was indirect (variable 347). The interaction situation, being under the scrutiny of observers, was a difficult place for the mother; there was no good way for her to invoke isolation, nor was physical punishment really available to her. Possibly the boys who would elsewhere have expected a punitive response to their tentative aggressions were encouraged by this environment to be more free. They did, however, keep the aggression indirect, perhaps by response generalization.

In contrast, physical punishment by the father appears to have an excitatory effect in the home (according to the father), which might be expected, and a slight inhibitory effect in the nursery school.

Both in the mother-child interaction and in the doll play, aggression is clearly reduced by the father's punishment. The mother's physical punishment has little effect on boys.

Ridicule also tends to have a facilitating effect in the home—especially for aggression reported by the parent who does *not* do the ridiculing!—but otherwise is an inhibitor of everything but tattling.

The mother's use of isolation and ridicule, then, appears to have some influence on boys' aggression, isolation tending to reduce it at home and to facilitate it outside, and ridicule tending toward the opposite effects. The father's use of physical punishment increases his son's aggression toward him, but tends to decrease aggression in the nursery school and the MCI.

Isolation appears to have no effect on girls' aggression, but the mother's physical punishment tends to increase interpersonal aggression in the nursery school, especially the (more feminine) prosocial form. The effects of ridicule are difficult to assess; mainly they are nil.

Our findings with respect to method of punishment may be quickly summarized. The effects of maternal isolation and ridicule on boys appear to be excitatory and inhibitory, respectively, outside the home, but physical punishment by the mother seems to be little related to any form of aggression. The common finding of an association between physical punishment at home and aggression outside the home is given no support at all in boys, but is demonstrated in girls regardless of which parent does the punishing. There are no clear indications that the agent of punishment is a determining factor in the influence of punishment, although in both sexes the relevant correlations with respect to physical punishment are larger with the like-sexed parent than with the unlike-sexed parent.

Permissiveness for Aggression

The theoretical implications of parental permissiveness for aggression are more simply established than those for punishment. Permissiveness is behavior seen by the child as a signal to proceed with whatever act he is motivated to perform at the moment. It is as much negative in quality as positive, however, in the sense that it is also an absence of signals to refrain from the act. In some instances, it may even represent a positive incitement to action.

We should expect that a child who has been treated permissively will have learned to react to his parents freely when his instigation to aggression is aroused. Moreover, we should expect the parents to have become cue stimuli serving as such instigation. Hence, children whose parents permit aggression should behave more aggressively at home and in the parents' presence than children whose parents are not permissive.

We should also expect the amount of aggression expressed outside the home to be less. Since permissively treated children do not suffer the added frustration of having their aggressive acts interfered with, they have less strength of response available for stimulus generalization. Furthermore, since severity of punishment is negatively related to permissiveness, such children tend to suffer less punishment, and hence have less conflict drive to facilitate outside aggressions.

In *Patterns of Child Rearing*, it was shown that where the mother's permissiveness for aggression was high, her report of aggression in the home was also high. When the influence of three other variables (punishment for aggression, use of physical punishment, and maternal coldness) is held constant by partial correlation, the zero-order r of .23 is raised to .35. In the follow-up sample from that group (Sears, 1961) in which the analysis was broken down by sex of child, the r of .23 became .19 for girls and .27 for boys.

In the present data (Table 21), there is satisfactory replication of this finding for the boys ($r = .40$), but not for the girls.

The same effect from father's permissiveness is clearly revealed in the boys; it relates .51 to his report of the boy's aggression at home. But again the girls do not exhibit the association where the parental measure used is an interview scale.

The other main expectation—that parental permissiveness will be negatively related to aggression in the nursery school—is clearly supported by the correlations between the same-sexed parent's scale and the various measures of nursery school aggression. The influence of the father on the boy (variable 59) is markedly stronger than that of the mother on the girl (variable 58), if one may judge from the sizes of the correlations. The chief difference seems to be that the mother has less influence on her daughter's antisocial and interpersonal forms of aggressive behavior; her effect on tattling and other prosocial behavior is as strong as or stronger than that of the father on the boy.

A possible explanation for this weaker mother-daughter relation lies in the greater influence of the father's punishment of aggression as a determinant of antisocial aggression. In Table 19 there is evidence that for both sexes, but especially for the girls, the *opposite-sexed parent* is more influential than the same-sexed parent. (The relations among the various relevant parent scales are shown in Appendix K, Table K3.) Thus, with respect to girl's antisocial aggression, father's punishment and mother's permissiveness both contribute to the variance (16 per cent and 4 per cent, respectively) in the same direction as that indicated by the correlation between them ($-.57$). If we hold constant the father's influence, however, the partial correlation for the mother's influence on the girl is .04, or essentially zero. The converse relationship, a partial correlation holding the mother's influence constant, is .36, little less than the original .40.

One generalization that may be drawn from our findings on antisocial or interpersonal aggression in the nursery school is that the father's permissiveness (for boys) and punishment (for girls) are the main deter-

TABLE 21
Permissiveness for Aggression:
Correlations with Fourteen Child Aggression Measures

Aggression Measures	Var. No.	Mother Inter- view (58)	Father Inter- view (59)	Mother Attitude Scale (169)	Mother's Demands for Aggres- sion (55)	Father's Demands for Aggres- sion (56)
GIRLS						
Parent Interviews						
Aggression toward mother	W	00	−07	−16	41	−27
Aggression toward father	X	−27	−02	12	04	17
Behavior Unit Observation						
Injury to objects	192	15	37	26	04	20
Total antisocial	194	−20	04	−03	13	−38
Tattling	197	−44	−14	−12	05	10
Total prosocial	198	−51	−18	−21	28	01
Direct interpersonal	Z	−35	05	−09	14	−28
Observer Rating	214	−05	08	21	−16	−34
Mother-Child Interaction						
Directness	347	07	−08	−16	15	−12
Self-aggression	350	12	00	25	33	48
Fantasy aggression	351	−24	00	−28	41	07
Real outer-directed	Y	20	09	33	−13	−07
Permissive Doll Play						
Total thematic, I	290	26	38	21	−07	−54
Total thematic, II	291	16	07	−07	−17	−45
BOYS						
Parent Interviews						
Aggression toward mother	W	40	15	30	54	39
Aggression toward father	X	−27	51	07	−27	19
Behavior Unit Observation						
Injury to objects	192	−08	−41	−09	−03	04
Total antisocial	194	−10	−47	−09	−01	09
Tattling	197	−01	−17	12	−44	30
Total prosocial	198	−20	−51	−28	−17	05
Direct interpersonal	Z	−10	−56	−17	06	04
Observer Rating	214	−09	−46	−04	−05	33
Mother-Child Interaction						
Directness	347	22	20	05	−05	−05
Self-aggression	350	−05	14	06	−13	09
Fantasy aggression	351	01	03	29	−06	22
Real outer-directed	Y	01	−36	12	−09	45
Permissive Doll Play						
Total thematic, I	290	14	−02	07	01	−15
Total thematic, II	291	−04	05	−05	−01	21

minants. The mother's behavior is strongly influential on girls only for the (more feminine) prosocial aggression, where both her permissiveness and her punishment are influential. On the other hand, aggression in the home is excited by both permissiveness and punishment in spite of their mutual negative relation, although punishment is more influential than permissiveness for girls.

In the mother-child interaction, the mother's presence, even in the nursery school setting, provides substantial opportunity for stimulus generalization. There is little evidence to support the expectation that there would be a positive relation of aggression to permissiveness, however. For girls, there is an r of .20 between real outer-directed aggression (MCI) and mother's permissiveness, but for boys the correlation is zero. For both sexes, there is also a small positive correlation with the mother attitude scale of permissiveness. However, since the effects of home punishment (Table 19) are all slightly negative, the suggestion might be made that the MCI, being neither "home" nor "nursery school" completely, became the battleground for various other determinants of aggression, including the amount of aggression displayed there by the mother; this would perhaps account for our being unable to demonstrate the influence of longer-term parental behavior as measured by the interview.

Primary Identification

The form of aggression we conceived to be the most representative of a growing primary identification was the prosocial. As mentioned earlier, this is the aggression form parents most often display to children—the form that characterizes adults as contrasted with children. If our original hypotheses concerning the origin of primary identification are correct, the extent to which children have developed prosocial aggression should be positively related to their dependency and adult role behavior, and to the parents' warmth, high demands for mature behavior, use of love-oriented discipline, use of relatively non-permissive discipline, and verbal reference to the parents themselves as models of good behavior.

With adult role, we faced the problem of a strong, inherent, sex-typing distortion; with prosocial aggression at this age, we do not. Adult role is difficult to use as a measure of maturing in boys, since it is predominantly a feminine (or at least maternalized) form of behavior and therefore conflicts with masculinity. In the case of prosocial aggression, the intercorrelations with other forms of nursery school aggression are about the same for both sexes, and there is no correlation whatever with the summary sex-typing score of masculinity-femininity. By age twelve, however, prosocial aggression becomes feminine (Sears, 1961).

Many of the correlational data for testing the series of primary identification hypotheses have already been given. First to be considered is dependency; Appendix K, Table K5, shows positive relations with the mature and active forms of dependency in both sexes, although the coefficients are significantly larger for the girls. There are also consistently positive relations with adult role measures in both sexes (except for the "feminine" category of real adult work for boys). The role of rated activity level is unimportant; partialled out, it reduces the girls' correlations somewhat but not the boys'. The hypothesis that dependency and adult role are correlates, then, receives unequivocal support.

The second hypothesis relates to warmth. There were six scales, two relating to father and four to mother, that measured some aspect of warmth. None for boys and only one for girls (warmth of father to daughter) is of significant size, and that one is negative. The hypothesis receives no support.

The third hypothesis supposes the influence of high demand for mature behavior. This question was examined in the earlier discussion of pressure and restrictiveness. Prosocial aggression is not correlated significantly with any of the 21 scales examined, although tattling (one of the prosocial categories) in girls is related to two father scales in the right direction. The support for the hypothesis seems less than minimal.

The fourth set of variables to be considered is the group of love-oriented disciplinary techniques comprising isolation, reasoning, and praise. (Withdrawal of love was even less successfully measured in the present study than in the *Patterns* research; we have not been able to use the scale at all.) Reasoning by either parent is entirely unrelated to prosocial aggression in either sex. Isolation by mother is positively related (.45) in boys. Praise by father is negatively related (−.61) in girls. In other words, of the ten possible correlations, two were significant at the .05 level, one favoring and one negating the hypothesis.

The fifth hypothesis, concerning non-permissiveness, was examined in the preceding section. To the extent that aggression itself is the behavior not permitted, non-permissiveness is clearly related in both sexes

to the occurrence of prosocial aggression. There are other permissiveness scales to be examined, of course—especially those relating to sex
(eight scales), independence (two scales), and dependency (two scales).
In addition, there is the mother's non-permissiveness factor scale, which
is a summary of all these scales. None of these thirteen measures is significantly related to prosocial aggression in either sex.

The final scale to be considered is that of the parents' verbal reference to themselves as models for the child. Neither the father's nor the
mother's scale is correlated more than .10 with prosocial aggression in
either sex of child.

The dependency hypothesis, then, still looks promising, but of the remaining hypothesized parent determinants to prosocial aggression *conceived as a product of primary identification,* only non-permissiveness
for aggression relates in expected fashion. The interpretation of that relationship in terms of simple learning and action principles seems more
parsimonious, but the pervasive influence of one parent or the other in
the excitation and inhibition of aggression forms other than the prosocial
provokes a strong suspicion that something having to do with models
of family roles is at least as important as our theoretical dimensions of
frustration, permissiveness, and punishment.

An Inductive Analysis

To pursue the search for whatever mechanisms may account for the
structure of aggression in these young children, we shall turn from hypothesis testing to hypothesis formation, following the procedure used
in previous chapters with dependency and adult role. For aggression,
however, there are substantially more separable forms of expression than
there were for either of the other two classes of behavior. Not all are of
equal importance, of course, and our examination will be limited to the
two syndromes isolated in the analysis of interrelations among forms of
aggression, and to the category of injury to objects, which is useful for
clarifying the process of aggression development in girls.

The two tables that follow (22 and 23) list all the variables (both
child-behavioral and parental) that correlate at a significance level of
.05 or better (i.e., .43 for boys, .46 for girls) with the aggression measures composing the syndromes. The correlates of injury to objects will
be taken up later. The significantly correlated, non-aggressive, child-
behavior variables are included in these two tables in order to provide

a broader behavioral context for the aggression. The child measures are from the parents' reports, the nursery school, and the mother-child interaction. The permissive-doll-play variables have been omitted, since there are few of them that correlate significantly with the overt aggressive behavior measures; moreover, the relation of fantasy to reality in the domain of aggression encompasses more territory than we can cope with in the present context.

The Boys' Syndrome

The clustered aggression measures forming the boys' syndrome are those listed across the five columns of Table 22. They are entirely independent of one another, so far as their manner and time of measurement are concerned, though the observers who made the BUO measurements (Z and 192) also made the observer rating (214) later; Z and 192 correlate .83 and .51, respectively, with 214, as shown in Table 18. We should bear in mind also that the father's report of aggression in the home is *negatively* related to all four other measures.

There are two ends to this cluster, of course. The labels of its component measures emphasize aggressive behavior, but a low score on the syndrome is equally meaningful. Boys seen by their fathers to be non-aggressive at home are shown by our observations to be nevertheless quite aggressive outside the home, not only toward their peers (in the BUO) but even toward their mothers (in the MCI). On the other hand, boys who tend to be aggressive in the home, according to the father, are relatively non-aggressive outside. In order to draw the correlational findings together into a more lifelike description than that provided by a tabular listing, we shall treat the high-scoring and low-scoring boys as representatives of two *types* of boy, recognizing as we describe "him" (whether the aggressive or the non-aggressive extreme) that "he" is simply an abstraction from the correlations, not to be found in nature exactly as described. The same principle applies to generalizations made about his child-rearing experiences and the personality qualities of his parents. For the descriptions, we shall draw mainly on the information presented in Table 22, but shall cite also a few correlated variables not included there because their *r*'s do not quite reach the .05 level of significance, but which should not be ignored. We shall describe the "aggressive boy" first, and his non-aggressive counterpart second.

The aggressive boy. The boy who scores high on the aggression syndrome has a high activity level that manifests itself in both physical movement and social interaction. He is gregarious, outgoing, and outer-directed in his play at the nursery school. His interactions are not of the passive-dependent type, by any means, and he shows little or no narcis-sistic oral or masturbatory activity ($r = -.41$ with Z). On the contrary, he displays maturity of manner and a seriousness about accepting re-sponsibility; whatever active dependency he does show is of the nega-tive rather than positive attention seeking kind. He is a vigorous, run-about, rough—but nurturant—youngster viewed as distinctly masculine by the observers. (The other measures of sex typing all support this last statement, but non-significantly; we suspect some stereotyping in the observers' conception of masculinity, but the correlations with the other measures offer justification for their ratings.)

This boy is no paragon of masculine virtue, however, He displaces his aggression by injuring objects, he expresses negative attention seeking along with his adult role maturity, and he cannot (or at least did not) resist temptation, a failure most clearly displayed in the achievement-oriented game of ring toss ($r = -.40$ with Y).

At home, according to his father, the boy is quite unaggressive toward the parents. He freely expresses affection toward his mother but *not* toward his father (all five relevant coefficients are negative but non-significant). He also shows little dependency toward his father, and the father perceives no resemblance to himself ($r = -.40$ with X) in spite of an apparent father-son similarity in aggressiveness. This is probably an accurate judgment on the father's part, because the aggressive boy's father is overtly quite aggressive at home and has low aggression anxi-ety, whereas his son is aggressive only away from home. In the mother-child interaction, the boy's mother judged his behavior *not* to corre-spond with his behavior at home, another probably correct estimate, since the boy did show high aggression in the MCI. (The mother was not asked to judge solely on aggression, of course, but to consider in her judgment everything the child did during the first session of the MCI.)

In spite of the evidence for current *non-aggressiveness* at home, the parents describe the boy's earlier conduct as poor with respect to four types of misbehavior at home: fibbing, taking others' things, playing with fire, and teasing animals. And at age four, when he does something wrong, they perceive him as tending to hide it rather than confess to it.

An interesting relation to the mother was displayed in the MCI. When

TABLE 22

Boys' Aggression Syndrome: Correlations of the Five Variables with Other
Child Behavior Measures, and with Parent Interview and
Mother-Child Interaction Measures, at Level $p < .05$

(Where a sign alone is shown, the r is greater than .25 but less than .43.)

Child Behavior Measures and Parent Measures	Var. No.	Father Rating (X)	MCI (Y)	BUO (Z)	Inj. to Objects (192)	Obs. Rating (214)
Child Behavior: Parent Interviews						
Good conduct on four problems: pooled .	52	+	−57		−	
Source of power (mother high): pooled .	81	−51			+	
Source of nurturance (mother high): pooled	82	−		53	+	44
Confession of wrongdoing: mother . . .	87		−44			
Expression of affection toward mother . .	116	−			50	
Dependency on father	123				−47	
Behavior Maturity Scale: mother	170			+	47	43
Child Behavior: BUO, Assessments, Observer Rating						
Negative attention seeking (BUO) . . .	187				58	
Being near (BUO)	221	+		−47	−	−58
Orality (BUO)	223	+			−46	−48
Physical contact seeking (observer rating)	215	50	−	−49	−60	−57
Activity level (observer rating)	217	−	+	65	56	85
Social interaction level (observer rating) .	218	−	44	66	49	76
Total adult mannerisms (BUO)	178	−48	+	+	+	44
Nurturance (BUO)	182			53		+
Total fantasy adult role (BUO)	185	−43		50	+	50
Resistance to temptation, total	211	+	−46		−	
Acceptance of responsibility (hamster) . .	226	−		+	46	+
Tension following deviation (red light) .	231			51	+	+
Masculinity (observer rating)	203	−		50	47	56
Child Behavior: MCI						
Bids for attention: mother busy	336		60			
Bids for attention: mother attentive . . .	337			−49		−
Interest in adult role	360	47				
Tension	366	−	50	+	+	+
Mother Behavior: Interview						
Permissiveness for social sex play	32	−44	+		53	+
Expects child to take responsibility . . .	48	−	49	67	49	69
Use of isolation (for punishment)	66	−	+	62		51
Use of deprivation of privileges	69				43	
Sex stereotyping of parents' roles	79		−44	−57	−	−59

TABLE 22 (continued)

Boys' Aggression Syndrome

Child Behavior Measures and Parent Measures	Var. No.	Father Rating (X)	MCI (Y)	BUO (Z)	Inj. to Objects (192)	Obs. Rating (214)
Importance of teaching right and wrong .	83			43		
Rewarding of confession	93	−58		+	+	
High psychological vs. tangible reward . .	98					46
Empathy for child	131	−			43	
Warmth: mother's parents	157		−46	−	−	
Mean age of expected independence (Winterbottom Scale)	171			−48	−51	48
Father Behavior: Interview						
Pressure for conformity to standards . . .	46		−50			
Overt aggression in home by father . . .	54			54		45
Demands for aggression to peers	56		45			+
Permissiveness for aggression toward parents	59	51	−	−56	−	−46
Use of physical punishment	68	49	−			
Relative strictness of parents (mother high)	75			−49	−	−67
Mother Behavior: MCI						
Sees MCI as achievement situation . . .	3	−	44			
Punishment for independence	325	−	44			
Directiveness	326	−		−48		
Warmth	330	−50	+	+	+	+
Involvement in telephone game	332	−51				
Involvement with puzzles	333		45			
Pressure for obedience	341	−	47		47	
Pressure for achievement	353		+	+		45
Punishment for low achievement	355	−	51	+		+

the mother was busy, bids for attention accompanied the boy's aggression. When she was attentive, they did not necessarily ($r = .10$). The lower correlation with frequency of bids for attention under the attentive condition suggests that the boy is dependent on his mother mainly under conditions of frustration—the dependency does *not* generalize to a non-frustrating situation.

So much for the aggressive boy's behavior. Now what about the child-rearing experiences that helped to produce it? There are several qualities that can be traced through the parent interviews and the MCI. First, with respect to the mother-son relationship, there is evidence that the mother takes an active interest in and responsibility for the boy's development, and has high standards for him. She expects him to take responsibility, she believes it important to teach him the meaning of right and wrong, and on the Winterbottom Scale she indicated her belief that he should acquire independence at an early age. She was judged by the observers as viewing the MCI as an achievement situation for the boy. She actively involved herself in both the puzzles and the telephone game, pressed the boy for obedience and high achievement, and punished him when he failed and when he was too independent to suit her. In other words, she is responsive and interested, and presses for effective socialization, just as her interview scales suggest she does at home.

With all these pressures, however, she is in most respects neither directive nor punitive. Indeed, she tends to be permissive about sex play, uses isolation and deprivation of privileges rather than ridicule ($r = -.41$ with Z) as a means of punishment, and in general uses psychological forms of reward for good behavior rather than more tangible ones. She is less strict than her husband, but is more frequently the agent of discipline ($r = -.41$ with X). She feels empathy for the boy, and both she and her husband agree that she is probably seen as the source of nurturance (as well as power) in the family. Although the interviews did not show her to be especially warm, she was judged so in the MCI. In view of her strong pressure for socialization, her interest in the boy, and the relatively gentle manner of her treating him, it is not surprising that she succeeded (according to her own lights, at least); she judged him, on the Behavior Maturity Scale, to be quite mature.

The father is not very strict, either, and does not press for conformity to standards in general, but his attitudes toward aggression are sharply defined. He is quite non-permissive of aggression toward the parents but demands aggression toward other children. He himself is overtly aggressive in his relations with the boy, and has low aggression anxiety, but this aggressiveness is definitely *not* displayed through the use of physical punishment. Moreover, he has a tendency to use himself as a model for good behavior, and his wife evaluates him highly.

The non-aggressive boy. The boy who represents the other end of the distribution on the aggression syndrome measures is the youngster who is aggressive toward his parents (according to the father), but non-aggressive in the nursery school.

The mother of this boy is restrictive in the inhibitory sense, if one may judge from her non-permissiveness with respect to sex play. But the father seems to play a more active and more dominating role than the mother, and the effects of physical punishment, coupled with high permissiveness for aggression, suggest that the boy suffers substantial frustration at the hands of his father but expresses the consequent aggression directly.

One might be tempted to interpret the low nursery school aggression as indicating low facilitation from the safely expressed aggression toward parents, were it not for the correlates of such inaction. The boy scores high on orality, masturbation ($r = -.41$ with Z), being near, and seeking of physical contact. He is non-gregarious and physically inactive. Unlike the aggressive boy, he is believed to perceive his father as the source of power and nurturance in the home, and his father tends to be his disciplinarian. He is somewhat dependent on his father and more affectionate toward him than toward his mother. In fact, the behavior of this boy would seem to be an excellent example of the outcome of defensive identification.

Interpretation. If we assume that the type of aggression represented by the high extreme of the aggression syndrome is essentially masculine, and that masculinity is a product of the boy's identification with the father, then the primary identification theory derives considerably more support from the above description of child-rearing correlates than it did when the same correlates were examined as antecedent to prosocial aggression. The aggressive boy's father is an aggressive model who is admired by the much-loved mother ($r = .39$ with 214), and who instructs the boy to behave aggressively toward his peers. There is evidence of non-permissiveness, of (non-punitive) pressures for maturity and responsibility, and some indication of maternal warmth. These are the hypothesized variables of primary identification.

When stated in this way, however, the theory-data consistency hides three important points. First, what dependency the boy shows is toward the mother and definitely not toward the father. Second, the mother, not the father, is believed to be seen as the source of both nurturance and power, and is the chief disciplinarian. Third, the pressures for achievement and maturity also come from her, not from the father. Only the non-permissiveness for home aggression comes from him. Unless one assumes that non-permissiveness for aggression is the main determinant of identification—which no one has done, to our knowledge—the child-rearing conditions described here are mainly appropriate for primary identification with the mother. *The father's main contribution appears to be as the model whom the boy emulates, not as the initial producer of the identification process.*

The significance of this point lies in its implications for both primary and defensive identification. According to various recent formulations of the former (e.g., Bronfenbrenner, 1960; Mowrer, 1950; Mussen and Rutherford, 1963; Sears, 1957; Sears, Maccoby, and Levin, 1957), the initial identification of the child is ordinarily with his mother. It is she who establishes the conditions that create the habit of *role practice*. Once this process has been established, the quality or nature of the future identification-induced behavior is determined by the nature of the behavior displayed by whatever models the child has available. In the present instance, there appears to be evidence for the effective development of identification by the mother and an effective utilization of the father as the model.

The completion of the process of defensive identification should be accompanied by a shift of the boy's affectionateness and dependency from the mother to the father, by his reevaluation of the parents' roles so that the father is now seen as the source of nurturance and power, and by his adoption of the father's style of (prosocial) aggression. The non-aggressive boy seems a better candidate for defensive identification than the aggressive boy. He tends to be dependent on the father and does not express affection toward the mother, and he tends to show higher resistance to temptation than the aggressive boy. Also, he is reported to see his father as source of nurturance and power.[*]

[*] Mussen and Rutherford (1963) have shown that the more masculine first-grade boys, as defined by Brown's (1956) *It Scale*, report their fathers as sources of nurturance and power to a greater extent than the less masculine boys do. Their "source" reports were obtained from the reactions of the boys themselves to nine structured doll-play episodes.

If our aggressiveness syndrome is a measure of masculinity, a parallel finding from our study should be that the aggressive boy sees father, not mother, as source of nurturance and power. There are certain differences between Mussen's work and ours, however, that render the differing results less antagonistic than they seem on the face. His boys (aged five years, six months, to six years, six months) were a little more than a year older than ours, and therefore presumably emerging from the Oedipal conflict with completion of defensive identification, whereas ours were very likely in the midst of the conflict and in process of settling definitely on males as models. Further, Mussen's measure of perceived sources was a direct one, obtained from the boys themselves. Ours was inferential, obtained from the parents; regardless of how accurate ours might have been, it could scarcely have been sensitive to rapid perceptual changes in the boys.

In the measurement of sex typing, we used the *It Scale*, also, but its correlations

On the other hand, he does not show high prosocial aggression, nor is he masculine. Quite the contrary.

Whereas his father is non-aggressive, and does not demand that the boy be aggressive toward peers, he permits aggression toward himself, and provides physical punishment as a model of prosocial aggression. There is no evidence that he is held up as a good model either by himself or by the mother, however.

Our conclusion is that although a high score on the forms of aggression making up the boys' syndrome is associated with the father's aggressive modeling behavior, the processes responsible are not defensive identification but, rather, three others:

1. Imitation of the father as an aggressive male model.
2. Drive facilitation by non-permissiveness for expression of aggression in the home.
3. Response facilitation by paternal "demand" for expression of aggression toward peers.

The low aggression of the boys at the other extreme of the syndrome can be accounted for by:

1. Imitation of the father as a non-aggressive male.
2. Permissiveness for aggression at home, and hence a lack of drive facilitation for such behavior outside the home.
3. Lack of "demand" for aggression toward peers.

We incline to the view that the non-aggressiveness outside the home, the nursery school passivity, and the narcissism and immaturity are collateral effects of physical punishment by the father and a general lack of pressure toward socialization by the mother. In Chapter 6, however, we shall examine further the aggressive components of defensive identification, in connection with guilt and other aspects of conscience.

The Girls' Interpersonal Aggression Syndrome

The girls' expression of aggression is less integrated into a cluster than the boys', but the group of nursery school interpersonal aggression categories (direct physical, direct verbal, verbal disapproval) and the unin-

---

with the five indices of the aggression syndrome ranged from −.06 to .30, with a median of .03. Obviously it was not measuring the same kind of masculinity as either the syndrome or the observer rating. We have been unable to replicate the Mussen and Rutherford findings with the *It Scale*, using our parent interview measures of child's perceived source of power and nurturance; these two scales correlate .10 and −.12, respectively, with the boys' *It Scale* scores.

TABLE 23

Girls' Aggression Syndrome: Correlations of the Two Variables with Other
Child Behavior Measures, and with Parent Interview and
Mother-Child Interaction Measures, at Level $p < .05$

(Where a sign alone is shown, the r is greater than .25 but less than .46.)

Child Behavior Measures and Parent Measures	Var. No.	BUO (Z)	Observer Rating (214)
Child Behavior: Parent Interviews			
Age of child	1	+	51
Reported sexuality in child: mother .	33	54	+
Child Behavior: BUO, Assessments, Observer Rating			
Positive attention seeking (BUO) .	219	61	57
Attention getting (observer rating) .	216	59	71
Activity level (observer rating) . .	217	72	86
Social interaction (observer rating) .	218	69	74
Giving facts and demonstrating knowledge (BUO)	175	52	+
Total adult mannerisms (BUO) . .	178	58	48
Nurturance (BUO)	182	55	+
Total real adult role (BUO)	184	61	+
Total fantasy adult role (BUO) . .	185	+	49
Resistance to temptation (QuRu) .	208	−	−47
Resistance to temptation, total score	211	−	−52
Evidence of internal conflict (hamster situation)	227	−51	−52
Child Behavior: MCI			
Tension	366	−47	−
Mother Behavior: Interview			
Proportion of caretaking in infancy .	11	−65	−59
Rigidity of scheduled feeding . . .	14	−51	−47
Permissiveness for indoor nudity . .	23	+	62
Agent of discipline (mother high) .	73		47
Relative strictness of parents (mother high)	75		49
Reward for adult role behavior . .	108	+	50
Warmth toward child	118	+	50
Affectional demonstrativeness toward child	120	+	70
Reward for dependency	126	+	51
Empathy for child	131	+	46
Severity of current separation from mother	142	+	49
Positive evaluation of mother role .	143	−	−47
Warmth: mother's parents	157	60	+
Pressure for independence (Winterbottom Scale)	172	−61	−46

TABLE 23 (continued)
Girls' Aggression Syndrome

Child Behavior Measures and Parent Measures	Var. No.	BUO (Z)	Observer Rating (214)
Father Behavior: Interview			
Resentment of this pregnancy . . .	10	65	+
Pressure for conformity to standards	46		−46
Aggression anxiety	63	+	48
Satisfaction with child's socialization	107		63
Expectancy of sex differences in behavior	113	49	60
Reward for sex-appropriate behavior	115	65	67
Mother Behavior: MCI			
Punishment for independence . . .	325	−50	−
Punishment for aggression	342	−	−52
Pressure and reward for adult role behavior	359	50	

cluded tattling category correlate quite highly with one another. In this grouping, tattling appears to take the place held by injury to objects in boys. Two of the girls' categories are antisocial and two are prosocial aggression; the impression evoked is that of a highly person-oriented kind of aggression. The observer rating reflects the same behavior to a considerable extent.

Table 23 lists the correlates of the girls' interpersonal aggression summary score (Z) and the observer rating (214). Tattling has been omitted from consideration here because its child-rearing correlates differ so markedly from those of the other interpersonal aggression variables; only one of its ten correlates of .46 and above is the same as any of those for the Z and 214 measures. Moreover, although tattling is an unusually interesting form of aggression because of its resemblance to certain adult behaviors falling more or less under a label of "moral righteousness," it occurred quite rarely in these young children and we doubt that our data are adequate for a sound analysis of either its behavioral correlates or its antecedents.

The girl who is high on interpersonal aggression is very active, and displays mature dependency behavior. This is reflected not only in positive attention seeking but in the several forms of adult role behavior as well, including nurturance, adult mannerisms, and giving facts. Parallel with the social orientation and high activity implied in these categories is a low exhibition of the more passive and immature, perhaps narcissistic, forms of behavior: being near ($r = -.44$ with Z), touching and holding ($-.43$ with Z), and masturbation ($-.41$ with Z). The main distinction between the girls' interpersonal aggression cluster and the boys' aggression syndrome lies in the clear association of positive attention seeking with the girls' structure, a quality notably absent in the boys'.

The maturity of the girl who exhibits high interpersonal aggression is indicated by the positive correlations with age, the several measures of adult role, and at least one sex-typing measure; there are also low positive relations with the Behavior Maturity Scale (.27 and .17). Furthermore, the girl is judged by the parents to resemble the mother ($r = .42$ with Z), and the father reports that deviant behavior is usually followed by confession (.42 with 214). Nonetheless, despite her maturity, the girl is low in resistance to temptation in the assessment situations, as is the high-aggression boy.

Among the parents' reports about the behavior of the girl in the home, we find the mother reporting much social nudity ($r = .42$ with 214) and a high degree of sexuality, qualities not surprising in a little girl whose mother is rated as quite permissive of indoor nudity and shows little modesty herself ($-.45$ with 214). The father unaccountably reports *little* nudity ($-.43$ with 214).

This combination of overt interpersonal aggressiveness with various forms of activity and mature dependency—especially nurturance—is strongly reminiscent of Murphy's finding (1937) of significant positive correlation between aggression and sympathy. Kagan and Moss (1962, Appendix 32B) have provided tabular representation of negative relations between peer-directed aggression and passive dependency, and positive relations between the former and activity. We have already remarked on the similarity between the boys' and girls' clusters in the present data.

When we examine the child-rearing experiences of the high-aggression girl, however, we find certain sharp differences from those of the high-aggression boy. In general, the girl's mother shows high permissiveness (or reward) and low punitiveness with respect to all the major socialization areas except aggression. The rigidity of scheduled feeding was low during the child's infancy, and current treatment of sex (especially modesty), dependency, independence, and adult role are all quite permissive. The mothers' handling of aggression does not conform to this principle, if one judges only from the interviews, though in the MCI these mothers were non-punitive of their daughters' aggressions. In addition to this general permissiveness, the mother imposes low demands and restrictions, as evidenced by low expectation for the girl to take responsibility ($r = -.40$ with 214), low restrictions with respect to house and property ($-.39$ with 214), and contentment with a late age for developing independence (Winterbottom Scale).

She is a warm mother, and she is demonstrative. But she is not comfortable in her home life, as reflected by her low evaluation of the mother role, and her low evaluation of her husband ($r = -.40$ with Z). This disenchantment is perhaps responsible for her having done proportionately little caretaking of her daughter in infancy, and for the inconsistency in her current caretaking practices and attitudes ($-.43$ with each). She is out a great deal, and her current separation from the child is high.

The father is also permissive with respect to dependency ($r = .45$ with 214) and independence ($.40$ with 214), and exerts low pressure for conformity. With respect to aggression, however, the father is somewhat punitive ($.44$ with Z), possibly because he himself seems to suffer some aggression anxiety. This attitude corresponds well with his belief that sex differences may be expected in the behavior of children, and with his tendency to reward sex-appropriate behavior. The father is less strict than his wife, and the mother is generally the agent of discipline. All in all, the father is quite satisfied with his daughter's socialization.

Interpretation. The combination of warmth, affectionateness, and broad permissiveness of the mother is tailor-made to produce an active and maturely dependent girl, as will be recalled from the analyses in the preceding chapters on dependency and adult role. The correlated maternal behavior, however, has a flavor quite different from that of the list for positive attention seeking. Although there is the same permissiveness, especially with respect to sex, there is no indication of maternal concern with child-rearing *toward a goal*. The mother's philosophy seems really to be more laissez-faire than simple permissiveness, a point of view that might well stem from discomfort with her own lot. Not only is there no pressure for socialization and achievement, but there is also both current and past history of ignoring the girl or being separated from her.

If the warmth and permissiveness are effective in producing dependency, then the separation not only supplements the strengthening of the dependency instigation (by frustration and conflict drive) but also adds instigation to aggression. The fact that the mother is the chief agent of discipline and is also the stricter of the two parents may have led to an ambiguous situation in the girl's relation to the father. Actually, there is a non-significant tendency for the father to be seen as the source of nurturance.

In this context, the father's tendency to punish aggression presents the girl with some additional frustration. This frustration, coupled with the child's image of her mother as an aggressive model, may have been sufficient to increase the instigation to peer-directed need-affiliation.

The girls' cluster of interpersonal aggression offers questionable support for the primary identification theory. The dependency pattern, established and vigorously maintained by the mother, is certainly represented appropriately. The ordinary interpretation of high demands (as a condition for creating contingency of love) would lead one to look for pressures, restrictions, achievement orientations, and non-permissiveness for aggression. These are not to be found; on the contrary, we find evidence of caretaking inconsistency and a tendency toward a possibly neglectful withdrawal from the girl; at best, there is no pressure for achievement and social growth. So far as modeling is concerned, however, the mother tends to be on the overtly aggressive end of the distribution herself ($r = .39$ with 214), and the daughter's aggressiveness could be interpreted as imitation.

If this interpretation is correct, then the father would seem to be responsible ultimately for establishing a firmer sex typing than has so far been achieved at this age. His expectation of sex differences and rewarding of sex-appropriate behavior could be important influences. He may have already been responsible for whatever femininity has been achieved. On the other hand, male aggressiveness represents a risk to the girl's femininity.

Injury to Objects

The directing of aggression toward inanimate objects rather than toward people has all the earmarks of displacement. There are two main kinds of such behavior—one, the overdetermined reaction to an actually frustrating object (the paint that spills, or the sand castle that crumbles), and the other, the damaging or attacking of objects that belong to someone else (kicking over someone's block tower, or running off with some needed toys in the dress-up corner). Both represent physical rather than verbal expression, and both are fundamentally antisocial in nature. Injury to objects achieves its aggressive effectiveness by attacking a deeply valued concern of our society—the acquisition and protection of *things*.

In boys, injury to objects is highly correlated with other outer-directed forms of aggression, and is clearly part of the syndrome discussed earlier. For the data in Table 22, this variable was included with the other categories forming the cluster; the data need not be repeated here. The boy who injures objects as a means of aggressing is active, mature, and masculine. There is pressure in the home for him to become more responsible and independent. His dependency on his demanding father is low, and he shows affection to his empathic and sexually permissive mother.

Injury to objects is essentially masculine. In the nursery school, it occurred much more frequently among the boys than among the girls (Table 17; $p < .001$), as did all other forms of antisocial aggression, and represents 18.2 per cent of all aggressive acts by the boys; in contrast, it constitutes only 8.3 per cent of the girls' aggression. Furthermore, injury to objects by boys correlates .23 with the boys' summary score of masculinity; and by girls, −.35 with femininity. Although neither figure is significant, the difference in directions confirms the interpretation of injury to objects as primarily a masculine form of behavior.

What are the child-rearing experiences for girls, then, that are associated with the development of this inappropriately sex-typed behavior? Descriptively, the little girl who directs aggression at objects is apparently at loggerheads with herself in the maturing process; she is immature in some ways and mature in others. She appears to have been an incipient tomboy but she lacks the activity (−.24) and social interactiveness (−.29) of the boys who display this behavior. Her immaturity is represented by the frequent use of the passive form of dependency ($r = .43$ with being near), and a low use of adult mannerisms (−.39). Also, she shows little reaction to her discovery that she has failed her "responsibility" in the hamster situation (−.62). On the other hand, although there are small negative correlations with all the other forms of adult role behavior, nurturance is positively correlated with injury to objects, a relationship that suggests an element of maturity. To summarize, the girls who rank high on this particular form of masculine aggression appear to be having difficulty in maturing, especially with respect to appropriate sex typing.

Among the child-rearing variables significantly associated with injury to objects, there is no evidence of an undue amount of either frustration or punishment. There is no indication that the supposed displacement from people to objects is the product of fear induced by punishment at home—either for aggression or for any other changeworthy behavior—nor is there any suggestion of the spilling over, into the peer group, of aggressiveness that has been suppressed at home. Indeed, this type of aggression in girls appears to be quite unrelated to the theoretical variables we have examined.

Once again, however, the issue of models enters the picture. The father is the relevant parent in most of the variables significantly correlated with injury to objects (Table 24). The father-daughter relationship is a positive one, involving much interaction between them. The father is believed to be seen as the source of nurturance by the daughter, and her dependency on him is relatively high (.40). He, in turn, places little pressure on her for maturity in taking responsibility (−.44) or in being neat and orderly. He is permissive about her sexuality, and sees her as displaying a good deal of it, especially in the form of running around the house nude.

These attitudes of the father suggest a sexual connotation in his relationship to his daughter. It is interesting to note that the mother does not seem to be aware of the sexuality of the girl (.06); this lack of perception stems perhaps from the fact that her own parents are not at all open about sex. In any case, the important affective relationship is between father and daughter.

One aspect of modeling is not revealed in the table because the rele-

TABLE 24

Injury to Objects by Girls (192):
Correlations with Parent Interview and Mother-Child
Interaction Measures at Level $p < .05$

8. Stability of the current home situation: pooled	−64
10. Resentment of this pregnancy: father	−46
27. Reported amount of child's social nudity: father	57
34. Reported sexuality in child: father	54
37. Openness about sex: mother's parents	−50
42. Pressure for neatness and orderliness: mother	−47
43. Pressure for neatness and orderliness: father	−51
82. Source of nurturance (mother high)	−50
127. Reward for dependency: father	64
151. Amount of father's interaction with child: pooled	49

vant correlations do not quite reach the .05 significance level. The mother's self-esteem correlates $-.38$ with injury to objects, whereas her evaluation of the father correlates .41. With respect to the more feminine girls' aggression syndrome, just the opposite relations obtain; the correlations with Z and 214, respectively, are .18 and .18 for mother's self-esteem, and $-.40$ and $-.34$ for her evaluation of the father. Tattling, another feminine form of aggression, is similarly related, correlating .57 with mother's self-esteem and $-.02$ with mother's evaluation of father. The consistency of these relationships suggests that the little girl tends to use as a model the parent more esteemed by the mother.

There is a similar relationship, in boys, between mother's evaluation of father and the boy's choice of masculine or feminine forms of aggressive behavior, but the relation to mother's self-esteem is reversed, and all the relevant coefficients are too small to warrant quoting them.

Interpretation. Injury to objects is an essentially masculine form of aggression. The little girl high in this form of aggression is partly mature, partly immature. Although she is nurturant, as befits a mature feminine role, she is also somewhat immaturely dependent and poorly sex-typed. Her father's warmth, permissiveness, and low demands facilitate her affectionate dependence on him. Her mother tends to devaluate herself and to esteem the father highly. The father, in other words, is in an exceptionally strong position to serve as a model for his daughter; and since the father does not expect sex differences in behavior, the girl can develop the masculine form of aggression without interference.

If this interpretation of injury to objects as a product of modeling is correct, the theory of primary identification—as we have presented it— suffers another blow. Again there is support for dependency as a prerequisite, but again we find no evidence for the high demands and contingent love anticipated by the theory. However, the significance of the mother's esteem for the father may be quite important. In the case of tattling, the girl models herself after the self-esteeming mother; with injury to objects, the modeling follows the mother's esteem for the father. We suggest that *the parent more esteemed by the mother tends to be the model for the girl.*

Discussion

Sex differences in both the structure of aggression and its child-rearing antecedents stand out as clearly in the aggression data as they did in the dependency and adult role data. In contrast with these behaviors, however, aggression appears to be more highly integrated (more nearly a unitary trait) in boys than in girls. Even so, within both sexes there are discriminably different aggressive behavior systems, with tattling and injury to objects being strongly differentiated from other forms of aggression for boys and girls, respectively. We have concluded that the former is reasonably characterized as feminine and the latter as masculine.

Two other kinds of differences have to do with the child-rearing correlates of aggression. One of these is the differential influence of the two parents, a factor especially evident also in connection with the various forms of dependency. The other is the quality of the parents as models.

We have earlier seen evidence that the same-sexed parent is largely responsible for determining the development of dependency behavior, with the exception that negative attention seeking and reassurance seeking in girls are influenced by the father. In the case of adult role behavior, mothers are generally more influential than fathers for both sexes, though for boys there is some variation in this relationship among the different categories, some (e.g., adult work) being more under the mother's influence than others. In the case of aggression, no such simple generalization can be made at all, because the role of models is so important.

By its nature, aggression can be measured easily in the parents, whereas dependency and adult role behavior cannot. The discussion (in the interview) of disciplinary methods and parents' attitudes toward their children's aggressive behavior provides a revealing impression of the parents' own styles and intensity of aggression. Parent scales measuring punitiveness and permissiveness, as well as those estimating hostility toward the child, overt aggressiveness, and aggression anxiety, are indicative of the extent to which each parent displays aggression before the child. In other words, we know something of their qualities as *models* for aggressive behavior.

The influence of modeling is manifested in two ways in our data. One is a rather gross effect resulting from the intrusion of one or the other parent in the child-rearing process in some special way, with that parent's own sex-typed aggression inducing a similar type of behavior in the child. This influence is most clearly displayed when the intrusion— or perhaps better, the atypically active cooperation—is from the fathers of girls. Among the dependency categories, negative attention seeking is an example in point, and among the aggression categories, injury to objects is another.

Similar effects of mothers on boys, such as we have seen with adult role, are less clearly discernible in the area of aggression, though tattling may offer an example. Tattletale boys were separated from their fathers in infancy (.47), and are affectionate (.51) toward their nurturant mothers (.55). The mothers are themselves relatively non-aggressive (demanding aggression to peers, −.44; suffering aggression anxiety, .57), and one may speculate that for this reason the boys adopt the verbal and attenuated (somewhat feminine) form of aggression. It is notable that these boys show high adult role in the two largely verbal categories (giving facts, .46; adult mannerisms, .60), but do not show the non-verbal maternal type (adult work, −.19).

In general, the effects of a heavy intrusion by a parent into the rearing of a child of the opposite sex appear to be most evident in the kind of behavior most typical of that sex of parent. Thus, the mother's effect on the boy is most discernible in his adoption of verbal adult role behavior and feminine forms of housework, and the father's effect on the girl is most notable in her display of negative attention seeking and injury to objects (the masculine form of aggression).

The second way in which modeling appears is in the direct correlation of the extents to which parent and child express aggression openly; in terms of the two syndromes described earlier, the boy's aggression is related to the father's, and the girl's (insignificantly) to the mother's. The same-sexed parent is the model. With respect to injury to objects, however, girls relate more to their fathers than to their mothers.

That the parent-child correlation exists is obvious, but the question arises why one parent rather than the other should become the model. One variable that may be crucial in this development is the extent of the mother's esteem for herself and for her husband, especially in the case of girls. The child seems to model himself (or herself) after the more mother-esteemed parent. The mother of the high-aggression-syndrome boy has a (non-significantly) high evaluation of the father; the mother of the high-aggression-syndrome girl has high self-esteem; the mother of the tattling girl has high self-esteem; and the mother of the object-injuring girl has high evaluation of the father. The principle holds for girls in all instances, and minimally so for boys.

One possible interpretation of these relationships can be derived indirectly from the work of Bandura (Bandura and Walters, 1963) on factors affecting children's adoption of a model's behavior. Ross (1962) showed that highly dependent nursery school children are influenced more by a model than less dependent children are. In the present instance, the more aggressive girls are also more dependent—the syndrome-aggression girls maturely so, and the object-injurers immaturely and passively so. If *esteem* may be interpreted as an indicator of the parent deemed by the mother the appropriate model, then the girl's response is effective.

This reasoning is somewhat questionable in that it does not account for the mother's ability to influence the girl's perception of who should be her model. The problem would be easily solved if we could assume, simply, that a girl identifies with the mother and then transfers the identification to the father (or imitates him as a model, in Bandura's terms), but such an assumption begs our original question: what are the sources of such identification?

In our examination of adult role behavior, we were led to the conclusion that such behavior could be understoood as a simple adoption, perhaps by imitation, of the kinds of parent-approved behavior that would maintain a comfortable dependency-nurturance relationship between the child and the parents, especially the mother. It seemed that adult role behavior could indeed be classified as a form of mature maternalized dependency, for all practical purposes. At the least, it is a sound index of the child's dependency.

In the case of the girl's aggression, however, we are driven a step further by the mother's apparent influence as a determiner of the model to be imitated. This *pre-imitation* process leaves us with a tentative conclusion that there is some process which serves to make the child more responsive to the values and the sanctions of the same-sexed parent. This hypothetical process is what we have called primary identification, but our data on girls' aggression bring us no closer to an understanding of its origins in child rearing than we were before. Aggression simply exemplifies the influence of such a hypothetical process.

Summary

The common finding that boys show more antisocial aggression than girls, both in the nursery school and in doll play, has been replicated. There are no significant differences in amount of prosocial aggression in either of these settings, although this form of aggression constitutes a larger proportion of the girls' total output of aggression than of the boys'. There is no evidence of a sex difference in amount of aggression shown at home or in the mother-child interaction.

There is a significant correlation between age and tattling in boys, and an almost significant one between age and real interpersonal aggression in girls.

The interrelations among the various measures of aggression suggest that there is a greater integration (i.e., a more consistent trait structure) in boys than in girls. In general, the direct and active forms of aggression, especially the antisocial forms, seem to characterize the masculine-sex-typed boys, whereas the interpersonal, verbal, and prosocial forms seem to characterize the girls. Tattling can be described as a feminine form of aggression, and injury to objects as masculine.

An examination of the correlations between certain theoretically significant child-rearing variables and the fourteen measures of children's aggression permitted the testing of several hypotheses, and led to the following conclusions:

1. Among four types of frustration, only one appeared to be related to aggression. There is a little evidence that current pressures and restrictions in the home are associated with higher direct aggression and lower indirect and attenuated aggression in boys, whereas the opposite holds for the girls. Infant frustrations, current separation from the parents, instability of the home, and parental inconsistencies in child rearing are not related to aggression in any systematic way.

2. Punishment for aggression by either parent of either sex of child tends to increase aggression in the home non-significantly, and there is no clear indication of any inhibiting effect on even the most severely punished children; this finding replicates that of Sears, Maccoby, and Levin (1957). No evidence has been adduced in support of the proposition that severe punishment for aggression facilitates projected, displaced, or attenuated aggression.

3. Permissiveness for aggression toward parents results in an increase in aggression in the home (replicating previous findings) and a reduction of aggression in the nursery school.

4. Prosocial aggression was used as the dependent variable in a test of the hypotheses concerning the child-rearing antecedents of primary identification. Again, as with adult role, the predicted correlation with

dependency was found, but there is little support for the remainder of the hypothesized relationships.

An inductive approach was taken to the question of antecedents for the boys' syndrome of direct outer-directed aggression, the girls' syndrome of interpersonal aggression, and the girls' use of injury to objects. The relationships discovered are not subject to abbreviated summary, but the following general conclusions have been reached:

1. Non-permissiveness in the home is associated with low aggression toward the parents, but with high aggression in the nursery school.

2. Girls apparently perceive which parent is the more esteemed by the mother, and tend to pattern their aggressive behavior after that of the esteemed model.

3. The intrusion of the opposite-sexed parent into a child's rearing tends to establish certain elements of that parent's behavior in the child. The influence of mothers on boys is more strongly exhibited with adult role behavior, and the influence of fathers on girls is more pronounced with aggression.

5. Sex Typing and Gender Role

Sex typing is the process by which a child develops role behavior appropriate to his ascribed gender. Although not all the qualities of behavior that differentiate the sexes can be assumed to derive from this process, there is good reason to believe that a substantial number of them do. Hampson (1965) has shown, for example, that pseudohermaphrodites adopt whichever gender role is ascribed to them in early infancy, regardless of their endocrinological or anatomical status. A baby may have virtually all the biological qualities of one sex, but if for reason of some minor anatomical deviance the child is labeled as of the other sex, and is reared as if it were of this other sex, it will develop most of the personality qualities appropriate to the ascribed gender. The implication of these findings is that the *ascription* of a particular gender label at birth initiates a complex set of treatments (by the parents and siblings and various others) that establishes the attitudes, feelings, interests, tastes, mannerisms, traits, and habit structures characterizing children of that gender in the particular culture in which the child's rearing occurs. Sex typing is the process by which the hypothesized treatments produce the indicated outcome.

For a number of reasons, sex typing has been interpreted by non-psychoanalytic theorists as an instance of primary identification. Gender roles are very broad and very subtle. It would be difficult to imagine that any kind of direct tuition could provide for the learning of such elaborate behavioral, attitudinal, and manneristic patterns as are subsumed under the rubrics of masculinity and femininity. Furthermore, these qualities are absorbed quite early and are highly resistant to modification. It has been shown, for example, that sex-typed characteristics of aggression in doll play are discriminable in three-year-olds (P. Sears, 1951), and Hampson has found that pseudohermaphrodites who are reared under one gender label for two and a half to three years can be shifted only partially, and not always successfully, to the other gender thereafter. The evident importance of models in producing appropriate sex typing is another reason for interpreting the process as an instance of identification. The absence of the father during a boy's third and fourth years of life has been shown to feminize the boy's expression of aggression (P. Sears, 1951), and even the quality of the mother's feelings about the absent father appears to affect the kind of influence the absence exerts (Bach, 1946).

Although Sigmund Freud's discussion of the resolution of the Oedipus complex (1924) and Anna Freud's analysis of the defensive process she has labeled identification with the aggressor (1936) both suggest that masculinity may be attributed to the defensive identification process, the age at which gender role differentiation is detectable—and its reversibility no longer accomplishable—throws considerable doubt on the importance of such a process for sex typing.

If we were to follow the reasoning for defensive identification, we would leave unsolved the problems of how girls become feminine and how boys develop their irreversible masculinity by age three. This is not to deny the significance of such a process, nor to suggest that it cannot affect the development of masculine and feminine roles, but rather to suggest, on the strength of the evidence concerning the onset of sex typing, that the Oedipus complex may be of only secondary importance in the establishment of gender role behavior.

The fact that psychoanalytic investigation finds extensive evidence of the influence of defensive identification may be another instance of the general principle that retrospective examination of genetic psychological processes tends to reveal mainly those aspects that involve persisting conflicts. Psychoanalysis is a method peculiarly effective for this purpose, but although it easily provides information concerning the conflictual aspects of development, it is probably less useful for discovering or elucidating the non-conflictual processes. Primary identification, involving mainly the modeling process, is far less conflictual than defensive identification, and hence is less easily disclosed by the retrospective method of psychoanalytic investigation.

The evidence for the importance of modeling in the sex-typing process consists largely of observations of parallelism in the behavior of parents and their children. In a definitive summary of the relevant data, Bandura and Walters (1963, Chapter 2) have shown that such parallels occur in many behavior qualities, including aggression, dependency, withdrawal, autism, sex anxiety, and guilt. In most of the reported researches, these parallels are between parents and children of the same sex, and more often between fathers and sons. From these studies it is not possible to discover clearly the conditions that induce the parallelism in behavior. The inference can of course be made that the father is normally a more appropriate model for the boy, and the mother for the girl, but this inference leaves us just where we were—asking what the social or other conditions may be that are conducive to imitation of the same-sexed parent's behavior.

Some indications of the paternal qualities important for this process in boys have been suggested in a set of researches by Mussen and his collaborators (Payne and Mussen, 1956; Mussen and Distler, 1959, 1960; Mussen, 1961; Mussen and Rutherford, 1963), who have shown that the fathers of highly masculine boys, ages six through high school, are viewed by the boys as rewarding and affectionate, on the one hand, and as possessing strength and power, on the other. Somewhat similarly, P. Sears (1953) found that the five-year-old sons of warm and affectionate fathers tended to adopt the father role in doll play to a greater extent than the sons of colder, more distant fathers. In an experimental situation, Bandura and Huston (1961) were able to demonstrate the more general principle that nurturance of the child by the model increases the probability that the child will imitate the model's behavior.

A second finding from the Sears study is of particular relevance to the question of why boys come to adopt the father's role rather than the mother's. Sears found that where the boys' mothers were warm and affectionate, and also devalued the father, the boys tended to adopt the mother role in doll play. One possible implication of devaluation is that, in the child's perception, the father is rendered less powerful, a point of some significance in connection with an ingenious experiment by Bandura, Ross, and Ross (1963), who showed that a child tends to imitate the behavior of the model who is more powerful and therefore more able to control desirable resources. Where the father has power, one might expect his children to imitate him, and his son, at least, to be more like him, i.e., masculine.

Before attempting to test these very tentative hypotheses concerning the determinants of modeling and gender role adoption, we must define the various measures we have considered as indices of masculinity and femininity, and examine the relationships among them.

Measurement of Gender Role

The measurement of masculinity and femininity presents a particular problem that has not been solved satisfactorily in this study or, to the best of our knowledge, in any other with children of this age. This is the problem of measuring each of the two gender roles *independently* of the other. Whatever the mechanism by which these qualities are learned, the usual conditions of family life provide ample opportunity for a child to model himself after both parents. If conditions are especially favorable for such modeling, the child can develop relatively high degrees of both masculinity and femininity. Although it is common to conceive of these role qualities as psychological opposites, they are in fact composed of so many behavioral, attitudinal, and affective components that it is entirely possible for a child to adopt at least some of the attributes belonging to each of them. Thus he can be, in some degree, both masculine and feminine.

Unfortunately, the element of *choice*—choice between actions or between things—is inherent in all but one of our gender role measures, and when the choice occurs, it is between a masculine action or thing and a feminine action or thing. Thus, our toy-preference measure pits masculine toys against feminine toys, and the performance of male-type actions in doll play is at the expense of female-type actions. There is some variation among our different measures in the degree to which a masculine choice precludes a feminine one, but we have no instance of total independence. For example, in our version of Rabban's (1950) toy-preference test, a child's score can range from totally masculine (he selects all the male toys first) to totally feminine (he selects all the female toys first); selection of any toy precludes selection of any other, and the final score lies somewhere on the single dimension of masculinity–femininity. On the other hand, in permissive doll play, there are five dolls among which the child makes his choice for agent of each action sequence, and although choosing the father doll for a given sequence precludes choosing the mother doll for that sequence, there are three other dolls that may be chosen or ignored; hence the total frequency of use of any given doll is not inherently negatively correlated with that of any other single doll. (In fact, for both sexes in the present study there is a *positive* correlation between father and mother dolls in frequency of use as agents of routine activities.)

We have obtained fourteen measures of behavioral attributes that have some relevance to gender role. Five of these are observational or assessment measures obtained in the nursery school setting. *All five of these scores represent measures of masculinity for boys and of femininity for girls:* i.e., measures of the degree to which the children display appropriate gender role.

Eight other measures are of agent choices and sex-typed actions performed in permissive doll play, and one is from the mother-child-interaction situation. These nine doll-play and MCI scores have *not* been adjusted so as to be measures of sex typing; they simply indicate the frequency or amount of the behavior designated. We have not converted such measures as "frequency of use of father doll as agent" to measures directly indicating masculinity or femininity because we had no adequate evidence in advance permitting us to make such an interpretation.

Observations and Assessments

The It Scale (Brown, 1956) (199). A sexless stick-figure drawing of a child is called "It." The subject uses "It" to make preference selections in three sets of cards. In the first set, "It" chooses eight pictured toys from among sixteen shown, half the toys being masculine and half feminine. The second set of cards is arranged in eight pairs, each pair consisting of either a male and a female object (e.g., men's and women's shoes) or a male and a female person; "It" selects the preferred picture from each pair. In the third set, the child selects from among four picture cards the character "It" would like to be: a boy, a girlish-dressed boy, a boyish-dressed girl, or a girl. The score for the It Scale can range from completely masculine to completely feminine.

The test-retest reliability of the It Scale is quite satisfactory. Borstelmann (1961) tested 32 children of each sex on two occasions, a month apart, and obtained correlations between the test and retest scores of .80 for boys and .64 for girls.

Area usage score (200). The nursery school and playground were mapped into 45 play areas; the mapping was done on a purely phenomenal basis, the areas including such differentiable things as "the swings," "the dress-up corner," "the packing boxes," and "the sand pile." Each area was given a number designation, and during the behavior unit observation the area location number was recorded for each half-minute period. On the basis of the first 230 minutes of observation of the forty children, twenty of each sex, a percentage value was determined for each area, reflecting how many of its "inhabitants" were girls and how many were boys.° Areas that were used 65 per cent or more by one sex (and 35 per cent or less by the other) were defined as "sex-typed areas." The definition produced nine masculine and eight feminine areas. A masculinity or femininity score was calculated for each child by dividing the number of half-minute intervals during which he or she played in the *appropriate* sex-typed areas by the total number of intervals he or she spent in *any* of the sex-typed areas, whether appropriate or not.

The consistency of this measure over the summer was virtually zero. (For boys the median was .12, and for girls −.01, by the method described in Appendix D.) We have retained it simply because it correlates positively with two of the other measures in boys and with three of them in girls. Furthermore, a comparison of area usage by the TTh children with that by the MWF group yields a *rho* of .53 between the masculine-feminine area-ranking orders for the two groups.

Pictures test (201). In this test, adapted from Fauls and Smith (1956), the child indicates his preference between two play activities presented to him in the form of pictures placed side by side on the table in front of him. There are twelve such pairs; in both alternatives for each pair, the child pursuing the play activity is of the same sex as the subject. (Thus, separate sets of cards are used for testing boys and girls, although the alternative pairs in both sets picture the same play activities.) In a typical pair, one alternative shows the child taking a doll for a walk in a doll buggy, and in the other the child is playing cowboy with appropriate costuming and gear. The obtained score for the measure is simply the total of sex-appropriate choices made. Borstelmann's (1961) test-retest reliability coefficients were .37 and .38 for boys and girls, respectively (see Appendix J).

Toy preference and satiation test (202). In this test, fourteen toys are ranged in a line on the floor. The child chooses one after another, in order of preference, until he has chosen eight. The toys used were as nearly like those of Rabban (1950) as we could secure. Rabban's toys were carefully standardized so that seven appealed predominantly to boys, seven to girls, and in Rabban's study the test as a whole, scored simply as the

---

° For this calculation, one of the 21 boys in our sample was excluded by lot, and one non-sample girl was added to our 19 girls; she was a child on whom these observational measures had been obtained but who was not otherwise included in the study.

number of sex-appropriate choices made, discriminated between the sexes at the .001 level of significance. Borstelmann's (1961) test-retest reliability coefficients were .76 for boys and .62 for girls (see Appendix J).

After the child has completed his eight choices, the experimenter removes all the toys except two, the first-chosen toy of appropriate sex and the first of inappropriate sex. He then leaves the child in the room alone to play with the toys. An observer notes the time that elapses before the child shifts from the appropriate toy to the inappropriate. This satiation-time score was used to break tied scores between children of a given sex; it has not itself been retained for the analysis (see Appendix J).

Observer rating (203). Separate five-point scales were used for boys and girls. The boys' scale ranged from (1) a sissy, to (5) entirely masculine, a buck; the girls' ranged from (1) a tomboy, to (5) a coquette, a clinging vine. The four observers rated each child at the end of the summer, and the average of these independent ratings was used as the child's score for masculinity or femininity. The six possible intercorrelations among the four individual ratings ($N = 40$) range from .53 to .80; the median correlation corrected by the Spearman–Brown formula is .88, which represents the reliability of the measure used.

Total standard score (204). The standard scores for all these measures except the It Scale (i.e., for measures 200, 201, 202, and 203) were combined to provide an overall measure of masculinity and femininity. The It Scale was excluded from the total score because of its uniformly zero relationship, in girls, to the other four measures.

Doll-Play Measures

The doll-play sessions, described in Chapter 1 and Appendix F, yielded four pairs of measures relevant to gender role.

Father as routine agent (240, 241). These scores, for the first and second sessions, respectively, represent the percentage of father agent among all non-aggressive acts by all agents.

Mother as routine agent (242, 243).

Male-typed routine adult work (278, 279). This score is the percentage of routine acts (regardless of agent) representing male-typed adult work (e.g., shop projects, mechanical fixing, other house construction or moving, car activity, going to work).

Female-typed routine adult work (280, 281). Examples of female-typed work are cooking, cleaning, care of clothes (washing, mending, etc.), bedmaking, other housekeeping.

Mother-Child-Interaction Measures

The telephone game in the MCI (described briefly in Chapter 1) yielded one gender role measure.

Child's willingness to adopt opposite sex role (364). The telephone game required the child to perform several roles, two of which (one a parent, the other a child) were to be of the opposite sex. The tape was rated on a four-point scale ranging from (1) active resistance, to (4) complete willingness.

Organization of Gender Role

Sex Differences

The presentation of data on sex typing requires special care. As mentioned earlier, all our measures of gender role except the observer rating were obtained with instruments that provided scores ranging from low (feminine, or at least non-masculine) to high (masculine). Because we refer in the present research to a construct of *appropriate* sex typing, we have *reversed* the girls' scores on all the obtained nursery school and assessment measures so that a high score for a girl represents high femininity just as a high score for a boy represents high masculinity. Elsewhere in our report we need not go behind these masculinity-femininity scores; here we shall return, in Table 25, to the raw scores for three of the measures (199, 201, 202) in order to indicate the effectiveness of the instruments in distinguishing between the sexes. Means for the observer rating (203) and the total standard score (204) cannot be included because both measures were initially prepared as sex-appropriate measures. Means for the area-usage measure (200) have been excluded for a different reason. This measure is discriminative between the sexes, of course, but because the sex-typed areas were defined on the basis of the first 230 minutes of observation of the same children, the difference between the means is a function of our own procedure. One girl was slightly more masculine by this measure than the three least masculine boys, but otherwise there was no overlap. This measure, like the observer rating and the total score, has significance only for intrasex comparisons.

The remaining scores in Table 25 are presented in units that are identical for boys and girls, since the girls' scores have not been reversed to

TABLE 25

Gender Role Measures: Means, Standard Deviations, Significance of
Sex Differences, and Correlations with Age

*(Values for assessment measures are raw scores; those for doll play are actual per cents;
those for MCI are ratings. An asterisk on the p-value indicates girls greater than boys.)*

Gender Role Measures	Var. No.	Boys		Girls		p (2-tail)	r with Age	
		Mean	S.D.	Mean	S.D.		Boys	Girls
Assessments and Rating								
"It" scale	199	64.52	16.72	31.89	20.39	<.001	−08	−10
Area usage score . . .	200	−	−	−	−	−	−04	04
Pictures test	201	5.62	1.80	1.84	1.46	<.001	24	09
Toy preference	202	6.24	1.03	2.63	1.53	<.001	20	22
Observer rating . . .	203	−	−	−	−	−	48	−35
Total standard score . .	204	−	−	−	−	−	44	00
Permissive Doll Play (Routine)								
Father agent, I	240	9.00	4.85	13.63	5.79	.01*	−17	07
Father agent, II . . .	241	6.10	4.35	10.05	5.63	.02*	−07	28
Mother agent, I . . .	242	7.48	5.91	13.11	5.17	.001*	01	−03
Mother agent, II . . .	243	5.52	5.37	14.47	7.86	<.001*	05	13
Male adult work, I . .	278	6.05	4.72	8.26	3.73	.10*	−25	−38
Male adult work, II . .	279	6.05	5.38	7.16	5.98	n.s.*	−09	45
Female adult work, I .	280	1.62	2.66	3.74	3.02	.02*	−06	45
Female adult work, II .	281	.81	1.80	3.58	4.03	.01*	01	05
Mother-Child Interaction								
Willingness to adopt opposite sex role . .	364	5.57	1.40	5.42	1.76	n.s.	−05	06

provide femininity scores. The figures for variables 240 through 281 are frequencies (per cent) comparable to those given for doll-play measures in Chapter 3, and those for 364 are arbitrary scale values derived from the tape ratings.

The It Scale, the pictures test, and the toy preference and satiation test all provide excellent discrimination between the sexes.

Among the permissive doll-play measures, there is a rather unexpected finding, namely, that in two presumably male areas (use of father doll as routine agent and performance of male-typed routine adult work) the girls were higher than the boys. Previous studies (e.g., P. Sears, 1951) have generally found a large difference favoring the girls in frequency of use of the mother doll, but little sex difference in use of the father doll. We do not know whether previous studies have measured the frequency of sex-typed adult work categories in doll play, but because the agent and work categories are highly correlated, we had fully expected the boys to display as much as or more masculine work than the girls. In general, the girls exhibited no more adult role behavior in the nursery school than the boys, but displayed much more in doll play. Both sexes showed a slight reduction in use of parent dolls as agents in the second session of doll play, a finding reported in earlier studies (P. Sears, 1953), and there was a similar decrease in the frequency of adult work.

The non-significant mean difference between boys' and girls' scores on willingness to play the inappropriate gender role in the telephone game suggests that neither sex was more bothered than the other about sex typing.

Age Differences

The correlations of the various measures with age (Table 25) suggest that the observers perceived the older boys as more masculine and the younger girls as more feminine. The other interesting point about the age correlations is the pair of session-to-session changes, for the girls, in male-typed and female-typed adult work. The reciprocal directions of the coefficients suggest that the older girls *increased* male work and *decreased* female work on the second session, whereas the younger girls did the opposite. This supposition is directly verified by a comparison of the means for the nine oldest girls with those for the ten youngest. The older group performed 6.44 per cent male-typed work at the first session, and increased this to 9.22 per cent at the second; the younger group, conversely, dropped from 9.90 per cent to 5.30 per cent. The changes in female-typed work are reciprocal.

Relations among Gender Role Measures

The intercorrelations among the various sex-typing and gender role measures are shown in Table 26. The median correlation among the five nursery school and assessment measures is .36 for girls and .15 for boys. This difference in medians hides the fact that all the girls' other measures correlate near zero with the It Scale, even though their intercorrelations are quite high, ranging from .32 to .71. For the boys, however, the median reflects fairly accurately the level of intercorrelation. This higher integration of femininity than of masculinity is similar to the phenomenon seen earlier in our examination of dependency and adult role, and is certainly in accord with an expectation that the boys would be slower in developing a stable gender role structure because of their need to shift from an early identification with (or modeling after) the mother to a later identification with the father.

The eight doll-play measures provide a surprising reversal of this principle. Although frequency of use of the father doll agent is positively related (in the same session) to that of the mother agent for both boys and girls, the boys' correlations are definitely higher. In performing male and female adult work, the girls' correlations are scarcely above zero, but the boys' have a median of .37. Further, the cross-correlations between use of the parent dolls and performance of adult work are higher for boys. These differences cannot be accounted for by any consistent differences in the distributions of scores for the two sexes; as can be seen in Table 25, the standard deviations for most of the doll-play measures are larger for the girls. An examination of correlations involving various agents of aggression as well as of routine behavior, and of various combinations of agents (such as adult, child, male, female), indicates that there is a consistent tendency for the session-to-session correlations for girls to be lower than for boys.

One reason for this—or at least one associated phenomenon –is the systematic difference between older and younger girls in these session-to-session changes (mentioned above in the discussion of age differences). The tendency shown by the older girls to increase masculine performance (and by the younger girls to decrease it) on the second session has the effect of lowering the inter-session correlations, and even of reversing their signs. We have not been able to discover a hypothesis that can satisfactorily account for these age differences. But the fact that girls generally have higher aggression anxiety (associated with child-rearing conditions more productive of such anxiety) might suggest that the permissiveness (anxiety reduction) perceived by the girls in the doll-play procedure introduces a stronger and more variable change in internal instigation from Session I to Session II for girls than for boys.

Now if we examine the correlations between the five assessment measures and the doll-play measures, we find that for boys the correlations are preponderantly negative, regardless of which agent is involved, whether the adult work portrayed is male or female, or which session is considered. The median for the twenty correlations between agents and assessment measures is −.21, but the correlations with the total score (median = −.30) may well give a better representation of the matrix.

TABLE 26
Intercorrelations among Gender Role Measures
(*Girls above the diagonal, boys below*)

Gender Role Measures	Var. No.	Variable Number Assessments						Agents: Doll Play				Sex-Typed Work: Doll Play				MCI
		199	200	201	202	203	204	240	241	242	243	278	279	280	281	364
Assessments and Rating																
"It" scale	199	*	−06	13	−03	09	10	00	−52	−03	−64	14	−29	−13	−09	−22
Area usage	200	39	*	55	37	32	70	07	−46	−18	47	−34	−07	35	23	−42
Pictures test	201	53	30	*	69	71	93	06	−29	−14	11	−35	−25	−10	09	−53
Toy preference	202	−03	−03	20	*	36	76	31	−01	07	17	−37	−14	07	−22	−64
Observer rating	203	01	−01	29	09	*	74	−06	−34	03	12	−25	−25	−46	07	−47
Total score	204	42	48	78	47	57	*	07	−36	−10	22	−36	−24	−05	06	−64
Permissive Doll Play (routine)																
Father agent, I	240	03	−13	−11	−41	01	−34	*	19	49	14	−14	16	30	10	−07
Father agent, II	241	−19	−42	−19	−24	−23	−32	13	*	23	29	33	57	14	12	34
Mother agent, I	242	−04	30	−31	−49	−04	−22	48	24	*	26	01	−02	39	40	03
Mother agent, II	243	−21	−03	−28	−25	−29	−29	25	69	63	*	−27	38	40	40	−25
Male adult work, I	278	−07	−14	−10	−06	−04	−29	72	−12	11	04	*	08	−09	05	38
Male adult work, II	279	−29	−39	−14	−14	−07	−25	35	69	22	46	17	*	24	13	21
Female adult work, I	280	−21	−27	−18	−17	−07	−37	58	22	46	37	42	58	*	46	−02
Female adult work, II	281	−28	−26	03	−11	01	−22	49	18	20	39	32	30	56	*	18
Mother-Child Interaction																
Willingness to adopt opposite sex role	364	−43	−24	−26	−25	12	−28	53	25	13	37	45	39	24	28	*

The median for the twenty correlations between adult work and the assessment measures is −.14, and that of the four with the total score is −.27. For girls, the twenty correlations involving agents center exactly at zero, and those involving adult work have a median of −.14. The correlations of the eight doll-play measures with the total score do not change the findings. However, it is worth noting that, for the girls, the negative correlations are to be found with male role or work, and the positive ones with female, the generalization being clearer for performance of adult work than for agent.

These various conclusions about doll play are rather riskily impressionistic, but there is a consistent implication in them. In the earlier discussion of adult role (Chapter 3), evidence was presented that real adult work in particular, and other categories of adult role to a lesser extent, are feminine forms of behavior—mature, but feminine. Now it appears that taking adult roles or performing adult work in doll play has the same quality for boys—and they rejected it. Perhaps the most telling bit of evidence in support of this conclusion is the set of correlations between willingness to adopt the opposite sex role (364, obtained during the telephone game) and the assessment measures. The willingness measure is negatively correlated with four of the five assessment measures of masculinity (and −.28 with the total score), but is positively related to all eight measures from the doll play (median = .33). In other words, the masculine boys were unwilling to play the opposite sex role in the telephone game, and in the doll play did not use either male or female adult agents or perform either male or female adult work. When we recall the high positive correlations between these role choices in doll play and the BUO measure of real adult work in the nursery school, we cannot help concluding that sex of doll agent and sex-appropriateness of doll performances are simply not fully discriminated by boys; any doll-play adultness is associated with femininity—or, at least, with non-masculinity.

The relationships for girls are similar, but with an intriguing difference: playing the role of an adult male agent or performing adult male work is negatively related to femininity, but adult female role or work is positively related to it. Thus, adopting the opposite sex role in the telephone game was rejected by the more feminine girls ($r = -.64$ with total score); they refused to use the father doll as agent, or to perform adult male work; but they did tend (slightly) to perform the feminine role and work.

We conclude from this that the girls in our sample had developed a better discrimination of gender roles than the boys, and that, for the girls, adultness per se in doll play was not feminine, but female role playing or performance was.

Relations to Other Child Measures

Most of the significant relationships between the nursery school assessment measures of sex typing and the other measures of the children's behavior have been mentioned previously, in the appropriate chapters. They can be summarized readily, and a few further findings concerning the doll-play measures can be added. (See Appendix K, Tables K7 to K10.)

Dependency

In girls, negative attention seeking was seen to be a masculine form of behavior ($r = -.47$ with the total score for femininity). The little girls who sought attention in this way were also more willing to adopt the opposite sex roles in the telephone game (.39), and in the first session of doll play performed a high amount of male work (.46). Positive attention seeking, on the other hand, is a feminine form of behavior (.44 with the total score), and is associated with a refusal to adopt the opposite sex role ($-.44$) or to perform adult male work in doll play ($-.29, -.30$).

In boys, there is relatively little relation between masculinity and either negative or positive attention seeking, but the less active and more immature boys tended to achieve non-masculine scores on the various assessment measures. The total observed dependency and total masculinity scores are correlated $-.48$. In general, the boys who were high on being near were also less masculine, performed more adult work, and used more adult agents in doll play.

Adult Role

In girls, the high correlation between positive attention seeking and total real adult role behavior (.67) ensures that the latter category also would be positively correlated with femininity (.43). Interestingly enough, so are giving facts and knowledge (.48) and adult mannerisms (.41), even though both these categories, in boys, tend to be somewhat correlated with masculinity (.34 and .23, respectively, with the total score, but .60 and .50, respectively, with the observer rating).

But the really significant finding for boys, as we have mentioned earlier, is the negative correlation between real adult work and the total masculinity score ($-.61$). This finding, coupled with the uniformly positive correlations between the BUO adult work measure and the eight adult agent and work categories of doll play, supports our view that adultness in role-playing actions is an indicator of non-masculinity in boys, whether the behavior is performed in a real social context, such as the nursery school, or in the relative fantasy of permissive doll play.

Aggression

Since aggression is more commonly masculine in its occurrence, there is some surprise in the discovery that its more consistent relationships to sex-typing measures are found in girls. In the chapter on aggression, evidence was presented that injury to objects is an essentially masculine form of aggression, and tattling a feminine form. In girls, injury to objects correlates negatively with all the assessment measures of femininity ($-.35$ with the total score), and tattling correlates zero to positively with them all ($.48$ with the total score). The correlations between injury to objects and the various doll-play agent and adult-work scores are small in size and mixed in direction, but the correlations between tattling and the adult forms of work in doll play display (non-significantly) the same discrimination between male and female work that we saw in connection with the BUO category of real adult work; the highly tattling (more feminine) girls showed a slight tendency not to perform adult male work ($-.28$ and $-.27$ in the two doll-play sessions) but did tend to perform adult female work in the second session ($.01$ and $.42$).

In the boys, also, injury to objects is apparently a masculine form of behavior, though much less strongly so ($r = .47$ with observer rating, $.23$ with the total score, and $-.24$ with willingness to adopt the opposite sex role in the telephone game). All eight of the correlations between injury to objects and the doll-play adult agent and work scores are negative, ranging from $-.11$ to $-.51$, with a median of $-.17$; again there is no evidence of the boys' discriminating between male and female agents or work. Tattling shows no significant correlation with any of the sex-typing measures, which is not surprising since we concluded earlier that tattling is bound up with verbal maturity.

For neither sex are there significant correlations between any of the other measures of aggression and any of the sex-typing measures except the observer rating. This score, for boys, is positively related to almost all aggression measures, significantly so with all the physical and outer-directed measures. We interpret this to mean that the more overt aggressions were an important element in the observers' concept of masculinity.

Antecedents of Gender Role

Following the procedure of the previous chapters, we shall, for the antecedents of gender role, consider first the evidence relevant to certain hypotheses that have been developed from either theoretical bases or previous empirical work. These hypotheses relate mainly to modeling and imitation, and the effects of parental expectancy. We shall then examine the remainder of the obtained data in the light of the social learning process to discover what other parental influences may reasonably be hypothesized to contribute to the sex-typing process.

Nurturance and Power

As was indicated earlier, there is evidence from the work of Bandura, Ross, and Ross (1963) that nurturance and demonstrated power to control resources are two important qualities in the behavior of models who are imitated by children of preschool age. Although the experiments that demonstrated the influence of these variables were brief, and the imitation presumably transitory, one might expect that if a high degree of such personality or behavior qualities typified one or the other parent of a child, the child would imitate that parent more frequently and thus develop the gender role exhibited by that parent. Thus, if a boy's father is both quite warm and quite powerful, and the mother less so, the boy should develop—by imitation—the masculine qualities of the father. Conversely, if the father is relatively weak and non-nurturant, he should be less influential as a model, and the boy should be less masculine.

This hypothesis is deceptively simple, as one immediately discovers when attempting to test it. Unlike the Bandura experiments, in which the model's behavior was relatively simple, and was easily recognizable in its imitated form when performed by the child, the present study defines the "model's behavior" as the very complex quality of gender role exemplified in parental behavior. Furthermore, the measures of gender role in the children are not like any aspect of the parent's behavior that we measured. Thus, we can make only a very risky and distant leap from the assumed identities of father with masculinity and of mother with femininity when we consider the parents as the models in the proposition, for example, that if the father is more nurturant and more powerful than the mother, the child will use him as the more-to-be-imitated model, and will thus be more masculine.

In an attempt to develop a procedurally independent measure of the children's perceptions of the relative power and nurturance of each of the parents, two scales were constructed for rating these qualities from the parent interviews. One was a five-point scale described as "Source of power: Child's probable perception of greater source of power over environment. Who's boss in the family? Who can make decisions that stick?" Ratings could range from (1) father, with no ambiguity, to (5) mother, with no ambiguity. The other scale was described as "Source of nurturance: Child's probable perception of greater source of nurturance (sympathy, affection, emotional support)." Both scales were first rated separately from the mother and father interviews, and then a pooled rating was made by reexamining the interviews where the separate father and mother ratings were disparate. Rater reliability was high on both scales.

For neither sex of child is there a significant correlation between either of these scales and any of the six nursery school or assessment measures of gender role, nor is either scale related significantly to any of the doll-play or MCI measures considered here. Comparison of extreme cases—those high on mother as source of both power and nurturance, and those high on father—adds no further information in support of the hypothesis. When the nurturance variable is measured by the direct scalar estimates of the *warmth* of each parent, the results of comparison with the gender role measures are the same.

We conclude that either the analogy between our "model" interpretation of the sex-typing process and the experimental situation used by Bandura is faulty, or that our measures of a child's perception of power and nurturance depart too far from the operational measures by which Mussen had originally demonstrated this relationship to permit us to secure supporting evidence.

Although we incline to the latter interpretation, there is one additional negative finding that may throw doubt on the adequacy of our analogy. One might expect that if the two parental gender roles are very clearly stereotyped and therefore markedly different from one another, the effectiveness of the model function should be greater—the child should discriminate more easily, and his own gender role should develop more fully. From the interviews, we were able to make ratings on a scale called sex stereotyping of parents' roles. The high end of this scale was described by "Some things seen as definitely man's work, others as woman's; highly and clearly differentiated; some things up to father, others to mother." The low end was described by "No differentiation expressed; no particular activities more proper to one than the other sex."

The correlations between this scale, for both parents, and all the assessment measures of gender role in both boys and girls are approximately zero. It must be noted, however, that our measures of gender role are relevant to the general concepts of masculinity and femininity, not to the imitation of the children's own parents as models; thus the hypothesis is not given an unequivocal test by these correlations.

Parental Expectations

Another hypothesis stems from the conception of role ascription as a determinant of the adoption of gender role. We would anticipate that the more strongly the parents expect behavioral differences between girls and boys at age four, the stronger and more definite the ascription of gender would be in their own child, and the more rapidly the gender role behavior would develop. Both parents' interviews were rated on a five-point scale, one end of which indicates a belief in many and quite marked native sex differences at age four, and the other end a belief that there are none, that children are "just children" at this age.

There is moderate support for the hypothesis among the girls. All the correlation coefficients between the assessment measures and each parent's expectation rating were positive, those between the total score and the parent ratings being .41 for the mother's expectancy and .26 for the father's. Neither coefficient is significant, but since the two parents' scales are entirely uncorrelated with one another, the two correlations can perhaps be interpreted as giving modest independent support. However, since the comparable boys' values are .19 and −.16, the support for the hypothesis must be considered exceedingly modest indeed!

An Inductive Approach

An examination of the significant child-rearing correlates of the total gender-role measures suggests a set of hypotheses quite different from those related to modeling. Table 27 shows all the scales from the parent interviews and the mother-child interaction that correlate significantly with either the observer rating or the total score. For both boys and girls there are two obvious clusters, one relating to sex and the other to disciplinary methods and aggression.

Sex Anxiety

So far we have made no reference to sex behavior per se in connection with the sex-typing process. Presumably there are some causal relations between the physical fact of gender and the nature of the ascribed gender role. One such relation may lie in the contrast between the active quality of male sexual behavior and the passive quality of female sexual behavior. Although variations among individuals and among cultures are quite wide, the human male is usually the more active in initiating sexual interaction, the female contributing to the process by making herself attractive and available. In the copulatory act itself, and in the foreplay, the male is characteristically the more active. Although there may be a strong biological determination of this sex difference, the kinds of behavior and attitudes represented by activity-passivity are ones that can also be significantly influenced by training. One might expect, therefore, that any qualities of the child-rearing experiences that tend to provoke active sexual play would conduce to masculinity, whereas parental attitudes that tend to inhibit a child's exploration and seeking would conduce to femininity.

There is substantial support for this expectation in the data presented in Table 27. In every instance of a significant correlation between an interview scale and one or the other gender-role measure, permissiveness is associated with masculinity and non-permissiveness with femininity. *This relationship holds for both sexes.* There are ten of the seventeen sex scales in the boys' list of correlates, and six in the girls'. Since these six are all included in the boys' list, these correlations represent the almost unprecedented finding of a given set of child-rearing experiences operating in the same direction of influence for both boys and girls. Moreover, the influence of the two parents appears to have been about equal, some scales from both appearing in the list.

The positive relation between age and masculinity in boys presents no difficulties for the interpretation of the sex-permissiveness variables, since none of these is significantly related to age.

It seems clear that the more freedom these children had for sexual play (i.e., the more permissive the parents were), the more masculine (or non-feminine) they became. This would occasion no surprise if we had been measuring the children's active sex play itself, but the measures showing this effect are quite detached from such overt sexuality. The choices of toys and occupations, in particular, seem distant from sex behavior. Whatever the mechanism by which encouragement or discouragement of active sexual behavior was translated into the liking or disliking of other gender role activities, there is little doubt that discouragement produced a passive non-masculine quality in the boys' behavior and a passive femininity in the girls'. In both sexes, this quality may well have represented not only the femininity we measured by our various assessment measures, but also qualities of fearfulness and in-

TABLE 27

Gender Role Measures: Observer Rating (203) and Total Score (204):
Correlations with Parent Interview and Mother-Child
Interaction Measures at Level $p < .05$

(Where a sign alone is shown, the r is larger than .25 but less than .46 for girls or .43 for boys.)

	Femininity	
	203	204
GIRLS		
8. Stability of current home situation (pooled)	+	46
18. Level of demands for table manners	46	+
19. Severity of toilet training	53	+
24. Father's permissiveness for indoor nudity	−55	−
27. Amount of child's social nudity (father)	−48	−
32. Mother's permissiveness for sex play among children .	−59	−
35. Extent mother gives sexual information to child	−54	−
38. Mother's sex anxiety	50	
39. Father's sex anxiety	58	54
58. Mother's permissiveness for aggression toward parents .	−73	−57
60. Mother's use of punishment for aggression toward parents	53	62
65. Father's use of reasoning	−48	
72. Father's use of ridicule	+	52
95. Father's use of praise	−47	−
107. Father's satisfaction with child's socialization	−49	
127. Father's use of reward for dependency	−60	−47
160. Extent of mother's current dissatisfaction with her life .	+	49
161. Age of father	−55	−69
162. Age of mother	−57	−73
173. Mother's non-permissiveness: factor score	62	+
333. Mother's involvement with puzzles (MCI)	−	−46

TABLE 27 (continued)
Gender Role Measures: Observer Rating (203) and Total Score (204)

	Masculinity	
	203	204
BOYS		
1. Age of child	48	44
2. Child's behavior: correspondence between MCI and home	−48	
5. Severity of child's early separation from mother	51	
17. Severity of child's feeding problems	−47	−46
18. Level of demands for table manners	−59	−
19. Severity of toilet training	−	−45
23. Mother's permissiveness for indoor nudity	61	52
24. Father's permissiveness for indoor nudity	+	62
25. Mother's pressure for modesty indoors	52	−65
26. Amount of child's social nudity (mother)	44	+
27. Amount of child's social nudity (father)	+	50
28. Mother's modesty	−44	−
31. Father's permissiveness for masturbation		52
32. Mother's permissiveness for sex play among children . .	61	+
35. Extent mother gives sexual information to child	47	+
38. Mother's sex anxiety	−47	
44. Mother's strictness about bedtime behavior	−	−65
48. Mother's expectancy of child's taking responsibility . .	48	
49. Father's expectancy of child's taking responsibility . .	−	−47
51. Extent mother keeps track of child	−59	−43
60. Mother's use of punishment for aggression toward parents		−46
67. Mother's use of physical punishment	−	−51
68. Father's use of physical punishment		−47
75. Relative strictness of parents: mother high (pooled) . .	−49	−
91. Father's expectancy of conscience	56	57
106. Mother's satisfaction with child's socialization		46
110. Mother's use of punishment for adult role behavior . .	−43	
130. Child's anxiety and fears (mother)	−	−48
150. Mother's sociability	48	
167. Mother Attitude Scale: permissiveness for sex play among children		46
170. Child Behavior Scale: maturity (mother)	54	46
171. Winterbottom Scale: mean age of expected independence (high = low pressure for independence) (mother) . .	−56	−
322. Mother's pressure for child's independence (MCI) . .	56	+
326. Mother's directiveness toward child (MCI)	−49	−47
330. Mother's warmth toward child (MCI)	54	60
359. Mother's pressure for and reward of adult role behavior (MCI)		46
365. Mother's ease in situation (MCI)	46	

hibition that, when related to aggression, have been shown to be characteristically feminine (Sears, 1961).

Severity of Socialization

Certain of the other variables in Table 27 suggest that the child-rearing conditions imposed on these children may have been appropriate for inducing fearfulness in those children of both sexes whose scores were more feminine than masculine. For example, severity of demands for good table manners and severity of toilet training are associated with femininity, as is mother's punishment for aggression toward parents. The high use of physical punishment by either parent tends to feminize, significantly so in boys and only slightly less prominently in girls (.43 for mothers, .41 for fathers, with the total score).

It seems clear that both punishment and non-permissiveness are feminizing influences, and that sex and aggression are the spheres within which such child-rearing behavior had its effect on gender role as this was measured by our nursery school assessment methods.

Doll-Play Roles

The relationships between our doll-play measures and other measures of the children's behavior suggest that we were on a wrong track in our attempts to use the relative frequencies of either the same-sex agent or the same-sex adult routine responses as indicators of gender role. The evidence is clear that the use of parent dolls (regardless of sex) as agents of routine behavior is too closely related to adult role behavior to be used for gender-role measurement. The frequency of performing adult sex-typed routine acts falls under the same interdict. Our doll-play measures all appear to be indicators of some curious combination of femininity and adult role adoption. The further pursuit of their antecedents in the present context does not seem especially useful.

The Telephone Game

So far as boys are concerned, much the same may be said of the telephone game, in which a rating was made of the child's willingness to assume the opposite gender role. Although, as we would expect, this willingness is negatively correlated with the assessment measures of masculinity, it is also positively related to the feminine qualities of adult work as measured in both the social life of the nursery school and the fantasy life of permissive doll play (see Appendix K, Table K8). The few significant child-rearing correlates (Table 28) do not suggest any further clue to the origins of these combined personality qualities, although several non-significant ones (e.g., mother's and father's use of physical punishment, .35 and .39) are similar to the variables correlated with non-masculinity as measured by the total assessment score.

For the girls, however, the expected child-rearing antecedents clearly parallel those relating to both adult role behavior and femininity as measured by our nursery school assessments. The main child-rearing correlates of willingness to adopt the opposite sex role involve high permissiveness and non-punitiveness; since this measure is a reverse indicator of gender role, the correlates are actually the same as those of the other measures of femininity—non-permissiveness and punitiveness.

These findings support our earlier judgment that this telephone-game measure is a useful index of gender role. One further bit of evidence can

TABLE 28

Willingness to Adopt Opposite Gender Role in Telephone Game (364):
Correlations with Parent Interview and Mother-Child
Interaction Measures at Level $p < .05$

GIRLS

10. Father's resentment of this pregnancy	−58
24. Father's permissiveness for indoor nudity	52
39. Father's sex anxiety	−49
58. Mother's permissiveness for aggression toward parents	61
60. Mother's use of punishment for aggression toward parents	−61
67. Mother's use of physical punishment	−55
95. Father's use of praise	49
134. Father's achievement standards for child	54
145. Mother's caretaking consistency (with this child)	57
168. Mother Attitude Scale: use of punishment for aggression toward parents	−52
173. Mother's non-permissiveness: factor score	−52

BOYS

2. Child's behavior: correspondence between MCI and home	−43
9. Mother's resentment of this pregnancy	−67
37. Openness about sex shown by mother's parents	49
63. Father's aggression anxiety	−48
76. Strictness of mother	44
89. Signs of conscience as reaction to wrongdoing (pooled)	47
129. Father's use of punishment for dependency	52
153. Mother's evaluation of father	45

be added. Although the "willingness" measure was taken from the mother-child interaction, there are no MCI variables in its correlation list (Table 28). All the other child-behavior measures obtained in the MCI appear to have been influenced fairly strongly by the mother's behavior, if one may judge from the many significant correlations between mother and child MCI measures. In other words, the children's dependence, aggression, obedience, etc., seem to have been situationally influenced to a considerable extent. The lack of such correlates with the "willingness" variable suggests that it was more internally instigated, or at least less situationally determined.

Discussion

The origins of gender role suggested by these data are difficult to fit into a model of primary identification. The feminine girls were dependent in the mature verbal way (positive attention seeking), but the masculine boys were quite the opposite. Once again, as with adult role and prosocial aggression, we are impressed by the apparent femininity of the kinds of identification behavior associated with dependency.

The other relationships required by the theory are equally obscured in the data. There is no evidence that the feminine girls' mothers were warm, or set high standards (except for table manners), or used love-oriented discipline, or specified themselves as models. The masculine boys' parents, in the home, were not warm, nor did they use love-oriented discipline or refer to themselves as models. On the other hand, there is ambiguous evidence concerning their setting of high standards: pressures for good table manners, modesty, and strict bedtime rules were low, but the mothers expected the boys to take responsibility and the fathers expected them to have a conscience; and in the MCI, the mothers pressed for independence and adult role behavior, and were judged to be warm.

The box score for primary identification theory as an explanation of gender role is poor. For girls, the only proposition supported is the customary one of dependency. For boys, even that lacks support, and the propositions about warmth and high standards receive highly equivocal support.

In our search for an alternative explanation of individual differences in gender role development, our attention has become focused on the parents' control of sex and aggression. There is strong evidence that a non-permissive or punitive attitude toward such behavior is conducive to feminization of both boys and girls. We have suggested that the mechanism responsible for this effect is the inhibition of activity in the male (whose normal sex role requires activity) and the reinforcement or facilitation of passivity in the female. There is certainly no evidence of the latter process in our data, however; all the girls' gender role measures correlate positively with rated social-interaction level, the total score on femininity to the extent of .60. The comparable correlation for boys is .59. Physical activity and social interaction are both high in the appropriately sex-typed children of both sexes.

Sheer activity level, however, is an omnibus measure; it makes no distinctions among *kinds* of activity. The actions of highly feminine girls are, in fact, feminine: positive attention seeking, adult role, tattling, and prosocial and interpersonal aggression. These behavior categories are as highly correlated with activity level as with femininity. If we are to support the interpretation that non-permissiveness produces femininity in girls by reinforcing their passivity, then clearly passivity must be defined in some manner other than mere absence of motion or interaction. The only way such a definition can be given is in terms of male-appropriate behavior; the girl becomes passive with respect to masculine activity.

This definition, though no doubt correct, begs the question of how the masculine behavior is inhibited while the feminine is not. One promising answer is suggested by Kohlberg's theory of cognitive-developmental identification (1965). In a searching analysis of past findings concerning the antecedents and behavioral correlates of gender role, he has concluded that a child must have a *gender identity* before any reinforcements can influence gender role behavior. The child must label himself as a boy or girl first, so that *his own conception* of his gender role can thereafter determine the directions of behavioral change induced by environmental influences. Thus, if the girl labels herself a girl, and if she defines the girl role as incorporating positive attention seeking, adult role play, etc., she will interpret non-reward, non-permissiveness, and punishment as indicators that she must work harder and harder to build her feminine role repertoire. In this connection it should be noted that the feminine role almost invariably involves less exploration, less seeking of new experiences, and even less risk taking in games (Kass, 1964). Regardless of the amount of physical activity she may display, her repertoire of acts becomes more and more confined.

The boy's case is similar in certain respects. Once he has labeled himself a boy, and has developed a conception of what constitutes the male role, he will move in that direction under rewarding circumstances. The male role, however, is one that demands activity, flexibility, aggressiveness, and adventuresomeness. If he suffers non-permissive treatment with respect to sex and aggression, he will no doubt behave as the girl does; i.e., he will work harder to achieve the male role and to avoid the female role. But for the boy, this inhibition, this influence toward passivity and conformity, is antithetical to the role behavior he seeks to achieve, whereas for the girl it is appropriate to the outcome she pursues in her own behavioral development. The non-permissively treated boy may *try harder* to approximate the male role, but there are already two strikes against him: he is inhibited in his performance by his parents' non-permissiveness, and he is presented continuously with parental behavior that distorts his own conception of what constitutes male role behavior. And the distortion is in the direction of passivity and inhibition— i.e., femininity.

The fact that a high degree of appropriate sex typing is associated with high activity and social interaction suggests that the confusion created by inappropriate rearing experiences (non-permissiveness for the boy and permissiveness for the girl) may produce some immaturity. There is evidence to support this notion. In both sexes there is a small negative correlation between high gender role score and the immature form of dependency (being near); for boys, the correlation is $-.36$, and for girls, $-.25$. Likewise, maturity as measured by the Behavior Maturity Scale is positively related to both masculinity ($.46$) and femininity ($.22$). Although only one of these four correlations is significant, all are in the direction that suggests an association of poor gender role achievement with immaturity.

Perhaps the argument can also explain why masculinity develops more slowly than femininity. Permissiveness and non-punitiveness are not only reinforcing but also non-guiding. The feminine girl receives constant correction of her behavior because of the parents' non-permissiveness, but the exploring, seeking, experimenting, risk-taking, masculine boy is allowed to go his own way, at least in matters of sex and aggression. As a result, he has more opportunity to pursue inappropriate behavior as well as to be reinforced in his appropriate behavior. This freedom is congruent with his role in the long run, but may provide difficulties of discrimination in the early stages.

Following Kohlberg's analysis, one might speculate on still another reason for the slower development of the boy. Since the mother is the chief caretaker in the years when the child's gender identity is being established, she may have more influence on the role definition than the father. It may be, for example, that the relatively higher sex and aggression anxiety she experiences as a woman becomes infused into her guidance of the boy toward appropriate male role behavior. If this occurs, the boy is unlikely to obtain role clarification as early as the girl, and the goal of his self-training will therefore continue relatively unclear. It is worth noting, in this connection, that the more masculine boys had high early separation from the mother, low demands for table manners, and lenient toilet training—all conditions conducive to a non-feminine influence by the mother in the boy's infancy. Likewise, the most masculine boys were those whose mothers, as well as fathers, showed permissiveness for sex and aggression and eschewed physical punishment. In other words, the mother's influence in early as well as late childhood is clearly in evidence.

In presenting this rather general interpretation of our data on gender role, we are under no illusion that we have accounted for all the sex-typed differences *between* boys and girls. We do suggest, however, that our reasoning gives a satisfactory explanation of the individual differences, *within* each sex, in the rate of gender role achievement.

Summary

The extent of the children's development of gender role was measured by an observer rating and by five assessment procedures (including one introduced into the mother-child interaction). Analyses of the intercorrelations among these measures, and of their correlations with frequency of occurrence of both parent dolls as agents and sex-typed adult work in doll play, led to the following generalizations:

1. The intercorrelations among the girls' assessment measures are higher than those of the boys, as was the case with the measures of dependency and adult role.

2. On the doll-play measures, the boys' intercorrelations are higher, and the patterns of relationship suggest that the use of adult dolls as agents is a feminine quality for boys.

3. The girls discriminated between sex roles of adults better than the boys; whereas the use of *either* adult doll was an indicator of poor sex typing in boys, only the use of the father doll had that diagnostic value in girls.

The major child-rearing correlates of gender role are the clusters of parental sex-permissiveness scales and punishment for aggression. A closed, anxious, non-permissive attitude on the part of either or both parents was conducive to femininity in both sexes of children, as were the use of physical punishment and severe control of aggression. A hypothesis was proposed that permissiveness encourages the development of the active, adventurous, free-ranging quality of behavior that characterizes the male role, and that punitiveness creates pressure toward the more passive and conforming behavior that typifies the female role.

6. *Conscience*

As a concept, conscience lacks the operational precision of some of the other presumed consequents of the identification processes. The term, so ancient in moral dogma, is more of a chapter heading than a technical variable. In the present context we use it to refer generally to those qualities of children's behavior represented by the control of impulse and the reactions to loss of such control. In the research literature, these aspects of behavior are commonly referred to as resistance to temptation and feelings of fear, shame, or guilt concerning deviation (or anticipated deviation) from right and proper conduct.

In its customary usage, conscience has a structural connotation; it is a part of the mind that controls other parts, directing behavior in ways that are mainly inhibiting and self-punishing. "Thus conscience does make cowards of us all. . . ." When Freud systematized his structural conceptions, the functions of conscience were assigned to a superego. Although the homunculoid quality of the entity was retained, Freud's statements clearly define the superego's functions as those of internalized parental control. Very early (1914, p. 53), he said "The institution of conscience was at bottom an embodiment, first of parental criticism, and subsequently of that of society."

According to Freud's theory, identification is the process by which parental standards and punitiveness are internalized—primary (anaclitic) identification in the earliest years, and later, especially in the boy, defensive identification. By both mechanisms, the punitiveness of the parents is converted by the child into self-punishment, and the child learns to behave in ways suited to his parents' standards of conduct. Thus the anticipation of punishment—originally from the parents, later from the self—serves as the drive for developing resistance to the temptation to behave in ways antithetical to those standards. The successful avoidance of punishment reinforces the new behavior. Temptation cannot always be resisted, however; hence the self-punishment that ensues from deviation was included in the description of the superego's functions. In the initial stages of socialization, the child learns to expect retribution for his changeworthy behavior, and when he deviates he suffers fear. With increasing experience, and with more complex forms of punishment based on affronts to pride rather than physical pain or loss of love, the form of the emotional reaction to deviation comes to be shame; the fear is not of being physically hurt or rejected by the loving parents, but of having faults exposed to ridicule, of "losing face." Finally, with the fully developed superego, the anguish is in the form of true guilt and remorse involving loss of self-esteem, emotions which occur quite independently of the actual or anticipated reactions of others.

In addition to the feeling of distress following deviation—whether fear, shame, or guilt—there are likely to be various behavioral maneuvers designed to reduce them. Thus, the child may make amends or atone for the bad behavior; he may try to correct the outcome of his actions and eliminate the damage he may have done. Or he may seek to turn aside wrath through confession, a practice that would be self-defeating, of course, if the distress were from true guilt feelings occurring in the absence of a punitive agent! Or he may deny the deviation or conceal the fact that it has occurred at all. Beyond these normal responses of small children, Freud emphasized also various psychopathological reactions such as repression, projection, and depression, but we are less concerned in the present study with these psychodynamic elaborations than with the more typical overt methods of post-deviation conduct.

This theory, from which our own reasoning and research started, gives rise at once to the same questions we dealt with in each of the preceding chapters. The first question is whether or not the set of behaviors described does in fact exist as a unit. An implication of identification theory is that measures of resistance to temptation and guilt reaction to deviation should be positively correlated with one another. The child most likely to experience shame or remorse following deviation should be the one least likely to deviate at all, i.e., to give in to temptation.

An obvious prior question is whether there are positive relationships among different measures of resistance to temptation, or among measures of guilt.

A second main question has to do with the constellation of behaviors that would be expected to result from identification. Resistance to temptation is a form of impulse control, an inhibition of infantile changeworthy behavior. The child who is highly resistant should also be low on antisocial aggression, low on the immature and passive forms of dependency, and well along the road toward masculinity or femininity. Judging from what we have already learned of the feminine (or at least non-masculine) quality of certain "mature" behaviors, however, we should expect some disparity between the sexes: girls who show high resistance to temptation should also display high prosocial aggression, positive attention seeking, adult role behavior, and tattling, but low injury to objects; boys who are resistant, on the other hand, should eschew the feminine forms of behavior, and be maturely and masculinely aggressive.

The exact nature of this masculine aggression in four-year-old boys is not easily predictable from the theory. As we have noted (in Chapter 1, and further in Chapter 5), defensive identification promotes some absorption of feminine qualities as well as masculine qualities. The boy's love for the father, coupled with the denial of his hostility toward the father, leads the boy to adopt the mother's role. To what extent such a feminine identification would lead to higher prosocial (rather than anti-social) aggression is difficult to estimate.

Perhaps the theory should not be pushed to such precision. Freud was attempting to systematize his observations in terms of a set of intra-psychic processes, not to establish a testable theory of antecedent-consequent relations in which overtly experienced events brought about by parents are viewed as the determinants of overt behavior of children. There is, in fact, real question how far we are justified in going in any effort to translate the intra-psychic constructs into behavioral propositions.

This translation problem becomes even more acute with respect to the child-rearing correlates of conscience, which constitute our third main problem. The theory of anaclitic identification suggests that for both sexes there should be a positive relation between resistance to temptation and the four types of parent variables we have discussed previously. For boys, however, the theory of defensive identification suggests, in addition, a correlation of conscience measures with paternal punitiveness and hostility toward the son, and indications in either the parents' behavior or the boy's of conflict concerning sexuality. Freud's theoretical analysis was couched in terms of the redirection of libidinal energy, however, and he was concerned more with the general question of how boys cope with their feelings toward their fathers, than with the specific question of how the individual experiences of individual boys create variations in amount and type of aggressive conduct.

The testing of the first hypothesis, which concerns the trait structure of resistance to temptation, is relatively easy. Hartshorne and May's classical studies of honesty and deceit (1928) provide the methodological pattern, namely, the presentation of several somewhat similar temptation situations and the correlation of the children's scores on resistance. In school-age children, Hartshorne and May found low positive correlations among a number of assessment measures, and Burton (1963) concluded, after a re-analysis of the data, that the findings provided support for the conception of honesty as a trait. We have followed the same general procedure in our measurement of resistance to temptation; i.e., we have constructed several similar assessment situations and have determined the intercorrelations among the children's resistance scores.

Testing the predicted association of guilt with resistance is more difficult because of the measurement problems presented by the guilt concept. Guilt is an emotional response that cannot be recognized readily by an observer. Although we have been able to differentiate guilt from fear theoretically, the distinction is not at all clear in overt behavior. The only direct behavioral expression of guilt is in self-recrimination or self-punishment, and although test devices have been constructed for the measurement of such attitudes in older children, we have found none suitable for preschool-aged youngsters. Actual self-punishment is rare in most children of this age, and the degree of emotional upset overtly expressed after wrongdoing can be indicative of either fear or guilt. Even the various techniques for reducing guilt feelings are equally usable for avoiding parental punishment; confession and atonement, for example, may be used to ward off criticism.

Because of the ambiguity of such behavioral indices, we have used several types of measure in the hope that the interrelations among them, and the relations between them and such other measured variables as aggression and dependency, would reveal some of the many facets of post-deviation feelings and behavior that are commonly combined in the single term *guilt*.

The testing of the second main hypothesis, which concerns the relation of guilt and resistance to temptation to other forms of child behavior, is difficult in proportion to the problems that arise in the interpretation of the guilt measures. Testing the final set of hypotheses, which concern child-rearing correlates of the conscience measures, involves the added difficulty that the theory of defensive identification provides a much less well-defined set of predictions than the theory of primary identification. Though we can examine the data for presence or absence of the few predicted relations, an understanding of the nature of young children's conscience development will profit more from a frankly inductive inquiry.

Measurement of Conscience

Neither type of conscience behavior was directly measurable in the open play situation of the nursery school. The atmosphere of the school was relatively permissive, and the restrictions placed on the children were too few for "temptation" requiring "resistance" to occur frequently. By the same token, there were few opportunities for teachers or researchers to observe instances of "deviation," and hence little opportunity to judge deviation reactions. Some instances of negative attention seeking and aggression might well be considered deviations, and these were observable enough. On the other hand, the children no doubt varied in the extent of their familiarity with the customs of the school, their knowledge of what was right and wrong, and their possession of sufficient wit and experience to perform the wrong things out of sight of adults. Such observations as might have been made in the open nursery school would have been contaminated by these irrelevant sources of variance.

To secure measures of either type of behavior, some circumvention of the customary conditions of research observation was necessary. Three procedures were used. One made use of the parents, whose long, continuing observation of their children in the home gave them (we hoped) a better opportunity for evaluating the extent of development of the more subtle aspects of conscience behavior. The needed information was obtained during the interviews.

The second type of measure was a group of artificially created assessment situations in which certain needed conditions for observation and measurement could be established. For comparison among children, it was necessary to provide temptations that would have relatively uniform values for all the children, and would provide equal opportunities for yielding. Furthermore, so that tests of resistance might be as nearly as possible tests of internalized self-control, rather than fear of punishment for disobedience, it was necessary to present temptation situations that gave the children the impression there was little or no risk of getting caught for wrongdoing. Five assessment situations were designed for the measurement of resistance to temptation, and two for the measurement of reactions to forced deviation; one situation was used for both these purposes, and one (quoting rules) was also used for adult role behavior measurement, as described in Chapter 3.

The third procedure for securing conscience measures was a fantasy method. Since guilt is detectable mainly in terms of feelings, a device was needed that would induce children to express freely their feelings after deviation. The real-life assessment situations were unsuitable for this purpose, of course, since denial is one of the main behavioral reactions to deviation and is in direct opposition to the expression of feelings. A device was required, rather, that would evoke a mild and fantasy-level feeling of having deviated, and for which the appropriate response to the situation would be to describe the ensuing behavior and feelings. For this purpose, deviation doll play was used, a procedure that involves presenting a child with a story that stops incomplete at the point a child doll commits a misdeed. The child subject is then instructed to complete the story, telling "what happens next."

Parent-Interview Measures

Both the father and the mother were queried about their child's conduct, his trustworthiness, and his reactions after doing something wrong. (See Appendix A: mother interview, questions 21, 27, and 39; father interview, questions 16 and 30.) Three scales rated the child's tendency to confess and his degree of conscience development. The first two, rated separately from the two parents' interviews, estimate the extent of confession of wrongdoing to the father and to the mother. These two scales (variables 87 and 88) have been retained as correlates of other child-behavior measures, but have not been used otherwise.

Signs of conscience (89). The third scale is a pooled rating from both interviews, measuring the extent to which the child showed certain signs of conscience in his relations with his parents. The signs include confessing, acting guilty, expressing awareness of having done wrong after misbehavior, and admitting the impropriety rather than denying it. Hiding or other signs of fear were considered evidence of a low degree of conscience development, and atonement and making reparations were interpreted as indicating a high degree. Where the interview response suggested that confession or "fixing up" could be understood as an effort to avoid punishment, these behaviors were interpreted as evidence of low conscience development.

The conscience scale is the same as that used in the study *Patterns of Child Rearing* (variable III, 34). It is a five-point scale, ranging from "5. High guilt. Feels miserable when naughty; always confesses; never denies; shows strong need for forgiveness" to "1. No evidence of guilt. Hides, denies, doesn't seem unhappy when naughty; may try to shift the blame, repeat the act, or report the occurrence with no evident feeling of discomfort." As is apparent in the preceding paragraph, we were attempting to make a distinction between fear and guilt, i.e., between reactions to *external stimuli* that demand conformity and propriety and reactions to *internal standards* serving the same function.

The inter-rater agreement for this conscience scale is satisfactory; the mean of the agreements on the father and mother scales, from which the pooled rating was calculated, is 94 per cent by the Type III criterion (see Appendix B).

Resistance to Temptation (RTT)

Resistance to temptation was assessed on four occasions, producing six separate measures. Three of the four situations were set up in Room A (see Chapter 1); the fourth (the hamster situation) was set up in Room B. All but the QuRu situation were conducted by male researchers. The details of procedure, scoring, and reliability are given in Appendix H.

Candy temptation (205). The child is taken to a room by the experimenter, who invites him to play a "very special game." When they enter the room, E at once notices a large plate of candies on a table. He calls this to S's attention, making clear that the candy does not belong to "us," and "we" must not touch it. E then takes S into a corner and shows him three circles painted on the floor; they are to be used for the special game of "ring toss." At this juncture, E suddenly remembers a telephone call he has to make and tells S to wait and to play with a scattering of junk toys that lie in a box beside a chair until E returns. E leaves and the child remains alone for eight minutes. When E returns, he confesses that he has forgotten the game but will bring it with him in a few days and then they can play. RTT is measured by the degree of transgression S displays during the eight minutes.

Ring-toss game (206). A few days later E takes S to the same room again for the promised game. The candy has been replaced by a fine toy appropriate to the sex of the child. E lets S play with the toy for a few moments and then draws him away to play the "special game" of ring toss. The rules require the child to stand behind a chair at some distance from the rings. Suddenly E remembers *another* telephone call he has to make, and as he leaves the room (for eight minutes) he emphasizes the rule about standing behind the chair to throw the rings, and makes playing with the fabulous toy contingent on S's getting the rings in the circle. Two measures of RTT are obtained, one from the ring toss and one from the toy. The ring-toss resistance measure is based on the degree to which the rules for the game are obeyed.

Toy temptation (207). The score for RTT with respect to the toy is based on a scale similar to that for the candy episode, a scale relating to degree of transgression, i.e., the extent to which the child plays with the toy while E is out of the room.

Quoting rules situation (208). The QuRu assessment was described in Chapter 3. It consists of the child's being brought into a room and left there for two minutes with strict instructions not to play with the new toys that someone has left there. Then a younger stooge is sent into the room with permission to play with the toys. For the adult role measurement we were interested in the subject's techniques of control over the stooge, but for RTT a judgment was made of how strongly the subject was able to resist playing with the toys himself. There are five points in the little drama that are easily noted, and the RTT score is based on how soon and how extensively the child yields to temptation.

Hamster: latency of response (209) *and seriousness of response* (210). These two RTT measures were obtained in the disappearing hamster situation (which is described in the following paragraphs since it was designed mainly to permit measurement of guilt reactions to deviation). As will be seen, the child is left alone for twenty minutes, again in the presence of very tempting distractions, and with a tiresome duty to perform that does not permit him to respond to temptation. The latency measure is based on the number of minutes that pass before the child leaves his assigned duty, and the seriousness measure is based on the degree of completeness with which he gives up the duty.

RTT: total standard score (211). The scores for the six measures just described were converted to standard scores, which were then summed to provide an overall measure of a child's resistance to temptation.

Reactions to Deviation: Hamster and Red Light

Two assessment situations were created for measuring emotional up-set, atonement (fixing), confession, and denial as responses to forced transgression of duties or rules laid down by an adult. Both episodes were designed to create situations in which the child is in conflict be-tween obeying the strictures established by the adult researcher and disobeying them in order to gain some personal goal. In the case of the disappearing hamster, the personal goal is multiple—to get out of the painful duty imposed by the adult, and to satisfy the need to play with, examine, or control the other elements in the environment. In the case of the red light situation, stimulation is given the child to win at a game that is difficult; winning can occur only if the child breaks the rules of the game.

In both situations, the temptation was meant to be sufficiently severe that transgression would occur in all cases. This goal was achieved in the red light episode, but four of our forty subjects (one boy and three girls) maintained their self-control so effectively in the hamster episode that we were unable to secure measures of response to deviation.

Two measures of response to deviation were obtained from the ham-ster episode, two from the red light situation. The details of scoring, to-gether with a more complete description of both the assessment proce-dures and the measurement techniques, are given in Appendix I. The hamster situation was conducted by a male researcher, the red light situ-ation by a female researcher; both researchers were well known by all the children. The red light situation used Room A; the hamster situation used Room B, because of the desirability for direct access to both the main nursery school rooms and the play yard. The following paragraphs give brief descriptions of the two assessment episodes, and after each are listed the variables for which measures were obtained.

The Case of the Disappearing Hamster

The experimenter explains to the child that he is doing some work in the back of the nursery school and needs some help. When the child agrees, E takes him to a room where there are several exciting toys, a Bobo doll (a life-size, punchable, self-righting manikin), and a record player on a low table. All these things are on the far side of the room, away from the mirror. S is allowed to play with the toys briefly, just long enough to discover how interesting they are, whereupon E explains that he is building the lid of a cage for a pet hamster. The cage, a solid box with a metal floor, is in the corner of the room just under the mirror. E says the hamster keeps getting out of the cage, and please will S stand there, with a rolled-up magazine, and keep him in the cage until E can go outside and finish the lid? S agrees, of course, and E departs through the door into the yard—after starting the record player with an invigorating Sousa march that will finish shortly after he leaves the room.

Thus, S is faced with the responsibility of guarding the hamster for an unknown length of time (actually, twenty minutes) while the record finishes and grinds continuously and the entrancing toys furnish a constant temptation to leave his post. When the temptation becomes too great (and it did, for all but three of the girls and one boy), S begins to drift away from the cage. As soon as his attention is pretty completely withdrawn, the observer behind the mirror releases a catch and the hinged false floor of the cage drops down and spills the hamster into a padded compartment below. The observer then quickly releases his pressure on the floor, allowing it to spring back into place. It makes a click as it closes. When S hears this sound, he returns to the cage only to discover the hamster missing. (All of our subjects who drifted heard the click and responded in this manner.)

The children can be expected to react in various ways (as ours did). If S flees to the nursery school, E is alerted by the observer and goes after him, reassuring him and saying that the hamster has been quickly caught; S is taken back to the room to see for himself and to play with the toys. If S goes after E to tell him what happened, E returns to the room at once and together they search through some crumpled newspapers and cartons near the cage. E has an extra hamster in his pocket which he slips into the papers near S, who quickly discovers it. If S stays in the room after the disappearance, E waits eight minutes before returning, and then asks a series of standard questions that permit an estimate of the child's willingness to confess.

The recording of the data for both the resistance to temptation measures and the reaction to deviation measures was all done by the observer behind the mirror. The two RTT measures have already been described; they consisted of a time measure (how long before the child yielded) and a seriousness measure (how far away from the cage he went). The data relevant to deviation reactions were obtained entirely during the time following the disappearance of the hamster. Thirteen of the fifteen measures obtained (see Appendix I) were indicators of the child's responses to deviation, but only two have been used in their original form; others were used in the formation of summary scores for emotional upset, confession, and fixing, and will be described following the description of the red light assessment procedure.

Behavioral evidence of internal conflict (227). This scale was based on the amount of hesitation and apparent concern shown by the child toward deviation. A longer build-up before yielding was interpreted as a sign of greater conflict and hence stronger resistance (or conscience).

Strength of reaction to deviation (228). This scale was based on the speed and vigor of both the emotional reaction to the click and the return to the cage. The quicker and more vigorous reactions were interpreted as showing greater concern and stronger conscience.

The Red Light Situation

The researcher invites the child to go to a room to see an especially nice toy which he may play with if he can win at playing a new game that E will show him. The toy is a dog whose tail is the key to a wind-up music box. The game is a bowling game. Four pins are set up in one of the ring-toss circles in the corner of the room. A few feet away, a red ribbon is stretched from the wall to a standard, at a height above S's head. Just behind the ribbon there are three small chairs in a row, parallel to the ribbon. S's task is to stand between the chairs and the overhead ribbon and roll the ball to knock down the pins. The arrangement is very awkward and confining, and makes almost impossible the child's attempt to avoid reaching out beyond the ribbon when rolling the ball. Beside the pins there is an awesome box with a red light on it and a buzzer inside. S is told the "bowling machine" will count the score. He is also told that if he breaks the rule about staying behind the ribbon, the light will go on and the buzzer will sound. S is given a sample of the machine's reaction by E, who bowls from in front of the ribbon. S is also allowed to see how E turns off the machine (i.e., the buzzer and red light) with a switch. (All this rigmarole is governed by the observer behind the mirror, of course.)

When S has clearly understood the rules, E leaves the room; the machine will count the score. The alert observer then waits until S very obviously breaks the rules in some way, and then switches on the machine. If S flees the room, E, who is just outside, cajoles him into returning, asks certain standard questions to elicit confession, and then allows

S to play with the toy dog. If S does not flee, E enters the room after two minutes, and the same procedure is followed.

Nine scales were used for scoring reactions to deviation. Six of these have been used in their original form, and the six and some of the others were combined with certain hamster measures to form the summary measures of upset, confession, and fixing. The six scales are as follows:

Extent of rule following (229).

Extent of efforts to hide the deviation (by turning off the red light) (230).

Tension following deviation (rule breaking and/or hiding the deviation) (231).

Intensity of confession (232).

Spontaneity of confession (233).

Degree of denial of deviation (234).

Summary Scores

In order to secure scores based on both assessment situations, three summary scores were constructed by adding the standard scores of certain scales. The original scales used for this purpose are given in Appendix I.

Emotional upset (235). This score was obtained by adding the standard scores for (vii, 11) and 231. The former is a measure of emotional upset expressed by the child after the disappearance of the hamster, and the latter measures amount of tension after rule breaking in the red light situation.

Confession (236). This score was obtained by adding the standard scores for (vii, 14) and 232, and then subtracting those for 234. The first of these components is a measure of the degree of self-responsibility and self-blame expressed in the hamster confessions; the second measures the intensity of confession in the red light situation; and the subtracted component is the measure of denial of responsibility in the red light situation.

Fixing (237). This score was obtained by adding the standard scores for (vii, 10 and 17) and 230. These are the measures, respectively, for the extent and effectiveness of the child's original search for the missing hamster, the degree to which he participated in the search with the experimenter present, and the extent he hid the red light deviation by turning off the light and buzzer.

Deviation Doll Play

To obtain the deviation doll-play measures, we presented the child with the same doll house and dolls used in the two sessions of permissive doll play. The child was reminded of the procedure, but this time was told the experimenter would start some stories and he could finish them. The six stories are ones that represent common deviations, well understood by four-year-old children. They include knocking over a floor lamp with a ball, spilling juice at the table, grabbing the baby's toy away from her, getting up to play again after being put to bed, stealing cookies, and spilling father's nail box. Each story is acted out by the experimenter to the point of deviation. The experimenter then hands the child doll to the subject and asks him to show what happens next. The details of the procedure and scoring are given in Appendix F, and the nineteen scoring categories and their definitions need not be repeated here.

Organization of Conscience

Sex Differences

The pooled rating of conscience obtained from the parent interviews does not differentiate the sexes significantly; what difference there is favors the girls (see Table 29). The direction of the difference, but not the significance of its size, replicates the finding with the same scale reported in *Patterns of Child Rearing*, in which the difference in means was at the level $p = .03$. There are two differences between the present study and the previous one that may have a bearing on the comparison of results: the *Patterns* ratings were obtained from mother interviews only, and the children in that study were a year older than this group.

Only one of the six assessment measures of resistance to temptation shows a significant sex difference: the girls were more resistant in the QuRu situation. There is a slight difference favoring the girls on all five other measures, however, and the cumulative effect of these non-significant differences is evident in the highly significant difference on the total standard score for RTT. This is as predicted by the primary identification theory.

What differences there are on the red light measures also favor the girls, with tension following deviation showing the greatest difference. When behavior in both the hamster and red light situations is combined into the three summary scales, the emotional upset measure (which is based partly on the tension measure) shows a significant difference in

TABLE 29

Conscience Measures: Means, Standard Deviations, Significance of Sex
Differences, and Correlations with Age

*(Values for deviation doll-play measures are actual per cents; others are ratings.
An asterisk on the p-value indicates girls greater than boys.)*

Conscience Measures	Var. No.	Boys Mean	S.D.	Girls Mean	S.D.	p (2-tail)	r with age Boys	Girls
Parent Interviews								
Signs of conscience: pooled .	89	4.52	1.37	4.84	1.14	n.s.*	39	17
Assessment: RTT								
Candy temptation	205	2.52	1.34	2.86	1.10	n.s.*	22	−03
Ring-toss game	206	5.86	2.34	5.95	1.76	n.s.*	01	−59
Toy temptation	207	2.38	1.40	2.50	1.21	n.s.*	48	07
Quoting rules situation . .	208	2.57	1.22	3.42	1.35	.05*	37	−14
Hamster: response latency .	209	4.00	2.84	4.44	3.18	n.s.*	25	−07
Hamster: response seriousness	210	2.30	1.35	2.50	1.54	n.s.*	20	−23
Total standard score . . .	211	12.68	3.89	14.64	4.44	< .001*	39	−23
Assessment: Hamster								
Internal conflict	227	2.05	1.13	2.21	1.06	n.s.*	−23	09
Reaction to deviation . . .	228	3.52	1.43	3.21	1.64	n.s.	05	−13
Assessment: Red Light								
Rule following	229	2.76	1.02	2.84	1.23	n.s.*	35	62
Hiding the deviation . . .	230	3.00	1.27	2.68	1.17	n.s.	08	06
Tension following deviation	231	3.57	1.76	5.21	2.04	< .02*	−21	−50
Intensity of confession . .	232	1.86	1.17	2.53	1.14	< .10*	17	−17
Spontaneity of confession .	233	2.00	1.23	2.53	1.04	n.s.	26	−05
Denial of deviation	234	3.29	1.03	3.11	.64	n.s.	−31	27
Combined scores: Hamster and Red Light								
Emotional upset	235	3.24	2.24	5.79	2.19	< .01*	−06	−13
Confession	236	4.05	2.15	4.89	1.80	n.s.*	18	−17
Fixing	237	6.05	2.10	5.05	1.47	.10	15	44
Deviation Doll Play								
Caught: other	314	22.41	11.18	16.11	8.19	< .10	35	−01
Verbal punishment	318	4.72	5.22	7.91	5.23	< .10*	−26	52
Physical punishment . . .	319	23.55	11.90	9.15	8.70	< .001	40	−16
Isolation	320	3.16	5.80	7.64	6.05	< .05*	−01	26

favor of the girls. The confession measure shows a slight but non-significant difference in the same direction, and the fixing measure favors the
boys slightly. It is interesting to note that the more unacceptable (to
parents) kinds of reactions to deviation are slightly more frequent in the
boys; these measures include hiding and denial in the red light situation,
as well as fixing.

Of the nineteen categories of story completion scored in the deviation doll play, only four show sex differences worth reporting. These four have been listed in Table 29. The boys' emphases on getting caught by authority and on physical punishment, and the girls' on verbal punishment and isolation, reflect the customary finding (e.g., Bach, 1945). Only two other response categories were exhibited by a majority of the children—redefinition minus (312) and gets away with it (321)—and neither shows a sex difference.

In general, then, the sex differences in conscience behavior were not great; the girls showed more resistance to temptation and more emotional disturbance following deviation, and boys displayed more antisocial reactions to deviation.

Age Differences

The correlations of the various conscience measures with age, as given in Table 29, are mainly non-significant, though there are certain consistencies of direction worth noting. In general, the older boys appear to have been more resistant to temptation, whereas the younger girls were a little more so. The r's between age and the RTT summary score are appropriately representative. A comparison of the mean RTT score for the older and younger halves of each sex group, however, shows that the overall sex difference is provided by the younger children; the older boys and girls have almost identical mean scores, whereas the younger boys were substantially less resistant than the other three subgroups.

In the red light situation, there was a fairly strong tendency for the older children to follow the rules more closely, a difference that may well have derived from their greater physical and mental maturity, as well as from their greater general obedience to adult requests. The older children also showed less tension after they had deviated. The direction of the other very modest differences suggests an increasing tendency with age for the girls to react with fixing and denial.

In the deviation doll play, the sex-typical responses were stronger with age. For boys, verbal punishment decreased and physical punishment increased, whereas for girls the opposite trends appeared.

In general, then, within the eighteen-month age range of our group, the variations of conscience with age were not very great, though there was a tendency for the older boys to reach a degree of resistance to temptation equivalent to that of the girls, and for both sexes to become less disturbed by the experience of deviation and more typical of their own gender roles in the fantasy reactions to deviation.

Relations among RTT Measures

Our measures of resistance to temptation are the six obtained from the four assessment situations—candy, ring toss plus toy, QuRu, and hamster. Our expectations, both from a theoretical standpoint and from the Hartshorne and May (1928) findings, were that these measures would show moderate but not large intercorrelations. Hartshorne and May concluded that situational determinants contributed strongly to response variance in moral behavior tests. In order to reduce the situational contribution in the present research, we tried to make the circumstances as similar as possible within the limits of our facilities and personnel. The same male experimenter administered all the assessments except QuRu. All were performed in the same physical setting (Room A) except the hamster situation (Room B). In each instance, the situation was structured so that there was a specific rule, prohibition, or responsibility given to the child. All observations were made by a concealed observer, and no adult was ever present at the time of temptation. All of these similarities should have served to maximize the correlations among the measures.

On the other hand, there were certain clear differences among the situations that should have introduced idiosyncratic sources of variance and thus lowered the correlations. The QuRu, candy, and toy episodes all involved a specific prohibition against playing with a tempting object, but in QuRu there was the additional variable of another child's presence. In the ring-toss part of the toy game there was a set of rules to be followed, and the prohibition was breaking the rules rather than approaching an object. Furthermore, the ring toss introduced the achievement motive—a motive quite different from those aroused by the other situations. Finally, the hamster episode appealed to the child to assume a responsibility; he was not specifically prohibited from playing with the toys across the room, but to do so was to fail in the responsibility.

The net results of the similarities and differences are presented in Table 30, which lists the correlations among the six RTT measures separately by sex of child. The median of the fifteen r's is .28 for the girls, and .24 for the boys. Five of the measures were more highly correlated with one another than these figures suggest, however; if the candy measure is disregarded, the girls' median of the remaining ten r's is .44, and the boys' is .35.

TABLE 30

Resistance to Temptation: Correlations among the Six Assessment Measures

(Girls above the diagonal, boys below)

RTT Measures	Var. No.	Variable Number						
		205	206	207	208	209	210	211
Candy temptation	205	*	03	13	26	04	−02	40
Ring-toss game	206	13	*	23	45	53	72	72
Toy temptation	207	44	08	*	03	28	29	45
Quoting rules	208	20	35	39	*	44	48	76
Hamster: latency of response . . .	209	10	20	31	16	*	76	73
Hamster: seriousness of response . .	210	−09	35	24	40	55	*	78
Total standard score	211	50	61	66	65	61	63	*

Although only six of the 30 coefficients reach the .05 level of significance, the differences of the medians from zero are highly significant, and the consistency of the positive relationship suggests that we are justified in using the summary score as a measure of a moderately stable quality of resistance to temptation.

Relations among Reactions to Deviation

The two deviation assessment situations differed somewhat in the nature of the moral sanctions invoked. In the red light episode, the child's motive was to gain a prize, and the prohibition was breaking the rules of the game by which the prize could be won. In the hamster situation, the child's motive to be helpful and responsible to an adult was aroused, and the prohibition of playing with the entrancing toys was entirely implicit. The range and quality of the reactions to these two episodes were quite different. Some of the scales described in Appendix I produced truncated distributions that do not permit correlational analysis, and four of the children steadfastly avoided the hamster deviation; since three of these were girls, certain of the scales are ratable for only sixteen girls and twenty boys. An examination of all the possible scatter plots among the post-deviation measures obtained from the two assessment situations led to a decision to construct the three previously mentioned summary measures—emotional upset, confession, and fixing—in order to secure measures deriving from both situations.

This combining was done entirely on a rational basis, not on the strength of any internal evidence of consistency between the responses to the two episodes. With a single exception, the relations between the comparable measures obtained separately from the two episodes are of negligible size. The exception is the three scales which compose the fixing measure for boys, which intercorrelate .42, .49, and .58; two of the scales are from the hamster situation and the third is from the red light. No relationship between the emotional upset or confession measures secured in the two situations is appreciably greater than zero.

There is considerable question just what significance may obtain from summary scores created from uncorrelated measures. Perhaps situational determinants in different settings can mask small consistencies in behavior, but there is no guarantee of this. The procedure we have followed —the only one known to us under these conditions—is to use the summary scores in our analysis, allowing their effectiveness or ineffectiveness in generating meaningful relationships with other child-behavior or parent measures to determine whether they are appropriate or not.

The intercorrelations among the three summary reaction-to-deviation scores are presented in Table 31, along with those for the RTT summary score and the parent-interview measure of conscience. Only two of the girls' correlations are of significant size and none of the boys' are. There is some difference in the patterning of the relationships, however, which should be noted in preparation for later discussion of child-rearing antecedents. In both sexes, fixing appears to have been antithetical to resistance and to emotional upset. One might infer that a child who is able to secure some gratification by yielding to temptation is able also to do something reparative about his wrongdoing. Reciprocally, the child who has discovered how to ward off criticism by reparative methods might thus find it safe (and emotionally tolerable) to risk the yielding. (It

TABLE 31

Reactions to Deviation: Correlations among the Three Summary Scores for Emotional Upset, Confession, and Fixing, the Summary RTT Score, and the Parent-Interview Rating of Conscience

(Girls above the diagonal, boys below)

Reaction-to-Deviation Measures	Var. No.	Variable Number				
		89	211	235	236	237
Interview						
Signs of conscience: pooled	89	°	−06	45	12	−06
Assessment						
Total standard score (RTT)	211	18	°	06	−30	−72
Emotional upset, summary score . . .	235	−06	37	°	31	−29
Confession, summary score	236	−27	23	38	°	−08
Fixing, summary score	237	−31	−28	−25	31	°

must be recognized that fixing *can* be a product of *either* internalized guilt or fear of social consequences.) The positive correlation between fixing and age, in the girls, is certainly suggestive that maturity consists in part in knowing how to handle the situation adaptively once the "mistake" has been made.

There is some indication that confession may serve the same function for girls, though the negative correlation with RTT is much smaller, and there is a positive relation between confession and emotional upset. It looks perhaps as if confession may be an intermediate step between actual resistance and the very practical response of fixing. The little girls who yielded but were nervous about it confessed afterward rather than repair the damage.

This interpretation cannot account for the boys' intercorrelations, however, for their confession is positively related to both resistance and fixing. The correlations are not significant in size, but their direction suggests the possibility that, for boys, confession is linked more tightly to the inhibition of impulse—i.e., is more a part of the self-control system—than it is in girls, who would seem to use it as a post-deviation adaptive response. The positive relation between confession and fixing, in boys, may represent simply an earlier stage of conscience development, in which confession remains linked with resistance and fixing has not yet become as completely free of its relation to resistance as it has in the girls. An alternative interpretation might be that these boys were *farther along* in the development of a unitary conscience that combines resistance, emotional upset, confession, and fixing into a single structure, while the girls were still dealing practically with the effects of their deviation.

Curiously enough, the first interpretation would be appropriate to a theory of primary identification and the second to a theory of defensive identification. The slower development in boys is predicted from the anaclitic theory; the gradual freeing of the child at a later stage, with development of realistic discrimination between manipulative reparations and rigid resistance to temptation would not stem from that theory, but would be consonant with the general principle of behavioral differentiation. The defensive theory would predict that as the boy works through his Oedipus problem, he will form a more rigid and unitary conscience (superego); this would be reflected in the array of positive correlations obtained here. Further light will be cast on these alternative theoretical positions when we examine the child-rearing correlates of the various conscience measures.

Relations among Deviation Doll-Play Measures

An exhaustive analysis of all nineteen categories of the deviation doll-play responses has been made by Burke (1961), but is not needed for present purposes, since our main interest is in those fantasy categories that have parallels in measures drawn from the assessment situations. The chief question is whether the fantasy and reality measures were measuring the same behavior qualities.

Of the nineteen categories, only four occurred with sufficient frequency among the boys, and six among the girls, to provide distributions legitimately subject to correlation. Their intercorrelations are given in Table 32. None of these is a parallel to any of the three summary scores from the assessment situations, of course, but because of their relevance to aggression and to resistance to temptation, their correlations with the summary scores, RTT, and age are given in Table 33.

The relationships among the categories are not large except in the self-evident instances. For example, getting caught, for both sexes, is negatively related to getting away with it. Likewise, getting way with it is negatively related to physical punishment. However, what is a little more interesting, for its sex-typicality, is that getting caught is strongly associated with physical punishment in boys but not in girls; the girls show positive (though non-significant) correlations between getting caught and both verbal punishment and isolation. These different punishment consequences of getting caught are the same categories that show sex differences in mean frequency (Table 29).

TABLE 32

Deviation Doll Play: Intercorrelations among Four Categories
for the Boys and Six for the Girls

(Girls above the diagonal, boys below)

Doll-Play Measures	Var. No.	Variable Numbers					
		312	314	318	319	320	321
Redefinition minus	312	*	−29	40	−32	−23	27
Caught: other	314	−10	*	17	−19	28	−20
Verbal punishment	318			*	09	03	−41
Physical punishment	319	−38	60		*	22	−68
Isolation	320					*	−54
Gets away with it	321	06	−54		−60		*

TABLE 33

Deviation Doll Play: Correlations of Four Categories for the Boys and Six
for the Girls with Five Other Measures of Conscience and with Age

Doll-Play Measures	Var. No.	Interview (89)	RTT (211)	Emotional Upset (235)	Con-fession (236)	Fixing (237)	Age (1)
		GIRLS					
Redefinition minus	312	−03	−26	−10	−22	51	42
Caught: other	314	00	−30	32	13	−20	−01
Verbal punishment	318	08	−16	−23	−31	16	52
Physical punishment . . .	319	04	−08	−33	04	05	−16
Isolation	320	28	04	−07	22	−23	26
Gets away with it	321	−10	11	07	−29	05	−24
		BOYS					
Redefinition minus	312	−07	−23	15	29	17	−21
Caught: other	314	18	30	16	04	−41	35
Physical punishment . . .	319	20	37	−13	00	−39	40
Gets away with it	321	16	−28	−19	−36	19	−05

The relations of the doll-play categories to the assessment measures, as shown in Table 33, are about what might be expected by chance. Only one correlation coefficient reaches the .05 level of significance.

Seven other doll-play scales have been compared with the reality measures by another method. For each doll-play scale (e.g., confession), the boys and girls were each divided into two subgroups, those who *did* display the response at some time and those who *did not*. The mean age and mean ratings on each of the "real" conscience measures (parent interview, RTT, and the three assessment measures) for the pairs of subgroups were then calculated, and the significance of the differences between them determined by *t*-test.

The doll-play measures examined in this way were delay, confession, fixing, hiding, authority fixes, and, for boys only, verbal punishment and isolation. The results can be summarized very simply. Only *fixing* and *hiding* in doll-play are significantly related to any of the "real" measures; the boys who displayed each of these two forms of story completion also did a little more fixing in the hamster and red light assessment situations than the boys who failed to display them ($p = .10$). No such relation appears for the girls, and there is no relation between doll-play confession and assessment confession for either sex. With respect to *age*, the older boys displayed both confession ($p = .05$) and isolation ($p = .10$)

in doll-play more frequently, whereas the older girls displayed more delay ($p = .05$).

It would be hazardous, from these data, to try to reach firm conclusions concerning the relations of the so-called projective measures to responses obtained in socially realistic assessment situations. Certainly there is little evidence of a direct correspondence. The positive relation between the boys' fixing and hiding in doll-play and their fixing responses in the assessment situations is the only suggestion of a direct correspondence.

The nature of the data from deviation doll-play is largely responsible for the difficulty. The majority of the nineteen response categories occurred in too small a proportion of the children's protocols to permit their use in a correlational analysis. And when comparisons are made by the alternative method of examining subgroups showing presence or absence of a category, the number of cases in each is too small for secondary analysis by other statistical devices. Since the examination of child-rearing antecedents would run into even more severe limitations from the sample size, we regretfully discontinue consideration of these measures as indices of conscience.

Relations of Conscience to Other Child Measures

With the large number of child-behavior variables that have been discussed in previous chapters, the task of describing their relations to the conscience measures (as defined by Table 31) becomes too complex for simple listing of correlations area by area. Tables K7 through K10, in Appendix K, present the coefficients between the main conscience measures and the chief measures of dependency, adult role, aggression, and gender role. In the text here, we shall simply attempt to draw from the tables a picture of the children of each sex who showed high conscience, as our several measures define that term, without heavy reference to exact coefficients.

Boys

By both theories of identification, boys who show high resistance to temptation should be high on other forms of impulse control as well. They should be gentler and less violent, more adult in their role behavior, more mature, and more detached from their parents. The anaclitic theory suggests they should be more masculine as well, but the defensive theory provides a cautionary note to that proposition, suggesting that successful progress toward resolution of the Oedipus conflict should produce some adoption of the mother's (feminine) role. As will be seen, the evidence supports the latter expectation better than the former.

The boys who were high on RTT did indeed show a relatively high general impulse control. They were low on both negative and positive attention seeking in the nursery school, and they were low on bids for attention in the MCI when the mother was busy. Similarly, they tended to be (non-significantly) lower on the various BUO measures of aggression, especially injury to objects; in the MCI, they were non-aggressive toward the mother, and what aggression they did show tended to be indirect rather than direct. In doll play they were highly non-aggressive.

The evidence for an association of some degree of femininity with high RTT comes largely from the doll play. It will be recalled that the use of adult agents for routine activities was associated with several other feminine characteristics, as was the preferential use of the mother doll. The high-RTT boys used the adult agents frequently, especially in the second session, and there is clearly stronger correlation of RTT with use of the mother (rather than father) doll, and with performance of female (rather than male) adult-typed work.

In each of the above instances, the correlation is larger for second-session doll play than first, which suggests a tendency toward femininity that was somewhat suppressed and not fully exhibited under the more socially inhibiting circumstances of the first session. The fact that none of the gender role measures was related at all to RTT would seem to support the notion of suppression, as would the lack of correlation with both of the especially feminine forms of adult role behavior (real adult work and QuRu). It may be assumed that the first-session doll play corresponded more closely to the assessment situations and the normal environment of the nursery school than the second-session doll play did.

One other association may be relevant to this femininity point. There is a high negative relation between RTT and the parents' pooled interview rating of the extent to which the child imitated the parents, and a slight positive r with resemblance to mother but not with resemblance to father. Conceivably the parents may have sensed an underlying femininity in these high-RTT boys, and may therefore have denied the notion of imitation.

Further support for this possibility comes from an examination of the correlates of the imitation and resemblance scales with the three "guilt" measures. Although none of the latter correlates very highly with RTT, both confession and fixing also have high negative correlations with resemblance to father. Boys with a conscience did not look like daddy to daddy!

We have interpreted emotional upset (after deviation in the two assessment situations) as an indication of either guilt or fear of losing the love relationship with the parents or parent surrogates. There is only a little evidence bearing on this matter. The boys who showed high emotional upset tended to be higher on the aggression syndrome (in contrast with the boys high on RTT), but they were significantly *low* on directness of aggression toward the mother in the MCI. They were also low on bids for attention when the mother was attentive, which suggests that they were normally comfortable and non-demanding when the nurturant, affection-giving behavior of the mother was in evidence. The interpretation of emotional upset as a reflection of the fear of loss of love seems better supported than the autonomous, self-punishing, "guilt" interpretation.

When confession and fixing are considered in conjunction with emotional upset, the picture of high-conscience boys becomes better delineated. The overt forms of feminine gender role are no more correlated with them than with the two other measures, but again we find the positive relationships with the adult agents in the second session of doll play. Confession is associated with high prosocial aggression, which is scarcely surprising, for confession is a highly prosocial act. In general, fixing is associated with low aggression, as is resistance to temptation, which *is* surprising because fixing and RTT are somewhat negatively related to one another.

This fact brings us back to the question of whether emotional upset, confession, and fixing form a kind of dimension related to maturity. Although none of the three is at all related to chronological age, the sequence of correlations with the behavior maturity scale (170) is important to note: emotional upset ($r = +.20$), confession ($-.21$), and fixing ($-.45$). (As will be seen later, the girls' correlations fall in the opposite sequence.) In other words, the less mature boys tended to use confession and fixing, whereas the more mature boys tended to resist temptation longer (.20) and to show more emotional upset when they yielded.

These various relationships suggest that of the two alternative processes presented earlier, as possible explanations of the direction taken by the change in organization of conscience in this age group of boys, the one more supported by the data is that which proposes an *increase in unity of the various aspects of conscience.* This conclusion, like the finding of an apparent suppressed femininity in the high-conscience boys, is in accord with expectations based on the theory of defensive identification.

Girls

The expectations for the girls are similar to the boys' expectations that were based on anaclitic identification theory. That is, the girls with high conscience should be high also on dependency and adult role behavior, but effective impulse control should make them low on aggression, with preference given to the feminine and attenuated forms.

With respect to RTT, the expectations are moderately well fulfilled. The resistant girls were high on reassurance seeking, and low on negative attention seeking and both nursery school and doll-play aggression. They tended slightly to be indirect in their aggression toward the mother in the MCI, and to be self-aggressive in the MCI. They were also high on the use of adult agents for routine performance in doll play.

On the other hand, the expected correlations with adult role behavior in the nursery school and with mature feminine attention seeking do not appear, nor do any relations to the direct measures of femininity. It appears that these girls did have fairly high impulse control in the aggression sphere, and that they may have been somewhat insecure in their relations to others.

Unlike the boys, the girls show no correlations between RTT and emotional upset, and have clear negative correlations between RTT and the two manipulative responses to deviation in the assessment episodes, confession and fixing. It is unwarranted, therefore, to speak of "high-conscience" girls in any general sense, as we did with boys.

The dependency behaviors that correlate with emotional upset, however, are perhaps more of the sort to be expected than is the case with RTT. Again, reassurance seeking is strong, but so is positive attention seeking. Furthermore, there is a significant correlation with bids for attention, in the MCI, when the mother was attentive. The predictable positive relationships with several adult role measures also occur, including significant ones with giving facts and nurturance. One might hazard the guess that these girls who showed high emotional upset were quite insecure and much in need of nurturance and affection.

On the other hand, they tended to be fairly aggressive in the nursery school, especially in antisocial ways, and they showed little self-aggression in the MCI. By and large, one could not characterize them as having much impulse control, with respect to either dependency or aggression, and their low use of adult dolls in doll play suggests a lack of mature femininity.

As was suggested earlier, confession and fixing in girls appear to be purely manipulative ways of resolving difficulties arising from wrongdoing. Neither category of response is related significantly to any dependency, adult role, or gender role measures. The girls who used fixing, however, were high on doll-play aggression at both sessions, and were low on injury to objects, the masculine form of aggression in the nursery school.

If we consider RTT and emotional upset as two unrelated aspects of conscience, then we get two only partially satisfactory correspondences to the expectations from the theory. The RTT correlates suggest an insecure little girl with high impulse control of both dependency and aggression but without the signs of developing femininity, whereas the emotional upset correlates described an insecure little girl who *lacks* impulse control with both dependency and aggression.

Parents' Rating of Conscience

Nothing was said, in the preceding section, about the child-behavior correlates of the parents' pooled rating of conscience. There are very few, and they can be interpreted more easily in context with the child-rearing correlates.

In the *Patterns of Child Rearing* study, the conscience scale was based solely on mother interviews. Evidence was given for positive correlations between conscience and both maternal warmth (or acceptance) and love-oriented techniques of discipline (such as praise, isolation, reasoning, and withdrawal of love); correspondingly, the use of tangible rewards, deprivation of privileges, and physical punishment were negatively correlated with conscience. There was some slight indication of a positive relation between conscience and the rating of dependency obtained from the mother interviews, but this relation was apparent only when the influence of the acceptance-rejection dimension was partialed out. That dimension was not used in the present study, so no test of the replicability of that finding can be made.

Table 34 lists the child and parent measures that correlate at the .05 level of significance with the parents' pooled ratings of conscience. The *Patterns* findings are fairly well replicated for both sexes. Warmth, permissiveness, and the use of praise all appear prominently in both lists; there is evidence, too, of low use of physical punishment for girls, and of ridicule for boys. There are fifteen scales in the present study that reflect the notion of love-oriented vs. material-oriented discipline. Including the significant correlates in the table, all but one correlate in the expected direction for girls, and all but three for the boys, the medians being .21 and .08, respectively. The indicated relation between love-oriented techniques and conscience is as small in the present data as it was in the *Patterns* study, but is in the same direction.

Girls

Of considerably more interest, however, is the difference between boys and girls with respect to the parent agents involved in the child-rearing experiences represented by the listing in Table 34. For each, it was the parent of the opposite sex. In the girls' list there is evidence of praising and empathic support from the father, and a detachment from the mother. The mother was democratic in her attitudes, non-aggressive and non-punitive toward the child, and consistent in her caretaking. Unlisted are non-significant positive correlations with high self-esteem for both parents and with the mother's dissatisfaction with her current situation. Apparently she had felt somewhat this way from the start, for the father did a high proportion of the caretaking in the girl's infancy (.41), and the mother was currently still somewhat separated from her. The child, in turn, was non-demonstrative toward her mother.

The apparent positive relation to the father and negative (or at least neutral) relation to the mother is reminiscent of the Oedipal situation described in Chapter 2 with regard to the dependency category of reassurance seeking. And, in fact, the high-conscience girls showed an almost significantly greater amount of such behavior in the BUO (.42). They also tended to be higher on touching and holding (.26). In other words, they were somewhat insecurely and immaturely dependent. Coupled with the warmer attachment to the father than to the mother, this dependency might be expected to produce (via defensive identifica-

TABLE 34

Parent-Interview Rating of Conscience (89):
Correlations with Child-Behavior, Parent-Interview, and Mother-Child-
Interaction Measures at Level $p < .05$

GIRLS

47. Mother's use of democracy 48
53. Extent of overt aggression in home by mother . . . . −63
67. Mother's use of physical punishment . . . . −51
88. Extent child confesses wrongdoing (father) 55
95. Father's use of praise 52
99. Father's use of psychological (vs. tangible) reward 58
116. Child's expression of affection toward mother . . . . −46
132. Father's empathy for child 46
142. Severity of child's current separation from mother 46
145. Mother's caretaking consistency (with this child) 50
168. Mother Attitude Scale: use of punishment for aggression toward parents . −55
225. Degree of child's involvement in hamster situation . . . . −46
296. Use of living room: doll play, I . . . . −56
360. Child's interest in adult role (telephone and fishing games): MCI . . . 46
361. Child's resistance to adult role (telephone and fishing games): MCI . . −57

BOYS

2. Child's behavior: correspondence between MCI and home . . . . . . −45
12. Father's proportion of caretaking in infancy . . . . −44
14. Rigidity of scheduled feeding . . . . −46
22. Amount of thumbsucking child has shown . . . . −52
42. Mother's pressure for neatness and orderliness 59
58. Mother's permissiveness for aggression toward parents 45
71. Mother's use of ridicule . . . . −43
87. Extent child confesses wrongdoing (mother) 68
94. Mother's use of praise 50
100. Mother's permissiveness for independence 45
102. Mother's use of reward for independence 48
104. Mother's use of punishment for independence . . . . −46
118. Mother's warmth toward child 47
120. Mother's affectional demonstrativeness toward child 47
152. Extent of child's acquaintance with father's work (pooled) 44
164. Spaciousness of living space . . . . −50
173. Mother's non-permissiveness: factor score . . . . −49
174. Warmth of mother-child relationship: factor score 53
175. Giving facts and demonstrating knowledge (BUO) 53
184. Total real adult role (BUO) 58
196. Verbal disapproval of behavior (BUO) 51
286. Use of nurturance: doll play, I 54
287. Use of nurturance: doll play, II 44
297. Use of living room: doll play, II 46
334. Mother's involvement with fishing (MCI) 54
364. Child's willingness to adopt opposite sex role (MCI) 47
365. Mother's ease in situation (MCI) 58

tion) high adult role behavior, feminine forms of aggression, and strong gender role development. The only evidence to support this expectation lies in a correlation of .41 between the conscience rating and QuRu, and significant correlations with both measures of adult role behavior in the MCI. Actually, since the mothers of the high-conscience girls were clearly non-aggressive toward their daughters, the theory would not predict an especially high level of any kind of aggression, prosocial or otherwise. The one measure of aggression that does show a significant relation to the parents' rating of conscience is the rated aggression toward the father (.48). So far as gender role is concerned, there is no evidence of any relationship whatever between any of the measures of femininity and the rating on conscience.

Boys

Among the boys, the clear emphasis in Table 34 is on a close relationship with a warm and permissive mother who encouraged independence and (perhaps because her house was small!) pressed for neatness and order. There is an indication that this relationship began early, with a high proportion of caretaking by the mother (.37), and with low oral frustration.

There is no evidence that the high-conscience boys were more dependent, but this is scarcely surprising, since dependency in boys is a regressive response to punitive and cold treatment, especially by the father. These high-conscience boys had not had such treatment, and indeed the mothers used praise and reasoning (.32), and avoided such an ego-damaging practice as ridicule.

The outstanding behavioral characteristic of these boys is high adult role behavior. The parents saw them as resembling themselves. In the BUO, the boys scored high in giving facts and knowledge and in the feminine category of adult work; the correlation between rated conscience and total real AR is .58. The feminine quality of the adult role behavior is further indicated by high use of nurturance in both sessions of permissive doll play. In the MCI telephone game, they were willing to adopt the opposite sex role. In the nursery school, the only kind of aggression they showed significantly more often than other boys was verbal disapproval. As with the girls, however, there is no relation between conscience and the gender role rating or any of the gender role assessments.

Conclusions

These various child-rearing and child-behavior correlates of the parents' pooled ratings of conscience are as revealing of the parents' views of their children as of the children's behavior itself. Evidently the child who showed remorse, and who confessed his wrongdoings to the parent of the opposite sex, was seen as more closely attached to that parent. This attachment, coupled with warm and permissive treatment by the mother, led to a feminizing of the boy and to a need for reassurance in the girl.

Where the measures are comparable, the present data provide a good replication of the findings reported in *Patterns of Child Rearing*. The replication may prove of some value, retrospectively, in clarifying the interpretation of the conscience variable as examined in that study.

Resistance to Temptation

Boys

The relations between resistance to temptation and other child measures have already been discussed. We shall turn now to the apparent RTT child-rearing antecedents.

It will be recalled that the boys who ranked high on resistance to temptation tended to be the older and more mature members of the group. They showed little aggression in either the nursery school or doll play, and were neither aggressive nor dependent toward their mothers in the MCI. The nature of their doll play suggests a suppressed quality of femininity, and we have concluded that there is some reason for considering the RTT measure as an index of mature impulse control.

The next question is whether the child-rearing correlates of high resistance are those that might be expected from defensive identification theory. We would expect evidence of an ambivalent relationship between father and son, and non-permissiveness or punitiveness from the father for aggression in the home. The relationship between mother and son is difficult to predict.

The lower half of Table 35 lists the variables from the parent interviews that correlate with the RTT summary score. (There are no mother variables from the MCI whose correlations with RTT are significant.) There is certainly evidence of ambivalence on the father's part; he was affectionately demonstrative to the boy and also hostile toward him. There is no evidence of non-permissiveness or punitiveness, however,

TABLE 35

Resistance to Temptation (211):
Correlations with Parent Interview and Mother-Child
Interaction Measures at Level $p < .05$

GIRLS

  56. Father's demand for aggression toward peers 71
  72. Father's use of ridicule 51
  78. Extent of parents' disagreement abut child rearing (pooled) . . 46
 107. Father's satisfaction with child's socialization . . . . −68
 125. Father's permissiveness for dependency . . . . −61
 133. Mother's achievement standards for child 60
 150. Mother's sociability 47
 156. Strictness of father's parents . . . . −56
 157. Warmth of mother's parents . . . . −46
 322. Mother's pressure for child's independence (MCI) 50
 331. Mother's responsiveness to child (MCI) 59
 369. Mother's use of reasoning with child (MCI) 51

BOYS

   7. Severity of child's current separation from father . . . . . . −46
  13. Duration of breast feeding . . . . −46
  15. Severity of child's reaction to weaning . . . . −47
  17. Severity of child's feeding problems . . . . −47
  84. Father's stress on importance of teaching right and wrong . . . 45
 111. Extent child imitates parents (pooled) . . . . −50
 121. Father's affectional demonstrativeness toward child 52
 141. Father's hostility to child 60
 142. Severity of child's current separation from mother 68
 147. Parental discrepancy score . . . . −43

neither for aggression nor for anything else. An examination of a large number of other punishment, permissiveness, and reward variables reveals no correlations with RTT that even approach significance, and the directions of correlation appear to be ordered completely by chance.

An inductive look at the table encourages some interesting suggestions, however. First, the father believed in the importance of teaching the meaning of right and wrong. This variable appears with significant relations to the emotional upset and confession measures also, as will be seen in later tables. (It also correlates .40 with RTT in girls.) Second, there is indication of a reasonably gentle early oral-socialization experience. The duration of breast feeding was brief, which may be interpreted as non-frustrating (Sears *et al.*, 1957, pp. 86–90), and there was low severity of weaning (−.40). Third, the boy had a non-severe reaction to weaning, and later he had very few feeding problems. Fourth, although there is no evidence of a consistent difference between the parents in the amount of infant caretaking each did, there is an indication that at the time of the interview the boy was spending a good deal of time with his father but was rather severely separated from his mother.

These characteristics could be interpreted in at least two or three ways; we can suggest these hypotheses but cannot test them. The boy's relationship to the father appears to have been a close one, although the father seems to have been under some strain. But whether under strain because the mother had abdicated from closeness or because the father felt he must take responsibility is impossible to judge; the emphasis on moral teaching might suggest the latter. The mother's separation could have resulted either from her feeling that the boy was reaching a sexually stimulating age, and that she must put more distance between him and herself, or from a decision to let the father have his turn with the boy. These mothers of high-RTT boys were no more sex-anxious than other mothers—all the relevant r's are close to zero—but the boys were the older ones, and perhaps both motives were involved.

One other possibility should be considered, though there are no supporting data to recommend it. The lack of reaction to weaning, and the later lack of feeding problems, might be indices of a general passivity and an inability to overcome the suppressive influences of parental control. The low aggressiveness at age four would fit this constitutional interpretation. On the other hand, the observer ratings for activity level and social interaction correlate zero with RTT, and the correlation of RTT with self-aggression in the MCI is also zero.

One finding that gives a faintly Oedipal cast to this whole matter is the pair of non-significant correlations between RTT and the frequency of thematic doll play performed in the parents' bedroom of the doll house: .34 for Session I, and .23 for Session II. These coefficients are too small to be telling, and perhaps they reflect only the adult-agent preference shown by these boys. At the same time, we cannot help noting that the correlations with two other adult areas are lower: kitchen location, −.09 and .22, and living room, .03 and −.07. The comparable correlations for use of the children's bedroom are .25 and .31, however, not significantly different from those for the parents' bedroom. Perhaps it was the bedrooms that were provocative to the children.

In sum, the defensive identification theory is partly supported by the data—perhaps better by the child-behavior intercorrelations than by the child-rearing ones—but there is also a strong suggestion that the father's association with the boy, and his stress on the importance of teaching right and wrong, were important variables in producing resistance to temptation.

Girls

The high-resistance girls were also low on aggression in the nursery school and in doll play, and they too used the adult dolls as agents in doll play. They were the *younger* members of the girls' group, however, and they differed in one important respect from the boys—a high seeking for reassurance in the nursery school. Exercise of high impulse control might accurately characterize the high-RTT boys, but it will do for the girls only by adding the implication of insecurity.

Anaclitic identification theory leads us to expect a high association of resistance with the mature forms of feminine dependency, adult role, prosocial aggression, and feminine sex typing. These correlations do not appear, nor with one important exception, do we find evidence of the expected child-rearing variables in the upper half of Table 35. The only variable relevant to anaclitic theory that fulfills our expectations is mother's achievement standards. The father's standards tended to be high, too (.41).

As with the boys, the father seems to have been of great importance. There is no indication of ambivalence here, though, for the father was clearly dissatisfied with his daughter. He ridiculed her, was not permissive about her dependency, and demanded more aggression toward her peers. Perhaps there was some reason for his discomfort; these "good" little girls were rated low on both activity level (−.49) and social interaction (−.43) by the observers, and the parents' pooled rating of how well the child behaved about teasing animals suggests a certain amount of displaced aggression at home (−.39).

The prominence of the father, together with the girls' reassurance seeking in the nursery school, might suggest that we are seeing in the measure of resistance to temptation an indication of defensive identification based on an Oedipal conflict. It will be recalled (Chapter 2) that reassurance seeking appears to be the result of the father's sexual seductiveness. One might infer that high resistance is simply a product of the superego development deriving from a resolution of the conflict. There are three reasons for rejecting this interpretation, however. First, the girls who were highest on resistance were also the youngest, and although we know little about the exact age at which the Oedipal conflict is most severe in girls, we would expect it to be so nearer the fifth year than the fourth. In any case, the older girls should have shown more resolution (i.e., RTT) than the younger. Second, there is no correlation coefficient much above zero between RTT and any of the sex scales in the interview, for *either* parent, or for any of the three mother-attitude sex scales. That is, there is no indication of the paternal seductiveness found in connection with reassurance seeking. Third, there is no evidence of an ambivalent affectional relationship with the mother.

An alternative suggestion rests upon the origins of "virtue" in these little girls. It may have been the product of demands for high standards of achievement on the part of both parents (father's $r = .41$), and high pressure from the father for an understanding of the difference between right and wrong (.40), and to have been reinforced by the father's constant but non-punitive expression of dissatisfaction with the girl's progress. One supporting finding for this interpretation is the r of .40 between RTT and the amount of overt self-aggression shown by the girls in the MCI.

To summarize, resistance to temptation in these four-year-old girls appears not to have been a product of the processes implied by either theory of identification, but rather the product of the girls' efforts to meet the high standards of achievement prescribed by both parents and quite literally demanded by the fathers.

Emotional Upset, Confession, and Fixing

Our three summary scores for reaction to deviation conclude the analysis of conscience. Fixing will be seen to be so dissociated from emotional upset and confession as to warrant separate discussion.

Boys

Both emotional upset and confession were conceived to be measures of either guilt or fear as responses to wrongdoing. The two are somewhat positively correlated with resistance to temptation (.37 and .23, respectively) and somewhat with each other (.38). We were led to conclude, from an examination of the child-behavior correlates, that emotional upset is, for four-year-olds, the most "mature" reaction to deviation, confession somewhat less so, and fixing the least of all.

Tables 36 and 37 list the variables from the parent interviews and the

MCI that correlate with emotional upset and confession, respectively, at a level of $p = .05$ or better. There is one marked similarity in the apparent antecedents of RTT, emotional upset, and confession—the father's belief in the importance of teaching right and wrong. Between RTT and emotional upset, there are two other similarities—the brief duration of breast feeding and the severity of current separation from the mother.

The two non-reparative reactions to deviation—emotional upset and confession—had one very pronounced quality in common; both parents of "high-guilt" boys were non-permissive of sexuality. In addition, the mother was cold, and evidently somewhat rejecting, and succeeded in frustrating the boy's dependency in a number of ways. Her sex anxiety had led to proportionately low caretaking in infancy, she was often separated from the boy currently, she punished dependency, and she was quite sociable with other adults. These qualities, coupled with the fact that the families had more children, suggest a high level of dependency frustration. Not surprisingly, the "high-guilt" boys tended to be high in touching and holding in the nursery school, were reported high in dependency on the father, and were affectionate toward him (.40).

The parent measures show no significant indicators of punitiveness, but possibly the mothers' lack of overt aggression is an index of non-permissiveness about aggression. The mother-attitude scale and the interview ratings of permissiveness for aggression (for both parents) correlate from $-.14$ to $-.41$ (median $r = -.33$) with emotional upset and with confession.

Possibly the combination of non-permissiveness for both aggression and dependency produced a displacement of the former. In comparison with the impulse-controlling high-RTT boys, the "high-guilt" boys showed a good deal of aggression in the nursery school, but in the MCI they tended to be indirect in their aggression toward their mothers, and to indulge in fantasy aggression. It is interesting to note too, that the aggression expressed in doll play tended to be attributed to female agents rather than male. And again, as with resistance to temptation, there is a positive relation between the conscience measures and doll-play themes acted out in the parents' bedroom (Session I, .66), this time to the clear exclusion of the kitchen (Session I, $-.62$) and with no relation to the children's bedroom (Session I, .13).

To summarize, the two "guilt" measures and RTT are differentiated with respect to antecedents by the nature of the parents' affectional rela-

TABLE 36

Emotional Upset (235):
Correlations with Parent Interview and Mother-Child
Interaction Measures at Level $p < .05$

GIRLS

23. Mother's permissiveness for indoor nudity 58
29. Father's modesty . . . . −73
33. Sexuality in child (mother) 52
37. Openness about sex shown by mother's parents . . . . −49
42. Mother's pressure for neatness and orderliness . . . . −50
45. Mother's pressure for conformity to standards . . . . −67
48. Mother's expectancy of child's taking responsibility . . . . . −54
52. Child's level of conduct on four problems (pooled) . . . . . −49
66. Mother's use of isolation 56
79. Extent of sex stereotyping in parents' roles (mother) . . . . . −48
81. Source of power in home: mother high (pooled) . . . . . . −46
106. Mother's satisfaction with child's socialization 54
121. Father's affectional demonstrativeness toward child 51
124. Mother's permissiveness for dependency 58
126. Mother's use of reward for dependency 53
128. Mother's use of punishment for dependency . . . . −68
158. Extent mother disowns grandparents' child-rearing policies . . 50
159. Extent father disowns grandparents' child-rearing policies . . . 50

BOYS

13. Duration of breast feeding . . . . −43
23. Mother's permissiveness for indoor nudity . . . . −63
26. Amount of child's social nudity (mother) . . . . −45
28. Mother's modesty 44
34. Sexuality in child (father) . . . . −51
35. Extent mother gives sexual information to child . . . . −44
36. Extent father gives sexual information to child . . . . −53
38. Mother's sex anxiety 46
53. Extent of overt aggression in home by mother . . . . −44
66. Mother's use of isolation 44
83. Mother's stress on importance of teaching right and wrong . . . 43
84. Father's stress on importance of teaching right and wrong . . . 43
132. Father's empathy for child . . . . −44
142. Severity of child's current separation from mother 59
146. Mother's child-rearing anxiety . . . . −48
149. Father's self-esteem 46
154. Father's evaluation of mother . . . . −60
161. Age of father 55
165. Mother Attitude Scale: permissiveness for nudity . . . . . . −56
166. Mother Attitude Scale: permissiveness for masturbation . . . −47

TABLE 37

Confession (236):
Correlations with Parent Interview and Mother-Child
Interaction Measures at Level $p < .05$

GIRLS

102. Mother's use of reward for independence . . . . −54
121. Father's affectional demonstrativeness toward child 48
368. Mother's used of models with child (MCI) 57

BOYS

11. Mother's proportion of caretaking in infancy . . . . −64
23. Mother's permissiveness for indoor nudity . . . . −48
28. Mother's modesty 64
31. Father's permissiveness for masturbation . . . . −43
38. Mother's sex anxiety 46
64. Mother's use of reasoning . . . . −56
70. Father's use of deprivation of privileges 48
73. Relative frequency as agents of discipline: mother high (mother) −57
84. Father's stress on importance of teaching right and wrong . . . 55
88. Extent child confesses wrongdoing (father) . . . . −44
90. Mother's expectancy of conscience . . . . −44
94. Mother's use of praise . . . . −43
108. Mother's use of reward for adult role behavior . . . . −58
111. Extent child imitates parents (pooled) . . . . −50
118. Mother's warmth toward child . . . . −64
123. Child's expression of dependency toward father 48
128. Mother's use of punishment for dependency 52
131. Mother's empathy for child . . . . −58
136. Extent child resembles father (pooled) . . . . −62
143. Extent mother evaluates positively the mother role . . . . . . −46
150. Mother's sociability 48
163. Number of children in family 45
167. Mother Attitude Scale:
    permissiveness for sex play among children . . . . −43
174. Warmth of mother-child relationship: factor score . . . . . . −62
332. Mother's involvement in telephone game (MCI) . . . . . . −50
343. Mother's hostility to child (MCI) . . . . −49

tionships with the boy, "guilt" being associated with the mother's coldness and her restrictiveness toward sex, dependency, and aggression, and with the father's non-permissiveness about sex. With respect to child-behavior correlates, the high-RTT and "high-guilt" measures are differentiated by the level of overt and fantasy aggression shown, "guilt" being associated with several nursery school, MCI, and doll-play measures that suggest the parental attitudes had produced displaced and attenuated aggression and some conflict about sex.

Interview vs. assessment measures. It should be clear now why the assessment measures of emotional upset and confession do not correlate positively with the rating of conscience obtained from the parent interviews. The two sets of measures are related to completely different, even antithetical, sets of antecedents. If we consider the parents' reports a valid reflection of their sons' internalization of moral standards and guilt, then it is questionable whether we should apply the same term to the measures derived from the assessment situations. The latter measures, emotional upset and confession, seem to reflect anxiety over the expression of sexual and aggressive impulses, motivated by the threat of maternal rejection, a process having some general similarity to that implied by the psychoanalytic description of the mechanism of superego development. It is clearly not the process that seemed to be involved in the development of conscience as viewed by the parents, and (at least at this age) seems to have carried with it more effective deterrents to yielding to temptation, at least as we have measured resistance to temptation. We suggest that there may be at least two kinds of motivational systems for moral behavior whose operation can be observed in boys of this age. What the relative importance of these motives may be in later conscience development we can only guess, although Grinder's (1961) study suggests that resistance to temptation at later ages bears some relation to parents' earlier reports of conscience.

Fixing. The reparative response to deviation has been ignored until now in the discussion because it does not appear to belong to the same behavioral constellation as resistance to temptation, emotional upset, and confession. This exclusion seems further justified when we examine the significantly correlated interview variables in Table 38. Although the boys who scored high in fixing were neither older nor younger than the other boys, they were described by the mothers as being immature. And small wonder. Their fathers were warm, empathic, affectionally demonstrative (.41), and not hostile (−.41). There was no evidence of the ambivalence noted in the fathers of the high-RTT boys. There is no variable in the list, nor is there among a dozen unlisted but barely non-significant variables, that suggests any pressure for development—whether toward conscience, independence, achievement, or sex-appropriateness of behavior. There is no indication, either, of any pressure or restrictiveness concerning sex, aggression, or dependency. Indeed, there is no clue to any parental quality that would have induced these boys to mature. So evidently they did not.

TABLE 38

Fixing (237):
Correlations with Parent Interview and Mother-Child
Interaction Measures at Level $p < .05$

GIRLS

52. Child's level of conduct on four problems (pooled) 56
56. Father's demand for aggression toward peers . . . . −46
92. Extent child refrains from teasing animals (pooled) 65
116. Child's expression of affection toward mother 46
156. Strictness of father's parents 52
157. Warmth of mother's parents 58
158. Extent mother disowns grandparents' child-rearing policies . . −56
369. Mother's use of reasoning with child (MCI) . . . . −54

BOYS

78. Extent of parents' disagreement about child rearing (pooled) . −46
87. Extent child confesses wrongdoing (mother) . . . . −69
90. Mother's expectancy of conscience . . . . −56
97. Father's use of tangible reward . . . . −52
99. Father's use of psychological (vs. tangible) reward 44
103. Father's use of reward for independence . . . . −51
119. Father's warmth toward child 44
132. Father's empathy for child 46
134. Father's achievement standards for child . . . . −43
136. Extent child resembles father (pooled) . . . . −56
170. Child Behavior Scale: maturity (mother) . . . . −45

Girls

Just as with the boys, the girls' two measures of "guilt" are positively correlated with one another but are unrelated to resistance to temptation. And again, as with the boys, fixing is negatively related to RTT, but much more strongly so in this case. We shall consider emotional upset and confession first, though the latter must be largely ignored because it has almost no significant correlates from either the child or parent lists of variables.

Girls with high scores on emotional upset were extremely high in their exhibition of both positive attention seeking (the mature form of dependency) and reassurance seeking, in the expression of nurturance, and in both the antisocial and prosocial forms of aggression. Perhaps it is the conflicting masculine quality implied by the aggression that prevented them from being scored as either more or less feminine than other girls.

The child-rearing correlates listed in Table 36 suggest four themes: a highly positive and sexually tinged relationship between father and daughter, acceptance of sexuality and dependency by the mother, low pressure for any kinds of standards, and mother's satisfaction with her daughter. One may speculate that the sexual quality of the relation with the father created anxiety for the little girl, not only about her own sexual impulses but also about her relationship with her mother. We have suggested before that this may have been the root of the high seeking for reassurance that accompanied the father's free expression and both parents' permissiveness. Now we see high emotional upset following wrongdoing in the same girls.

There are two possible interpretations of the high adult role behavior shown by the high-upset girls. One is that they were attempting to model themselves after the mother as a means of warding off rivalrous aggression from her, and the other, that they were adopting adult feminine behavior as a dyadic response to the father's expressions of affection. Either explanation would be consonant with defensive identification theory. From the standpoint of anaclitic identification, however, the data are not so supportive. There is clear evidence of dependency, to be sure, but there is an equally clear indication that demands for conformity, neatness and order, and the taking of responsibility were low. The mothers did use isolation (a love-oriented technique), and they did not seem to have used physical punishment or to have placed any punitive restrictiveness on aggression. Their handling of sex and dependency was highly permissive and non-punitive, of course.

Fixing. The number of child-rearing correlates of fixing, as of confession, is so small for girls that little is suggested (Table 38). These high fixers were evidently quite good at home, in their parents' view, and affectionate toward their mothers, but what parental behavior may have been responsible is impossible to tell from these data.

Discussion and Summary

The data we have presented in this chapter are not relevant to the content of moral development, but relate to the structure of conscience and to the context of parent-child relationships in which it develops.

The development of conscience cannot be considered a unitary process in any simple sense. This is not to say there is no evidence of consistency among the various aspects of moral behavior we measured. There is substantial evidence of correlation among the experimental measures of resistance to temptation. Reactions to induced deviations were not consistent across situations, however, and there is little evidence of any integral connection between the measures of "guilt" and those of resistance to temptation; there are only low positive correlations in boys, and the corresponding relationships in girls are zero or negative. Thus avoidance of remorse and of loss of self-esteem seem not to have been powerful motives for resisting temptation in these four-year-old children.

There is no direct correspondence between measures of presumably identical aspects of conscience that were derived from different sources. Parents' reports of their children's degree of remorse after transgressions bear little relationship to "guilt" reactions in the experimental situations. Fantasy responses to deviation doll-play stories are not related in any obvious way either to the child's own behavior in a deviation situation or to parental perception of the child's reactions to deviations in the home. This last fact suggests the use of considerable caution in interpreting findings from studies that have relied solely or primarily on fantasy measures as indices of guilt or internalized control.

The limited consistency among our conscience measures must be viewed in relation to the age of the children in our sample. We chose to study four-year-olds for theoretical reasons; both primary and defensive identification theory define this age as crucial in the development of conscience. By the same token, it is an age of rapid and idiosyncratic transition from one stage or manifestation of these developmental processes to another, and there is a strong possibility that even the narrow age range of our group was sufficient, with our cross-sectional research method, to produce variations dependent on age that masked the orderliness of individual children's development. That age is by no means irrelevant to some of the findings is indicated by one major sex difference: the highest resistance to temptation was found among the *younger* girls but among the *older* boys. This fact suggested the possible interpretation that the girls at this age were becoming more discriminative and more situationally influenced in their moral behavior, whereas the boys were becoming more rigidly influenced by some unitary process such as that implied by defensive identification theory.

Other sex differences were noted also. As expected from the anaclitic theory, the girls showed stronger resistance to temptation on the cumulative measure of RTT, and showed more severe emotional upset following forced deviation. In the deviation doll play, boys tended more frequently to complete their stories by having the culprit caught by authority and punished by physical means. The girls, on the other hand, brought isolation and verbal punishment into greater use. Although these differences are in the same directions as differences in parental treatment of the sexes, they are far larger than the differences in treatment.

Resistance to temptation is closely related to non-aggressiveness in both sexes, and we have been led to conclude that it represents an index of general impulse control. The child-rearing correlates of this type of behavior are different for the boys and girls, however, and suggest the possibility that the boys were being much influenced by the fathers' close attention and moral training, whereas the girls were being influenced more by the mothers' high standards and positive discipline. The ambivalence of the boys' fathers fits the pattern to be expected from defensive identification, and the girls' relation with their mothers is more in accord with what might develop through primary identification.

The "guilt" reactions (emotional upset and confession) also present a difference in the parent-child relationships of the two sexes. The boys who showed high upset had mothers who tended to be cold, restrictive, and non-permissive about sex, and fathers who tended to be non-punitive but perhaps authoritarian. The girls, on the other hand, were strongly influenced by their fathers, and there was clear suggestion of a sexually tinged relationship that could be interpreted quite easily as involving an Oedipus conflict. Thus, again, the pattern of the data suggests defensive identification as a possible mediating process for the development of an important aspect of conscience.

7. Conclusions

The theories of anaclitic and defensive identification were originally derived from the retrospective associations of psychoanalytic patients. These theoretical accounts were intended to be descriptive of the apparent psychodynamics by which children resolve certain emotional conflicts, and in so doing absorb the restrictive and idealistic standards of conduct of their parents. Anaclitic identification described the way in which the very young child of either sex responds to the pain produced by the nurturant mother's gradual withdrawal of love and intimacy as the child matures. Defensive identification described the boy's normal method of coping with the intolerable conflict of love and hate for the rivalrous father in the Oedipus triangle. The outcome of the two processes, the formation of the superego, was posited for both sexes, but Freud acknowledged a suspicion that the rigidity and the punitive and retributive qualities of the superego are substantially less in the female than in the male. He implied that the earlier anaclitic process is less powerful than the later defensive one in creating internalization of prohibitions and the capacity for self-punishment, and that defensive identification is a characteristically masculine phenomenon.

The reformulation of identification theory, as presented in Chapter 1, was designed to make the consequences of these two hypothetical processes more accessible to behavioral investigation. In doing this, we became acutely aware of the difference between the purely descriptive statement of a psychodynamic process and a testable theory of behavioral development. Although the former contained suggestions of variables that might be included in the latter, it did not specify the conditions under which greater or lesser degrees of any particular behavioral product of identification would occur, nor did it define the variables responsible for the observable behavior changes. The reformulation of the theories—particularly that of anaclitic identification—was therefore less a translation of psychoanalytic language into behavioral terms than a conversion of a map of something seen into a set of operationally defined variables the interactions among which would account for the *development* of what was seen and for differences among individuals in the *rate* of that development. The research that followed must not be viewed as an attempted verification of psychoanalytic concepts, therefore, but as a testing of a behavioral theory that was suggested by psychoanalytic observations and was then constructed within the framework of an entirely different theoretical structure. Insofar as it deals with the specific child-rearing antecedents of development, and with the conditions determining individual differences in rate of development, it is less an extension of psychoanalytic theory than a new formulation. In emphasizing the distinction between *verification* and *hypothesis testing*, we are not in any sense denying the psychoanalytic parentage of the behavioral theory—the family features are too similar to permit that. We *are* trying to make explicit, however, that what hypotheses we have proposed— some of which have been unsupported by our findings—are hypotheses independent of, and in some instances irrelevant to, psychoanalytic formulations of the theories of identification.

Although the theories from which the research started were behavioral, the dependent variables selected were the several complex forms of action that were conceived to be the trait-like consequences of identification. No attempt was made to study directly the development of dependency, the origins of the imitative process, or the shift to role practice following the withdrawal of love and attention. In other words, the investigation was directed toward the testing of hypotheses derived from the presumed operation of the identification mechanism rather than toward the more direct and minute examination of the mechanism itself. As a result, whatever positive findings were obtained cannot be interpreted as *uniquely* supportive of the theories, but only as what were to be expected if the mechanisms in fact work as the theories imply. There is still a reasonable possibility that other mechanisms could account for the obtained outcomes.

The most profitable next research steps would seem to be in the direction suggested by Schaffer and Emerson (1964) and Walters and Parke (1965), i.e., an examination of the conditions determining both the development of attachments in early infancy and the facilitation or inhibition of imitation. Until these processes have been examined fully, there seems little likelihood that greater precision in the kinds of parent-child measurements we have used in the present study will aid materially in determining whether primary identification is a necessary or adequate theoretical construct for the explanation of such regularities in the socialization process as have been revealed here.

Primary Identification: Expectations and Results

The present research was designed to answer two kinds of questions, one kind about intercorrelations among the behaviors selected as examples of identification-mediated traits, and the other about the child-rearing antecedents of such behavior. Although the specific hypotheses concerning the latter now seem very inexact, and even naïve, in the light of the complexities uncovered in our analysis of the data, a summary statement of the results of our hypothesis testing is needed.

Child-Behavior Correlations

The first hypothesis was that there should be positive correlations among the child behaviors we presumed to be the products of primary identification. Our reasoning was that if a single process is responsible for these various forms of behavior, they should develop at a similar rate; thus, in a sample of children who vary among themselves in degree of development, the extent of development should produce positive correlations.

This reasoning should apply to girls without equivocation, but its accuracy for boys occasions some doubt. Both sexes are presumed to identify with the mother initially. Since there is no interruption in the girl's attachment, and no alternative mechanism introduced, girls should continue to show a high level of intercorrelation among the several behaviors. At some point in the second to fourth years, however, the boy would be expected to develop defensive identification with the father, and the consequences of this change in model would be superimposed on the initial products of primary identification. Thus it was expected that the boys might show less coherence than the girls among the primary-identification-mediated behaviors. To the extent that defensive identification had taken over the structuring of the kinds of behavior measured, there should be positive correlations between aggression (especially toward the father), masculinity, and resistance to temptation. The theory as presented in Chapter 1, however, was unable to predict the fates of dependency and adult role under the influence of defensive identification.

A precondition for testing the hypotheses concerning correlations among classes of behavior was that the various measures of any one class of behavior should be highly intercorrelated. For the girls, this requirement was fairly well met within four of the areas—adult role, aggression, gender role, and resistance to temptation. Among the boys, however, only aggression and resistance to temptation showed a similar degree of unity, whereas gender role showed substantially less, and adult role none at all, apparently because of the contamination of some of the measures with femininity, in the form of maternal adultness. In neither sex was there any correlation between measures of emotional upset obtained in the two separate assessment situations.

The final test of the intercorrelation hypothesis is presented in Table 39. The developmental aspect of primary identification theory required that the identification-mediated behaviors be not only positively inter-correlated but also related to dependency. In Table 39, positive attention seeking is included as the measure of dependency because it appeared to be the most prominent form in both sexes. For girls, these data give substantial support to the dependency aspect of the hypothesis; all of the variables except resistance to temptation are positively and significantly correlated with positive attention seeking. The other aspect of the hypothesis—the requirement for intercorrelations among the identification-mediated behaviors—does not fare quite so well, but, again with the exception of those involving resistance to temptation, the correlations range from zero to .60, with a median of .25.

For boys, however, there is little evidence of a primary identification cluster; only adult role and prosocial aggression are related positively

TABLE 39

Correlations among the Main Measures of Identification

(Girls above the diagonal, boys below)

Main Measures of Identification	Var. No.	Variable Number					
		219	184	198	204	211	235
Positive attention seeking (BUO)	219	°	67	52	44	−19	55
Total real adult role (BUO)	184	42	°	60	43	10	36
Total prosocial aggression (BUO) . . .	198	28	47	°	13	−21	25
Sex typing, total standard score	204	−14	−15	−04	°	−01	−03
Resistance to temptation, total standard score	211	−32	07	−13	10	°	06
Emotional upset, combined score	235	−21	05	37	01	37	°

to each other and to dependency. As we noted in Chapter 6, there is some evidence of a "conscience" cluster in boys, but both conscience measures (RTT and emotional upset) correlate *negatively* rather than positively with dependency, and neither is at all related to masculinity.

Possibly these data give evidence of the competing influences of primary and defensive identification. The sex differences in the size and patterning of the correlations are consonant with this view. On the other hand, the non-significant size of several of the girls' correlations suggests caution in their interpretation, and it is conceivable that at least some of the sex difference in size of correlation may be a function of the lesser coherence *within* the boys' behavior categories.

Child-Rearing Antecedents

In addition to dependency in the child, the primary identification theory required four kinds of parental behavior. As will have been noted frequently in the preceding chapters, the testing of hypotheses concerning child-rearing variables is by no means simple. The qualities described by the four labels we have chosen are complex, and in some instances are measured by several different interview scales or MCI categories. For example, "high demands" can be exhibited in a number of behavioral areas—by inhibition of changeworthy forms of dependency, sex, and aggression, by encouragement of independence, achievement, neatness and orderliness, and responsibility, by demands for good table manners, and so on. Although some of these parental qualities correlate positively with one another, not all do. Further, although husbands and wives tend to be similar on many dimensions of child rearing, the similarity is exceedingly small on the average, and it is possible for one parent to make high demands and the other to make low ones. Since our original hypotheses were imprecise with respect to both area of application of qualities (e.g., aggression vs. achievement) and agent of performance (father vs. mother), the final testing of relationships between parent and child behaviors must be equally inexact.

In spite of these difficulties, however, we have attempted to form decisions from the evidence supporting the theory. Table 40 indicates our best judgments of extent of agreement between actual and expected relationships. A *yes* means fairly unequivocal support. *Slight* means small non-significant correlations in the right direction. A *no* means that the relevant correlations are essentially zero, providing support neither for

TABLE 40

Evidence Obtained in Support of Hypotheses Concerning Child-Rearing Antecedents of Child Behaviors Presumed to Be Mediated by Primary Identification

Parental Child-Rearing Qualities	Identification-Mediated Behaviors					
	Positive Attention Seeking (219)	Total Real Adult Role (184)	Total Prosocial Aggression (198)	Sex Typing, Total Standard Score (204)	Total Standard Score, RTT (211)	Emotional Upset, Combined Score (235)
GIRLS						
Nurturance and warmth	yes	no	no	no	no	yes
High demands	equivocal[7]	equivocal[1]	equivocal[2]	yes	yes	opposing[3]
Love-oriented discipline	no	opposing	opposing	opposing	opposing[4]	no
Use of models and labels of behavior . .	no	equivocal[5]	no	slight	slight	slight
BOYS						
Nurturance and warmth	slight[7]	no	no	slight	no	no
High demands	no	slight	slight	equivocal[6]	no	equivocal[7]
Love-oriented discipline	no	no	no	equivocal[8]	no	no
Use of models and labels of behavior . .	no	slight	no	no	yes	yes

1 High on aggression control and expectancy of conscience, but father low on expecting conformity.
2 High on aggression control, but low on expecting conformity and independence.
3 Low on expecting conformity and on demands for neatness, and no evidence on aggression or achievement.
4 High on ridicule, but no evidence on praise, reasoning, or physical punishment.
5 High on belief in the importance of teaching right and wrong, but no evidence of use of models.
6 High on expectancy of responsibility, conscience, and independence, but low on aggression control.
7 No evidence on expectancy of responsibility, conscience, or independence, but high on aggression control.
8 Low on physical punishment, but no evidence on praise or reasoning.

the hypothesis nor for an alternative relationship. *Opposing* means that the evidence not only fails to support the expected relationship, but in fact suggests an opposing one. *Equivocal* means that there is some confirmatory evidence but also some correlations that are either zero or in the wrong direction; the footnotes explain the sources of disagreement. With the exception of the "slight" category, most of the judgments are essentially summary statements about data presented in detail in the earlier chapters, though we have reexamined the long lists of non-significant correlations in each instance to be sure that a few significant ones were not distorting a more general picture. Many behavioral qualities were, of course, exhibited more by mothers, and others more by fathers, but we have not made that distinction here, since this factor was not explicitly included in the original hypotheses.

The four types of parental behavior can be considered separately. *Nurturance and warmth* were evaluated in separate ways. There were several ratings of warmth from both the interviews and the mother-child interaction. There were no ratings of parental nurturance as such, but we have interpreted the sex- and dependency-permissiveness scales as representing a willingness for affection and intimacy. The results are quite clearly non-confirming in both sexes. This seems especially surprising for the girls, because there is substantial evidence of dependency permissiveness and some for sex permissiveness as correlates of positive attention seeking, which is closely related to all the identification behaviors but resistance to temptation. Among the boys, the positive implication of the "slight" rating on gender role derives from the high correlation with sex permissiveness, though neither dependency permissiveness nor warmth is related to masculinity.

High demands, as a concept, can apply to any area of conduct in which the inhibition of changeworthy behavior and the encouragement of mature forms can be clearly noted. In our evaluations in Table 40, we have taken into strongest consideration aggression control, demands for achievement, independence, conformity to standards, neatness and orderliness, and good table manners, and expectancies of conscience and of taking responsibilities. This very complex variable appears to be the best supported of the four, but the majority of relationships are not unequivocal. For the girls, the strict control of aggression is associated with all the identification-mediated behaviors except emotional upset, to which it is unrelated. For the boys, strictness of aggression control is non-significantly related to three of the behaviors, but is strongly opposed to masculinity. Thus we conclude that, except for boys' gender role, there is reasonable support for the hypothesis that high demands are associated with the more mature forms of child behavior.

Love-oriented discipline was evaluated in two ways, by presence of praise, isolation, and reasoning, and by absence of physical punishment and ridicule. There is little evidence of support for this hypothesis in boys, and quite general support for an opposing relationship in girls. With the small number of cases available we have not been able to test for replication the finding reported in *Patterns of Child Rearing* that high conscience was associated with love-oriented discipline only with warm mothers, though it is notable (Table 34) that there was strong support for the love-oriented-discipline hypothesis when the same interview measure of child's conscience used in the former study was used as the measure of conscience in the present one. Thus we have replication with one consequent measure, but not with the alternative independent measures included in Table 40.

The use of models and labels for good behavior was evaluated from four scales, two for each parent. Use of "models" relates directly to the extent of use of the parents as models, use of "labels" to the parents' belief in the importance of teaching the difference between right and wrong. Our interpretation of the latter is that such teaching involves labeling. There is evidence of a fairly pervasive correlation of such behavior with the various child measures.

Conclusions

We conclude that the evidence is fairly satisfactory for the existence of a constellation of behavior in girls that could be described as the product of some such process as primary (anaclitic) identification. Further, there is support for the developmental aspect of the theory that ascribes such development to high parental demands (particularly for control of aggression) and to the use of models and labels. There is no support for the hypothesis that nurturance and warmth are relevant to the process, however, and there is fairly strong evidence that love-oriented discipline is negatively related to the constellation.

For boys, although there is no evidence to support the notion of a cluster of primary-identification-related behaviors, it is interesting to note

that both the high-demands and models-and-labels hypotheses are somewhat associated with several of the child-behavior measures.

Primary Identification Theory Reconsidered

In spite of the rather limited support these findings give to the originally proposed theory of primary identification, the data display several
relationships that are nonetheless suggestive of such a process. The girls'
high correlations of positive attention seeking with all the identification-
mediated behaviors except resistance to temptation, the influence of the
father on some aspects of the girls' behavior, the intrusion of femininity
into the boys' adult role behavior, the association of femininity (or non-
masculinity) with immaturity in boys, and the evidently powerful influence of the degree and kind of parental control of the major behavior
systems (dependency, sex, aggression, and achievement) all suggest that
some process involving a dyadic relationship between parents and child
is influencing the child's modeling and his adoption of mature forms of
behavior. Some modification of our original hypotheses seems in order.

It was apparent from the intercorrelations among the five dependency
measures (Table 3) that the notion of a generalized trait of dependency
is indefensible. This conclusion is based on behavioral observations
made when the children were four years old, of course, and has no direct
relevance to the hypothetical process of dependency drive or habit formation in infancy. Our data have no value for determining whether or
not the *very early* strength of dependency is related to the later strength
of development of the identification behaviors. What is clear from the
present findings is that, by age four, *overt dependency behavior* does
not reflect a unitary drive or habit structure that can be interpreted as
the unique source of reinforcement for all the other behaviors we have
studied.

At the same time, we cannot ignore the pervasive positive correlation
of positive attention seeking in girls with the other measures—e.g., nurturance, real adult role, tattling, prosocial aggression, femininity, and
emotional upset (Appendix K, Tables K4 to K7). Within the category
of positive attention seeking, there is a reasonably good coherence or
unity (Gewirtz, 1954), and in the context of behaviors presented in
Table 39, it has the appearance of being closely associated with the development of maturely feminine behavior. With respect to child-rearing

antecedents, it differs from the identification-mediated behaviors in its lack of evidence for modeling and labeling, but it did have, as common correlates with them, nurturance and warmth and the typically high control of aggression (Table 40). We are inclined to consider positive attention seeking separately, therefore, and to ignore the other categories of dependency.

If the dependency motive or drive, as traditionally conceived, is not to be used as an indicator of the strength of the sources of reinforcement for identification, then the question of what these sources are must be reopened. From a theoretical standpoint, an operationally defined child-rearing variable would be more effective in the role of reinforcer than a hypothetical drive in the child himself. Our use of dependency motivation in this connection arose from an effort to convert Freud's cathexis, or attachment of the child to the mother, into a motivational system congruent with other concepts belonging to a behavioral type of theory. The child's attachment was the basis for the process of anaclitic identification, and dependency became the comparable link in the developmental process described as primary identification. Positive attention seeking, however, is simply another behavior, not fundamentally a better index of a drive than any of the identification-mediated behaviors, and the appropriate next step therefore appears to be to search for some common child-rearing correlate of all the child behaviors we have measured that are relevant to primary identification.

The recent work of Schaffer and Emerson (1964) calls attention to a promising lead. Returning to the concept of attachment, they sought determinants of the strength of development of this process in infants during the first year of life. Prominent in their findings was evidence that the caretaker's responsiveness to the child's actions strengthened the attachment. Since positive attention seeking may reflect a developed form of early attachment, consideration should be given to the possibility that parental responsiveness may be a significant child-rearing antecedent of the various other identification-relevant behaviors as well.

We had no measure of parental responsiveness as such, either from the interviews or from the mother-child interaction. We did not develop a responsiveness scale for the interviews because an attempt in an earlier study (Sears *et al.*, 1953) had failed to measure mother's responsiveness to child's aggression as a variable different from mother's punitiveness for aggression; the interview ratings for the two scales were so highly correlated that there was doubt they measured separate aspects of mother behavior. In the present instance, however, we are concerned with positive attention seeking rather than aggression, and thus with a form of child behavior less likely to instigate a punitive reaction from the parents. Some degree of reward rather than some degree of punishment is more likely to follow the child's behavior. Although we do not have a scale labeled responsiveness, the parent behavior from which ratings of *reward for dependency* were made is behavior relevant to the responsiveness hypothesis.

The reward-for-dependency rating was made separately for the mother (variable 126) and father (127) from the whole corpus of their respective interviews. The descriptive phrases that characterized the behavior being evaluated were "Extent to which the parent rewards the child's dependent acts, complies with his demands, and gives attention, help, or affection when the child solicits. The parents' reactions to emotional and instrumental dependency, and reactions when busy, are to be weighted equally. Both frequency and degree of reward are to be considered." The five-point scale for the rating ranges from "5. Tries always to comply; will stop whatever she is doing," to "1. Does not reward; tells child to do it himself, or suggests some alternative action."

One disadvantage of this scale, for our present purpose, is that it does not differentiate among the various kinds of dependency rewarded. As we have seen earlier, there is no reason to assume a unified trait of dependency, and therefore the amount of reward relates to the whole set of relatively unconnected behaviors. Since positive attention seeking is by far the most frequent form of dependency supplication, however, we may assume safely (though without direct proof) that the scales are mainly measures of responsiveness to that kind of mature dependency.

If we interpret the rating on reward for dependency as a measure of the degree to which reinforcement is provided for the child's positive attention seeking, we can consider it also to be a measure of the extent to which each parent is creating the appropriate learning conditions for identification, regardless of whether we follow Freud's theory or our own. Freud's (anaclitic) theory is based on the child's development of cathexis, or attachment; the parents' affectionate responsiveness is the appropriate condition for producing this quality. Our own (primary) identification theory is based on dependency, and the same parental behavior is evidently associated with the establishment of the mature form, positive attention seeking. Thus, in either case, we expect reward for dependency—considered as a measure of parental responsiveness—to be associated with the various forms of child behavior we have labeled as products of identification.

The pervasive occurrence of this single variable among the several lists of antecedents suggests that it may serve as a suitable substitute for dependency motivation in the child. From a theoretical standpoint, this substitution is very desirable, for it permits us to place all the antecedents in the realm of parent behavior, and thus avoid risks associated with the use of antecedent variables lying within the behavior constellation of the child, i.e., the risks inherent in introducing consequent-consequent relationships into antecedent-consequent theoretical formulas. The differential development of boys and girls, however, and the inconsistent appearance of mother's reward in some lists and of father's in others, makes evident the necessity for a cautious and critical examination of the findings before we rely on the new variable. Some relevant correlations are presented in Table 41.

The mechanisms of development are often highlighted more clearly by deviant behavior than by normal conforming behavior. In the present instance, we shall pursue this line, turning first to the child-rearing cor-

TABLE 41

Parents' Use of Reward for Dependency (126 and 127):
Correlations with Several Measures of Child Behavior

| | | Use of Reward for Dependency | | | |
| | | With Boys | | With Girls | |
Child Behavior Measures	Var. No.	By Mother (126)	By Father (127)	By Mother (126)	By Father (127)
Real adult work	179	56	23	22	−11
Nurturance	182	10	−37	21	17
Total real adult role	184	26	−27	15	−06
Negative attention seeking	187	−01	−25	18	60
Reassurance seeking	188	21	27	15	17
Positive attention seeking	219	−28	−09	50	00
Injury to objects	192	−16	−34	−12	64
Total antisocial aggression	194	−20	−34	48	33
Tattling	197	03	−30	20	−32
Total prosocial aggression	198	−14	−41	09	−30
Sex typing, total standard score	204	−28	−31	17	−47
Resistance to temptation, total standard score	211	15	−01	−35	−05
Quoting rules, total score	212	50	00	29	28
Emotional upset, combined score	235	14	−26	53	29

relates of girls' behaviors that are more characteristically masculine (or non-feminine): negative attention seeking, injury to objects, and non-feminine gender role adoption. As earlier discussions have shown, these three behaviors are all associated with father-interview scales that suggest a strong intrusion of the father into the girl's rearing. We know further that the father's influence on the girl does not necessarily produce masculine behavior, as witness its effects on reassurance seeking and emotional upset over deviation. The question, then, is: What is the special character of the father's intrusion into the lives of the little girls who showed a high degree of the three non-feminine measures?

Only two interview scales are common to all three lists of antecedents (Tables 5, 24, 27): stability of current home situation (variable 8) and father's reward for dependency (variable 127). These correlated negatively with each other ($r = -.62$); i.e., the more stable the current home situation was, the less the father responded rewardingly to his daughter's dependency.* The two scales are part of a cluster of significantly inter-correlated measures of paternal behavior. Included in the cluster are several measures that reveal the quality of the father's behavior: high proportion of caretaking in infancy, high sex permissiveness, high aggression permissiveness, high use of praise, low use of physical punishment, high warmth, high emotional demonstrativeness, high empathy, and low hostility to the child. The fathers of the masculinized girls (i.e., the girls who were high on the masculine forms of behavior) were warm, interactive, permissive, and understanding in their attitudes toward their daughters. These are qualities that might be expected to make the father seem the main source of nurturance to the girl, and thus to promote a strong attachment to him. The scale measuring the parents' belief about the child's perception of source of nurturance is in fact part of the same paternal cluster, and appears in the list of correlates of injury to objects. According to the experimental studies of Mussen and of Bandura, high nurturance is conducive to adoption of the nurturant person as a model. If this was the mechanism operating in the present instance, the father became more of a model than the mother, and the girl therefore became more masculine.

There is an alternative explanation of the relationships, however. It

---

* Home stability measured the expectation of "geographic" stability, i.e., the extent the family could expect to continue in their present home or community. In general, graduate students were less stable than other parents in this sense (though in no other), and the academic occupation led to the fathers' spending more time at home.

is notable that these masculinizing fathers were permissive of both sex and aggression, as well as rewarding of dependency, thus granting the girls freedom to behave uninhibitedly and, with respect to aggression and negative attention seeking, in a masculine way. The present data afford no way to choose between the modeling and direct reinforcement hypotheses, but there is an additional fact that perhaps supports the latter. There are many child-rearing variables on which the two parents are as likely to be dissimilar as similar, but aggression control is not one of them, nor is sex permissiveness. The parents of girls (it is less true for boys) tended to agree on their policies toward these two major areas of socialization; the mothers as well as the fathers were permissive of sex and aggression in the masculinized girls. The mothers did not exhibit the other forms of behavior shown by the fathers (specifically, neither permissiveness nor reward for dependency), but to the extent that the mothers were permissive of sex and aggression, the girls would have secured more practice and more direct reinforcement of the masculine type of activity.

We shall turn now to the obvious alternative source of clues to the dynamics of the process—the antecedents of the feminized (or at least non-masculinized) boys. There were three forms of these boys' behavior that appeared to have a feminine quality: real adult work, quoting rules, and non-masculine gender role. Only seven parent-interview variables correlate significantly with real adult work (variable 179) in boys; they are as follows:

    40. Mother's restrictions on house and property . . . . −58
    50. Extent mother's standards of obedience are realistic . . . . . −46
    75. Relative strictness of parents: mother high 43
    78. Extent of parents' disagreement about child rearing . . . . . −47
   122. Child's expression of dependency toward mother 55
   126. Mother's use of reward for dependency 56
   160. Extent of mother's current dissatisfaction with her life 45

The mother's use of reward for dependency appears at a significant level both in the above list and in Table 15 for quoting rules, and it is negatively correlated, though non-significantly, with masculinity ($r = -.28$). Thus we have here a phenomenon in the feminized boys parallel to that seen with the masculinized girls. Apparently, imitation of the parent of the opposite sex (or at least behavior suggesting such imitation) was related to a high degree of nurturance and responsiveness by that parent.

The qualities (for boys) of maternal behavior associated with reward of dependency are different from those (for girls) of paternal behavior, however. The rewarding mothers were also warm and demonstrative, low on household restrictions, high on keeping track of the boy, high on use of praise and reasoning, low on punishment of independence and adult role, and low on hostility to the child—but there is no evidence whatever of permissiveness (*or* non-permissiveness) with respect to sex and aggression. Thus the conditions for creating a warmly reinforcing parental person were established, but without associating these with support of sex and aggression. It is no surprise that real adult work and quoting rules are not at all correlated with any of the forms of aggression.

The general principle may be stated that *when the parent of the opposite sex rewards dependency, the child develops behavior qualities characteristic of that sex.*

When we examine the converse of this proposition, however, the results are not as clear. The influence of reward by the same-sexed parent— toward sex-appropriate conformity—is less evident, as the six variables just examined demonstrate. None of the three masculine behaviors *in boys* is associated with use of reward for dependency by the father; all three correlations are non-significantly negative, in fact. Of the three feminine behaviors *in girls,* all relate positively to reward by the mother, but none even close to significantly. Thus it seems that with respect to the behaviors that are especially strongly sex-typed, and clearly influenced in some children of each sex by the warmth and rewarding of dependency by the opposite-sexed parent (Pd), the same-sexed parent (Ps) had little or no effect. In other words, the principle stated above cannot be generalized, with respect to these particular behaviors, to a statement that *the rewarding parent* determines the direction of development.

This apparent failure of what would be a highly useful principle rests on a rather peculiar set of relationships. In both sexes, the correlations of the antithetical sex-typed behaviors with the direct measures of gender role are larger in the negative direction for the inappropriate sex than in the positive direction for the appropriate sex. For example, real adult work is negatively correlated with masculinity in boys more strongly ($-.61$) than it is positively correlated with femininity in girls ($.30$). There is evidently something specific about these behaviors that makes them peculiarly susceptible to infusion into the behavior of the opposite sex as a product of Pd's rewarding of dependency, but not into the behavior of the same sex by such rewards from Ps.

The constellation of generally feminine behaviors that compose the primary identification cluster for girls (positive attention seeking, real adult role, prosocial aggression, femininity, and emotional upset) provides another opportunity for testing the effects of reward by Ps. Table 41 lists the correlations between these behaviors and the scales for reward of dependency by mother and father. For girls, two of the correlations between the feminine behavior and the mother's use of reward for dependency are positive and significant (variables 219, 235), but the other three are virtually zero (variables 184, 198, 204). The influence of the father's reward is indeterminate, though the negative correlation with femininity is probably important. For the boys, all of these same behaviors are correlated negatively with father's use of reward for dependency, though none significantly. The negative correlation between father's reward for dependency and his son's masculinity is in opposition to the other four negative r's, of course, because each of the other four variables is a part of the *feminine* cluster. The influence of the mother's rewarding is as indeterminable here as the father's was with the girls.

The non-significant size of these various correlations makes any conclusion risky, though their directions suggest that the mother's influence was more significant for the girls, and the father's for the boys.

These findings suggest a possible hypothesis that *the strength of the basic feminine personality pattern in girls varies directly with the amount of rewarding dependency by Ps (the mother), but the strength of its infusion into the boy's personality varies inversely with the strength of such reward from Ps (the father).* If this should prove a valid proposition, we think its explanation will be that the girl is in less conflict, with respect to model, than the boy. The mother's rewarding of the girl has an influence proportional to the amount of it that occurs. The boy, on the other hand, has two models, one of which has held temporal primacy. The mother's rewarding of dependency strengthens his use of her as a model unless the father overcomes her influence by rewarding the boy's dependency himself. His influence is proportional to the extent that he does this.

Although we have couched this reasoning in terms of modeling, the same principle would hold for an explanation in terms of direct reinforcement. If the mother does more rewarding of the girl, the qualities rewarded will be strengthened. It may be taken for granted, we think, that most mothers of girls reward feminine forms of behavior, and shape their daughters to the end of being feminine, to a greater extent than they reward non-femininity. The mothers of boys undoubtedly have a cognitive picture of the masculine role, and no doubt try to support it. There is plenty of evidence outside the present study, however, to support the proposition that mothers whose husbands do not participate in child rearing have feminized sons. We can conceive that in spite of the cognitive map of the masculine role, mothers tend to shape their sons in a more feminine direction because non-aggressiveness characterizes femininity; the mothers are inhibited in their own aggression and dislike it in others, and would be non-permissive of their sons' display of it.

The fact that the cluster of maturely sex-appropriate behaviors is found in the girls and not in the boys accords with Freud's description of anaclitic identification. The findings on the influence of the two parents, however, are relevant to a reformulation of our original conception of primary identification. The qualities of behavior induced in children initially are essentially those that characterize the adult feminine role; they are maternal qualities. Qualities that characterize the adult male role must be superimposed on the original role learning. We hypothesize that the particular forms of maternal nurturance and responsiveness falling under the rubric *reward for dependency* provide the reinforcement for the initial feminization of both sexes. This role adoption may be by imitation of the maternal model or by direct reinforcement of mother-like behaviors. We predict, further, that the presence of siblings should provide additional models and reinforcers, and that the sex of the siblings should influence the rate at which feminization or masculinization occurs. The extent to which the father, or a male sibling, rewards dependency should determine the rate at which the feminine qualities are disrupted and replaced by others, ones more characteristic of the father or the sibling.

Although this conception of the primary identification process appears to be congruent with the behavioral outcomes found in our data for girls, and for the sex-inappropriate outcomes observed in the boys, it is not adequate to account for the continuing development of masculinity in boys—at least for masculinity as defined by our measures of gender role. The fact must be noted (Table 41) that, for boys, there are non-significant negative correlations between masculinity and the rewarding of dependency by *both* parents. Whereas the low reward from the mother fits the theory, that from the father is just the opposite of what should be expected. We can conclude only that the hypothesized mechanism of primary identification is not adequate in its present form to account for gender role development in the boy. This was a conclusion reached on more positive grounds in Chapter 5, of course.

Defensive Identification

Both the masculine role and the superego develop, according to Freud (1924), as a consequence of the boy's defensive identification with the father. In Chapter 6 we brought together what evidence there was for constellating child behaviors and parental attitudes that we interpreted as indicators of such a process. These include generalized impulse control (dependency, aggression, and resistance to temptation), emotional upset and confession after wrongdoing, inhibition of aggression toward the father, overt masculinity, and suppressed femininity. The data provided one severe disappointment with respect to the theory, however; the various assessment measures of resistance to temptation (RTT) correlate about zero, on the average, with the measures of masculinity, the correlation between summary scores of the two being only .10. Thus the basic expectation from the theory was not confirmed.

At the same time, there was some support for three hypotheses concerning relationships (with other variables) generated separately by RTT and masculinity. For example, there was a non-significant confirmation of the expectation that the more masculine boys would show less aggression to their fathers (r with $X = -.25$). However, with respect to RTT, the expected constellation of low dependency (r with positive attention seeking $= -.32$), low overt aggression (with Z, $-.23$; with Y, $-.46$), high emotional upset (.37), high confession (.23), and suppressed femininity (with adult agents in doll play: Session I, .25; Session II, .52) was confirmed, but again mainly by non-significant correlations. Further, there appeared to be evidence for a developing internalized control structure, involving RTT, emotional upset, and confession, that is related to behavioral maturity; i.e., the boys appeared to be moving toward a more rigid self-restraint and away from the instrumental solution of moral problems as represented by fixing or reparation in the deviation situations.

None of these findings are direct or immediate in their demonstration of the defensive identification process, but all of them may be called supportive in that they describe outcomes to be expected if such a process were operative.

We did not attempt to devise a developmental theory of defensive identification, i.e., one positing the child-rearing conditions that would produce variations in the rate of development of the process. That task seemed scarcely worthwhile in the prior absence of data concerning the structure of the conscience or superego. Even with such data available, and with the opportunity we have had to examine extensively the child-rearing experiences correlated with the development of conscience, a developmental theoretical model is difficult to construct.

Among the parent-child relationships evinced in our data, however, there are some that can be considered congruent with Freud's description of defensive identification. There is clear indication of the father's ambivalence toward the high-conscience boys, and of a high current separation of the boys from their mothers. The latter fact, coupled with the gentle early socialization these boys received, suggests that the conditions had been appropriate for establishing an early warm cathexis of the boys for their mothers; when the boys reached the age of four, the mothers found it necessary to break off this relationship. According to the data reviewed in the preceding section, this should lead to a weakening of the mother's influence as a model (or source of reinforcement), and presumably should make the son more susceptible to the influence of the father.

The other interview variables significantly correlated with the various boy behaviors forming the defensive identification cluster reveal only one consistency, namely the father's belief in the importance of teaching right and wrong. This variable correlates significantly with RTT, emotional upset, and confession. It relates only very slightly and non-significantly to low positive attention seeking and to the (feminine) use of adult dolls as agents in doll play. It is entirely unrelated to any form of aggression. Among boys' fathers, this variable correlates .45 with hostility toward the son, −.56 with father's aggression anxiety, and .46 with punishment of dependency. Beyond these three variables, it relates significantly only to the set of maternal variables involving coldness, non-permissiveness, sex anxiety, and the mother's consequently low proportional caretaking in infancy.

At best, these findings are only suggestive of some conditions that may lead to the constellation of behaviors that have often been interpreted as the products of defensive identification. It seems reasonable to infer that the boy who is denied a close and nurturant relationship with a cold and sex-anxious mother will turn to the father as a source of affection and support. If, however, he is met by expressions of hostility, and even some punishment of his dependent strivings, he will attempt to secure acceptance in any way he can; that way is no doubt indicated by the father's clearly enunciated standards of what things are right and wrong to do.

Whatever merit defensive identification may have as a psychodynamic account of conscience development in boys, it gains no support at all as an explanation of the development of masculine gender role. Here, as we have seen in Chapter 5, the important antecedents seem to be parental permissiveness of sexuality and aggression. We must agree with Sanford (1955) that although identification with the aggressor may be a clinically observable phenomenon occurring as an emergency defense under conditions of extreme threat, it has little to recommend it as an account of normal developmental processes.

A Brief Conclusion

The theory of primary identification required that a number of behaviors be highly correlated with one another in girls of age four, and that a less coherent behavioral pattern be presented by boys of that age. By and large, our data appear to confirm this expectation. Positive attention seeking, adult role behavior, prosocial aggression, emotional upset after wrongdoing, and femininity did form a cluster in the girls, though the correlations among them were by no means all significant in size. At the same time, it must be emphasized that one of the important elements of conscience—resistance to temptation—definitely did not belong with this group, in the sense that it did not correlate positively with the other measures. The expected lower coherence of these traits among boys appeared as a median intercorrelation of about zero.

The original formulation of the theory assumed that a dependency motivational system would provide the reinforcement of the imitative responses that constituted the new repertoire of actions composing more mature and more adultlike roles. There was no evidence in the data, however, that any unitary concept of dependency was justified. The small positive correlations among the dependency categories in girls were matched by zero or negative correlations in boys. The notion of a dependency drive as the source of reinforcement for imitation or modeling was abandoned, therefore, and an alternative index of reinforcement was sought among the child-rearing measures obtained from the parent interviews.

Of the four classes of child-rearing variables hypothesized as ante-cedents of the identification-mediated cluster of child behaviors, only high demands seemed to be rather generally correlated with the cluster. Considerable difficulty was encountered in testing the antecedent-con-sequent hypotheses, however, because there were so many possible par-ent measures that could conceivably serve as indices of the rather ab-stractly defined theoretical variables. In the end, the suggestion was made that use of *reward for dependency* was a suitable substitute for *dependency drive or habit* as a designation of the source of reinforce-ment for imitative responses. Evidence was available to indicate that such reward, when administered by the parent opposite in sex from the child, was effective in establishing behaviors inappropriate to the child's ascribed gender role. The evidence was less convincing that rewards by the same-sexed parent were effective in establishing appropriately sex-typed behavior.

On the bases of the intercorrelations among the various child behav-iors that were hypothesized to be mediated by a primary identification process, and the antecedent-consequent relationships displayed in the re-lations between child-rearing and child-behavior variables, we con-cluded that:

1. Children of both sexes initially adopt feminine-maternal ways of be-having. The mechanisms involved may include either a modeling pro-cess, the efficiency of which is based on the responsiveness of the mother, or direct tuition, either intentional and verbalizable or not.

2. The boy develops a cognitive map of the male role at some point in his first three or four years and begins to shape his own behavior to-ward that role. To the extent that he has male models available (e.g., the father), the boy will be efficient in this shaping. The male charac-teristics are superimposed on, and replace, the female characteristics adopted earlier. There is no evidence in our data, however, that the fa-ther's responsiveness to his son's dependency supplications is a signifi-cant determinant of the development of masculinity.

3. Masculinity and femininity both appear to be more influenced by parental attitudes toward the control of sex and aggression than by any aspect of the availability or the behavior of models. Masculinity is as-sociated with freedom of expression, and with parental non-punitiveness, whereas femininity is associated with the opposite. This principle holds for children of both sexes.

Several aspects of the data concerning conscience in boys were congruent with Freud's theory of defensive identification, but we have been unable to form a behavioral theory of this process comparable to that for primary identification, nor do the data appear to call for one. Since masculinity and the various qualities of conscience we measured proved to be unrelated to one another, there seems to be no pressing need for a single process to account for such diverse forms of behavior.

In summary, children's personalities appear to possess "something like" the kind of patterning of feminine-maternal qualities that we hypothesized in our theory of primary identification, but by age four this patterning in boys has all but broken down under the requirement that males model themselves after males. The anaclitic quality of the initial socialization process remains evident in girls at this age, but does not in boys. Whether the growth of masculinity in boys is largely a product of the male role map or of some process such as defensive identification will best be determined by research with boys just older and just younger than our boys. And for both sexes the needed clarification of the primary identification process will require examination of the conditions and consequences of attachment and imitation in the first two years of life. We must know more about the mechanism itself before we can go much beyond our present study of its consequences.

Appendixes

Appendix A. *Parent Interviews*

The questions making up the mother and father interviews are presented here exactly as asked; following each one are the probes used (as necessary) to develop full response. The planning, procedure, and reliability of these interviews are discussed in Chapter 1 and Appendix B.

Mother Interview

0. What happened in the room just now with X? [This question referred to the first mother-child-interaction session.]
    a. How did the games go?
    b. What did X do while you were doing the questionnaire?
    c. How did his behavior in the room compare with his behavior with you at home?
    d. What happened when he played the different roles in the telephone game—you, his daddy, etc.?

1. Now let's go back to the beginning. Can you remember how things were when you found you were pregnant with X?
    a. Was he planned for?
    b. Was it a good time to have a baby?
    c. How did you feel during the pregnancy?
    d. How did the delivery go?
    e. How much change did it make in your life when X came along?
    f. (How did you feel about this pregnancy in relation to your others?)

2. Did you have help after the baby came?
    a. How much did your husband help to care for X?

3. How was he fed, breast or bottle?
    a. Why did you decide to do it that way?
    b. What kind of a feeding schedule did you have?

4. When did you start weaning?

    a. How did you decide what was the right time?

    b. How did you go about it?

    c. How did X react?

    d. How long did it take?

5. What about X's eating now—is he a good eater?

    a. Have there ever been any feeding problems?

    b. What have you done about teaching him table manners?

    c. Do you insist he eat what's on his plate or just as much as he wants?

6. What about toilet training—how did you go about it?

    a. When did you start bowel training?

    b. How did it go?

    c. Were there any special problems that came up?

    d. How long did it take?

    e. How did X react?

    f. What did you do when he had accidents?

    g. What do you do now?

7. What about wetting—is he mostly dry at night now?

    a. How did you handle it when the bed was wet?

    b. When did X get to the point of being dry in the daytime?

    c. Do you think X caught onto the idea of not wetting or soiling, and was trying?

    d. When did this happen?

    e. What did your husband do about X's toilet training?

8. Can you remember any special habits X had as a baby, like rocking or thumbsucking?

    a. Does he have any now?

    b. What have you done about them?

9. How do you feel about X's running around without clothes on?

    a. Have you tried to get him not to do this?

    b. How?

    c. Do you let him see you undressed?

    d. Take him in the bathroom with you?

    e. Does your husband?

    f. Has X ever done anything or said anything about this that has embarrassed you?

10. Children seem to differ somwhat in the age at which they discover the parts of their body and start to examine and play with them. Can you remember how old X was when he began to notice his genitals?

    a. Did he start to play with them about that same time?

    b. How much does he do this now?

    c. How do you think this should be handled?

    d. What have you done with X?

    e. How has it worked?

    f. How important do you feel it is to prevent this in a child?

11. What about sex play with other children, such as looking at each other, or going to the toilet together, or giggling together—has this occurred?

    a. What have you done?

12. Do you think X knows about sex differences?

    a. Has he asked questions about where babies come from, and that sort of thing?

    b. How have you answered?

    c. (How did he react to your next pregnancy?)

    d. How do you plan to give him information about sex?

    e. When?

    f. What kind of information do you think is appropriate?

13. How much did you know about sex as a child?

    a. How did your parents handle these things with you?

    b. What about adolescence—did you know what to expect?

    c. What about menstruation—where did you get the information?

    d. How free were you to discuss these things with your parents?

    e. How is this different from what you are doing?

14. What about being neat . . . ?

15. How important do you think it is for him to be careful about marking on the walls and jumping on the furniture and things like that?

    a. What do you do about it if he does these things?

16. And how about teaching children to leave alone the things that belong to other members of the family?

    a. What have you done about this with X?

17. We'd like to get some idea of the sort of rules you have for X in general—the sort of thing he is allowed to do and the sort of things he isn't allowed to do. What are some of the rules?

    a. How about bedtime?

    b. How about making noise in the house—how much of that do you allow?

    c. How about the amount of time he can spend listening to the radio or watching TV programs?

d. How far away is he allowed to go by himself?

e. How about not going into the street?

f. Any other rules?

g. How are these decided on?

h. Do you think children should have a voice in making the rules?

18. Do you thing a child of X's age should be given any regular jobs to do around the house?

a. Does X have any regular jobs he is supposed to do? Are there some things around the house he is expected to take responsibility for? How is he about this?

b. [If yes] How do you go about getting him to do this?

c. How much do you have to keep after X to get him to do the things he is supposed to do?

19. Some parents expect their children to obey immediately when they tell them to be quiet or pick something up, and so on; others don't think it's terribly important for a child to obey right away. How do you feel about this?

a. How does your husband feel about strict obedience?

b. If you ask X to do something, and he jumps up right away and do it, how do you react?

c. Do you say something to him?

d. If he doesn't do what you ask, do you ever just drop the subject, or do you always see to it that he does it?

20. Do you keep track of exactly where X is and what he is doing most of the time, or can you let him watch out for himself quite a bit?

a. How often do you check?

21. There are some things that almost all children do sometime in their early lives that may present problems to their parents. What has X's history been with respect to these kinds of behavior:

a. Fibbing or telling tall stories?

b. Taking or using things that don't belong to him?

c. Playing with fire or matches?

d. Teasing or hurting animals?

22. What are the things that X does that bother you particularly?

a. How do you show it when you get annoyed with X?

b. [If restrained] Do you think X can usually tell how you feel?

23. Most parents come to a point once in a while when they just blow up at their children. Does this happen to you?

    a. What generally brings it on?

    b. How do you feel when this happens?

24. Some parents feel children shouldn't fight with other children in the neighborhood; others feel they should learn to defend themselves. What do you think about this?

    a. What have you taught X about fighting?

    b. How much does X fight with other children?

25. [If X has siblings] Would you tell me something about how X and his brother (sister) get along together?

    a. How do you feel about it when they quarrel?

    b. How bad does it have to get before you do something about it?

    c. How do you handle it when the children quarrel? Give me an example.

    d. Now how about when things are going smoothly among the children—do you do anything to show them that you have noticed this?

    e. [If yes] What sort of thing would you do?

26. Sometimes a child will get angry at his parents and hit them or kick them or shout angry things at them. How much of this sort of thing do you think parents ought to allow in a child of X's age?

    a. How do you handle it when X acts like this? Give me an example.

    b. [If this doesn't happen] How did you teach him not to do this?

    c. [If it does happen] How important do you feel it is to prevent this kind of angry behavior?

    d. How do you go about preventing it?

27. In general, what ways do you use of getting X to behave as you want him to?

    a. How much do you try explaining things to him and reasoning with him?

28. What do you think are the best ways of disciplining children?

    a. What seems to work best with X?

    b. Do you send him to his room, deprive him of things like watching TV or playing with a favorite toy?

    c. What about scolding; what kind of things would you say?

    d. What about making him feel silly or ashamed (like saying he's "too big a boy!")?

    e. Can you think of the last time he did something wrong, and describe just what happened and what you did?

    f. How do things like this make you feel?

    g. How often do you spank X?

    h. For what?

    i. How do you feel about spanking him?

29. How often do you tell X that you're going to have to punish him and then for some reason you don't follow through?

    a. What kinds of things might keep you from following through?

30. When X has to be disciplined, who usually does it, you or your husband (assuming both of you are there)?

    a. How strict is your husband with X?

    b. Does he ever do anything in disciplining X that you'd rather he didn't do?

31. In general, how well would you say you and your husband agree about the best way to handle X?

    a. Does he ever think you are too strict or not strict enough?

    b. Can you give me an example of a case where you didn't agree entirely?

32. We are wondering about who makes the main decisions about the children. In some families it is the father; in others, he leaves it all to the mother. How does that work out in your family?

    a. For instance, in deciding how far away from the house X is allowed to go by himself?

    b. How about health matters such as:

       1) calling the doctor

       2) or keeping him indoors for the day

       Who decides that?

    c. Who decides how much X should help you or his father around the house?

33. How about in other things besides things that affect the children—who generally makes the decisions in your family?

    a. How about money matters?

    b. Who handles the money, pays the bills, and so on?

    c. Who has most to say in deciding what you will do in your leisure time?

    d. How about if you were considering moving to a different house—who would have most to say about a decision like that?

34. In some families, the work is more or less divided up between what

the wife does and what the husband does. For instance, it will be the wife's job to wash dishes and the husband's job to mow the lawn and take care of the furnace. In other families everybody helps with everything. How is this in your family?

35. Do you think X understands pretty well these relationships between you and his father?
 a. Does he seem to go to you for some things and to his father for others?
 b. How about for sympathy?
 c. For permission to do something he wants to do?
 d. To get a new toy or clothes or something?
 e. Do you think he ever has the feeling or the idea that one of his parents is the *real* boss in the family?

36. We're interested in what kinds of ideas of right and wrong children get. How much do you think is possible to teach them at this age?
 a. How important is it?
 b. How have you gone about this with X?
 c. What kinds of examples of behavior do you use?
 d. Do you ever use specific people? For instance, yourself or your husband?

37. How does X usually react when he's done something wrong? Can you tell when he has?
 a. Does it seem to bother him, does he ever act sorry or ashamed?
 b. Does he ever come tell you when he's done something wrong?
 c. About what kinds of things?
 d. What do you do then?

38. What do you do if he's unusually good?
 a. Do you let him know you're pleased? How?
 b. Besides praising him would you give him something special, like something to eat, or a special privilege?

39. How much can you count on X to do the things he's supposed to do if you're not there to check up on him?
 a. Are there situations in which you can't trust him? What are they?
 b. Suppose you left him to watch something while you went away for a few minutes—how much could you count on him?

40. How important do you think it is for a child to learn to do things for himself?

    a. How have you tried to help X in this?

    b. Have there been some times when he has surprised you by how grown-up he seems?

41. Have there been any problems about his trying to act *too* grown-up, like using daddy's razor (trying on your shoes, or lipstick)?

    a. What have you seen him do?

    b. Does he ever try to make family decisions that you would rather he didn't? Does he sometimes act sort of bossy?

    c. Does he sometimes offer to take responsibilities that you think are beyond him at this age—such as staying alone, opening windows, crossing streets?

    d. How do you feel about his efforts to act grown-up?

42. In what ways would you expect a little boy to behave differently from a little girl?

    a. How early do you think boys and girls begin to show these differences in their interests and the way they act?

    b. Which do you think is easier to bring up?

    c. Which do you enjoy more?

    d. Have you taught X anything about how little boys should act differently from little girls [or vice versa]?

43. What kind of a child is X to live with—is he pretty easy to get along with?

    a. Are there times when he's a little upset or out of sorts? Can you give me some examples?

    b. What about when you're not feeling well?

44. Would you describe X as an affectionate child?

    a. How much do you cuddle him?

    b. How do you feel about this?

    c. How much attention does he seem to want from you?

    d. Does he seem to want more when he's done something wrong?

    e. How would you feel about giving it to him then?

    f. How do you generally react if he demands attention when you're busy?

    g. Does he seem to need to be with you most of the time or does he get along without you pretty well?

    h. How does he react when you have to be away?

45. What things do you most enjoy doing with X?

    a. Do you read to him or tell him stories?

    b. Do you tease or joke with him sometimes?

    c. How does he react to that?

46. How easy is it for you to talk to X?

    a. Does he ask questions quite a bit? What kind?

    b. How do you usually answer them?

    c. How much do you think he understands?

47. What things seem to frighten X especially?

    a. Have there been some times when he was badly hurt or frightened?

    b. How did he react?

    c. What did you do?

    d. Has he had any bad dreams?

    e. How often does he have accidents?

48. What sort of person would you like X to grow up to be?

    a. Whom does he most resemble?

    b. How much do you want him to be like his father?

    c. Like you?

    d. What do you think the chances are he will grow up to be this kind of person?

49. What plans do you have for schooling?

    a. What sort of work would you like him to do?

    b. What about getting along with people?

    c. Are there any particular activities you'll encourage him in?

    d. How much do you feel you can determine how these things will work out?

50. I'd like to get a fuller picture of how your life goes. How do you usually spend your week?

    a. What do you find time to do besides taking care of the children?

    b. What part of your day is most difficult for you?

    c. What is most pleasant?

51. Did you find that starting to have children made a difference in your interests and the things you shared with your husband?

    a. How much difference did it make in your social life?

52. Were you working before X was born?

    a. (How did you feel about stopping?)

    b. (Would you ever want to go back to work?)

53. Most mothers occasionally wish that sometimes they could get completely away from the children for a while. What about you?

    a. What do you do about this?

    b. How much time do you and your husband get to spend together these days?

54. What are the times that the whole family is together?

    a. What do you do together?

    b. Trips, or picnics, or visits to the zoo together?

55. How much time does X spend with his father?

    a. How much of this is alone with him?

    b. What do they do together?

    c. How much do you think X knows about what his father does at work?

56. How prepared for marriage do you feel you were?

    a. Have there been a good many things about running a home you have had to learn as you've gone along? Tell me about them.

57. Earlier I asked once about how your ways of doing things with X compared with your parents' ways of doing things with you. Can you tell some more about this?

    a. Feeding and table manners?

    b. Infant care and affection?

    c. Toilet training?

    d. Discipline?

    e. Responsibility and work?

    f. Goals and aspirations about school and career?

58. Would you say the ways you and your husband do things now with X are more similar to how things were done in your family or in your husband's?

    a. In what specific ways?

    b. How did this get worked out between you?

    c. What about religion?

Father Interview

1. First I'd like to ask just a little about X's early life. Where were you living and what were you doing at the time your wife became pregnant?

    a. Was it a planned pregnancy?

    b. Was it a good time to have a baby?

    c. How much change did it make in your life when X came along?

    d. Did you find that starting to have children made a difference in your interests and the things you shared with your wife?

    e. (If a first child) How did you feel about the responsibilities of becoming a father?

2. Was your wife working before X was born?

    a. How did you feel about her stopping?

    b. (If worked) Has she gone back to work, or would you like her to?

    c. Do you feel she is satisfied with her role as a mother?

3. How much did you help to care for X during his first year of life?

    a. Feeding?

    b. Toileting and cleanliness?

4. What kind of baby was X? Did he cry a great deal?

    a. [When he did cry] How did you handle this?

    b. Did you and your wife agree on this policy?

    c. Did either of you feel the other was too hard-hearted or too soft-hearted?

    d. Was he an affectionate baby?

    e. Were there any habits like thumbsucking that you felt were a problem?

5. Let's come up to the last year or so, now, with that same question; has X had any habits recently that have puzzled you or bothered you?

    a. Thumbsucking?

6. How do you feel about X's running around without clothes on?

    a. Have you tried to get him not to do this?

    b. How?

    c. Do you let him see you undressed?

    d. Do you let him in the bathroom with you?

    e. Does your wife?

    f. Has X ever done anything or said anything about this that has embarrassed you?

7. Children seem to differ somewhat in the age at which they discover the parts of their body and start to examine and play with them. Can you remember how old X was when he began to notice his genitals?

    a. Did he start to play with them about that same time?

    b. How much does he do this now?

    c. How do you think this should be handled?

    d. What have you done with X?

    e. How has it worked?

    f. How important do you feel it is to prevent this in a child?

8. What about sex play with other children, such as looking at each

other, or going to the toilet together, or giggling together? Has this occurred?

    a. What have you done?

  9. How much do you think X knows about sex differences?

    a. Has he asked questions about where babies come from, and that sort of thing?

    b. How have you answered?

    c. What kind of information do you think is appropriate?

  10. Now we want to change the subject—the question of being neat and orderly and keeping things clean. What do you expect of X as far as neatness is concerned?

    a. How do you go about getting him to do this?

  11. How important do you think it is for him to be careful about marking on the walls and jumping on the furniture and things like that?

    a. What do you do about it if he does these things?

  12. And how about teaching children to leave alone the things that belong to other members of the family?

    a. What have you done about this with X?

  13. Do you think a child of X's age should be given any regular jobs to do around the house?

    a. Does X have any regular jobs he is supposed to do?

    b. [If yes] How do you go about getting him to do this?

    c. How much do you have to keep after X to get him to do the things he is supposed to do?

  14. When you ask X to do something, does he obey immediately? What do you do when he doesn't?

    a. When he doesn't, do you ever just drop the subject, or do you always see to it that he does it?

    b. How does your wife feel about strict obedience?

  15. Most parents get annoyed at their children sometimes. How do you show it when you get annoyed with X?

    a. Do you think X can usually tell how you feel?

    b. How does X act when you really blow up at him? Give me an example.

    c. Are there any special things X does that are likely to make you blow up?

  16. There are some things that almost all children do sometime in

their early lives that may present problems to their parents. What has X's history been with respect to these kinds of behavior:

    a. Fibbing or telling tall stories?

    b. Taking or using things that don't belong to him?

    c. Playing with fire?

    d. Teasing or hurting animals?

17. What about showing anger at his parents? You know the kind of thing—hitting or kicking or shouting angry things at you.

    a. How do you handle it when X acts like this? Give me an example.

    b. [If this doesn't happen] How did you teach him not to do this?

    c. [If it does happen] How important do you feel it is to prevent this kind of angry behavior?

    d. How do you go about preventing it?

18. Are there any other things X does that bother you particularly?

19. Some parents feel children shouldn't fight with other children in the neighborhood; others feel they should learn to defend themselves. What do you think about this?

    a. What have you taught X about fighting?

    b. How much does X fight with other children?

20. In general, what ways do you use of getting X to behave as you want him to? How much do you try explaining things to him and reasoning with him?

21. What do you think are the best ways of disciplining children?

    a. What seems to work best with X?

    b. Do you send him to his room, deprive him of things like watching TV or playing with a favorite toy?

    c. What about scolding—what kind of things would you say?

    d. What about making him feel silly or ashamed (like saying he's "too big a boy!")?

    e. Can you think of the last time he did something wrong, and describe just what happened and what you did?

    f. How do things like this make you feel?

    g. How often do you spank X?

    h. For what?

    i. How do you feel about spanking him?

22. How often do you tell X that you're going to have to punish him and then for some reason you don't follow through?

a. What kinds of things might keep you from following through?

23. When X has to be disciplined, who usually does it, you or your wife (assuming both of you are there)?

a. How strict is your wife with X?

b. Does she ever do anything in disciplining X that you'd rather she didn't do?

24. In general, how well would you say you and your wife agree about the best way to handle X?

a. Does she ever think you are too strict or not strict enough?

b. Can you give me an example of a case where you didn't agree entirely?

25. We are wondering about who makes the main decisions about the children. In some families it is the father; in others, he leaves it all to the mother. How does that work out in your family?

a. For instance, in deciding how far away from the house he's allowed to go by himself?

b. How about health matters, such as:

1) calling the doctor

2) or keeping him indoors for the day

Who decides that?

c. Who decides how much X should help you or his mother around the house?

26. How about in other things besides things that affect the children—who generally makes the decisions in your family?

a. How about money matters?

b. Who handles the money, pays the bills, and so on?

c. Who has most to say in deciding what you will do in your leisure time?

27. In some families, the work is more or less divided up between what the wife does and what the husband does. For instance, it will be the wife's job to wash dishes and the husband's job to mow the lawn and take care of the furnace. In other families everybody helps with everything. How is this in your family?

28. Do you think X understands pretty well these relationships between you and his mother?

a. Does he seem to go to you for some things and to his mother for others?

    b. How about for sympathy?

    c. For permission to do something he wants to do?

    d. To get a new toy or clothes or something?

    e. Do you think he ever has the feeling or the idea that one of his parents is the *real* boss in the family?

29. We're interested in what kinds of ideas of right and wrong children get. How much do you think is possible to teach them at this age?

    a. How important is it?

    b. How have you gone about this with X?

    c. What kinds of examples of behavior do you use?

    d. Do you ever use specific people—for instance, yourself or your wife?

30. How does X usually react when he's done something wrong? Can you tell when he has?

    a. Does it seem to bother him, does he ever act sorry or ashamed?

    b. Does he ever come and tell you when he's done something wrong?

    c. About what kinds of things?

    d. What do you do then?

31. What do you do if he's unusually good?

    a. Do you let him know you're pleased? How?

    b. Besides praising him, would you give him something special, like something to eat or a special privilege?

32. How important do you think it is for a child to learn to do things for himself?

    a. How have you tried to help X in this?

    b. Have there been some times when he has surprised you by how grown up he seems? Can you give me an example?

33. Have there been any problems about his trying to act *too* grown-up, like using your razor (trying on your wife's shoes, or lipstick)?

    a. What have you seen him do?

    b. Does he ever try to make family decisions that you would rather he didn't? Does he sometimes act sort of bossy?

    c. Does he sometimes offer to take responsibilities that you think are beyond him at this age—such as staying alone, opening windows, crossing streets?

    d. How do you feel about his efforts to act grown-up?

34. Now about the ways boys act differently from girls:
    a. How early do you think boys and girls begin to show these differences in their interests and the way they act?
    b. Which do you think is easier to bring up?
    c. Which do you enjoy more?
    d. Have you taught X anything about how little boys should act differently from little girls [or vice versa]?
    e. Does X have any particular likes or habits that seem too girlish [boyish]?
    f. Do you think he will naturally outgrow them, or are you making some effort to change them?
35. Would you describe X as an affectionate child?
    a. How much do you cuddle him?
    b. How do you feel about this?
    c. How much attention does he seem to want from you?
    d. Does he seem to want more when he's done something wrong?
    e. How would you feel about giving it to him then?
    f. How do you generally react if he demands attention when you're busy?
    g. Does he seem to need to be with you most of the time or does he get along without you pretty well?
    h. How does he react when you have to be away?
36. What things do you most enjoy doing with X?
37. What sort of person would you like X to grow up to be?
    a. What do you think the chances are he will grow up to be this kind of person?
38. What plans do you have for schooling?
    a. How much do you feel you can determine how these things will work out?
39. How much time does X spend with you?
    a. How much of this is alone with you?
    b. What do you do together?
    c. How much do you think X knows about what you do at work?
40. I'd like to ask about how your ways of doing things with X compare with your parents' ways of doing things with you. How about:
    a. Discipline?
    b. Responsibility and work?
    c. Goals and aspirations about school and career?

Appendix B. *Interview Coding and Reliability*

The two raters, both experienced in coding interview material, were trained on several pretest interviews. When they appeared to understand all the concepts fully, and to be agreeing on nearly all their judgments, they began the coding of the research interviews. This task was performed independently, and after each block of five to ten interviews they compared their ratings and discussed any serious disagreements. When a disagreement was no greater than one point on a five-point scale, the two ratings were simply averaged, but in the few cases in which it was greater, a joint decision was reached by reexamination of the interview. When an interview failed to provide adequate information for rating a particular scale, the datum involved was recorded as "Not Ascertained" on that scale. The entire group of forty mother interviews was rated first, and the forty father interviews second.

Since disagreements of no more than one point (i.e., ratings on adjacent points) were averaged, not discussed, a five-point scale could be automatically expanded to a nine-point scale, the even-numbered points accommodating those cases on which disagreement occurred; on a five-point scale, for example, if a mother was rated "2" by one rater and "3" by the other, the "2.5" average would fall at "4" on the nine-point scale. For the half dozen seven-point scales, the raters eliminated all disagreements and converted their ratings to nine points. With a few minor variations, then, all interview scales in their final form provided nine-point distributions.

Rating Types

There were two kinds of ratings, one an individual rating of the response of the mother or father concerned, the other a *pooled* rating based on the relevant material contained in both parents' interviews.

The individual-parent ratings have been used, and interpreted, as measures of the parents themselves. In most instances, such scales refer to some aspect of parental behavior or attitude, such as permissiveness for aggression. In a few cases, however, they refer to the child's behavior, such as amount of nudity child shows in the home. These "child-behavior" scales have also been interpreted (usually) as being relevant to the parent (i.e., to his perceptions) rather than to the child, although for some scales (e.g., each parent's report of how much aggression the child shows toward him) we have tentatively interpreted the ratings as referring to the child's behavior because there is good reason, in these cases, to expect the child to behave differently toward the two parents.

The pooled ratings were used as measures of several kinds of child behavior; we have used the pooled measure where we sought as objective a measure as possible of the child's actual behavior in the home, and were *not* seeking an indirect measure of the parent by estimating the individual parent's *perception* of the child. The scales based on information pooled from both parents' interviews are noted in Appendix C by ("P") following the title.

Reliability Types

Three types of rater reliability have been calculated, each using "per cent agreement" as the unit in which reliability is expressed. The three types represent three levels of stringency. Separate calculations have been made by each type for each subject's mother and each subject's father and for each scale. The *subject* measure indicates the per cent of agreement betwen the two raters (before discussion) on the 161 scales rated from each mother's interview, and similarly on the 119 from each father's interview. The *scale* measure cuts the analysis in the other direction, indicating the per cent agreement among the ratings of the forty mothers or the forty fathers on each of the scales separately. The reliability values obtained by the two kinds of calculation permit discrimination among parents, on the one hand, and among scales, on the other; thus we may evaluate how reliably a parent was measured, or how reliably a scale measured a given variable.

The three types of reliability measurement are as follows: I, the most stringent, measures per cent of *exact* agreement, regardless of whether a rating is on the numerical scale or is an "N.A." rating; II also measures *exact* agreement, but disregards instances of "N.A." ratings by either rater; III measures agreement to the extent that ratings occur at *the same or adjacent points* on a scale, with "N.A." judgments again disregarded. The medians and ranges of the three types of reliability measures for subject evaluations and for scale evaluations are given in Table B1.

Although each of the three types of measurement has its use, the third is probably the most relevant to the data actually used in the research. It measures agreement within one point on the rating scales, and since disagreements of that size were averaged without discussion, the final scale scores actually represent measures based on that degree of error tolerance. Type III reliability is therefore the type given for each scale in Appendix C.

The median reliability indicators are entirely satisfactory in all cases, for both *subjects* and *scales*, and of course all instances of disagreement beyond the tolerance implied in Type III were corrected by discussion. However, the ranges given in the table for Types I and II reliabilities show that the relatively non-stringent Type III indicator is hiding some real weakness in coding, a weakness resulting only partly from the occurrence of "N.A." ratings. In the reliability column of Appendix C, an asterisk has been appended to the Type III figures for scales for which the Type II "per cent agreement" is below 60 per cent.

TABLE B1

Reliability of Interview Ratings: Medians and Ranges of Per Cent Agreement
on Mothers and Fathers, and on Mother and Father Scales,
Calculated by Three Formulae

Category Measured	N	Type of Reliability (Per Cent Agreement; See Text)					
		I		II		III	
		Median	Range	Median	Range	Median	Range
Mothers	40	72.5	54–82	72.5	58–83	97.5	89–100
Fathers	40	77.5	60–87	72.5	63–87	97.5	95–100
Mother scales . . .	161	67.5	35–100	67.5	35–100	97.5	74–100
Father scales . . .	119	72.5	37–100	72.5	37–100	100	87–100

Appendix C. *Parent and Child Variables*

In the course of this study, 556 variables were coded. Of these, 246 were parental and 310 were child. However, some of the parent measures proved to have unacceptably low reliability, and the behavior represented by some of the child measures occurred so infrequently that its measures were of limited value. After discarding these, there were 373 variables remaining, 184 parental and 189 child. These constitute the list that follows. An index to text and table citations of the variables follows immediately after the list.

The data analysis required a correlation matrix of these 373 variables, separately by sex of child. For all but three of the child variables an obtained score was available for every child, but in more than a third of the parent-interview measures there were one or more "not ascertained" cases. In such instances, the median score, calculated separately for boys' and girls' parents, was substituted for the non-scalar value.

The list of variables is to be interpreted as follows:

Column 1. The variable number in the correlation matrix. These numbers are used to identify variables in the text. When a roman arabic combination (e.g., VI, 22) appears in the text, it refers to a variable that was not included in the correlation matrix; the numbers are deck and column identifiers in the original storage decks for the study (on file at the Laboratory of Human Development, Stanford University).

Column 2. The name of the variable. For the interpretation of mean differences between groups, and the directions of correlations, the high end of a scale or measure is indicated by the name of the scale. Thus, on variable 1, "age of child," older children have higher scale numbers; on 211, "resistance to temptation: total standard score," a high number reflects high resistance to temptation. For a few variables involving comparison between parents, a statement is included to indicate which parent is at the high end of the scale; e.g., on 81, "source of power in home: mother high," a low score indicates father and a high score, mother.

Column 3. For parent interview and questionnaire scales only, the number of cases for which scalar judgments were available. The number of "not ascertained" cases is the difference from 40. (Data were obtained for all forty children on all but three of the child variables.)

Column 4. For parent interview scales only, the per cent agreement between raters according to the Type III criterion described in Appendix B. Reliability figures were not calculated for final pooled ratings; for these, the figure given is the mean of the two reliability indices for the initial separate ratings of each parents' interviews. An asterisk (*) on a reliability figure indicates that the Type II index was below 60 per cent. (Reliability calculations for child variables are described in the succeeding appendixes.)

List of Variables

Var. No.	Name of Variable	N	Reliability

Variables Derived from Parent Interviews and Mother Questionnaires

(See also Chapter 1 and Appendixes A and B. Letters in parentheses indicate derivation from mothers', fathers', or pooled responses; where these letters are omitted, the source of the response is implicit in the name of the variable.)

Var. No.	Name of Variable	N	Reliability
1.	Age of child (M)	40	
2.	Child's behavior: correspondence between MCI and home (M)	40	95*
3.	MCI seen by mother as achievement situation for child	40	100*
4.	Mother's tension concerning MCI	40	98
5.	Severity of child's early separation from mother	39	95
6.	Severity of child's early separation from father	38	99
7.	Severity of child's current separation from father (P)	40	99
8.	Stability of current home situation (P)	40	100
9.	Mother's resentment of this pregnancy	38	84*
10.	Father's resentment of this pregnancy	40	88
11.	Mother's proportion of caretaking in infancy	40	95
12.	Father's proportion of caretaking in infancy	40	100*
13.	Duration of breast feeding (M)	37	100
14.	Rigidity of scheduled feeding (M)	37	100
15.	Severity of child's reaction to weaning (M)	39	100
16.	Severity of weaning (M)	39	97
17.	Severity of child's feeding problems (M)	40	98
18.	Level of demands for table manners (M)	38	100*
19.	Severity of toilet training (M)	39	97*
20.	Severity of child's reaction to toilet training (M)	37	97
21.	Frequency of current bedwetting (M)	40	97
22.	Amount of thumbsucking child has shown (P)	40	100

Var. No.	Name of Variable	N	Reliability
23.	Mother's permissiveness for indoor nudity	37	97
24.	Father's permissiveness for indoor nudity	36	100
25.	Mother's pressure for modesty indoors	37	97
26.	Amount of child's social nudity (M)	38	94
27.	Amount of child's social nudity (F)	38	100
28.	Mother's modesty	40	100
29.	Father's modesty	40	98°
30.	Mother's permissiveness for masturbation	39	95
31.	Father's permissiveness for masturbation	39	100
32.	Mother's permissiveness for sex play among children	36	91
33.	Sexuality in child (M)	40	100
34.	Sexuality in child (F)	40	100
35.	Extent mother gives sexual information to child	40	100°
36.	Extent father gives sexual information to child	40	100
37.	Openness about sex shown by mother's parents (M)	40	100
38.	Mother's sex anxiety	40	93°
39.	Father's sex anxiety	40	98°
40.	Mother's restrictions on house and property	40	100
41.	Father's restrictions on house and property	39	100
42.	Mother's pressure for neatness and orderliness	39	97°
43.	Father's pressure for neatness and orderliness	38	100
44.	Mother's strictness about bedtime behavior	37	100°
45.	Mother's pressure for conformity to standards	40	85°
46.	Father's pressure for conformity to standards	40	98°
47.	Mother's use of democracy	39	100
48.	Mother's expectancy of child's taking responsibility	40	100
49.	Father's expectancy of child's taking responsibility	39	100
50.	Extent mother's standards of obedience are realistic	38	97°
51.	Extent mother keeps track of child	39	100
52.	Child's level of conduct on four problems (P) (fibbing, taking others' things, playing with fire, teasing animals)	40	97
53.	Extent of overt aggression in home by mother	40	100
54.	Extent of overt aggression in home by father	40	100
55.	Mother's demand for aggression toward peers	40	95
56.	Father's demand for aggression toward peers	39	95
W.	Mother's perception of child's aggression toward parents	40	100
X.	Father's perception of child's aggression toward parents	40	100
57.	Child's aggression toward parents (P: W + X)	40	100
58.	Mother's permissiveness for aggression toward parents	39	97
59.	Father's permissiveness for aggression toward parents	38	97
60.	Mother's use of punishment for aggression toward parents	37	100
61.	Father's use of punishment for aggression toward parents	38	97
62.	Mother's aggression anxiety	40	95
63.	Father's aggression anxiety	40	100
64.	Mother's use of reasoning	40	100
65.	Father's use of reasoning	38	98°

Var. No.	Name of Variable	N	Reliability
66.	Mother's use of isolation	39	100
67.	Mother's use of physical punishment	40	100
68.	Father's use of physical punishment	40	100
69.	Mother's use of deprivation of privileges	38	97°
70.	Father's use of deprivation of privileges	38	97
71.	Mother's use of ridicule	37	96
72.	Father's use of ridicule	38	100
73.	Relative frequency as agents of discipline: mother high (M)	40	100
74.	Relative frequency as agents of discipline: mother high (F)	40	100
75.	Relative strictness of parents: mother high (P)	40	100
76.	Strictness of mother	40	93
77.	Strictness of father	40	100°
78.	Extent of parents' disagreement about child rearing (P) . .	40	96°
79.	Extent of sex stereotyping in parents' roles (M)	39	95°
80.	Extent of sex stereotyping in parents' roles (F)	39	97°
81.	Source of power in home: mother high (P)	40	98
82.	Source of nurturance: mother high (P)	40	98
83.	Mother's stress on importance of teaching right and wrong .	40	100
84.	Father's stress on importance of teaching right and wrong .	40	100°
85.	Mother's use of people as models of good behavior	38	97
86.	Father's use of people as models of good behavior	36	94°
87.	Extent child confesses wrongdoing (M)	40	100
88.	Extent child confesses wrongdoing (F)	40	100
89.	Signs of conscience as reaction to wrongdoing (P)	40	94
90.	Mother's expectancy of conscience	39	97°
91.	Father's expectancy of conscience	38	95
92.	Extent child refrains from teasing animals (P)	40	100
93.	Mother's use of reward for confession	38	91°
94.	Mother's use of praise	40	88°
95.	Father's use of praise	38	95°
96.	Mother's use of tangible reward	40	95°
97.	Father's use of tangible reward	39	95
98.	Mother's use of psychological (vs. tangible) reward	40	95
99.	Father's use of psychological (vs. tangible) reward	40	100
100.	Mother's permissiveness for independence	40	95°
101.	Father's permissiveness for independence	40	98°
102.	Mother's use of reward for independence	40	98°
103.	Father's use of reward for independence	40	95
104.	Mother's use of punishment for independence	39	87°
105.	Father's use of punishment for independence	39	100
106.	Mother's satisfaction with child's socialization	40	93°
107.	Father's satisfaction with child's socialization	40	98°
108.	Mother's use of reward for adult role behavior	38	78°
109.	Father's use of reward for adult role behavior	40	95°
110.	Mother's use of punishment for adult role behavior	37	92°
111.	Extent child imitates parents (P)	40	96

Var. No.	Name of Variable	N	Reliability
112.	Mother's expectancy of sex differences in behavior	40	95°
113.	Father's expectancy of sex differences in behavior	39	95°
114.	Mother's use of reward for sex-appropriate behavior	40	100°
115.	Father's use of reward for sex-appropriate behavior	39	95°
116.	Child's expression of affection toward mother	39	95°
117.	Child's expression of affection toward father	40	98
118.	Mother's warmth toward child	40	83°
119.	Father's warmth toward child	40	98
120.	Mother's affectional demonstrativeness toward child	40	90°
121.	Father's affectional demonstrativeness toward child	40	98
122.	Child's expression of dependency toward mother	40	90°
123.	Child's expression of dependency toward father	40	100
124.	Mother's permissiveness for dependency	40	95
125.	Father's permissiveness for dependency	40	98°
126.	Mother's use of reward for dependency	40	95
127.	Father's use of reward for dependency	40	98
128.	Mother's use of punishment for dependency	39	87°
129.	Father's use of punishment for dependency	40	88
130.	Child's anxiety and fears (M)	40	95°
131.	Mother's empathy for child	40	95°
132.	Father's empathy for child	40	98°
133.	Mother's achievement standards for child	40	90°
134.	Father's achievement standards for child	40	92°
135.	Extent child resembles mother (P)	38	94
136.	Extent child resembles father (P)	37	90°
137.	Extent of mother's influence on child	40	100°
138.	Mother's directiveness toward child	40	100
139.	Father's directiveness toward child	40	100°
140.	Mother's hostility to child	40	93°
141.	Father's hostility to child	40	100
142.	Severity of child's current separation from mother (M) . . .	40	98
143.	Extent mother evaluates positively the mother role	40	100
144.	Continuity of mother's goals with the mother role	39	95°
145.	Mother's caretaking consistency (with this child)	40	98°
146.	Mother's child-rearing anxiety	40	88°
147.	Parental discrepancy score	40	N.A.
148.	Mother's self-esteem	40	88°
149.	Father's self-esteem	40	93°
150.	Mother's sociability	38	97
151.	Amount of father's interaction with child (P)	40	98°
152.	Extent of child's acquaintance with father's work (P) . . .	40	98°
153.	Mother's evaluation of father	37	97°
154.	Father's evaluation of mother	40	95°
155.	Strictness of mother's parents	39	100
156.	Strictness of father's parents	36	97°
157.	Warmth of mother's parents	37	94°

Var. No.	Name of Variable	N	Reliability
158.	Extent mother disowns grandparents' child-rearing policies .	40	98
159.	Extent father disowns grandparents' child-rearing policies .	38	95
160.	Extent of mother's current dissatisfaction with her life . . .	40	100
161.	Age of father (P)	40	
162.	Age of mother (P)	40	
163.	Number of children in family (M)	40	
164.	Spaciousness of living space (M)	40	100
165.	Mother Attitude Scale: permissiveness for nudity	40	
166.	Mother Attitude Scale: permissiveness for masturbation . .	40	
167.	Mother Attitude Scale: permissiveness for sex play among children	40	
168.	Mother Attitude Scale: punitiveness for aggression toward parents	40	
169.	Mother Attitude Scale: permissiveness for aggression toward parents	40	
170.	Child Behavior Scale: maturity (M)	40	
171.	Winterbottom Scale: mean age of expected independence (high = low pressure for independence) (M)	40	
172.	Winterbottom Scale: number of items checked (high = high pressure for independence) (M)	40	
173.	Mother's non-permissiveness: factor score	40	
174.	Warmth of mother-child relationship: factor score	40	

Variables Derived from Observation of Children

(For BUO, see Chapter 1 and Appendix D; all BUO variables are real except those specifically identified as fantasy. For assessment situations, see Chapters 3, 5, and 6, and Appendixes G, H, and I; for sex-typing tests, see Appendix J; for observer ratings, see Appendix E.)

175. Giving facts or demonstrating knowledge (BUO)
176. Real adult mannerisms (BUO)
177. Fantasy adult mannerisms (BUO)
179. Real adult work (BUO)
180. Fantasy adult work (BUO)
182. Nurturance (BUO)
184. Total real adult role (BUO)
185. Total fantasy adult role (BUO)
187. Negative attention seeking (BUO)
188. Reassurance seeking (BUO)
189. Direct physical aggression (BUO)
191. Direct verbal aggression (BUO)
192. Injury to objects (BUO)
193. Mischief (BUO)

194. Total antisocial aggression (BUO)
196. Verbal disapproval of behavior (BUO)
197. Tattling (BUO)
198. Total prosocial aggression (BUO)
199. "It" Scale (sex typing)
200. Area usage score (sex typing)
201. Pictures test (sex typing)
202. Toy preference and satiation test (sex typing)
203. Sex typing: observer rating
204. Sex typing: total standard score
205. Candy temptation (RTT)
206. Ring toss game (RTT)
207. Toy temptation (RTT)
208. Quoting rules situation (RTT)

209. Hamster: latency of response (RTT)
210. Hamster: seriousness of response (RTT)
211. Resistance to temptation: total standard score
212. Quoting rules: total raw score
213. Quoting rules: stooge rating of persistence
214. Aggression: observer rating
215. Physical contact seeking: observer rating
216. Attention getting: observer rating
217. Physical activity level: observer rating
218. Social interaction level: observer rating
219. Positive attention seeking (BUO)
220. Touching and holding (BUO)
221. Being near (BUO)
222. Masturbation (BUO)
223. Orality (BUO)
224. Total observed dependency (BUO)

225. Degree of involvement (hamster)
226. Acceptance of responsibility (hamster)
227. Behavioral evidence of internal conflict (hamster)
228. Strength of reaction to deviation (hamster)
229. Extent of rule following (red light)
230. Extent of efforts to hide deviation (red light)
231. Tension following deviation (red light)
232. Intensity of confession (red light)
233. Spontaneity of confession (red light)
234. Degree of denial of deviation (red light)
235. Emotional upset: summary score (hamster and red light)
236. Confession: summary score (hamster and red light)
237. Fixing: summary score (hamster and red light)

Variables Derived from Permissive Doll Play

(See also Appendix F. Each variable exists separately for each of the two sessions of doll play; the two identifying numbers refer to Sessions I and II, respectively.)

238, 239. Activity level
240, 241. Father as routine agent
242, 243. Mother as routine agent
244, 245. Boy as routine agent
246, 247. Girl as routine agent
248, 249. Baby as routine agent
250, 251. Adult as routine agent
252, 253. Child as routine agent
254, 255. Male as routine agent
256, 257. Female as routine agent
258, 259. Father as aggression agent
260, 261. Mother as aggression agent
262, 263. Boy as aggression agent
264, 265. Girl as aggression agent
266, 267. Baby as aggression agent
268, 269. Adult as aggression agent
270, 271. Child as aggression agent
272, 273. Male as aggression agent
274, 275. Female as aggression agent
276, 277. Use of routine role

278, 279. Use of male-typed routine adult work
280, 281. Use of female-typed routine adult work
282, 283. Use of routine toileting
284, 285. Total routine adult role
286, 287. Use of nurturance
288, 289. Total use of antisocial aggression
290, 291. Total use of thematic aggression
292, 293. Use of kitchen
294, 295. Use of toilet
296, 297. Use of living room
298, 299. Use of parents' bedroom
300, 301. Use of children's bedroom
302, 303. Use of garage
304, 305. Use of shop
306, 307. Use of yard or street (out of the house)

308, 309. Total use of unusual agents and objects (O, En, Eq, S; see Appendix F.)

310, 311. Child-subject as agent

Variables Derived from Deviation Doll Play

(See also Appendix F.)

312. Redefinition minus
313. Delay
314. Caught: other
315. Apology and fixing
316. Hiding

317. Authority fixes
318. Verbal punishment
319. Physical punishment
320. Isolation
321. Gets away with it

Variables Derived from Mother-Child Interaction

(See also Chapter 1. Variables marked with an asterisk were rated at the close of each session by the two observers. The remainder were scored from the tapes. Except where indicated, the measures were based on the full hour of interaction.)

322. Mother's pressure for child's independence
323. Mother's restriction of child's independence
324. Mother's use of reward for child's independence
325. Mother's use of punishment for child's independence
°326. Mother's directiveness toward child
327. Child's independence of mother
328. Mother's use of reward for child's dependency
329. Mother's use of punishment for child's dependency
°330. Mother's warmth toward child
°331. Mother's responsiveness to child
°332. Mother's involvement in telephone game
°333. Mother's involvement with puzzles
°334. Mother's involvement with fishing
335. Child's expression of dependency on mother
°336. Frequency of child's bids for attention: mother busy
°337. Frequency of child's bids for attention: mother attentive
°338. Frequency of child's bids for attention: 336 + 337

339. Child's warmth toward mother
°340. Child's involvement in telephone game
341. Mother's pressure for child's obedience
342. Mother's use of punishment for child's aggression
343. Mother's hostility to child
344. Child's disobedience to mother
345. Child's direct aggression toward mother
346. Child's indirect aggression toward mother
347. Directness of child's aggression toward mother
348. Child's outer-directed physical aggression
349. Child's outer-directed verbal aggression
350. Child's direct self-aggression
351. Child's fantasy aggression
352. Child's willingness to adopt deviant child role
353. Mother's pressure for child's achievement
354. Mother's use of reward for child's achievement
355. Mother's use of punishment for child's low achievement
356. Child's achievement standards

357. Mother's concern with neatness
*358. Mother's concern with water play and clean-up
359. Mother's pressure for and reward of adult role behavior
360. Child's interest in adult role (telephone and fishing games)
361. Child's resistance to adult role (telephone and fishing games)
362. Child's concern with sex appropriateness

363. Child's willingness to adopt self-role
364. Child's willingness to adopt opposite sex role
*365. Mother's ease in situation
366. Child's tension
*367. Child's activity level
368. Mother's use of models with child
369. Mother's use of reasoning with child

Summary Scores on Child's Aggression

(For W and X, see variable 57.)

Y. Real outer-directed aggression (MCI: sum of variables 344, 345, 346, and 348)

Z. Direct interpersonal aggression (BUO: sum of variables 189, 191, and 196)

Index to Variables

Text and table citations of the above variables are listed below. The variable numbers are indicated in boldface type; page numbers for text citations and/or table numbers for table citations follow in light type. Where variables listed in tables are also discussed in the adjacent text, only the table citations are given. It should be noted that the citations, particularly in the text, often employ neither the precise wording of the variable list above nor the number designations of the variables. Text citations in the Appendixes are not listed; table citations in the Appendixes are listed only for Appendix K.

Appendix D. *Behavior Unit Observations (BUO)*

The behavior unit observations (BUO) were designed to secure time-sampling frequency measures of dependency, prosocial and antisocial aggression, adult role behavior, oral movements, and masturbation. A set of predefined categories was prepared in advance, four observers were carefully trained in its use, and a fairly high level of observer reliability was achieved before data collection began.

Behavior Categories

The behavior categories are of two general kinds, designated as *real* and *fantasy*. The real categories measure behavior evidently intended by the child to have the kind of manipulative or stimulative effect that a verbal description of the action would imply. For example, real direct physical aggression is behavior that appears to be motivated by intention to hurt the object, perhaps another child. The fantasy categories measure behavior that presumably is *not* expected to have the kinds of effects a verbal description would imply. Thus, fantasy direct physical aggression might be exemplified by a pretended shooting with a machine gun or pistol. The fantasy forms of behavior occur in play context, whereas the real forms are part of a child's actual social and manipulative sequence of behavior. Only a few of the real categories have fantasy counterparts; all such pairs are in the adult role and aggression areas. However, as can be seen in the discussion of findings on adult role, in Chapter 3, the distinction is an important one.

The 29 categories listed here do not include several (mainly fantasy forms) that were discarded during the study or afterward. These were categories that occurred too infrequently to permit adequate observer reliability or to provide a useful frequency distribution within our sample of children. Indeed, several of those listed here have such severely skewed distributions that they cannot be introduced into the correlation matrix. (These are indicated by their lack of the initial arabic code number.) Thus, the categories finally used for our data analysis are not completely exhaustive of the classes to which they refer. For example, since fantasy direct physical aggression (mentioned above) is one of the discarded categories, the class of aggression behavior is not exhaustively represented. The categories probably do include, however, more than 99 per cent of all the behavior that could be allocated to each of the classes.

Obviously, the 29 listed categories were not intended to exhaust a child's total repertoire of actions, but were limited to the kinds of behavior we were interested in. In the list of categories following, the initial arabic designation is the identifying number of the variable as used in the text (and as listed in Appendix C). The roman and arabic numerals in parentheses are deck and column identifiers from the data-storage punched cards used for this study. Except where specifically identified as fantasy, all categories are measures of real behavior.

Adult Role

(vi, 5) *Positive goodness.* Calling attention to goodness of self or of group; making a point of following a rule; of being neat, tidy, clean, orderly; of conforming to own understanding of teacher's wishes; calling attention to praiseworthy actions.

175. (vi, 6) *Giving facts and demonstrating knowledge.* Teaching or guiding another with the intent of helping to train. *Examples*: Boy explains to an adult "why the sand sucks in the water." Boy speaks to another boy who is using sandpaper incorrectly: "This is the sand side. You're rubbing on the paper." Boy says to teacher, "This fell over because it had nothing to hold it up." *Disregard*: Simple observations and statements meant to disparage or to demonstrate another's ignorance. Girl sitting on a swing observes to herself: "There's sand everywhere you go." Child says: "This clay is gucky." "That's an airplane, stupid."

176. (vi, 7) *Real adult mannerisms.* Employing characteristically adult postures, gestures, tone of voice, language, vocabulary, etc.; exhibiting interpretive or indirect imitation, or pseudosophistication. *Examples*: Boy calmly comments to himself, "Jesus Christ." "Clear the area, clear the area," says boy, and motions for all to leave. "I've had 15 minutes here, that's enough," says girl, and shrugs her shoulders and leaves. "Confidentially, Jane," girl whispers coyly into ear of neighbor.

177. (vi, 8) *Fantasy adult mannerisms.* Acting like an adult in a "pre-

tend" context. *Examples*: Child dresses up in adult clothes, walks back and forth, but performs no specific acts of adult work. Uses terms "mother" or "sister" clearly to denote dominant-submissive roles, though without any specific action, such as "Now sister, we really should . . ."

179. (vi, 10) *Real adult work.* Spontaneously assuming the responsibility of work appropriate to an adult, including tasks necessary to maintain activity in progress in the nursery school. *Examples*: Child straightens paints and arranges colors on all four easels. Comes to stove and cleans up water found there. Helps to keep place tidy: picks up nails and blocks. Realizes, during construction period, that children are running out of nails; goes to look for more. *Disregard*: Nurturant responses, such as protecting and comforting, and such independent responses as getting equipment or Kleenex for self, or tying own shoes.

180. (vi, 11) *Fantasy adult work.* Performing work appropriate to an adult, in play context. *Examples*: Child pretends to be: cowboy rounding up cattle, truck driver, fireman, mother getting dinner or cleaning house, teacher preparing juice, service station attendant.

(vi, 13) *Imitating.* Repeating adult-like actions or words in exact form or with slight modification. *Examples*: Child continually glances at the teacher's Easter egg, and using the same colors makes one as nearly like it as possible. Teacher says, "It's a good day for suntans," and child says, "It's a good day for swimming." "As soon as there is water all around it, it's an island," child repeats after adult. "This is the way my father saws," boy says as he demonstrates. Also includes behavior directed at supporting the adult in his role. *Examples*: Boy who did not assist in juice preparation says, "We forgot to put the crackers on." "Didn't you hear? She wants us to come in." *Disregard*: Such behavior as simply following an adult around, or engaging in the same activities when there is no evidence he is attempting to perform the common activity precisely as the adult is (e.g., child sits down by an adult who is playing the piano and begins to play at random).

182. (vi, 14) *Nurturance.* Voluntarily guiding or assisting another with the intent of being helpful or performing a service. *Examples*: Child offers supplies: "You may use this paper." Explains ongoing game to new arrival. "Oh, I can get him for you," offers boy to girl chasing runaway hamster. Also includes reacting to the perceived dependence of another with mothering, comforting, protecting behavior. *Examples*: Child comforts the crying of an upset child. Strokes the hair of a smaller child while

listening to a story. Praises another's work or person. *Disregard*: Routine duties such as passing crackers or napkins, or comments such as "It's juice time, if you want to know," for which the motive is not helpful service.

(vi, 15) *Nurturance (fantasy)*. Nurturance in a play context, or nurturant behavior directed toward an inanimate object; hugging or protecting dolls or stuffed animals.

(vi, 17) *Rule stating*. Showing concern that rules should be kept; citing rules directly and by inference. *Examples*: "You're not supposed to hit smaller children." "Don't bang the window." "Stop that; that's not the way to play games." Boy looks at second boy and tells a third, "He's a bad boy; he's taking too many pieces of wood." *Disregard*: Commands or statements that are specific to the child or the situation and have no general application, such as: "Color it this way." "Get out of my way."

Dependency

187. (vi, 21) *Negative attention seeking*. Getting attention by disruption, aggressive activity with minimal provocation, defiance, or oppositional behavior; opposing and resisting direction, rules, routines, and demands by ignoring, refusing, or doing the opposite. *Examples*: Child skips through block corner kicking at the children's constructions. Child waves a saw threateningly by another's neck until stopped by teacher. Child hits at teacher to get her attention. Teacher asks child to put cup in wastebasket; child says "No" and leaves. *Disregard*: Aggressive acts expressive of strong frustration, such as child in block corner hitting boy who has just kicked over his large block castle.

188. (vi, 25) *Reassurance seeking*. Apologizing, asking unnecessary permission, or seeking protection, comfort, consolation, help, or guidance. *Examples*: Child says "I'm sorry." "Andy, I'm having trouble with this puzzle." Child runs up to teacher: "He is going to hit me." "Could you help me dig?" "See, I'm keeping my paints on the easel."

219. (vi, 71) *Positive attention seeking*. Seeking praise, seeking to join an in-group by inviting cooperative activity, or actually interrupting a group activity in progress. *Examples*: Child says, "Do you like my picture?" "Yesterday I went to a birthday party," boy interrupts group hearing story. "I can build the longest train in the whole nursery school." Onlooker to group at sand box: "Hey, let's go blow bubbles."

220. (vi, 72) *Touching and holding.* Non-aggressive touching, holding, clasping onto others. *Examples*: Child walks around with teacher, holding her hand. Holds onto teacher's skirt during story time. Rests head on neighbor's lap during story time.

221. (vi, 73) *Being near.* Following or standing near a particular child or a group of children or a teacher. *Examples*: Child scurries to get seat next to teacher during juice. Follows another child from activity to activity. Stands quietly by teacher and watches others playing. *Disregard*: Leaving one activity to join a preferred activity, or engaging in interaction that has some joint activity as an aim.

Antisocial Aggression

189. (vi, 27) *Direct physical aggression.* Hitting, throwing, withholding objects, pulling, taking things away from a child, i.e., the use of force toward another person.

(vi, 28) *Direct physical aggression (fantasy).* The same, but in a play context. *Example*: Shooting machine gun or pistol.

(vi, 30) *Physical Threat.* Using threatening gestures.

(vi, 31) *Indirect physical aggression.* Damaging property of another child.

191. (vi, 32) *Direct verbal aggression.* Name calling, jeering, threatening, uttering angry talk, derogating status, commanding vigorously.

(vi, 33) *Indirect verbal aggression.* Muttering angrily to self, telling another child about grievance but without asking assistance.

(vi, 34) *Vicarious aggression.* Enjoying or ignoring another's discomfiture or hurt.

192. (vi, 35) *Injury to objects.* Displaced or non-person-directed aggression, such as smashing constructions or spilling paints.

193. (vi, 36) *Mischief.* Mischievous disobedience, such as throwing cups in the wrong place, or scattering sand.

Prosocial Aggression

196. (vi, 40) *Verbal disapproval of behavior.* "That's bad; you can't do that."

197. (vi, 41) *Tattling.* Calling attention to another child's misbehavior, but without asking help.

(vi, 42) *Asking retribution.* Asking an adult to punish another child.

Self-Stimulation

222. (vi, 74) *Masturbation.* Handling the genital area, or pressing or rubbing against an object that appears to provide genital stimulation; "riding" a chair or table edge, or a broomstick.

223. (vi, 75) *Orality.* Manual-oral contacts in the absence of food intake.

Procedure

The remainder of this appendix discusses BUO recording and scheduling, observer reliability, trait consistency, and construction of scores. In the discussion of observer reliability and trait consistency, reference is made to *summary scores* (we have also called them *total scores*) for adult role, dependency, and antisocial and prosocial aggression. These are combinations of the above categories; their construction is described in the final section of this Appendix.

BUO Recording

Each observer was provided with a clipboard for BUO recordings. At the top of the clipboard was a battery-powered timing device that flashed a small bulb briefly every half-minute. The recording blank consisted of four rows of five boxes each. The observer followed his target child unobtrusively for a ten-minute period, and at each flash of the light made decisions about five matters, as they related to the preceding half-minute, and recorded a symbol for each in a box. The five matters considered were:

1. The child's *location* in the nursery school. This was recorded in terms of 45 numbered locations on a map of the nursery school. Location was always recorded, regardless of whether any other symbols were appropriate, since the location was used in developing one measure of sex typing (see Chapter 5).

2. The *behavior category* that best described the dominant behavior of the child during the half-minute. If none of the categories was applicable, no symbol was entered in the box. Thus, although *location* could be specified for every observation unit, *category* could be noted only when one of the listed behaviors was the dominant form. About 30 per cent of the periods provided a category notation. By *dominant* was meant the longer lasting, the more vigorous, or the more central to what else the child was doing. It will be noted that the categories fall under six general headings: adult role, dependency, antisocial and

prosocial aggression, orality, and masturbation. Double scoring, i.e., recording a given half-minute of action as two different behavior categories, was permitted only when (a) one was an adult role category and the other an aggression category, (b) both were aggression categories, or (c) one was either orality or masturbation. Or, to put it the other way around, double scoring was not permitted *within* the adult role group of categories or the dependency group, or between dependency and anything else except orality and masturbation. When double scoring did occur, the time unit was counted for both categories scored, but this occurred so rarely that its influence on the data is nil. Our reason for avoiding double scoring is that it doubles the weighting of some time periods and thus makes the obtained percentages of unequal significance.

3. Whether the child was alone or with others, i.e., whether or not he was engaged in non-interactive play away from what the observer judged to be any immediate possibility of social interaction. This category was designed as a rough index of a child's tendency to withdraw from his social surroundings, but the data obtained have not been used in the present study because the observer rating for social interaction level, described in Appendix E, seemed satisfactory.

4. The *object* of the behavior category, noted for the adult role, aggression, and dependency categories, e.g., nurturance toward *a girl*, aggression toward *equipment*, being near *the teacher*. The following categories of objects were distinguished: boy, girl, teacher, observer, other adult, play equipment or other physical object, animal, self, and no object (e.g., spilling sand in mischief).

5. Whether the teacher was present or absent, recorded for aggression categories. (These data have not been analyzed for the present study.)

BUO Scheduling

One serious defect in time-sampling observations, when taken in the free-activity situation of the nursery school, is that stimulus conditions are seldom the same for any two children or at any two moments in time. Partly this is "chance," of course; not all children are in the same spot when the teacher asks for help, when another child starts crying or explodes angrily, or when any one of many other types of stimulus events occurs. (Indeed, with respect to some behavior categories, this factor is so important in determining a child's behavior that the naturalistic time-sampling method cannot be used at all; we found, for example, that "temptations" were so infrequently and unequally presented that we could not measure resistance to temptation in the nursery school setting itself.) But to some extent the lack of equivalence of stimuli is a function of the subject child's own predisposition to action. A counterphobic boy invites admiration or envy for his daring on the jungle gym, while a timid girl offers a stimulus more appropriate to nurturance when she expresses fear of the swings. These responses from others—envy and nurturance, here—provide some part of the environmental stimulation for each child.

Although there is no way to eliminate these two sources of error from time-sampling observations designed to measure relatively stable behavioral dispositions, or traits, it is possible to minimize them by careful randomizing of the time and place of the observations. This procedure reduces biases introduced by observers' tendencies to seek "easy" or "interesting" conditions for observation; for example, a social context is often a more demanding situation from the observer's standpoint, and she might well prefer to watch a child engaged in solitary play, or she might feel she has been watching a particular child too often in solitary play and thus pick him for observation when she notes that he is in a group. Likewise, some parts of the school session offer more stimuli to one kind of behavior than another, and if one child is customarily observed early in the morning and another late, these systematic stimulus variations could produce significant bias in the frequency with which the various responses were observed.

To avoid such difficulties in the present research, an effort was made to observe each child not less than three times in each of the seven weeks. This was intended to eliminate bias resulting from temporal change in the children themselves. This precaution proved fortunate, for Vitz (1961) has shown that there was a significant increase in adult role behavior for both sexes during the seven weeks of our research period, and a decrease in antisocial aggression for boys. A few exceptions to the plan, caused by absences resulting from brief illness, affected the data base in two ways: the control of the temporal-change factor was not entirely complete; and the finally obtained number of observation time units varied somewhat for different children within each of the two attending groups. For the MWF group, the maximum was 42 ten-minute periods, the minimum, 30, and the mean, 38. For the TTh group, the comparable figures were 30, 23, and 27. Thus the mean number of recorded observation time units per child in the MWF group was 760, and in the TTh group, 540.

Since there were four observers, each presumably with idiosyncratic sensitivities and blind spots, it was important that each contribute an equal share to the total observations of each child. To this end, we prepared observation schedules that strictly specified a given time of a given day for each observation of each child. Different schedules were given each observer. Each schedule was constructed initially with a table of random numbers, each child being represented once. (Separate schedules were drawn up for the MWF and TTh groups, of course.) The four schedules (one per observer) were then compared, and a few changes in sequence were made for two purposes: one, to ensure there would be no overlap in times at which any two observers were watching one child; and the other, to make certain that observation periods for each child were equally allocated to the three thirds of the nursery school session (9:00 to 9:50, 9:50 to 10:40, and 10:40 to 11:30). A new schedule, constructed similarly, was given to each observer when the preceding one was completed. When a child was absent, he was placed on an alternate list, and a substitute child was selected from the original list, in order if possible, but in any case from the same time period.

The teachers, volunteer mothers, and other experimenters were also given copies of the schedules first thing in the morning. They were asked not to *initiate* contact with a child during his observation period, though they might *respond to his initiations* in customary fashion. When a selected child's own mother was present the day he was being observed, she was asked to find an inconspicuous way of being out of his vicinity for the twenty minutes preceding his observation, as well as during it.

Observer Reliability

Measures of agreement among the observers were obtained on three occasions: the last day of the first week, just before the start of formal data collection; the last day of the fifth week; and the last day of the sixth week. All these tests were done with the MWF group of children, because time pressures were less with them than with the TTh group.

On each occasion, each observer was paired with each of the other three for three or four ten-minute observation periods, each pair simultaneously observing and recording the behavior of the same child. In all, 63 pairs of these simultaneous ten-minute periods were collected, representing 10.5 hours of recorded behavior. The observer agreement can be reported for each of the three occasions separately, and for the total of the occasions as an estimate of reliability for the summer as a whole.

The level of agreement was computed as a per cent value by the formula:

$$\frac{2 \times \text{number of agreements}}{\text{total judgments recorded by observer 1 plus total by observer 2}}$$

The record for each half-minute observation consisted of a maximum of five decisions (as described above). Three of these *judgments* were used in the reliability calculation; separate calculations were made for *alone* and *location* judgments. In calculating the denominator, a *judgment* was counted only when some item was recorded; blank periods (in which nothing relevant to the scoring system occurred) were not included. The term *agreement* is based upon frequency and timing (as will be explained) within each ten-minute period of the recording—separately—of behavior category, object, and (for aggression only) presence or absence of teacher. Thus, if both observers agreed that the child performed "182. Nurturance" during the seventh half-minute interval of a period, this was counted as one agreement. However, if one observer recorded "teacher" as object of the act and the other recorded "no object," no agreement was counted, even though two additional judgments (observer 1 plus observer 2) were added to the denominator in the formula. Leeway from exact agreement was allowed in only one type of circumstance; if identical observations were recorded with a timing discrepancy of no more than two half-minute periods, they were counted as agreements. This latitude was permitted because of the physical difficulty of maintaining exact beginning and ending coordination between the two observers for the ten-minute period. Of course, if categories were recorded in different sequence by the two observers, no agreements were counted, even if the actual frequencies of the items were the same in the two reports.

Table D1 shows the reliability measures obtained on each occasion and for all three combined. The noticeable improvement over the summer no doubt resulted from the discussion among observers, after the preceding reliability tests, of the reasons for their disagreements.

Separate values can be calculated also for each behavior category, for combinations of categories (e.g., total adult role), or for all categories

TABLE D1

Observer Reliability on All Categories Combined

Occasion	Number of Ten-Minute Periods	Number of Judgments Recorded	Per Cent Agreement
First week 20		530	72
Fifth week 21		659	82
Sixth week 22		534	87
Total 63		1723	81

combined. Of the ten adult role categories, one did not occur at all during the reliability sessions (positive goodness), one had 40 per cent agreement and only five occurrences (stating a rule), and the others ranged from 67 per cent to 100 per cent. Of the five dependency categories, one had 40 per cent and only five occurrences (negative attention seeking), and the other four ranged from 67 per cent to 82 per cent. Of the eight antisocial aggression categories, two did not occur at all (indirect verbal and vicarious), one had 50 per cent (direct verbal), one had 60 per cent (mischief), and the other four ranged from 67 per cent to 90 per cent. Of the three prosocial aggression categories, one did not occur (asking retribution); verbal disapproval of behavior had 59 per cent, and tattling had 80 per cent. Masturbation did not occur at all; orality had 85 per cent agreement.

For the four major types of behavior, the total number of times each was reported by any of the observers, and the per cent of these that represented agreements, are as follows:

> Adult Role: 394 times; 86 per cent
> Dependency: 139 times; 78 per cent
> Antisocial Aggression: 128 times; 70 per cent
> Prosocial Aggression: 23 times; 61 per cent

The reliability of judging location (see Chapter 5) was 86 per cent. The discrepancy from perfection arose from three factors: a child would change location halfway through a half-minute period; the 45-area map was inadequately differentiated; and the map would be rendered inapplicable because of some child's having moved equipment in such a way as to invalidate the map's area divisions.

Although the reliability estimates for some of the less frequently occurring categories are below an acceptable level, those for all the main combinations of categories (classes of behavior) and the larger individual categories are satisfactory. An examination of the instances of disagreement shows that, for adult role and aggression, about half involved the question to which of two categories an action should be allocated within that main heading, and half were simply omissions; there was not a single instance of an action's being ascribed to an aggressive category by one observer but put in another major category by the other. Disagreements on dependency behaviors resulted 58 per cent from omissions by one observer, 25 per cent from differences in judgment of how long (how many half-minute intervals) the dependency action continued, and only 16 per cent from disagreement on type of dependency. The latter figure contrasts with 46 per cent for adult role and 49 per cent for aggression.

In general, then, we are justified in being relatively most confident of the *combined* categories for adult role, antisocial and prosocial aggression, and orality, and in the *individual* categories of dependency (except negative attention seeking). As is shown in Chapter 2 (and reiterated in Chapter 7), the correlations among these dependency categories are so low that we are somewhat skeptical of whether a combined score for dependency is useful, especially in boys. Less confidence can be placed on individual categories within the adult role and aggression classifications.

Trait Consistency

Since the behavior-category observations were designed to be used as measures of traits, or predispositions to perform specific types of action, we must raise the question of how consistent a given child was with respect to his frequency of displaying each of the types. There are two ways of answering the question, one by comparing the separate observers' scores for the full summer, the other by comparing the (total) scores obtained at different times during the summer by all four observers combined. Neither method of analysis gives a dependable answer, for both suffer the attenuation resulting from observer unreliability. With the data available, however, there is no way to correct for this attenuation; hence the degree of consistency reported here may be considered a minimum estimate.

For the first method, a score for each of the forty children, on each of the variable classes shown in Table D2, was computed from the records of each observer separately. This score was the number of occurrences of a variable (e.g., adult role) divided by the number of observations made of that child. Since the latter number varied from child to child and from observer to observer, there is no cumulative constancy in the denominator that would distort the distributions for correlational purposes. For each variable, each of the four observers' scores for each of the forty children was correlated with each of the other observers' scores. Using the method of z-transformation, a mean of these six correlations was obtained, as shown in the first column in Table D2. Since the scores are composed of the total observations of the research (not the observer-reliability measures described in the preceding section), each observer's scores are entirely independent of those of the other three. Each observer's scores, in other words, represent approximately one-fourth of the final measure for a given child. Hence, a corrected coefficient (Spearman-Brown), based on the increase of the mean intercorrelation to a value assuming four times as much data, is appropriate. These corrected values are shown in the second column.

TABLE D2

Mean Intercorrelations for Forty Children Between Four Observers' Scores on
Five Major Variable Classes, and Between Totals of Four Observers'
Scores at Three Time Periods, with Spearman-Brown
Corrections of Both Sets of Values

Variable Classes	Between Four Observers		Between Three Time Periods	
	Mean r	Corrected r ($\times 4$)	Mean r	Corrected r ($\times 3$)
Adult role	.45	.77	.48	.73
Dependency	.42	.74	.36	.63
Antisocial aggression	.58	.85	.56	.79
Prosocial aggression	.41	.74	.54	.73
Orality	.73	.92	.77	.91

The second method of evaluating consistency involves the computing of a score on each variable for each child for each of three time periods (weeks 2–3, 4–6, and 7–8), using the observations of all four observers; the method of computation is the same as that described above. The values given in the third column of Table D2 are the means of the three possible intercorrelations between the three time periods. In the fourth column are the Spearman-Brown corrections.

The latter measures of trait consistency (third column) are very similar to those obtained by intercorrelating the scores obtained separately by each of the four observers during the whole seven weeks (first column). The largest difference is that for dependency, which is somewhat lower in the time-period comparison; as already mentioned, there are other reasons for doubting the usefulness of this "total dependency" score. For the other four variables, the consistency measures seem reasonably satisfactory.

These raw correlations reflect not only the consistency of the children, of course, but the degree of reliability of the observers. The final corrected values given here probably represent a reasonable estimate of the stability of the measures we must work with, even though we cannot be sure exactly how much of the obtained instability is a function of inadequate observation. Biasing the estimates in the opposite direction, however, is the fact that the first four variables listed in Table D2 are not totally independent; i.e., when a dependency response was recorded, neither an adult role nor an aggression response could be recorded. Even though double scoring was permitted—but rarely occurred—with certain of the behavior classes, the finiteness of the number of observation categories into which all four classes had to fall induces some spurious raising of the intercorrelations *within* each class. That this particular character of the procedure was probably of little influence is suggested by the fact that many time units contained none of our categories and hence provided a kind of behavioral vacuum (from a measurement standpoint only!) in which each category could expand or contract its frequency independently of the others' frequencies.

Our best conclusion about trait consistency cannot be very precise. There appears to be sufficient evidence to warrant fairly strong reliance on the observational measures for the major variables (except total dependency), and the observer reliability for the individual dependency categories (except negative attention seeking) is sufficiently high to warrant using them separately.

Construction of Scores

The final scores constructed for use in data analysis were of two kinds, those for the individual categories listed earlier, and those for combinations or classes of these categories (summary, or total, scores). The individual category scores were obtained by dividing the total number of times a category was recorded for a given child (by all four observers during the full seven weeks) by the total number of half-minute periods the child was observed. This score was expressed to three decimal places. Then the distribution of the forty children's scores was divided into ten equal class intervals in order to be suitably distributed for storage on punched cards. A careful examination of every distribution in the research disclosed no instance in which this class-interval division distorted the distribution of raw scores. Since the absolute (raw) scores of our many measuring procedures have no significance in themselves, *all means and standard deviations throughout are presented in terms of these ten-class-intervals scales.*

Summary scores—we have also referred to them as "total" scores— were identically constructed, except that the numerator is the total frequency of all the categories listed under a major variable. The summary scores relevant to the behavior unit observations are as follows:

184. (vi, 18) *Total real adult role.* Sum of vi, 5, 6, 7, 10, 13, 14, 17.

185. (vi, 19) *Total fantasy adult role.* Sum of vi, 8, 11, 15.

224. (vi, 76) *Total observed dependency.* Sum of vi, 21, 25, 71, 72 ,73.

194. (vi, 37) *Total antisocial aggression.* Sum of vi, 27, 29, 30, 31, 32, 33, 34, 35, 36.

(vi, 38) *Total antisocial aggression (fantasy).* Sum of vi, 28, and a few other fantasy categories with too few frequencies to warrant separate recording; this total score does not, in fact, differ significantly from vi, 28, direct physical aggression (fantasy).

198. (vi, 43) *Total prosocial aggression.* Sum of vi, 40, 41, 42.

Appendix E. *Observer Rating Scales*

Since the four observers were in continuous contact with all the children for all eight weeks of summer school, and had about equal opportunity to observe each one, it seemed wise to supplement the behavior unit observations with rating scales on some of the same measures, as well as on two other important variables. For one of the latter (physical activity level) there was no comparable measure; for the other (social interaction level) we did not trouble to extract a score from the BUO data. These variables are important because certain forms of behavior, such as aggression, dependency, and adult role, characteristically show substantial positive correlation with activity. This is particularly the case when measures of these substantive variables are obtained in the free-moving situation; a child who moves more and makes more social contacts has more opportunity to make every kind of reaction to others, including aggression, etc. As can be seen in Table E1, observer reliability proved to be excellent.

The Rating Scales

The rating scales are all five-point scales; each dimension was defined, as indicated below, but separate descriptive labels were not provided for each of the five points. The observers, working independently, rated all the children on each scale on the last day of school. The scale names and definitions are as follows:

203. (vi, 50) *Sex typing.* Masculinity ranges from highly masculine (a "buck") through average, then effeminate, to a "sissy." Femininity ranges from a "coquette" or "clinging vine" through average, then somewhat boyish, to a "tomboy."

214. (vi, 66) *Aggression.* Going past some commonly accepted limits by acts directed against children or adults. *Examples:* Pinching, biting, pushing others; throwing sand, mud, blocks; spilling water; spitting at others; bumping into others; grabbing things; ruining others' work or play; taking up a role that justifies doing these things (e.g., being a pi-

rate, an animal); teasing, threatening others (verbally or with gestures); belittling others, hurting other child's pride (e.g., "You are a baby"); deliberately spilling water, paint; tipping over puzzle boxes; spilling beads; throwing, kicking blocks, toys; throwing blocks at bird cage; sweeping things off the table; knocking planks, ladders.

215. (VI, 67) *Physical contact seeking.* Frequency of seeking contact or trying to be near teacher or other adult. *Examples:* Sits on the lap of an adult. Grabs adult's skirt. Asks: "Pick me up." "Hold my hand." Sits next to teacher at juice time or when reading a book. Glances at teacher often while playing with clay or cutting out. Climbs or slides only if an adult is present.

216. (VI, 68) *Attention getting.* Seeking notice, praise, approval, or help. *Examples* (seeking notice): Child exclaims: "Lookit." "See?" "You know what?" "Are you my friend?" "I want some ice." Also includes attention seeking by negative means (e.g., yelling loudly and throwing blocks, so as to be certain of attracting an adult) and any behavior aimed at getting an adult to occupy herself with the child. *Examples* (seeking praise or approval): Child exclaims: "Look, I did it all by myself." "Look at me, I'm right on top." "Pretty, isn't it?" showing a picture he has just painted, or something he has made out of clay. "Watch me," when he displays some skill. "I drank all the juice." "I washed my hands." *Examples* (seeking help): Any sort of service or assistance the child tries to get from others. "Put on my coat." "Help me down." "You do it." "Where does this go?" when working on a puzzle. Child shows his hands ("Dirty") and expects someone else to clean them. Child seeks protection and assistance from others when attacked or when something has been taken away from him.

217. (VI, 69) *Physical activity level.* Intensity and frequency of all physical movements, including walking, running, swinging, and autistic movements of jumping, whirling, swinging arms, or jiggling; also regards amount of movement from place to place in the yard and school, and the rapidity and vigor of movements. *Disregard:* Whether movements or actions have any obvious goal, or whether they are socially oriented.

218. (VI, 70) *Social interaction level.* Intensity and frequency of social interactions, including speaking, asking for cooperation in play or work, playing interactively, communicating through gestures or other non-verbal means, being with other children or adults in an interactive manner. *Disregard:* Amount of physical movement, non-interactive "being near" (i.e., merely staying in a "popular" location, without interacting).

Observer Reliability

The mean inter-observer reliability coefficients are given in the first column of Table E1; these are the averages of the six *r*'s between each observer and each other one, using a *z*-transformation. The final scores used for data analysis are the means of the scores attributed to each child by all four observers combined. Hence, correction by the Spearman-Brown formula (×4) is appropriate as a means of estimating the reliabilities of the measures actually used in the research. These also are given in Table E1.

Again, as in the behavior unit observations, dependency had relatively poor reliability. Of the two dependency scales, physical contact seeking is the better; it combines the kinds of behavior listed as touching and holding and being near, which showed 82 per cent and 67 per cent agreement, respectively, in the BUO reliability calculations. These two BUO categories are positively correlated (.71 for girls, .13 for boys), so their

TABLE E1

Reliability of Rating Scales: Mean Intercorrelations among Four Observers, and Spearman-Brown Correction for Totaled Ratings by All Four (N = 40)

Observer Rating Scales	Var. No.	Mean *r*	Corrected *r* (×4)
Sex typing	203	.66	.88
Aggression	214	.63	.87
Physical contact seeking . .	215	.53	.82
Attention getting	216	.39	.72
Physical activity level . . .	217	.76	.93
Social interaction level . . .	218	.80	.94

TABLE E2

Intercorrelations among Observer Rating Scales

(Boys above the diagonal, girls below)

Observer Rating Scales	Var. No.	Variable Number					
		203	214	215	216	217	218
Sex typing	203	°	.56	−.83	−.30	.66	.80
Aggression	214	−.07	°	−.57	.15	.85	.76
Physical contact seeking .	215	.41	−.07	°	.56	−.58	−.72
Attention getting	216	.46	.71	.44	°	.21	−.01
Physical activity level . .	217	.21	.86	.02	.82	°	.82
Social interaction level . .	218	.40	.74	.03	.85	.91	°

combination in a single rating scale seems not to have done violence to the unity of behavior, at least in girls. The final corrected coefficient of .82 on the rating scale is fairly satisfactory. The case with attention getting is much less satisfactory. As its definition indicates, this rating scale combines the two classes of behavior recorded separately in the BUO as negative and positive attention seeking. Whereas the latter had a reliability of 82 per cent agreement, the former's reliability was only 40 per cent. Combining the two in the single rating scale evidently created confusion for the raters, for the raw mean coefficient is only .39. One further comment is in order: these two dependency rating scales proved to be positively correlated (Table E2), although there was a tendency toward zero or even negative correlations between the relevant BUO categories representing the same dimensions of behavior (Table 3, Chapter 2). The reliabilities for the physical activity and social interaction scales are excellent.

Appendix F. *Doll Play*

The two sessions of permissive doll play and the session of deviation doll play all used the same dolls and doll house, and all were conducted by the same woman experimenter. They all used the same room (Room B). The room was bare except for the doll-play equipment, which consisted of an open-topped, one-story doll house and a Standard Family of five dolls (father, mother, boy, girl, baby). The house was 24 × 38 inches, made with plywood floor and walls. It contained non-movable furniture appropriate to the various rooms. The dolls were constructed of pipe cleaners and cloth. They were laid out in front of the house.

Permissive Doll Play

The actual variables drawn from permissive doll play are presented in Appendix C, and are not repeated here. The many details of technique, scoring and coding, observer reliability, and trait consistency are presented in the following pages.

Technique

After suitable rapport between the experimenter and the subject has been established, E invites S to go to "the other room." E sits on the floor beside the dolls, suggesting that S might like to sit beside her. E says: "See this doll house? It has rooms like your house does." And pointing to each room in turn: "See, here is the living room, the kitchen, the bathroom. And here is mother and daddy's bedroom, and this is the children's bedroom. Out here is the garage, and this is daddy's workshop." Then, pointing to each doll in turn: "And here are the people who live in this house—here is the daddy, and the mother, and the boy, and the girl, and the baby. These people live in that house just like you live in your house, and you can make them do *anything* you like in that house. They can do *anything* you want them to." A pause, then: "I wonder what they're going to do."

As soon as S picks up a doll and starts playing, E begins scoring. She maintains a *moderate* interaction level of five to seven interventions per five-minute period. The first session is terminated after 20 minutes by E's smiling suggestion that "We'll come back and play again another day." The second session is presented to S as a resumption, but when E and S sit down before the doll house, E repeats the same comments as before. Session II also lasts 20 minutes.

Scoring and Coding

Of the forty children, five terminated their play in Session I before the 20-minute period was finished (one child after 15 minutes, three others after 17 minutes, and one after 19). At the second session, four children stopped the play before the full 20 minutes was up (one child after 12 minutes, one after 15, and two after 18), and one child refused to stop until after 25 minutes. Although these variations in time obviously had dynamic significance, they did not interfere with formal measurement, for all the measures we have used are proportions based on the total number of acts actually performed.

The subject's behavior was scored in behavior units rather than time samples. By this method, the unit is considered to be an act—thematic or non-thematic—which in its most complete form is represented by an */agent/doing something/*to an *object/* (e.g., "The daddy turns on the TV"; "The mommy gives the baby a bath"). Not all actions have an agent (e.g., "The boy gets wet"); even more may lack an object (e.g., "The mommy is sleeping"). All have an *act,* however.

In recording the continuous flow of behavior, the observer splits up the flow into units, each unit containing agent, act, and object. A new behavior unit starts whenever there is a change in any one of these three elements. Thus, "The daddy reads and reads and reads" does not involve more than one unit, but "The daddy reads and then turns on the TV" is two units. So is "The mommy feeds the baby and the daddy," and "The boy goes to the toilet and then washes his hands," and "The mommy spanked and so did the daddy." In each of these examples there is a change of one or another of the three *elements* in the sequence.

The ongoing activity portrayed by S is recorded as a series of notations specifying for each act: (a) agent (if any), (b) type of act, or behavior category, (c) object (if any), and (d) location in the house (if apparent).

The agent and object categories are as follows:

F   – Father doll.
M   – Mother doll.
B   – Boy doll.
G   – Girl doll.
bb – Baby doll.
FM – Parent dolls as a pair.
Ch – B and G dolls; may include bb.
Gr – Group of three or more dolls.
Fr – Friends and relatives.
Y   – Persons non-affiliated to the family; incidental characters.
O   – Animals, spirits, demons (wolves, Easter bunny, devils).
En – Environmental forces (catastrophes: fires, storms; or a time or season, such as middle of night, usually considered as *agent*).
Eq – Equipment and furniture, usually considered as *object*.
S   – Child-subject who is doing the doll play.
E   – Experimenter.

The behavior categories are:

R   – Routine role performance (the largest category in number of responses), defined by Yarrow (1948) as "thematic behavior reproductive of routines 'carried on' in the average home: eating meals, washing dishes, sleeping, bathing, dressing, caring for the baby, sitting in the living room, listening to the radio, father or mother going to work, children going to school, etc. . . ." Also includes casual commands and conversations, and social interaction not affectively toned (e.g., the mother may say, "Go to bed now, children," or the father may say, "I have to go to work").
Rm – Male-typed adult work: shop projects, mechanical fixing, other house construction and moving, car activity, going to work.
Rf – Female-typed adult work: cooking, cleaning, caring for clothes (washing, mending, etc.), bedmaking, other housekeeping.
Ra – Adult work or recreation, not sex-typed: reading the paper, playing cards, going to a party.

Rt — Routine role performance: toileting (*not* bathing).

N — Nurturance: giving help, reward, love, affectionate contact, or protection (e.g., mother rocks the baby; children kiss daddy good-bye; mother bandages a hurt knee).

D — Dependency: seeking help, reward, love, affection, or protection (e.g., baby climbs on father's lap; children ask a favor or a privilege; mother wishes father were home).

MC — Mutual companionship: playing games, dancing together, having friendly conversations (mother and father talk things over), going on walks together, having picnics.

H — Happy feeling states: the boy feels glad; the family is having fun; the baby loves her present.

P — Prestige: attribution of status to a doll (e.g., the aunt has a new car; the father says, "We'll get a television, too"; a nursery school child describes doll children returning to school in the afternoon "because they're in the First Grade and don't have to take naps").

C — Compliance: direct obedience to a command when subject so states (e.g., "The mother told them to wash their hands, and they went and got them nice and clean").

Am — Aggressive mischief: performing forbidden acts, disobedience, etc. (e.g., girl hides from father; baby throws cookies on floor).

Ava — Verbal aggression: threats, derogations, ridicule, aggressive explosions (e.g., boy feels mad; girl taunts mother with "You can't make me!"; father and mother quarrel over bills).

Avd — Verbal discipline: scoldings, threats of punishment (e.g., mother says, "You're a naughty boy for doing that," or father says, "If you break a window again, you'll get a licking").

Apd — Physical discipline: spankings, deprivations, punishments (e.g., the girl is sent to bed for being naughty).

Ai — Physical injury to persons or equipment: boy knocks down girl; baby smashes lamp; storm kills family.

Au — States of uncomfortable feeling: doll is sick, sad, lost, scared, or frustrated (e.g., mother can't find baby who ran out of grocery store; father has a headache).

X — Tangential (non-thematic) activity.

XA — Tangential aggression.

The location categories are:

K   – Kitchen
T   – Toilet
L   – Living room
Bp – Parents' bedroom
Bc – Children's bedroom
G   – Garage
S   – Shop
Y   – Yard or street; out of the house

Scores for the many variables listed in Appendix C were computed separately for each session by dividing the frequency of occurrence of a given item (agent, action, object, or location), or combination of items (e.g., antisocial aggressions, or adult dolls as agents of routine performance) by the total number of act units performed by the child during that session. This type of proportion score was required because the activity level (i.e., the total number of units) varied so greatly from child to child; the range in the first session was from 1.9 to 5.1 per minute, and in the second session, from 2.0 to 4.3. So far as activity level is concerned, the problem of scoring free doll play is essentially the same as that for the BUO discussed in Appendix D; the scores are similarly constructed except that the BUO category scores use *time* units for the denominator whereas the doll-play scores utilize *act* units.

The activity-level measures for the two sessions of doll play (238 and 239) and the observer ratings of activity level in the nursery school (217) are correlated, −.22 and .09 for boys and .08 and .21 for girls. The correlations between the two sessions of doll play are .29 for boys and .55 for girls.

Observer Reliability

One experimenter did all the doll-play sessions. Scoring consistency was tested by training an observer, who sat with E and S, to score simultaneously and independently. The O sat on the floor near the equipment so as to see the activity clearly. She was introduced as someone interested in how children played; the children were entirely accepting of her presence. Several preliminary sessions were scored and discussed by E and O until it was fairly certain that categories were understood and behavior was being broken down into units in essentially the same way.

In order to determine per cent agreement between E and O, the scoring of two twenty-minute sessions of doll play for each of five subjects was compared by the formula:

$$\frac{2 \times \text{number of agreements}}{\text{total units recorded by experimenter plus total by observer}}$$

The total number of agreed-upon units for the five subjects was 724, ranging from 128 to 202 for individual children. This range represents, for each subject, the total units in two twenty-minute sessions. The subjects presented a wide range of response: two of them gave primarily stereotyped and sex-typed routine responses; two gave a variety of responses over many categories; the fifth gave almost entirely aggressive or tangential responses.

Per cent agreement was first computed, separately for each child, for total units recorded, in order to determine the degree to which E and O agreed in breaking the twenty minutes of behavior into similar units. For the five subjects, these values ranged from 82 per cent to 93 per cent. For the units on which E and O agreed, per cent agreement was then computed separately for agents, action categories, objects, and locations, and for those actions scored specifically as aggresison.

Among the five children, the scorers' agent agreements ranged from 86 per cent to 100 per cent; object agreements from 91 per cent to 100 per cent; action agreements from 74 per cent to 98 per cent; location agreements from 94 per cent to 98 per cent; and aggression agreements from 63 per cent to 100 per cent. These values are as high as, or higher than, similar measures in previous doll-play studies, and are quite adequate for the present purposes.

Trait Consistency

A number of previous studies (Hollenberg and Sperry, 1951; P. Sears, 1953) have shown that the performance of doll play appears to have different effects on different children. The permissive quality of the E's behavior introduces an anxiety reduction factor that has a positive effect on the frequency of aggressive acts, and a variable effect on the choice of doll agents, depending on the child-rearing attitudes of the child's mother. Therefore, the usual technique of comparing scores on two performances has dubious value as a means of measuring trait consistency. However, for what the figures may be worth, the correlations between scores on the first and second sessions are given in Table F1 for a number of the major scoring categories.

TABLE F1

Correlations of Scores on Some Significant Permissive-Doll-Play Variables
Between Session I and Session II, Separately by Sex of Child

Permissive-Doll-Play Variables	Variable Numbers	Boys	Girls
Activity level	238, 239	.29	.55
Father as agent of routine performance . .	240, 241	.13	.19
Mother as agent of routine performance . .	242, 243	.63	.26
Father as agent of aggression	258, 259	.42	−.13
Mother as agent of aggression	260, 261	.15	−.17
Routine male-typed adult work	278, 279	.17	.08
Routine female-typed adult work	280, 281	.56	.46
Use of nurturance	286, 287	.34	.63
Total use of thematic aggression	290, 291	.42	.53
Use of parents' bedroom	298, 299	.10	.09
Use of children's bedroom	300, 301	.54	.31
Use of garage	302, 303	.13	.04

Deviation Doll Play

The woman who served as E for the permissive doll play performed
the same role for the deviation doll-play session. The same doll house
and dolls were used. A list of the variables drawn from deviation doll
play, and the details of technique, scoring, coding, and reliability calculation are presented in the following pages.

Technique

The initial instructions are given after E and S are seated before the
equipment, as follows: "You remember about this doll house and the
dolls, don't you? They're just like the last time you were here, but today
we're going to do something different with them. I'm going to tell you
the beginnings of some stories and you can show me and tell me about
how the stories end."

During the beginning phase of each story, E places the dolls in appropriate places while saying, for example, "Now let's pretend that the
mother is in the kitchen; daddy is in the shop; . . ." The child doll of the
same sex as S is kept in hand, and active, during the story, and then is
handed to S at the end of E's telling. In the following descriptions of the
stories, the first statement indicates the location of the dolls, the symbols
Cd and Cs being used to refer to the child dolls of opposite sex from, and
same sex as, S, respectively. The stories as told here are for a boy; the pro-
nouns relating to the active child doll are reversed for girl subjects.

Ball and floor lamp. Mother in kitchen; father in shop; Cd in living room; baby in cradle in bedroom. The story: "This boy is playing in the living room with a ball. Daddy says, 'It's all right to play ball here, but be very careful not to hurt anything,' and goes into his shop. The boy is having a lot of fun but he isn't as careful as he should be and the ball hits this floor lamp and knocks it over. Now you take the doll and show me and tell me how the rest of the story goes."

Spilling juice. Father in bathroom; baby and Cd in kitchen; mother in kitchen and then empties garbage. The story: "This boy is in the kitchen eating breakfast. He doesn't like his juice but his mother tells him that he has to drink it. Then the mother goes out to empty the garbage. He is so mad at her that he knocks over the glass and spills the juice all over the table. Now you take the boy and show me how the rest of the story goes."

Grabbing baby's toy. Mother in bedroom, then goes to kitchen; father in shop; Cd in living room; baby in bedroom. The story: "Mother and the little boy are watching the baby play with its favorite toy. The mother says to the boy, 'You watch the baby for a while 'cause I have to get dinner.' Then she goes into the kitchen. Well, the little boy watched the baby playing with that toy and he wanted it, and so do you know what he did? He grabbed it away from the baby and the baby started to cry. Now, you take the little boy and show and tell me about what happened then."

Bedtime disobedience. Mother in living room; Cs and Cd in their bedroom; baby in cradle; father in children's bedroom and then in living room. The story: "It's getting very late and the children are playing in their room. The father comes in and tells them that it's bedtime and puts them to bed. Now, this little boy knew he was supposed to be asleep, but do you know what he did? Well, he got out of bed and began playing again. Now, you take him and show and tell me about the rest of the story."

Stealing cookies. Father in living room; Cd in children's bedroom; baby in parents' bedroom; mother in kitchen and then in living room; Cs in chair beside table. The story: "This little boy is in the kitchen watching his mother make some cookies for a big people's party. She puts the cookies on the table to cool and tells the boy, 'Don't eat any because they are for the big people's party.' But when the mother goes into the living room the boy reaches over to the cookies and takes a few. Now, you take the boy and show me how the rest of the story goes."

Spilling nail box. Father, mother, baby, and Cd in living room. The story: "The boy goes into the living room and asks the father if he can go and play in his shop. The father says, 'Yes, you can play in the shop, but you must be very careful.' The boy goes into the shop to play. He is reaching for a hammer up on the shelf and he knocks over a box of nails and they go all over the floor. Now, you take the boy and show me the rest of the story."

Scoring and Coding

It is common in deviation doll play that a child gives more than one ending or completion to an incomplete story. Sometimes this results from his redefining the story or the seriousness of the deviation, after his first completion, but other times it appears to be a compulsive continuation of an attempt to reduce the conflict implied by the deviation, as if one solution were not enough. Therefore, the number of *units* of story completion varies from one child to another.

The completions were all scored, regardless of how many there were. The categories used are given below. A given completion could be scored with more than one category. The final score for a child on a given category is a per cent value calculated by dividing the frequency with which it was used by the total number of category scorings recorded. Thus, a child might give a total of nine completions for the six stories. Among these nine, there might be twenty aspects of the completions that warrant a scoring of one or another category. If two of these twenty are physical punishment, the final score for that category is 10 per cent. In the final coding, the distributions of such per cent scores were converted to ten class intervals, as was done with the BUO and permissive-doll-play per cent scores, for more convenient use with the punched cards.

Categories

Nineteen categories of deviation doll play were defined as measurable variables; ten of these were retained for the final analyses. The categories are as follows:

312. (IX, 20) *Redefinition minus* (R—). The subject distorts or retells the story stem in such a way as to make the deviation more severe; a story in which there is a repetition of the deviant act is also scored R—.

313. (IX, 21) *Delay* (D). The subject is unwilling or unable to complete the story without prompting and urging by E, and may use various irrelevant and distracting behaviors to avoid continuing; score D also for long periods of silence.

(ix, 22) *Confession*: elicited (EC) or spontaneous (SC). Child admits or confesses that he was responsible for the deviant act, whether or not he *was* responsible, whether or not he has been charged or accused.

(ix, 23) *Denial*: response (RD), implicit (ID), or spontaneous (SD). Child denies responsibility for the deviation in response to an accusation, or by failing to respond when confession is solicited by authority, or denies voluntarily before he is even implicated.

(ix, 24) *Tattling* (Tat). A peer of the child tells an authority that the child has committed a deviant act.

(ix, 25) *Omnipotent: other* (OO). The subject implies or states that authority learns child is guilty of the deviation in some unspecified or mystical way, such as: "Oh, mothers always know when you do something bad—they can just tell."

314. (ix, 26) *Caught: other* (O). Authority finds out child is responsible by some means other than those enumerated above, most commonly by direct observation.

315. (ix, 27) *Apology* (A) and *Fixing* (F). The child spontaneously apologizes for the deviation, or he spontaneously restores or "undoes" the deviant act, or volunteers to help do so.

316. (ix, 28) *Hiding* (H). Child hides himself or the evidence from an authority; this excludes fixing and restoring.

317. (ix, 29) *Authority fixes* (AF). The authority either fixes or helps fix, repair, restore, or undo the deviant act, either spontaneously or at the request of the child; if authority and child work together, AF may be scored together with F or FF on a single story.

(ix, 30) *Authority forgives* (OK). An authority forgives the child for deviating, either spontaneously or upon request by the child.

(ix, 31) *Referral to other authority* (Ref). An authority, knowing that the child has deviated, refers the child to another authority for discipline, or threatens to do so.

(ix, 32) *Forced fixing* (FF). The child is forced to fix, restore, or undo the deviant act by an authority.

318. (ix, 33) *Verbal punishment* (VP). An authority scolds the child, asks why he did it, tells him never to do it again, or threatens punishment for repetition of the deviant act.

319. (ix, 34) *Physical punishment* (PP). An authority spanks or otherwise hurts the child physically; confinement, isolation, denial of privilege, etc., are *not* classified as physical punishment.

320. (ix, 35) *Isolation* (Iso). The child is forced to remain *alone* for

a time as punishment; confinement in the presence of the authority is not isolation.

(ix, 36) *Cries* (Cry). The child in the story (not the subject telling the story) cries.

(ix, 37) *Prevention, control* (PC). Authority controls the child's behavior externally; emphasis is not on teaching child nor on punishing him, but rather on making it environmentally impossible for the deviation to occur again.

321. (ix, 38) *Gets away with it* (GA). The deviation is never discovered, or the child is never implicated, or the child is never punished in any way; the subject must perceive that a deviation has occurred.

Observer Reliability

Observer reliability was developed in the customary manner, and the reliability, as measured by per cent agreement between E and an observer, was considered acceptable at the time. The records of this process have been lost, however, and exact figures cannot be given here. The reliability estimated for a comparable procedure performed in our laboratory may be found in Wurtz (1959, p. 232); he obtained 96 per cent agreement on the coding of 55 completions.

Appendix G. *Adult Role: Quoting Rules (QuRu)*

Only one assessment situation was designed for the measurement of adult role playing. This situation, quoting rules (or QuRu), is a realistic little episode in which the subject child is given a restrictive rule, then placed in a social conflict with a younger child who has been given a permissive rule. The subject is shown some very stimulating toys and given a strict injunction not to play with them while the experimenter is out of the room. Then he is left alone for two minutes (a period that provided us incidentally with an assessment of S's resistance to temptation). To add to this psychic burden, the younger child, who has previously been told he *may* play with the toys, is then sent into the room with him. They remain alone there together for five minutes. Thus, S is faced with another child's breaking a rule that he himself would like to break but is disciplining himself not to. His methods of restraining and controlling the stooge child are evaluated for their adult quality, with quoting the restrictive rule being considered the primary evidence of adult behavior.

The Setting

The experiment room (Room A) was prepared for the test by placing a child's low table under a window at the left of the entrance and a child's chair against the wall at the right. Beside the chair was a box containing a few distinctly "beat-up" old toys: four small rectangular blocks, one cylindrical block, a wooden truck, three broken crayons, a piece of drawing paper, and a used puzzle from the regular nursery school collection. Across the room on the table, however, were some exceedingly attractive new toys: two new puzzles, a big fire engine with removable accessories, and a girl's play outfit consisting of a new hat in a hatbox, high-heeled shoes, and a purse. These were placed in standard positions on the table, the puzzles back against the wall and the other things lined up across the front.

Technique

The test situation requires two experimenters and a younger (stooge) child who is not a subject in the research. E1 (male, in our research) introduces the child to the situation, then retires to record observations; E2 (female, in our research) works with the stooge child. The duration of the test is 20–25 minutes.

The subject is approached in the schoolroom or on the playground by E1 and told by the latter that he has a special toy he wants to show S, suggesting that they go to another room to see it. When they get inside, E1 draws S immediately to the table, saying, "Here are some brand-new toys that are going to be for the nursery school later on, but right now don't play with them, because they might get broken if you do." He shows S how the toys work, and adds, "See, they're pretty good toys, and they're sure going to be a lot of fun to play with when they're in the nursery school." He then leads S over to the box of old toys and says he has to go out to his car to get the special toy he has promised. "While I'm gone you wait for me here. O.K.?" After some sign of assent, E1 says, "While I'm gone, here are some toys you *can* play with." He then mentions that it might take him a little while to get the special toy, but S should wait here for him, because the toy is really terrific.

Two minutes elapse, with S alone in the room and E1 recording observations from behind the one-way mirror. In the meantime, E2 has been readying the stooge child (call him X) for his part in the show. This consists of telling X that there is a special surprise treat for him in another room; would he like to see it? After the to-be-expected affirmative reply, E2 takes X over to the door and, without opening it at once, says: "I have to go outside to get the surprise, so will you wait for me in this room? O.K.? And while you're waiting for me, there's a whole bunch of brand-new toys inside on a table; you can play with them till I get back." For a moment E2 describes the toys in glowing terms; then, opening the door, she says, "I'll be back real soon!" She lets X into the room as quickly as possible, and if X asks about S's presence, says, "That's all right; he's waiting for someone else."

Enter the crisis. The two children are now alone together for five minutes, during which E1 continues to record observations from behind the mirror.

At the end of this period, E2 returns with a new book. She sits down with X and reads it to him; when it is done, they leave the room together, E2 telling S to stay there, that E1 will soon return. After two more minutes, E1 *does* return and *does* bring a fine toy, which S is allowed to play with as long as he wishes. He never does get a chance to play with the forbidden toys (unless E2 has permitted it, to keep peace!), and eventually the toys *do* turn up in the nursery school (in our case, in the last week of school after all the QuRu work was done), and the children *do* get a chance to play with them.

During these various interchanges between the two E's and two children, a good deal of ingenuity is required of the E's to (a) avoid letting S feel discriminated against, (b) keep S from blaming X after the session is over, and (c) terminate the session with gentle feelings of satisfaction on the part of both children. Tattling must be tolerated when E2 returns, and explanations must be given why E2 did not know the special toys are forbidden territory. (When our stooges got ruffled feelings from the encounter, they had to be smoothed out; for since there were only half as many younger children in the group as there were subjects, each of the younger ones had to be an X on two occasions. The occasions were kept as far apart as the schedule would permit.)

Observation Procedure

For measurement purposes, this episode falls conveniently into four parts: (1) the initial two minutes while S is alone and faced with the conflict between his desire to play with the forbidden toys and his wish to observe the rule enunciated by E1 (this period was used for measuring resistance to temptation); (11) the five-minute period after X enters the room and starts playing with the forbidden toys, during which time the two children are alone together; (111) the seven-minute period after E2 returns with a little book to read to X (and to S, if he wishes to listen); and (1v) the final two minutes after E2 and X both leave, and S is once more alone, waiting for the return of E1.

An observer behind the mirror (E2 briefly, then E1 for the remainder of the session) recorded the behavior of all who were in the room from the moment S was introduced to the situation and left alone (Part 1) to the final two minutes when S was again left alone (end of Part 1v). The recording was done in half-minute units, for the sake of maintaining a time reference, but the notations provided a complete running account of the episode, not a time-sampling measurement. Soon after the data were collected, the observer (E1), working from these records, dictated a running account of the events of the session, with appropriate coding of names and subject numbers to assure complete anonymity of each description. These were then transcribed. Seven months later, when time had eliminated most of the observer's (E1) memory of the tests, he and another assistant scored these accounts independently on the scale described below as "vi, 63: Adult role qualities."

Examples of Taped Accounts

Two of the transcribed accounts, one of a high adult role girl and one of a low adult role boy, presented as they were edited by the observer from the transcriptions of his commentary, will illustrate the kinds of behavior available for measurement.

High Adult Role Girl

Part I. After the instructions, and just before E1 leaves, S says, as she points at the microphone, "Look at that," and then, "Well, I stole a matchbook, once," apparently quite irrelevantly, except that she evidently expects this situation to be one that will test her obeying of rules. During Part I she wanders about. She looks at the new toys—she's quite curious about them. Then she withdraws, plays a little bit with the old toys, and looks around, trying to find E1.

Part II. When X enters, S says: "Don't touch those—we can't play with those—those are for the nursery school next year. John said we mustn't touch those, and when he comes he'll bring another surprise for both of us." S then leaves the room and gets a chair for X and brings it back in—she's rather restless and excited, and really expects a surprise for both of them, and is quite successful at preventing X from playing with the new toys, as X never again makes a real attempt. And while they're sitting there, rather restless, excited, waiting, S gives considerable nurturance to X, and says, "We mustn't touch those toys, but let's go look at them," and they do go over and look at them, and again she says, "Now, let's not touch them—let's just look." At the very end of Part II, she does finger the toys, assuming, I guess, that perhaps this will be the surprise, that they will, after all, get to play with the new toys.

Part III. E2 enters, and S says nothing at all. She doesn't pay any particular attention to E2, and although X is now encouraged to play with the toys, S says nothing; she simply observes. As the story starts, S listens intently to the story, occasionally interrupting with a mild amount of attention seeking, and then as she listens to the story, she pounds on the chair with one of the old blocks. At the end of the story she asks, "Is John coming pretty soon?" and the others leave.

Part IV. S spends most of this time intently preoccupied with the search for E1. She goes to the window; she goes to the door and opens it, leans out, looks, listens, actually walks out into the hall, and then comes back; she goes to the window and looks out for E1, then goes back to the door, and finally leaves the room in search for E1.

Summation. Overall, then, she was quite successful with a compliant X. It is hard to say how much effort she would have expended with a more determined X. Her approach was rather mature; she offered considerable nurturance, offered other toys, got a chair for X, and promised another surprise when E1 returned. She appears to be a good manipulator and a subtle manipulator of other children, in terms of getting at their motivations in a rather adult way.

Low Adult Role Boy

Part I. S is relatively interested in the old toys; he makes the old puzzle, then plays with the old blocks.

Part II. When X enters, S says, "John said not to touch those," but without much conviction. He then says, "Don't go near those—please don't—don't touch those." X, however, is rather persistent—has in fact been in the setting before—and within two minutes both of them are playing quite cooperatively together with the new toy, the fire engine. The play continues until the fire engine breaks—that is, until several parts come off that are hard to replace. Immediately, S withdraws to the old toys, while X starts to put away the new toy, trying to replace the parts so that they look as they were at the beginning. S remains with the old toys, casually mentioning, toward the end of this part of the session, "John doesn't want us to touch those anyway."

Part III. When E2 enters, S is at first dependent. He states the rule, wonders why E2 is in there. Then, as E2 starts to read, S goes back to the old toys, and plays with them, rather contentedly, as he listens to the story. Then, as E2 begins to make it clear to X that it's all right to play with the new toys, S joins in and they both play with the new toys, but not until S has checked with E2 to make sure it's all right for him also to play with the new toys. He remains rather dependent on E2 through this period of playing with the new toys until the end of Part III.

Part IV. S plays with the old toys throughout the period. Once, he looks at the new toys, but then returns to the old toys, and pounds on his foot with one of the blocks. He does not play with the new toys at any time in this part.

Scoring for Adult Role

Four scores, plus a summary score and a stooge rating, were obtained from this episode, but they are by no means independent of one another. The first three depend on the set of predetermined categories, relating to rule quoting and control of X, in terms of which the behavior was recorded. These predetermined categories were (a) using *self* as authority (quoting rules, commanding, threat of tattling, threat of aggression, reasoning); (b) using the *experimenter* as authority (actual tattling, threats of E's intervention); (c) *physical deterrence*, aggressive or otherwise; and (d) *counter-offers* or inducements to stay away from the toys. The six scores obtained—only the last two were retained for analysis—are as follows:

(vi, 60) *Latency of rule quoting.* A simple two-point scale indicating the occurrence or non-occurrence of any kind of rule quoting during the first half-minute of Part II (immediately after the entrance of X, and before X's own behavior could have much effect on S).

(vi, 61) *Frequency of rule quoting.* A six-point scale ranging from no use of self or experimenter authority or physical deterrence to extended use of all three; based on the first 120 seconds of Part II.

(vi, 62) *Quality of rule quoting.* A seven-point scale ranging from no effort by S to control X, through mere assertion, and then assertion plus reasoning and counter-offers, to actual participation with X in using the old toys as a substitutive device; based on the first 120 seconds of Part II.

(vi, 63) *Adult role qualities.* An overall seven-point rating, based on the dictated running accounts, indicating simply how many of seven characteristics occurred (regardless of how often or how extensively each occurred)—characteristics considered to be indicative of adult role performance, comprising: reasoning, counter-offers, persistence of efforts, nurturant rather than rejecting attitude, intense rather than mild or passive reaction, self-controlled rather than emotional performance, and prosocial rather than antisocial aggression.

212. (vi, 64) *QuRu: total raw score.* The sum of the raw scores of the above four scales (vi, 60, 61, 62, 63). Raw scores, rather than standard

TABLE G1

Intercorrelations among the Quoting-Rules Measures of Adult Role

(Boys above the diagonal, girls below)

QuRu Measures	Var. No.	VI, 61	VI, 62	VI, 63	VI, 64 (212)
			Variable Number		
Frequency . . . . . . VI, 61		°	.47	.53	.77
Quality . . . . . . VI, 62		.20	°	.38	.77
Overall . . . . . . VI, 63		.55	.68	°	.83
Total (212) . . . . VI, 64		.66	.81	.94	°

scores, were used because the number of steps on each scale was the largest number that could be reliably discriminated, and it was desired to weight each of the four contributors according to its capacity for discriminating. The standard distributions for the three longer scales were, for girls, (61) 1.28, (62) 1.66, and (63) 1.80, and for boys, 1.02, 1.21, and 1.53. The contributions of the three longer scales to the total score are reflected in their correlations with it, as show in Table G1, which also shows the correlations between them for each sex separately. These intercorrelations range from .20 to .68 for the girls, and from .38 to .53 for the boys; the correlations of each scale with the total are of the order that would be predicted from their slightly differing standard deviations.

213. (VI, 65) *Stooge (X) rating of persistence.* A five-point rating of X's persistence in attempting to play with the toys.

Observer Reliability

Detailed records of the training of the observer were not kept. He and another observer practiced the half-minute recording simultaneously and independently, using a carefully defined set of behavior categories, for several pretest sessions. Their agreement was close to perfect on the last two sessions before data collection began. The same observer (who was also E1) recorded the sessions for all forty subjects of the research proper.

The reliability of scoring the overall measure (VI, 63) from the dictated running accounts of each session was determined in two ways. We determined first whether two raters would agree on the presence or absence of each of the seven behavior characteristics that were being counted. The transcriptions for two children were used for practice, and then the agreements on the remaining 38 children were counted. Since there were seven categories and 38 children, there were 266 judgments to be made. Scoring the protocols independently, the two raters agreed on 85 per cent of the judgments.

The second question is of the extent of agreement on the final rating attributed to each child. This rating was simply the sum of the behavior items judged present. There was exact agreement on the seven-point scale for twenty children, agreement within one scale point for an additional sixteen, and disagreement (two points apart) on just two children. For each sex separately, as well as for both combined, these figures correspond to computed reliability coefficients (r) of .87.

For cases in which there was disagreement, the raters re-examined the protocols together and reached agreement on a final rating.

Since the judgments required for the frequency and quality scales were essentially the same as those for the overall scale, the 85 per cent agreement on individual behavior items may be taken as a measure of the reliability of those scales also.

Trait Consistency

Our imaginations boggled at the problem of developing a consistency measure for this assessment episode. The nature of the experience was such that it could not be repeated for a test-retest measure, and the duration was too brief to permit an internal measure. The only alternative would have been comparison with a similar episode that could be scored in the same way. As may be seen in the text of Chapters 5 and 6, this proved a quite satisfactory method for getting measures of trait consistency for resistance to temptation, guilt, and sex typing. Unfortunately, we could not design a duplicate episode for adult role—and indeed did not try very hard to, since the corresponding BUO measures seemed sufficiently elaborate. As will be seen, however, the correlations of BUO measures with these from the quoting rules episode are negligible in size, and we are left uncertain whether these QuRu scores are representative for the children's behavior in "similar" situations.

Appendix H. *Resistance to Temptation (RTT)*

There were four assessment situations designed to measure a child's resistance to temptation. Two of these yielded two measures, so that we have had available six measures of RTT. The sum of the standard scores of all six measures, based on all forty subjects, has provided the RTT total standard score (variable 211).

Quoting Rules (QuRu)

It will be recalled (Appendix G) that S was taken to the experimental room by E1 and left there alone for two minutes (Part I) with instructions not to play with the new toys. Then X, the stooge who *had* permission to play with the toys, was sent into the room by E2, and the two children were alone together for five minutes (Part II). At the end of this time, E2, who was the permissive authority with respect to X's playing with the toys, returned to the room for seven minutes (Part III). Finally, she and X left the room and S remained there alone for another two minutes (Part IV).

Quite aside from the adult role aspects of this assessment situation, there was an RTT aspect of interest—the strain placed on S to resist the temptation to play with the initially forbidden toys. First he was alone with them, then with another child who tried to play with them, then with both the child and a permitting adult, and finally alone with the toys again. The point in this sequence of increasing temptation at which S *did* play with the toys provided a measure of RTT.

A simple five-point scale was sufficient to indicate the degree of resistance:

1. Yields while alone in Part I.
2. Yields first time during Part II.
3. Yields first time during III, and continues during IV.
4. Yields during III, but does not continue during IV.
5. Never yields.

On the basis of the point in time (in whatever part) at which yielding first occurred, it was possible to discriminate somewhat more finely than the five main points, and ultimately a ten-point distribution was obtained. This ten-point scale constituted variable 208. Two coders' independent evaluations of the typescript descriptions of the children's behavior produced 95 per cent agreement within one point on the ten-point scale.

Candy Temptation

The candy temptation situation was the first of two linked together as if parts of a single episode involving the child and the experimenter. In the first part, E invites S to go to a special room to play a very special game with him. "Unforeseen circumstances" finally prevent the playing of the game, however, and E promises they will have another chance in a few days. The second part occurs as planned, and the game is finally played, as will be seen in the subsequent description of the toy and ring-toss temptation situation. The same male E served on both occasions, of course, and the same female was the observer in both cases.

The Setting

This assessment took place in Room A, which was bare of furniture except for a child's low table under the window on the left side of the room and a child's chair against the wall on the right side of the room near the door. On top of the table, spread neatly on the left side, was a stack of mimeographed papers. On the right side of the table was a three-part candy dish filled with three different kinds of candy: gumdrops, jelly beans, and M&M's. Some paper napkins were next to the dish.

On the floor beside the child's chair was a small cardboard box containing four rectangular blocks, one cylindrical block, a wooden bus, a plastic plate, and a dish with four broken crayons in it. Laid on top of the box was a jigsaw puzzle, and on top of that a blank sheet of drawing paper.

On the floor in the far right corner of the room were painted three colored circles about 18 inches in diameter. They would later be part of the game.

Technique

After a brief friendly conversation out in the nursery school, E takes S into the room and closes the door. E at once draws S's attention to the candy, saying in a surprised tone of voice: "Hey, look at that! Someone's left his stuff here; I thought we were going to have this room all to ourselves." They go to the table and look at the candy. E says: "I wonder who left this here; we'd better not touch anything, because it doesn't belong to us. Right?" E makes sure he gets an affirmative answer, to be sure S understands.

E then says, "Well, let me show you the game that we came to play—it's over here," and he leads S to the circles. "Look at these pretty circles. We're going to use them in our game." Then, pointing to the circles in turn, E asks S, "What color is this?"

When they are finished, E leads S to a position behind the chair, saying: "Now we've got to come back here to play our game. We play it from behind this chair." Suddenly E looks up at the wall clock and then turns to S and says: "Gee, I just remembered that I've got to make a phone call from the office. I'll tell you what—you wait here until I get back and then we'll play the game." E shows S the box of toys and says: "Here are some toys you can play with until I get back. I won't be too long, and you wait for me. But keep the door closed so no one else comes in, because this is a special room for just *you* and *me*." E then leaves, closing the door behind him.

S is left alone in the room for eight minutes. When E returns, he says, "I'm sorry, but I forgot to bring the game with me, but the very next time I come I'll bring it with me and then we can play it for sure." E then takes S back into the nursery school, but before he leaves for the day, he stops to remind S that they will play the game next time E comes back to school.

Scoring and Reliability

An observer in the observation chamber wrote a minute-by-minute description of S's actions during the eight minutes S was alone, and at once rated him on the following five-point scale (which constitutes variable 205):

1. Complete transgression: S either eats some of the candy or puts it into his pockets.

2. Partial transgression: S touches the plate and/or the candy, and may pick the candy up, but does not eat it; S puts the candy back.

3. Active resistance to temptation: S is acutely aware of the candy and focuses on it at least once for fifteen seconds or more. S may go over

to the table and look at the candy, or he may ignore the table and look out the window over the table or he may ignore the table and look at the pictures on the observation room wall to the immediate left of the table. In general, S is attracted toward the table or the area immediately surrounding it.

4. Passive resistance: S shows some awareness of the candy and may look at the table briefly, but in general the table is not differentiated from the rest of the room.

5. Complete resistance: S ignores the table completely; pays no attention to it (presumably indicative of lack of interest in it).

The forty individual protocols were transcribed, with code numbers to disguise the children's identities, and were then rated independently by another coder several months later. The reliability of these ratings can be reported in two ways. There was perfect agreement between the coders on 90 per cent of the estimates, and the r between the two ratings for all the children was .97.

Toy and Ring-Toss Temptations

A few days after the candy-temptation episode, E seeks out S again and has a friendly talk with him, reminding him of the game they missed before, and indicating that at last they can play it. The two then go to the experiment room (Room A again).

The Setting

This time the low table and the chair were in the same places, but the box of uninteresting toys had been removed, and the papers and candy on the table had been replaced with a fabulously exciting toy. For boys, this was a rocket missile base with many moving parts, and for girls it was a very fine baby-doll set.

Technique

On entering the room, E leads S immediately to the table, saying: "Look what we've got here. How do you like it?" E introduces the toy as either a "rocket missile base" or a "doll that cries real tears and wets her diaper." E then shows S some of the different parts of the toy, picking them up as he says: "See, here's a helicopter, and here's a tank," or "See, here are her booties, and here's an extra diaper."

E then tells S, "Go ahead, you can play with it." He lets S play with the toy for a minute or two until S is just starting to get involved. E then says: "Hey, you know this isn't the game we came to play with, so let's play that game and *maybe when we're done you can play some more with this.*" E then picks up a set of three rings (like quoits) and says, "We're going to use these in our game." E leads S to the circles painted on the floor in the corner of the room. "See, we're going to throw these little circles into the big ones." E throws one while standing right next to the circles, and then hands the other two rings to S, telling him to try. This process is repeated several times until S attains a fair degree of proficiency. During these trials E constantly praises S's efforts.

Then E says: "Now to play this game we have to go back here behind the chair. You must stand behind this chair and throw the little circles into the big circles. If you can get all of them into the big circles—why, then you can play with the toy over there (pointing) for as long as you want to." E, still holding the rings, walks quickly over to the wall clock, looks at it, and says: "Gee whiz, do you remember last time I had to make a phone call from the office? Well, I've got to make another one now. I'll tell you what—while I'm gone you throw the rings from behind the chair and leave them where they fall, and when I come back we'll see how you did. If they're all inside the big circles you can play with the toy for as long as you want. But remember, you must throw from behind the chair, O.K.?" After receiving some sign of assent, he says: "You wait for me and I'll be back soon and we'll see how you did. But keep the door closed so that no one else comes in, because this is a special room for just *you* and *me.*" E then hands the rings to S and quickly leaves the room.

S is left in the room alone for eight minutes, while the observer makes the same kind of running description she has made for the candy temptation.

When E returns, he notes the position of the rings. If they are not in the circles, he makes an excuse that he has made a mistake and placed the chair too far away. By one device or another, he gives the child a feeling of success, and then allows him to play with the fabulous toy to his heart's content.

Scoring and Reliability

Two scales were used for measuring resistance—one for resistance to playing with the toy, and one for resistance to breaking the rules to achieve success at the ring toss. For the toy (variable 207), the following five-point scale was used:

1. S plays with the toy.

2. S touches the toy briefly and/or picks it up briefly, but does not play with it. The emphasis is on touching and/or holding rather than playing.

3. S shows acute awareness of the toy, focusing on it at least once for fifteen seconds or more. He may approach the table closely, but no part of the toy is touched, although the table may be.

4. S shows some awareness of the toy, and may glance at it briefly (less than fifteen seconds) but in general does not differentiate it from the rest of the room.

5. S ignores the toy completely; pays no attention to it.

For the ring-toss game, a nine-point scale was constructed (variable 206). It was based on the occurrence or non-occurrence of three types of rule infraction: placing the rings by hand or foot instead of tossing, not staying behind the chair when tossing, and tossing more or less than three times. The exact combinations used for scoring the nine scale points are shown in Table H1.

A placing-rings infraction includes any method of putting the rings in the circle other than tossing (e.g., kicking with feet, or pushing or sliding in with hands or feet). A chair infraction includes any throwing from in front of the chair. Placing the rings after throwing from behind the

TABLE H1

Scoring for Ring-Toss Game

	Rule Observance		
Scale Point	Placing Rings	Staying Behind Chair	Using Three Throws
1	broken	broken	broken (less than)
2	broken	broken	obeyed (exactly)
3	broken	broken	broken (more than)
4	broken	obeyed	broken (less than)
5	broken	obeyed	obeyed (exactly)
6	broken	obeyed	broken (more than)
7	obeyed	broken	broken (more than)
8	obeyed	obeyed	broken (more than)
8 (alternate) . . .	obeyed	broken	obeyed (exactly)
9	obeyed	obeyed	obeyed (exactly)

chair does not involve a chair infraction, nor does going to pick up the rings in order to throw them again. The infraction occurs only when the child is actually throwing the rings.

Scale points 1, 2, and 3 represent the most serious deviation. Scale points 4, 5, and 6 represent deviation that is not as serious, mainly because the chair rule has not been broken. Scale points 7, 8, and 9 represent various degrees of resistance in which the child does not place the rings but may break one or both of the other rules. None of our children was able to throw the rings into the circles; therefore, all had a reason for breaking the rules.

The reliability of coding on these scales can again be expressed in terms of per cent agreement and correlation between raters. The procedure was identical with that for the candy temptation. On the toy scale, the figures were 92 per cent agreement, and $r = .99$. On the ring-toss scale, they were 87 per cent agreement, and $r = .93$.

RTT Measures from Hamster Situation

Hamster: Latency

In the disappearing hamster situation (described in Appendix I), a measure (variable 209) was taken of the number of minutes that elapsed before S left his post beside the hamster's box and went to look at the toys. (See hamster score sheet, Time Before Deviation.) The longer the time, the higher the resistance to temptation.

Hamster: Seriousness of Response

An observer noted where in the room, and to what objects, S went when he left the box. The room was mapped into areas that could be coded in terms of distance from the box. (See item 2, under Deviation, on the hamster score sheet, in Appendix I.) The closer the child stayed to the hamster box, the greater his resistance to temptation was assumed to be (variable 210).

Appendix I. *Guilt Assessments*

Two assessment situations were designed to provide measures of the children's reactions to situations in which they disobey adult instructions. In one instance, *the disappearing hamster* situation, the deviation from proper behavior was induced by making the stimulus conditions for doing something else simply too strong to resist; this situation also provided two of the measures of resistance to temptation (see Appendix H). The other assessment situation, *the red light,* provided physical circumstances that made deviation inevitable, and immediately evident to the child; there was no opportunity for resistance. In both situations, however, the deviation occurred in the absence of the adult authority, and there were opportunities for measuring such coping methods as confession, hiding, and fixing or restitution.

The Disappearing Hamster

For this situation, the child is taken to an experimental room (Room B) by a friendly male experimenter, who asks the child to help him. He says he is building a box for his hamster, but that the lid is not yet finished. The hamster is in a box in the corner of the room, and E asks S to stand guard, keeping the hamster from escaping, while E goes outside to finish the box lid. E then leaves S alone. There are many entrancing toys in the room tempting S to succumb to these stimulational values and leave his post beside the hamster. (All but four of our children left their post.) A false floor in the hamster box is instantly released by the observer, who is recording the action from behind the mirror, and the hamster slides into a padded compartment below. The floor's springing back into place makes a slight noise, and S returns to look in the box, only to find the hamster missing. The details of equipment, procedure, recording, and scoring follow.

The Setting

In the room were two tables, one against the wall to the left as E and S entered through the nursery school door, and the other against the wall to the right midway between the door and the observation mirror. Over this table hung a large wall clock. On the table was a phonograph; the record was playing when the child entered and the album cover was on the table. The other table was bare. In the extreme left-hand corner, against the observation window, was the hamster cage, with a cardboard cover across the top of the cage and a rolled-up magazine lying beside it. On the floor, in the half of the room nearest the nursery school door, were a jet plane that shoots bullets, a helicopter that flies, a hand puppet, and a large Bobo doll (an inflated, punchable, standup toy). Scattered around the room were various cartons and boxes (providing hiding places for the "escaped" hamster). There was also another door, midway on the left wall, through which the experimenter would leave, and which opened onto an outside courtyard.

Technique

After E establishes rapport with S, he says, "Say, I'm doing some work in the back. Could you help me with it?" If S seems hesitant, E also mentions that there are some toys there that S can play with. No mention of the specific work is made.

E leads S into the experimental room through the nursery school entrance. He first shows S the jet plane and how it fires bullets. If the child does not seem interested in the jet, E demonstrates the helicopter or the puppet. S is allowed about three minutes to play with the toy. During this time E starts the record going. The phonograph is set to stop shortly after E leaves the room.

At the end of the three minutes, E introduces S to the hamster: "This is my hamster. I'm building him this cage but I don't have the top built yet, so I have to watch him very closely. (E removes the cardboard cover and tosses it to the floor.) He is very valuable to me and I don't want him to get out. If I don't stay right here and watch him, he climbs up the sides and gets out. When I have to leave him alone, I put that paper over the top but still he sometimes escapes. Now, I have to go outside for a little while to do some work on the top of the cage. Will you watch to see that my hamster doesn't get out while I'm gone? (Waits for affirmation from child.) Good! If the hamster starts to climb out you just gently push him back down with this rolled-up magazine. (Demonstrates for S.) I'll be back in about twenty minutes, I guess (E walks over to the clock), which will be about when the big hand gets to here (shows S vaguely). I'll knock when I come back and you can open the door for me; it works easily. (E demonstrates with the outside door.) This other door goes back to the nursery school (E opens the door), but there's no one here to bother you. Thank you very much for helping me like this. Don't forget, I'm counting on you to see that the hamster doesn't get out while I'm gone." E leaves, after a glance to make sure that all the toys have been put back, and that S has nothing he can occupy himself with while watching the hamster.

If S does not deviate within 25 minutes, E returns to the room and relieves him of further responsibility. (Four of our children held their post the full 25 minutes.)

If S does deviate by walking away from the hamster, the observer drops the floor of the box. If the child remains in the room eight more minutes, E returns. If S leaves the room to seek E, however, E returns with the child at that time. If S leaves the room and returns to the nursery school, E goes after him into the school and explains that everything is all right, that the hamster often gets out, that E has found him, and that S may now come back and play with the toys for a while if he'd like to.

If S leaves his post but does not leave the room, and E returns eight minutes later, E gives S four chances to confess. E's entering the room gives the child his first chance. If S says nothing, E goes immediately to the far corner of the room (away from the hamster), and, kneeling on the floor, gives S his second chance, saying, "How did it go?" If no answer is given, or no confession made, then E gives S his third chance by asking, "Did the hamster try to climb?" If the expected answer is still not given, E asks (for the fourth chance), "Is everything all right?" In any case, E does not refute S's statement. In the event that after the four chances S still has not admitted the hamster's disappearance, E walks over to the hamster's cage to put back the cardboard cover, and "notices" the hamster's disappearance. When this occurs, or when S admits the hamster is gone (during his four chances), or if S seeks out E before the eight minutes are up, E says: "That's O.K., he gets out all the time. He must be around here someplace; let's look for him."

During the ensuing search, E, who has carried another hamster in his pocket, lets the second hamster go free and waits until S discovers this one himself among the debris on the floor (perhaps with some subtle guidance by E). When this occurs, E says: "Oh, good! I'll put him back in his cage and put this cover over the top to try to keep him in. Well, thank you very much for helping me. Would you like to play with some of these toys now?" S then plays with the toys until E feels he has sufficiently recovered from his experience.

Scoring

This very complex procedure required several weeks of planning and many pretests in order to make it realistic and objectively scorable. The following score sheet was developed by two observers working together; no specific observer-reliability series was performed, but the scoring procedure was made firm only after the observers were in full agreement on its details, and were confident of its level of objectivity.

HAMSTER SCORE SHEET
(Where alternative answers are presented, circle one number or response.)

RAPPORT PERIOD (including instructions)

1. Child's interest in toys and situation:
       1. low   2. medium   3. high
2. Child's interest in hamster:
       1. low   2. medium   3. high
3. Child's attention to instructions:
       1. poor   2. medium   3. good
4. Child's approach to responsibility showed:
   1. willing, active, positive acceptance
   2. positive, though somewhat passive acceptance (which may have been elicited by E)
   3. neutral response; neither accepted nor rejected responsibility
   4. some evidence of resistance or of looking for other alternatives
   5. active rejection of responsibility

TIME BEFORE DEVIATION

Time in minutes:_____

DEVIATION

1. Child's deviation was:
   1. sudden
   2. after brief anticipation
   3. after marked or moderate period of ambivalence
   4. after long gradual buildup
2. Child's deviation was to which area and object?_____
3. Child reacted, when hearing noise from cage, by:
   1. being startled, jumping
   2. being startled, then freezing
   3. looking up

    4. showing curiosity

    5. minimal or very slow reaction

4. Child returned to hamster cage:

    1. quickly

    2. with moderate speed

    3. slowly or circuitously

    4. not at all

POST-DEVIATION BEHAVIOR

1. Child's facial expression at time of discovery showed:

    1. shock, extreme upset or emotion

    2. some concern or upset

    3. no change or noticeable expression

2. Child assimilated disappearance:

    1. immediately

    2. after short latency

    3. after some delay in comprehending situation

3. Child's level of activity after accepting hamster's disappearance was:

    1. intense, rushing, high motility

    2. moderate activity

    3. inactivity or extremely slow movement

4. Child's search was:

    1. realistic and thorough

    2. realistic but not thorough

    3. brief or cursory

    4. a slight looking around, not a real search

    5. non-existent

5. During eight minutes, child's evidence of concern over deviation was:

    1. marked and intense throughout

    2. very intense at outset, but diminished

    3. low at outset, but increased to intense level

    4. intense at outset, decreased, then increased again

    5. moderate throughout

    6. low throughout

    7. low or moderate at outset, then disappeared

    8. not apparent at first, then appeared later

6. Child's final resolution was to:

    1. leave and go back to the nursery school

    2. open the door to the experimenter to report

    3. continue to search for entire period

    4. remain inactive until E returned, sitting or standing

    5. show conflict about 1 or 2 above, but remain in situation

    6. start (or continue) playing with the toys

    7. break down emotionally and cry

    8. whimper or pout

    9. get very aggressive

7. If child confessed, was it:

    1. spontaneous?

    2. elicited after first query?
    3. elicited after second query?
    4. elicited after third query?
8. If child confessed, was it:
    1. realistic?
    2. a partial report?
    3. a total lie or fantasy?
9. If child confessed, was self referred to as:
    1. responsible for deviation?
    2. partly responsible for deviation?
    3. not responsible at all?
    4. not referred to?
10. Child blamed hamster's disappearance on:
    1. hamster
    2. experimenter
    3. cage
    4. other, or unknown, power or influence
    5. self, plus one of the above
    6. self only
11. Child's confession included defense, excuse, or justification:
    yes_____   no_____
11a. Child's confession included explanation of behavior after deviation:
    yes_____   no_____
12. Child's attitude toward experimenter was to:
    1. wait for reaction, expectantly or watchfully
    2. act sorry or repentent
    3. act aggressive or hostile or defiant
    4. act dependent
    5. act cold or indifferent
    6. show no reaction
13. Child's part in searching for the hamster was:
    1. eager and active participation
    2. some efforts to help
    3. slight look, but no real participation
    4. refusing or refraining help
14. Child's reaction to finding the hamster was:
    1. joyous, excited, pleased
    2. mild, positive
    3. neutral, no effect
    4. evident lack of interest
15. In post-play, child showed this degree of perseveration about hamster's disappearance:
    1. frequent
    2. some
    3. none
16. In post-play, child mentioned or went over to the hamster:
    1. frequently
    2. once or twice
    3. not at all

Variables Coded

Fifteen variables were coded from the data provided by the above scoring form. In the description of each variable below, the source of the data is given by reference to the item number on the scoring form. A high rating implies a high degree of the variable described in the scale title (and, in turn, high ratings in the component scoring-form items). Following are the variables:

225. (vii, 5) *Degree of involvement in the hamster situation.* Scale: 1 to 7. Based on average of Rapport Period items 1, 2, and 3.

226. (vii, 6) *Acceptance of responsibility for hamster.* Scale: 1 to 5. Based on Rapport Period item 4.

227. (vii, 7) *Behavioral evidence of internal conflict about deviation.* Scale: 1 to 4. Based on Deviation item 1.

228. (vii, 8) *Strength of reaction to deviation cue* (i.e., noise from box). Scale: 1 (weak) to 5 (strong and quick). Based on combined scores from Deviation items 3 and 4.

(vii, 9) *Strength of reaction to discovery that hamster is missing.* Scale 1 (weak, unconcerned) to 4 (shock and strong upset). Based on combined scores from Post-Deviation items 1 and 3.

(vii, 10) *Extent and quality of search for missing hamster.* Scale: 1 (none) to 5 (realistic and thorough). Based on Post-Deviation item 4.

(vii, 11) *Evidence of emotional upset after disappearance of hamster.* Scale: 1 (low) to 5 (marked and intense throughout the eight minutes). Based on Post-Deviation item 5.

(vii, 12) *Child's final behavioral resolution after hamster's disappearance.* Non-scalar. Coded directly from Post-Deviation item 6.

(vii, 13) *Spontaneity of child's confession upon E's return.* Scale: 1 (elicited after third query) to 4 (spontaneous). Based on Post-Deviation item 7.

(vii, 14) *Degree of self-responsibility and blame expressed in confession.* Scale: 1 (none) to 6 (fully and solely). Based on combined scores from Post-Deviation items 9 and 10.

(vii, 15) *Defensive reduction of seriousness of deviation by excuse, or explanation of behavior after deviation.* Scale: 1 (none) to 4 (much). Based on Post-Deviation items 11 and 11a.

(vii, 16) *Attitude toward E upon E's return.* Non-scalar. Coded directly from Post-Deviation item 12.

(vii, 17) *Extent of effort to find hamster with E present.* Scale: 1 (refused or refrained) to 4 (eager and active). Based on Post-Deviation item 13.

(VII, 18) *Degree of positive affect expressed at finding hamster.* Scale: 1 (uninterested) to 4 (joyous, excited, pleased). Based on Post-Deviation item 14.

(VII, 19) *Amount of post-situational concern or persevering over disappearance of hamster.* Scale: 1 (none) to 5 (frequent mention and going to box). Based on combined scores from Post-Deviation items 15 and 16.

The Red Light Situation

The child is taken to an experiment room (Room A) with the promise of being shown a surprise toy if he will play a game first. The game is a bowling game which has been set up with such physical obstacles that the child is almost forced to break a rule specifying where he must stand when he rolls the ball. Behind the bowling pins, there is a "bowling machine" that is alleged to count his score. However, he is warned that if he breaks the rule about where he must stand, a red light on the "bowling machine" will go on and a buzzer will sound. (The light and buzzer are controlled from the observation chamber.) E then leaves the room, and an observer behind the mirror awaits the child's first accidental step past the foul line. As soon as this occurs, he flashes the light and sounds the buzzer. The child has already been shown a dummy switch that turns off the light and thus hides his deviation from E when E returns. Two minutes after the deviation, E returns and questions S about what has happened.

The Setting

A yellow circle was painted on the floor of the room opposite the observation booth. Four small bowling pins were placed together inside the circle.

A strip of red ribbon, suspended 41 inches above the floor, was attached at one end to a hook on the wall to the right of the entrance to the room, and at the other end to the top one of two wooden boxes. The ribbon was placed 55 inches from the yellow circle. A row of three small chairs was placed 11 inches behind the ribbon, the backs of the chairs facing the ribbon. The rule for the bowling game required the child to stand behind the ribbon and in front of the row of chairs, the space being large enough that he could follow the rule, but small enough to maximize his difficulty in knowing whether he had broken the rule or not. The ribbon was placed at a level above the child's head to increase his difficulty in knowing whether he had deviated.

A "bowling machine," which consisted of a box with a wooden door, an enclosed buzzer, and a visible red light and dummy switch attached to the top of the box, was placed on the floor against the wall behind the circle in which the bowling pins were placed. The observer in the observation booth could signal the "rule-breaking" deviation by turning on the light and sounding the buzzer for a second by means of switches in the booth. Inside the wooden box was some "nothing" equipment the experimenter could consult to determine the child's "score."

Technique

Establishing the deviation. E brings the child to the room, saying: "I'd like to show you the game we have today. You roll this ball and try to knock down these pins. You stand here and roll the ball like this." E acts out the motion, standing in front of the ribbon, close to the pins. "Here, you try it."

The child is given practice trials in front of the string, at gradually increasing distances from the pins, until he learns the technique and has some successes at knocking down pins from different distances. He is encouraged by E with such phrases as: "Good. Now try to roll it from here." "Good, you knocked some more down."

After the child has knocked down the first pin or pins, he is told, "When you knock some pins down, you put them back in this circle." He is encouraged to do this each time during the practice trials. After several practice trials, E says: "Now you've learned how to play, and it's time for the real game. If you knock down a lot of pins in the real game, you'll get to see a surprise. Would you like that? All right. In the real game, you should hurry and play fast so you can knock down a lot of pins, so you can see the surprise. Now do you see that red string? In the real game, the rule is that you must stand back here behind this red string when you roll the ball. You must remember to do that. The wrong thing to do is to go in front of the string before you roll the ball. If you do the wrong thing—if you don't stay behind the string—the machine will make a noise and that red light will go on. Here, I'll show you."

E rolls the ball, allowing his arm to cross under the string. O turns on the light and buzzer, leaving the light on and sounding the buzzer for a second. E says: "Oh, oh! See what happened. I did it the wrong way. I didn't stay behind the string, so the machine made a noise and the light went on. But that won't happen if you stay behind the string. Now I'll get the machine all set."

E goes to the "bowling machine" and pulls the dummy switch, making sure the child is watching the procedure. (O turns off the light.) E then hands the ball to S, saying, "Here, you try it, and remember to stay behind the string."

After further practice, and emphasis on the rules, E says: "Well, you know all about how to play the game, so you can play it all by yourself, can't you? I have to go outside the room to talk to someone for a few minutes, but you can go ahead and knock down a lot of pins so you can see the surprise. When you knock any pins down, put them back in the circle. You keep playing and I can tell from the machine how many pins you knocked down. I'll be back in a few minutes. We'll leave the door closed so no one will bother you while you're playing. When I come back, I'll knock and you let me in, O.K.? If you need me I'll be outside the room."

After the child begins to play, O watches for the first trial on which it seems the child will have difficulty knowing whether he has crossed beyond the string or not. On this trial, O turns on the light and buzzer, turning the buzzer off after a second but leaving the light on. If the child attempts to turn off the light with the dummy switch, O turns off the light, but if the child does not turn the light off, it is left on permanently. On the succeeding trials, O does not turn on the buzzer and light unless the child clearly is not attempting to obey the injunction about staying behind the string. However, if S deliberately disobeys, O repeats the buzzer and light signals. Again, if S presses the dummy switch, O turns off the light.

Observing reactions to deviation. As soon as O induces the first deviation by sounding the buzzer and turning on the light, he signals this fact to E, who waits two minutes and then returns to the room. If the child leaves the room after his deviation, to look for E or to return to the nursery school, E meets him outside the door. Whether E first meets the child inside or outside the room, he gives S time to make spontaneous remarks, and in any case takes him back to the room immediately so that O can hear and record S's remarks.

If the light is off and S does not spontaneously discuss the light-and-buzzer deviation, E asks him, "How was the game?" E then elicits S's report on the sequence of events by asking a series of "what" questions: "What happened?" "What did you do after that?" "Did you do anything else?" "What?" E also asks a "how" question ("How did that happen?") about each situation aspect described by the child in response to the "what" questions. The "what" and "how" questions are designed to elicit the child's report concerning (a) the rule-breaking deviation (i.e., staying behind the string and the light-and-buzzer event) and (b) his hiding response (i.e., his turning off the light, if he did so).

If the "what" and "how" questions do not elicit the necessary information about (a) and (b), E also asks "why" questions, e.g., "Why did you turn off the light?" All these questions are probes, and are used only as needed to ensure a full response from S.

Closing the episode. After the necessary responses have been secured from S, E says, "Now, I'll go see if you knocked down enough pins so you can see the surprise." E opens the wooden door on the front of the bowling machine, looks inside and says: "Almost enough for the surprise. Let's knock them down one more time."

In the following trials, E attempts to help the child alleviate his feelings concerning the deviation and/or hiding in a way suitable for the particular child. If S has confessed, or is upset, or fearful of the light and buzzer, or doubtful of his ability to stay behind the string, and shows reluctance to roll the ball from there, E might say: "Well, we all make mistakes. Sometimes it's kind of hard to stay behind the string. Let's try it this time in front of the string so we won't have to worry about the noise and the light." He lets the child roll the ball until he knocks down some pins, praises him, and tells him he can now see the surprise. If it seems the child is willing to roll the ball again from behind the string, and can gain mastery of the situation by doing so, E has him roll from behind the string. In any case, after he knocks down some pins, E praises him and shows him the surprise.

If the child has confessed neither the rule-breaking deviation nor the hiding response, it is more difficult to alleviate his feelings. E attempts to have him roll the ball from behind the string, and then, after he has knocked down some pins, E praises him for doing this and shows him the surprise; thus S is rewarded for doing the "right" thing rather than for his deviation or hiding. If a child who has not confessed is unwilling to roll the ball from behind the string, he is encouraged to roll it from in front, praised for knocking down some pins, and shown the surprise.

While playing with the promised surprise, S had further opportunity to ventilate his feelings. E says, "That's a nicer noise (referring to the music) than that old machine, isn't it?" (Our surprise was a toy dog with a windup spring inside that played a music box and activated the tail in a rotary manner to make the dog roll over.)

Scoring and Coding

The initial scoring was done by the observer. He recorded the child's verbal communications to E and also all of S's behavior while E was out of the room. However, as soon as the session was completed, E and O conferred with respect to the verbal communications, E reading the list of them that O had written down in sequence. This provided an opportunity for corrections and additions of statements made by S that O had not heard or had misinterpreted. E and O then immediately made independent judgments on categories A and C in the following list of scoring categories:

A. Verbal reaction to rule-breaking deviation; i.e., not staying behind the string. (Subjects were given separate scores for spontaneous and elicited reaction in these categories, as many scale items being checked as necessary for describing all the child's behavior.)

1. Confession of deviation—without defense or excuse for the act.
2. Confession of deviation—with defense serving to minimize or justify the deviation.
3. Statement of events, i.e., that the light went on and/or the machine made a noise, without attributing causation.
4. Projection of causation for the event.
5. Denial of event—implicit, i.e., no mention of the light-and-buzzer event.
6. Denial of event—explicit.

B. The hiding response to rule-breaking deviation (while the child was alone in the experimental room).

1. Hiding 0: no attempt to hide evidence of "rule breaking."
2. Hiding 1: one or more motions with hand toward the dummy light switch, but did not touch.
3. Hiding 2: pressed the switch.

4. Hiding 3: pressed switch more than once, after deliberately deviating by rolling from in front of the string after the experimentally induced deviation had occurred.

C. Verbal reaction to the hiding response. (This does not apply to subjects scoring in category B.1 above.)

1. Confession of hiding—without defense.
2. Confession of hiding—with defense.
3. Denial of hiding—implicit.
4. Denial of hiding—explicit: i.e., stating that light went off, without confessing personal responsibility.

D. Amount of tension following rule-breaking deviation and/or the hiding response (while the child was alone in the experimental room). (Indications of tension and of tension-reducing mechanisms were the basis of these ratings. Behaviors were scored as either *moderate* or *marked*. Both *intensity* and *frequency* were considered in making the ratings.)

1. Vocal tension: talking to or scolding self, crying, whining, sighing, coughing, whistling.
2. Facial tension: affective facial expression (anxious or fearful, guilty, angry, frowning, sad).
3. Postural tension: freezing or immobilization, drooping of shoulders, hands over ears, or startle reflex following the light and buzzer.
4. Locomotor tension: body movements, e.g., restrained and hesitant "V.T.E." movements toward the machine or the door, moving around the room, flight. (Scored as *extreme* if child left room.)
5. Autoerotic behavior: finger- or thumbsucking, masturbation, etc.

Nine scales were constructed for converting these scoring observations to quantitative indicators of dimensions that seemed theoretically relevant to the general problem of reaction to deviation. The first and third scales (VII, 20 and 22) were coded independently by E and O from the written protocols of the sessions. For all forty subjects, exact agreements were obtained on 100 per cent of the ratings for VII, 20, and on 95 per cent of the ratings for VII, 22. The remaining scales were coded by mechanical transformations of the original scoring categories. The nine scales follow:

(vii, 20) *Resistance to accepting responsibility for fulfilling the rule to stay behind the string.* Scale: 1 (none) to 3 (complete ignoring of rules at once).

229. (vii, 21) *Extent of rule following.* Scale: 1 (no attempt to follow rules even on first trial) to 5 (followed rule at least until fifth trial).

230. (vii, 22) *Extent of efforts to hide deviation by turning off red light.* Scale: 1 (no instance) to 5 (repeated deviation with hiding).

231. (vii, 23) *Amount of tension following deviation* (rule breaking and/or hiding). Scale: 1 (no indication) to 9 (several tension signs judged to be *marked*).

(vii, 24) *Leaving the room* (presumed to be flight). Scale: 1 (no flight) to 3 (leaves less than a minute after initial deviation).

232. (vii, 25) *Intensity of confession of deviation.* Scale: 1 (no confession) to 4 (strong; offers no defense).

233. (vii, 26) *Spontaniety of confession of deviation.* Scale: 1 (no confession) to 4 (completely spontaneous when E returns).

234. (vii, 27) *Degree of denial of deviation.* Scale: 1 (confession, with or without defense, but no denial) to 4 (strong denial, or complete projection).

(vii, 28) *Degree of verbal admission of hiding the deviation.* Scale: 1 (complete denial) to 3 (full confession without defense).

Observer Reliability

Since E did not observe the behavior listed under scoring categories B and D above, only O's record of those events is available. Therefore, scoring reliability was determined only for the categories listed under A and C. For those under A, there were twelve possible recordings, including both spontaneous and elicited reactions in each of the six listed categories, and more than one category could be judged to have occurred in a given child. The per cent of exact agreement between E's and O's positive (independent) judgments on 37 children was 88.5 per cent. On the judgments under C, the comparable value was 95.2 per cent. (Three children were observed by both E and O, but the judgments were not made independently, so these cases could not be included in the reliability correlations.)

Appendix J. *Gender Role (Sex Typing)*

There were five measures of gender role. *Area usage* is described in Appendix D, the *observer rating scale* in Appendix E; Brown's "It Test" was given and scored as described in the published instrument in Brown (1956). Two other assessments situations for gender role were revised from published instruments and therefore require description here; each produced a single retained measure.

The Pictures Test

This test, adapted from that of Fauls and Smith (1956), was designed to provide a preference measure for two sets of role activities, sex role and adult role. Eight line drawings, on cards 6½ × 8 inches, picture activities that are appropriate or inappropriate to the sex of the child being tested, or display adults or children performing acts that are age-appropriate. These eight cards are presented in pairs, with instructions to the child to indicate which of the two activities he would prefer to do. Twelve comparisons are offered. Separate sets of cards are used for boys and girls, identical in all respects except that the child in the pictures is a boy in one set and a girl in the other.

Technique

S is taken to a small testing room and seated across a child-size table from E, who says: "We're going to play a little game with some cards. I'll show you two pictures, and you get to pick one of them. Here's one just for practice. (E displays two pictures of a dog playing). Which one do you think the doggy likes to do best? Fine, I think so too. Now shall we play the real game? O.K., here's the first one."

E then describes the pictures in the first pair as he holds them up in front of S, asking, "Which one do you like to do best?" The procedure is the same for all twelve pairs except that the descriptions are abbreviated whenever a picture appears for the second or third time.

The pictures all show a child of the same sex as S in each of eight activity settings. Near the edge of each picture are a male and a female adult, identified by E as: "His (her) mother and daddy are watching him (her)."

Pictures

In the pictures, the activities and their settings vary in three ways: half are of a child playing and half are of a child helping with adult work; half are sex-appropriate and half are sex-inappropriate; half are indoors and half are outdoors. The following list gives the content of each picture, and in parentheses indicates the variations represented.

1. Child constructing houses and buildings with blocks. (Masc., child, indoors.)

2. Child playing cowboy with costume, boots, hat, and gun. (Masc., child, outdoors.)

3. Child playing house with little table, chairs, and dishes. (Fem., child, indoors.)

4. Child taking doll for a walk in a doll buggy. (Fem., child, outdoors.)

5. Child helping daddy hammer, saw, and paint things in the shop. (Masc., adult work, indoors.)

6. Child helping father wash the car. (Masc., adult work, outdoors.)

7. Child helping mother cook, bake, and wash dishes. (Fem., adult work, indoors.)

8. Child helping mother hang up washing on the clothesline. (Fem., adult work, outdoors.)

The pictures are presented in pairs as follows:

* I. 3 vs. 1	V. 1 vs. 7	* IX. 7 vs. 5
* II. 2 vs. 4	* VI. 4 vs. 8	* X. 2 vs. 6
* III. 5 vs. 1	VII. 3 vs. 5	* XI. 7 vs. 3
* IV. 6 vs. 8	VIII. 8 vs. 2	XII. 6 vs. 4

Scoring and Consistency

The degree of preference for activities appropriate to the child's own sex (variable 201) is measured by counting the frequency of sex-appropriate choices made on the eight starred pairs. It will be noted that each picture is presented twice, once in comparison with a child play activity and once with adult work. The scores can range from zero to eight, but with our subjects the obtained distributions for boys ranged from two to eight, and for girls, four to eight.

The remaining (unstarred) comparison pairs were intended for use in securing a measure of preference for adult role. This measure was abandoned, however, when Borstelmann (1961) discovered that test-retest reliability of the adult role measure was approximately zero. The comparable estimate of trait consistency over a one-month period for the sex-typing measure was .37 for boys and .38 for girls.

Toy Preference and Satiation

The toy preference test, modeled after that of Rabban (1950), measures the degree to which a child prefers appropriately to inappropriately sex-typed toys. It yields two measures: first, the proportion of choices of male vs. female toys, and second, the time required for the child to become satiated while playing with his first-choice toy.

The Toys

Fourteen attractive toys were obtained, seven female typed and seven male typed. The male toys were as follows:

1. A plastic toy submachine gun, with moving triggers, but silent.
2. A plastic highway road scraper, with adjustable blade.
3. A metal San Francisco cable car with friction motor.
4. A plastic tugboat with moving side wheel and piston rod.
5. Three miniature lead soldiers: a flag bearer, a marching rifleman, and a soldier on horseback.
6. A set of five small metal airplanes.
7. A metal dumptruck with spring dump mechanism.

The female toys were as follows:

1. A baby doll with feminine clothes and miniature nursing bottle.
2. A doll crib with moving side.
3. A doll Bathinette with moving top and folding legs.
4. Two purses, one child size and one doll size.
5. A doll Baby-tenda (feeding chair, folds into table).
6. A set of tea dishes: two cups, two saucers, silverware, and teapot.
7. A wicker doll buggy with movable canopy.

(The crib, Bathinette, Baby-tenda, and buggy all had plain dolls in them, but they were much less attractive and manipulable than the baby doll listed as the first item in the list.)

All the toys met the following criteria for attractiveness:

1. All had at least one moving part.

2. None had more than two distinct possible types of manipulation.

3. All were clearly sex-typed, having been selected in close agreement with the toys used in Rabban's study and, where necessary, after consultation with toy salesmen.

4. None of these toys or any closely similar to them were available in standard equipment of the nursery school.

5. All of them appeared, on pretest, to be attractive to children of nursery school age.

Technique

The toys are laid out in a line, spaced eight inches apart, on the floor of the testing room before the child is brought into the room. For each of our forty children, they were placed in the following order, left to right, the masculine and feminine toys alternating:

1. Gun (m)
2. Baby doll (f)
3. Road scraper (m)
4. Crib (f)
5. Cable car (m)
6. Bathinette (f)
7. Tugboat (m)
8. Two purses (f)
9. Toy soldiers (m)
10. Baby-tenda (f)
11. Five airplanes (m)
12. Tea set (f)
13. Dump truck (m)
14. Doll buggy (f)

When the child comes into the room, E says: "Would you like to see all the new toys? See all the new toys we have for the nursery school? Let's play a game, and then you will have a chance to play with any of these toys you like. Before we do that, though, let's make sure you know what all these toys are. This one is a gun; this one is a doll; this one is a road scraper; etc. Now I'll tell you what we're going to do. Look over all the toys very carefully and tell me which one of all these toys you would like to play with most of all. O.K. Give that one to me and I'll put it over here. (E puts the toy on a table.) Now, of all the toys that are left, tell me which one you would most like to play with. O.K., give it to me and I'll put it over here. Now show me another toy you like the best of all the ones that are left. O.K., I'll put that one over here too." This process continues until the child has made eight choices. An observer records each of the choices as the child makes it.

Then E says to the child, "Now we have a little job to do before you can play with the toys you chose." E collects all the toys, with the child's help, and places them in a big box, saving out only the child's first-choice toy and the first-chosen toy of inappropriate sex type. These are designated as "first choice" and "first inappropriate choice." E then places these two toys on the floor ten feet apart, saying, "Here is the toy you picked as the one you would most like to play with, so now you can play with it. Go ahead and play with it as long as you like, and I'll be back in a few minutes." E then picks up the box of remaining toys and leaves the room. At this instant the observer starts a timer in order to record the time elapsing before the child tires of his first-choice toy and, crossing the room, touches the first-inappropriate-choice toy.

E then returns to the testing room, greets the child, and gives him an opportunity to play with the toys for a few minutes.

Scoring and Consistency

One point is given for each sex-appropriate toy chosen in the first eight choices. The score is, therefore, a masculinity or femininity score (variable 202), depending on the sex of child. The possible range is from one to seven; the satiation scores were used only to break ties within each sex.

Rabban reported test-retest reliability (i.e., trait consistency) of .61 for four-year-olds, and .75 for five-year-olds. Borstelmann (1961), using the same toys as were used in the present test, obtained test-retest correlations over a one-month period of .76 for boys and .62 for girls. The age range was three years, four months, to five years for each sex, with a median of four years, two months, which was eight months younger than our group.

Appendix K. *Supplementary Tables*

This appendix comprises ten tables of correlations and intercorrelations supplementary to the data in the text. All are referred to in the text where appropriate.

TABLE K1

Intercorrelations among BUO Aggression Measures

(Measures combined for the Z summary score are indicated by a superscript.
Girls are above the diagonal, boys below.)

BUO Aggression Measures	Var. No.	Variable Number							
		189	191	196	192	197	193	194	198
Direct physical^z	189	✿	66	29	−12	58	28	75	32
Direct verbal^z	191	50	✿	52	−31	49	28	80	46
Verbal disapproval^z	196	61	49	✿	03	47	49	59	94
Injury to objects	192	46	36	33	✿	−18	09	15	−03
Tattling	197	26	10	15	−06	✿	15	44	62
Mischief	193	30	23	04	63	−11	✿	53	46
Total antisocial	194	85	64	50	75	12	63	✿	52
Total prosocial	198	66	44	79	31	49	03	55	✿

TABLE K2

Intercorrelations among MCI Aggression Measures

(Measures combined for the Y summary score are indicated by a superscript.
Girls are above the diagonal, boys below.)

MCI Aggression Measures	Var. No.	Variable Number							
		344	345	346	348	347	350	351	349
Disobedience^y	344	✿	74	88	83	−16	15	17	58
Direct toward mother^y . . .	345	37	✿	83	72	15	−11	11	67
Indirect toward mother^y . . .	346	85	46	✿	83	−24	13	14	60
Outer-directed physical^y . .	348	74	36	61	✿	−06	06	17	61
Directness, toward mother . .	347	−30	32	−43	−23	✿	−18	−17	08
Direct self	350	11	−04	−01	−10	−26	✿	35	22
Fantasy	351	24	34	21	33	15	02	✿	33
Outer-directed verbal	349	21	41	25	23	28	05	72	✿

TABLE K3

Intercorrelations among Fourteen Measures of Parental Discipline, and of Permissiveness and Punishment for Aggression

(Girls' parents above the diagonal, boys' parents below)

Parent Measures	Var. No.	Permissiveness					Punishment				Discipline				
		58	59	169	55	56	60	61	168	342	66	67	68	71	72
Permissiveness for aggression toward parents:															
Mother	58	*	48	53	−25	−12	−66	−57	−53	−05	−07	−49	−54	−30	−05
Father	59	33	*	65	−41	−02	−26	−60	−38	−34	−32	−39	−38	−09	01
Mother Attitude Scale	169	67	63	*	−54	17	−40	−48	−76	−51	06	−55	−51	−29	−04
Demand for aggression toward peers:															
Mother	55	48	−03	10	*	10	20	36	37	35	−26	34	07	25	07
Father	56	−22	−10	14	−18	*	31	−05	−10	−03	−14	04	27	14	31
Punishment for aggression toward parents:															
Mother	60	−66	−24	−55	−15	47	*	40	59	−04	04	60	65	58	16
Father	61	−36	−16	−25	−12	02	22	*	25	12	27	54	40	28	33
Mother Attitude Scale	168	−47	−41	−71	−08	−42	22	28	*	44	−13	54	49	62	13
Mother-Child Interaction	342	−27	−28	−29	03	−03	−03	03	18	*	−06	19	29	−07	10
Use of isolation:															
Mother	66	−19	−55	−34	18	10	25	06	50	03	*	−23	14	−17	06
Use of physical punishment:															
Mother	67	−33	−17	−21	−01	56	62	06	15	16	47	*	64	57	15
Father	68	−01	26	12	10	11	16	36	15	−10	07	35	*	39	06
Use of ridicule:															
Mother	71	−52	−10	−61	−17	07	45	41	29	31	−08	30	04	*	19
Father	72	−03	−27	09	−14	48	20	11	03	−18	20	35	16	−21	*

TABLE K4

Adult Role with Dependency:
Correlations Between Some Principal Measures of Each

		Dependency Measures								
Adult Role Measures	Var. No.	Negative Attention Seeking (187)		Reassurance Seeking (188)		Positive Attention Seeking (219)		Touching and Holding (220)		Being Near (221)
		Boys	Girls	Boys	Girls	Boys	Girls	Boys	Girls	Boys Girls
Real adult work	179	07	−08	−09	25	−10	11	11	13	34 12
Nurturance	182	31	02	03	20	02	75	60	−10	−22 −03
Total real adult role . . .	184	22	−06	−07	30	42	67	38	−16	−14 −18
Total fantasy adult role .	185	08	01	−40	−20	19	07	−02	−23	−23 −28
Quoting rules, total score .	212	−07	21	36	10	04	19	02	40	−16 27
Adult as routine agent, doll play I	250	−22	−56	11	11	−07	17	08	−04	33 −18
Adult as routine agent, doll play II	251	−14	−24	06	−10	−26	−38	47	−11	41 −15

TABLE K5

Aggression with Dependency:
Correlations Between Some Principal Measures of Each

		Dependency Measures								
Aggression Measures	Var. No.	Negative Attention Seeking (187)		Reassurance Seeking (188)		Positive Attention Seeking (219)		Touching and Holding (220)		Being Near (221)
		Boys	Girls	Boys	Girls	Boys	Girls	Boys	Girls	Boys Girls
Toward parents (mother's perception)	W	12	41	−14	18	20	−06	18	05	−05 23
Toward parents (father's perception)	X	11	−26	18	43	01	18	08	08	31 −03
Direct inter-personal (BUO)	Z	21	17	−06	16	19	61	20	−43	−47 −44
Injury to objects (BUO)	192	58	27	−25	29	15	14	−33	01	−36 43
Tattling (BUO)	197	−27	−14	−04	35	29	54	06	−10	−15 −23
Real outer-directed (MCI)	Y	11	19	18	−03	−08	−08	−05	−22	−16 −16
Total thematic, doll play I	290	38	39	−35	−37	24	−01	−21	−37	−47 −18
Total thematic, doll play II	291	40	18	41	−12	28	20	12	07	01 −12

TABLE K6

Aggression with Adult Role:
Correlations Between Some Principal Measures of Each

		Adult Role Measures						
		Doing Real Adult Work	Nurtur- ance	Total Adult Role		QuRu, Total Score	Adult as Routine Agent in Doll Play	
				Real	Fan- tasy		I	II
Aggression Measures	Var. No.	(179)	(182)	(184)	(185)	(212)	(250)	(251)
		GIRLS						
Toward parents (mother's perception) . . .	W	25	−10	−11	06	44	21	02
Toward parents (father's perception) . . .	X	18	22	26	32	20	02	33
Direct interpersonal (BUO) .	Z	36	55	61	33	−05	−03	−15
Injury to objects (BUO) . . .	192	−11	49	23	−21	−04	−15	08
Tattling (BUO)	197	21	45	58	−07	−14	20	05
Real outer-directed (MCI) . .	Y	−22	−12	05	34	24	−16	−25
Total thematic, doll play I . .	290	−02	−04	−10	26	02	−56	−44
Total thematic, doll play II . .	291	00	−01	04	00	17	−31	−80
		BOYS						
Toward parents (mother's perception) . . .	W	10	28	45	−07	51	13	−27
Toward parents (father's perception) . . .	X	−02	−18	−04	−43	03	11	35
Direct interpersonal (BUO) .	Z	−25	53	40	50	07	−18	−22
Injury to objects (BUO) . . .	192	−05	15	11	34	04	−21	−48
Tattling (BUO)	197	−19	−04	33	−05	35	−30	−17
Real outer-directed (MCI) . .	Y	−32	08	−18	24	−03	−38	−50
Total thematic, doll play I . .	290	−03	21	14	−08	11	−44	−28
Total thematic, doll play II . .	291	−18	31	13	−22	27	−32	−32

TABLE K7

Gender Role and Conscience with Dependency:
Correlations Between Some Principal Measures of Each

Gender Role and Conscience Measures	Var. No.	Dependency Measures									
		Negative Attention Seeking (187)		Reassurance Seeking (188)		Positive Attention Seeking (219)		Touching and Holding (220)		Being Near (221)	
		Boys	Girls	Boys	Girls	Boys	Girls	Boys	Girls	Boys	Girls
Gender Role											
Observer rating	203	25	−51	−59	18	11	30	04	21	−48	−05
Total standard score	204	−14	−47	−27	−08	−14	44	−18	17	−36	−25
Telephone: willingness	364	−11	39	−07	39	04	−44	28	16	−20	34
Conscience											
Interviews: pooled	89	−05	12	−27	42	10	08	28	26	−25	19
RTT: total standard score	211	−40	−49	−13	44	−32	−19	36	−02	06	06
Emotional upset: summary	235	−16	18	23	56	−21	55	16	06	−18	16
Confession: summary	236	01	14	19	03	03	09	56	01	−09	15
Fixing: summary	237	05	27	04	−39	−11	−07	14	−01	25	−21

TABLE K8

Gender Role and Conscience with Adult Role:
Correlations Between Some Principal Measures of Each

Gender Role and Conscience Measures	Var. No.	Adult Role Measures						
		Real Adult Work (179)	Nurturance (182)	Total Real Adult Role (184)	Total Fantasy Adult Role (185)	Quoting Rules, Total Score (212)	Adult as Routine Agent, I (250)	Adult as Routine Agent, II (251)
GIRLS								
Gender Role								
Observer rating	203	52	25	48	32	01	07	−03
Total standard score	204	30	31	43	19	−03	08	03
Telephone: willingness	364	−05	−25	−23	−39	−11	−06	−03
Conscience								
Interviews: pooled	89	00	04	−01	08	−27	−03	−11
RTT: total standard score	211	01	00	10	−29	−22	40	49
Emotional upset: summary	235	13	48	36	−21	−05	−05	−29
Confession: summary	236	07	10	−12	04	26	−07	−22
Fixing: summary	237	21	−12	−04	26	07	−04	−12
BOYS								
Gender Role								
Observer rating	203	−20	33	35	56	02	−08	−30
Total standard score	204	−61	−09	−15	02	−11	−47	−37
Telephone: willingness	364	29	16	15	18	−19	45	40
Conscience								
Interviews: pooled	89	31	34	58	22	06	13	−04
RTT: total standard score	211	05	−08	07	−31	−04	25	52
Emotional upset: summary	235	−02	22	05	−05	07	22	44
Confession: summary	236	−25	36	15	07	−07	00	44
Fixing: summary	237	10	−01	−20	−04	−11	07	26

TABLE K9

Gender Role and Conscience with Aggression:
Correlations Between Some Principal Measures of Each

Gender Role and Conscience Measures	Var. No.	Aggression Measures							
		Toward Parents		Injury to Objects		Tat-		Total Thematic	
		Mother (W)	Father (X)	BUO (Z)	Objects (192)	tling (197)	MCI (Y)	I (290)	II (291)
GIRLS									
Gender Role									
Observer rating	203	−08	33	10	−31	38	−08	−23	05
Total standard score	204	−28	24	21	−35	48	−22	−22	19
Telephone: willingness	364	13	−17	−30	29	−22	02	−01	06
Conscience									
Interviews: pooled	89	15	48	−02	06	11	08	03	09
RTT: total standard score	211	−29	22	−38	34	02	−19	−72	−66
Emotional upset: summary	235	09	17	35	25	36	03	−06	−02
Confession: summary	236	56	02	02	23	−15	10	25	15
Fixing: summary	237	20	−21	37	−49	12	16	46	58
BOYS									
Gender Role									
Observer rating	203	21	−33	50	47	25	18	28	−15
Total standard score	204	04	−25	19	23	26	37	29	05
Telephone: willingness	364	−09	07	28	−24	−14	−18	−11	−41
Conscience									
Interviews: pooled	89	15	−28	35	−04	05	−19	10	−25
RTT: total standard score	211	−01	27	−23	−42	15	−46	−34	−58
Emotional upset: summary	235	−38	−24	38	16	02	−06	−06	−15
Confession: summary	236	−19	17	11	−13	10	−09	−08	06
Fixing: summary	237	00	08	−28	−12	−06	17	23	28

TABLE K10

Gender Role with Conscience:
Correlations Between Some Principal Measures of Each

Gender Role Measures	Var. No.	Inter-views: Pooled: (89) Boys	Girls	RTT, Total Score (211) Boys	Girls	Emo-tional Upset: Summary (235) Boys	Girls	Con-fession: Summary (236) Boys	Girls	Fixing: Summary (237) Boys	Girls
Observer rating	203	38	−05	02	13	−03	−01	−01	02	−02	−13
Total standard score	204	−04	−21	10	−01	01	−03	−06	06	08	15
Telephone: willingness	364	47	38	14	16	11	04	12	−27	15	05

References

References

References marked with an asterisk (*) relate to this research project.

*American Psychological Association (1963) The conscience of a child. New York: Mayer-Sklar. Film, 30 minutes.

Bach, G. R. (1945) Young children's play fantasies. *Psychol. Monogr.*, 59, No. 272.

Bach, G. R. (1946) Father-fantasies and father-typing in father-separated children. *Child Develpm.*, 17, 63–80.

Bandura, A., and Aletha C. Huston (1961) Identification as a process of incidental learning. *J. abn. soc. Psychol.*, 63, 311–18.

Bandura, A., and R. H. Walters (1959) *Adolescent aggression.* New York: Ronald Press.

Bandura, A., and R. H. Walters (1963) *Social learning and personality development.* New York: Holt, Rinehart, and Winston.

Bandura, A., Dorothea Ross, and Sheila A. Ross (1963) A comparative test of the status envy, social power, and secondary reinforcement theories of identificatory learning. *J. abn. soc. Psychol.*, 67, 527–34.

Bishop, Barbara M. (1951) Mother-child interaction and the social behavior of children. *Psychol. Monogr.*, 65, No. 328.

Borstelmann, L. J. (1961) Sex of experimenter and sex-typed behavior of young children. *Child Develpm.*, 32, 519–24.

Bronfenbrenner, U. (1960) Freudian theories of identification and their derivatives. *Child Develpm.*, 31, 15–40.

Brown, D. G. (1956) Sex-role preference in young children. *Psychol. Monogr.*, 70, No. 421.

*Burke, Margaret P. (1961) Conscience development in nursery school children as revealed through fantasy. Unpubl. master's thesis, Stanford Univ.

Burton, R. (1963) The generality of honesty reconsidered. *Psychol. Rev.*, 70, 481–99.

Cain-Levine Social Competency Scales (1963) Palo Alto: Consulting Psychologists Press, Inc. (Prepared by L. F. Cain, F. F. Elzey, and S. Levine.)

Dawe, Helen (1934) An analysis of 200 quarrels of preschool children. *Child Develpm.*, 5, 139–56.

*Dowley, Edith M. (1960) Doing research in a nursery school. *J. nursery Educ.*, 16, 22–25.

Durett, Mary E. (1959) The relationship of early infant regulation and later behavior in play interviews. *Child Develpm.*, 30, 211–16.

Fauls, L. B., and W. D. Smith (1956) Sex-role learning of five-year-olds. *J. genet. Psychol.*, 89, 105–19.

Freud, Anna (1936) *The ego and the mechanisms of defense.* London: Hogarth Press, 1937.

Freud, S. (1914) On narcissism: an introduction. *Coll. Papers, 4,* 30–59.

Freud, S. (1917) Mourning and melancholia. *Coll. Papers, 4,* 152–70.

Freud, S. (1921) *Group psychology and the analysis of the ego.* New York: Liveright.

Freud, S. (1923) *The ego and the id.* London: Hogarth Press.

Freud, S. (1924) The passing of the Oedipus-complex. *Coll. Papers, 2,* 269–76.

Gewirtz, J. L. (1954) Three determinants of attention seeking in young children. *Monogr. Soc. Res. Child Develpm., 19,* No. 2 (Serial No. 59).

Gewirtz, J. L. (1961) A learning analysis of the effects of normal stimulation, privation, and deprivation on the acquisition of social motivation and attachment. In B. M. Foss (Ed.) *Determinants of infant behavior.* New York: Wiley, pp. 213–83.

Glueck, S., and Eleanor Glueck (1950) *Unraveling juvenile delinquency.* Cambridge: Harvard Univ. Press.

Green, Elise E. (1933) Friendships and quarrels among preschool children. *Child Develpm., 4,* 237–52.

Grinder, R. E. (1961) Parental childrearing practices, conscience, and resistance to temptation of sixth-grade children. *Child Develpm., 33,* 803–20.

Hampson, J. L. (1965) Determinants of psychosexual orientation. In F. A. Beach (Ed.) *Sex and behavior.* New York: Wiley, pp. 108–32.

*Harsanyi, Anne (1960) Identification of young children as measured by teachers' rating scales. Unpubl. master's thesis, Stanford Univ.

Hartshorne, H., and M. A. May (1928) *Studies in the nature of character.* vol. I: *studies in deceit.* New York: Macmillan.

*Hatfield, J. S., Lucy Rau, and R. Alpert (1965) A study of mother-child interaction. In preparation.

Heathers, G. L. (1955) Emotional dependence and independence in nursery school play. *J. genet. Psychol., 87,* 37–57.

Hilgard, E. R. (1949) Human motives and the concept of the self. *Amer. Psychol., 4,* 374–82.

Hollenberg, Eleanor, and Margaret Sperry (1951) Some antecedents of aggression and effects of frustration in doll play. *Personality, 1,* 32–43.

Huschka, Mabel (1942) The child's response to coercive bowel training. In S. Tompkins (Ed.) *Contemporary psychopathology.* Cambridge: Harvard Univ. Press, pp. 36–48.

Jersild, A. T., and F. V. Markey (1935) Conflicts between preschool children. *Child Develpm. Monogr.,* No. 21. New York: Columbia Univ. Press.

Johnson, Elizabeth Z. (1951) Attitudes of children toward authority as projected in their doll play at two age levels. Unpubl. doctoral dissertation, Harvard Univ.

Kagan, J., and H. A. Moss (1962) *Birth to maturity.* New York: Wiley.

Kass, N. (1964) Risk in decision making as a function of age, sex, and probability preference. *Child Develpm., 35,* 577–82.

Kohlberg, L. (1966) A cognitive-developmental analysis of the formation of sex-role concepts and attitudes. In Eleanor E. Maccoby (Ed.) *Sex differences and sex typing.* Stanford: Stanford Univ. Press. In preparation.

Lefkowitz, M. M., L. O. Walder, and L. D. Eron (1963) Punishment, identification and aggression. *Merrill Palmer Quart., 9,* 159–74.

Maccoby, Eleanor E. (1959) Role-taking in childhood and its consequences for social learning. *Child Develpm., 30,* 239–52.

Maccoby, Eleanor E. (1961) The taking of adult roles in middle childhood. *J. abn. soc. Psychol., 63,* 493–503.

McCord, Joan, W. McCord, and E. Thurber (1963) Effects of maternal employment on lower-class boys. *J. abn. soc. Psychol., 67,* 177–82.

McCord, W., and Joan McCord (1956) *Psychopathy and delinquency.* New York: Grune & Stratton.

Merrill, Barbara A. (1946) Measurement of mother-child interaction. *J. abn. soc. Psychol., 41,* 37–49.

Miller, N. E. (1948) Theory and experiment relating psychoanalytic displacement to stimulus-response generalization. *J. abn. soc. Psychol., 43,* 155–78.

Milton, G. A. (1958) A factor analytic study of child-rearing behaviors. *Child Develpm., 29,* 382–92.

Moore, T., and L. E. Ucko (1961) Four to six: constructiveness and conflict in meeting doll play problems. *J. child Psychol. Psychiat., 2,* 21–47.

Mowrer, O. H. (1950) *Learning theory and personality dynamics.* New York: Ronald Press.

Mowrer, O. H. (1960) *Learning theory and the symbolic processes.* New York: Wiley.

Murphy, Lois B. (1937) *Social behavior and child personality.* New York: Columbia Univ. Press.

Murray, H. A., Jr. (1938) *Explorations in personality.* New York: Oxford Univ. Press.

Mussen, P. (1961) Some antecedents and consequents of masculine sex-typing in adolescent boys. *Psychol. Monogr., 75,* No. 506.

Mussen, P., and L. Distler (1959) Masculinity, identification, and father-son relationships. *J. abn. soc. Psychol., 59,* 350–56.

Mussen, P., and L. Distler (1960) Child-rearing antecedents of masculine identification in kindergarten boys. *Child Develpm., 31,* 89–100.

Mussen, P., and E. Rutherford (1963) Parent-child relations and parental personality in relation to young children's sex-role preferences. *Child Develpm., 34,* 589–607.

Payne, D., and P. Mussen (1956) Parent-child relations and father identification among adolescent boys. *J. abn. soc. Psychol., 52,* 358–62.

Rabban, M. (1950) Sex role identification in young children in two diverse social groups. *Genet. Psychol. Monogr., 42,* 81–158.

Robbins, Lillian C. (1963) The accuracy of parental recall of aspects of child development and of child rearing practices. *J. abn. soc. Psychol., 66,* 261–70.

Ross, Dorothea (1962) The relationship between dependency, intentional learning, and incidental learning in preschool children. Unpubl. doctoral dissertation, Stanford Univ.

°Rowe, Patricia (1961) A nursery school teacher's part in a research project. *J. nursery Educ., 16,* 65–70.

Sanford, R. N. (1955) The dynamics of identification. *Psychol. Rev., 62,* 106–18.

Schaffer, H. R., and Peggy E. Emerson (1964) The development of social attachments in infancy. *Monogr. Soc. Res. Child Develpm., 29,* No. 94.

Sears, Pauline S. (1951) Doll play aggression in normal young children: influence of sex, age, sibling status, father's absence. *Psychol. Monogr., 65,* No. 323.

Sears, Pauline S. (1953) Child rearing factors related to the playing of sex-typed roles. *Amer. Psychol. 8,* 431. Abstract only.

Sears, R. R. (1951) A theoretical framework for personality and social behavior. *Amer. Psychol., 6,* 476–83.

Sears, R. R. (1957) Identification as a form of behavioral development. In D. B. Harris (Ed.) *The concept of development.* Minneapolis: Univ. of Minn. Press, pp. 149–61.

*Sears, R. R. (1960) Reporting research to parents. *J. nursery Educ., 16,* 25–32.

Sears, R. R. (1961) Relation of early socialization experiences to aggression in middle childhood. *J. abn. soc. Psychol., 63,* 466–92.

*Sears, R. R. (1963) Dependency motivation. In M. R. Jones (Ed.) *Nebraska Symposium on Motivation: 1963.* Lincoln: Univ. of Nebr. Press, pp. 25–64.

*Sears, R. R. (1965) Development of gender role. In F. A. Beach (Ed.) *Sex and behavior.* New York: Wiley, pp. 133–63.

Sears, R. R., Eleanor E. Maccoby, and H. Levin (1957) *Patterns of child rearing.* Evanston, Ill.: Row, Peterson.

Sears, R. R., J. W. M. Whiting, V. Nowlis, and Pauline S. Sears (1953) Some child-rearing antecedents of aggression and dependency in young children. *Genet. Psychol. Monogr., 47,* 135–234.

Siegel, Alberta (1956) Film-mediated fantasy aggression and strength of aggressive drive. *Child Develpm., 27,* 365–78.

Smith, Henrietta T. (1958) A comparison of interview and observation measures of mother behavior. *J. abn. soc. Psychol., 57,* 278–82.

*Vitz, P. C. (1961) Some changes in behavior of nursery school children over a period of seven weeks. *J. nursery Educ., 16,* 62–65.

Walters, R. H., and R. D. Parke (1965) The role of the distance receptors in the development of social responsiveness. In L. P. Lipsitt and C. C. Spiker (Eds.) *Advances in child development and behavior,* vol. ii. New York: Academic Press.

*Weinberger, G. (1959) The measurement of resistance to temptation. Unpubl. master's thesis, Stanford Univ.

Whiting, J. W. M. (1944) The frustration complex in Kwoma society. *Man, 115,* 140–44.

Whiting, J. W. M., and I. L. Child (1953) *Child training and personality: a cross-cultural study.* New Haven: Yale Univ. Press.

Winterbottom, Marian R. (1953) The relation of childhood training in independence to achievement motivation. Unpubl. doctoral dissertation, Univ. of Michigan.

Wurtz, K. R. (1959) The expression of guilt in fantasy and reality. *J. genet. Psychol., 95,* 227–38.

Yarrow, L. J. (1948) The effect of antecedent frustration on projective play. *Psychol. Monogr., 62,* No. 293.

Index

Index

(See also Index to Variables, Appendix C.)

Action theory, 60–61, 66, 69, 114, 149
Activity level, 39–40, 195, 313; see also variables 217, 218, 238, 239
Adult role: definition, 77, 80–81; measurement of, 80–84, 327–34; assessment (QuRu), 82–83, 327–34; permissive doll play and, 83, 86, 182–84; sex differences in, 84–86, 91–92, 108–9; age differences in, 87, 92; as a trait, 87–92, 108–9, 309–10; theory of, 77–80, 108–9; correspondence to identification theory, 96–100; and dependency, 78–80, 92–96, 110–11, 363; and gender role, 184–85, 366; and aggression, 126–28, 364; and conscience, 366; real, 101–3, 183; fantasy, 81, 92, 99, 103–4; in middle childhood, 76–77, 86, 96; feminine quality of, 92, 95–96, 105–8, 127, 183
Affiliation and aggression, girls, 127, 158–62
Age, 13, 38; see also variable 1
Age differences: in dependency, 35, 37–38; in adult role, 87, 92; in aggression, 121; in gender role, 180, 182; in conscience, 213, 219–20, 230–31, 239; in deviation doll play, 219–20
Aggression: measurement of, 116–19, 312–13; MCI measures of, 117–18, 147, 361; behavior unit observations of, 116–17, 361; permissive doll play and, 118, 185; deviation doll play and, 118; sex differences in, 119–21, 125; age differences in, 121; as a trait, 114, 121–23, 166, 309–10, 361; as identification-mediated behavior, 112–16, 147–49; modeling and, 155–57, 164–68; and dependency, 126–28, 363; and

adult role, 126–28, 364; and gender role, 185–86, 367; and conscience, 367; and permissiveness, 144–47, 362; and punishment, 135–44, 155–57, 362; boys' syndrome of, 122–26, 150–57; girls' syndrome of, 122–26, 157–62; and frustration, 115, 128–35; and need-affiliation, girls, 127, 158–62
Aggressive boy, description, 150–54
Alpert, R., iii, 15, 372
Ambivalence, father toward son, 228–30
Anaclitic identification, 1, 3–7, 112, 199–201, 217, 220, 241–42, 251, 262; see also Primary identification
Antisocial aggression (see Aggression)
Area usage score (gender role), 175; see also Behavior unit observations, variable 199
Attachment in infancy, 242, 250
Autonomy, 63–64

Bach, G. R., 119, 120, 172, 371
Baldwin, C. M., ii
Bandura, A., 4, 5, 140, 168, 172, 173, 186, 371
Barron, G. A., iii
Beavin, J., iii
Bedwetting (see variable 21)
Behavior unit observations (BUO): content categories, 22–23, 297–302, 310–11; schedule, 13–14, 303–5; method, 22–23, 297–311; recording, 302–3; reliability, observer, 305–8; trait consistency, 308–10; of dependency, 33, 300–301, 311; of adult role, 81–83, 298–300, 311; of aggression, 116–17, 301–2, 311; summary scores, 310–11; real vs. fantasy, 297–98